HERMETICA II

This volume presents in new English translations the scattered fragments and testimonies regarding Hermes Thrice Great that complete Brian Copenhaver's translation of the *Hermetica* (Cambridge 1992). It contains the twenty-nine fragments from Stobaeus (including the famous *Korē Kosmou*), the Oxford and Vienna fragments (never before translated into English), an expanded selection of fragments from various authors (including Zosimus of Panopolis, Augustine, and Albert the Great), and testimonies about Hermes from thirty-eight authors (including Cicero, Pseudo-Manetho, the Emperor Julian, Al-Kindī, Michael Psellus, the *Emerald Tablet*, and Nicholas of Cusa). All translations are accompanied by introductions and notes which cite sources for further reading. These Hermetic texts will appeal to a broad array of readers interested in western esotericism including scholars of Egyptology, the New Testament, the classical world, Byzantium, medieval Islam, the Latin Middle Ages, and the Renaissance.

M. DAVID LITWA is a research fellow at the Institute for Religion and Critical Inquiry in Melbourne, Australia. His recent books include: *Desiring Divinity: Self-deification in Ancient Jewish and Christian Mythmaking* (2016); *Refutation of All Heresies: Text, Translation, and Notes* (2016); and *Iesus Deus: The Early Christian Depiction of Jesus as a Mediterranean God* (2014).

HERMETICA II

The Excerpts of Stobaeus, Papyrus Fragments, and Ancient Testimonies in an English Translation with Notes and Introductions

M. DAVID LITWA

Institute for Religion and Critical Inquiry, Melbourne

Shaftesbury Road, Cambridge CB2 8EA, United Kingdom

One Liberty Plaza, 20th Floor, New York, NY 10006, USA

477 Williamstown Road, Port Melbourne, VIC 3207, Australia

314–321, 3rd Floor, Plot 3, Splendor Forum, Jasola District Centre, New Delhi – 110025, India

103 Penang Road, #05–06/07, Visioncrest Commercial, Singapore 238467

Cambridge University Press is part of Cambridge University Press & Assessment, a department of the University of Cambridge.

We share the University's mission to contribute to society through the pursuit of education, learning and research at the highest international levels of excellence.

www.cambridge.org
Information on this title: www.cambridge.org/9781316633588

DOI: 10.1017/9781316856567

First published 2018
First paperback edition 2022

A catalogue record for this publication is available from the British Library

ISBN 978-1-107-18253-0 Hardback
ISBN 978-1-316-63358-8 Paperback

For Sam, Annie, Alex, and Eve
שבת שלום

Contents

Preface

Despite widespread interest in the Hermetica across the globe, currently there does not exist a reliable and up-to-date English translation of the various Hermetic fragments and testimonies. Indeed, some of these fragments and testimonies remain generally unknown.

At the turn of the twentieth century, G. R. S. Mead made a translation of select fragments into Victorian English from now-outdated editions. The translation of the fragments by Walter Scott (1924) was based on his own re-written Greek text – a jungle of emendations and transpositions. When it came to testimonies, moreover, Scott did not actually translate the Greek or Latin texts. He only rendered into English (via Latin translations) texts originally written in Arabic.

The present translation serves a new generation of scholarly and lay readers of the Hermetica. It remains faithful to – though critically engaged with – the various manuscript traditions. Copious notes provide historical background, parallels, and references for further reading. Included also are many testimonies that Scott did not print. It is hoped that this volume will spark interest in the full reception history of the Hermetica, which must include Late Antiquity and the medieval period.

Here I gratefully acknowledge persons who read parts of the manuscript and offered helpful suggestions: Brian P. Copenhaver, David Runia, and Christian H. Bull. Christian Wildberg and Kevin Van Bladel also kindly answered my inquiries and provided guidance based on their expertise. My thanks also to Oxford University Press for the use of Van Bladel's translations of Arabic source materials.

Abbreviations

ANRW	Haase and others, eds., *Aufstieg und Niedergang der römischen Welt*
Ascl.	The Latin *Asclepius*
BSGRT	Bibliotheca Scriptorum Graecorum et Romanorum Teubneriana
CCAG	*Catalogus Codicum Astrologorum Graecorum*, 11 vols., 1898–1912
CCSL	Corpus Christianorum Series Latina
CH	*Corpus Hermeticum*
CH Deutsch	Holzhausen, ed., *Das Corpus Hermeticum Deutsch*, 2 vols., 1997
Copenhaver	Copenhaver, trans., *Hermetica: The Greek Corpus Hermeticum*, 1992
DGWE	Hanegraaff, ed., *Dictionary of Gnosis and Western Esotericism*, 2006.
DH	*Definitions of Hermes Trismegistus to Asclepius*
DK	Diels and Kranz, eds., *Fragmente der Vorsokratiker*, 6th edition
Disc. 8–9	*Discourse on the Eighth and Ninth* (NHC VI,6)
DPA	Richard Goulet, ed., *Dictionnaire des philosophes antiques*, 5 vols., 1989–
F	Codex Farnesius
FH	Hermetic Fragments from various sources
FHSG	Fortenbaugh, Huby, Sharples, and Gutas, eds., *Theophrastus of Eresus*, 1992
HHE	Mahé, *Hermès en Haute-Égypte*, 2 vols., 1978–82.
LS	Long and Sedley, eds., *The Hellenistic Philosophers*, 2 vols., 1987
MSS	Manuscripts
Mystique	Festugière, *Hermétisme et mystique païenne*, 1967

NF	Nock and Festugière, eds., *Corpus Hermeticum*, 4 vols., 1945–54
NHC	Nag Hammadi Codices
NHS	Nag Hammadi Studies
NRSV	The New Revised Standard Version of the Bible
OF	Bernabé, ed., *Orphicorum et Orphicis similium testimonia et fragmenta*, 2005
OH	Oxford Hermetic Fragments
OLD	P. G. W. Glare, ed., *Oxford Latin Dictionary*. 1968–82
OTP	Charlesworth, ed., *Old Testament Pseudepigrapha*, 2 vols., 1983–85
P	Codex Parisinus gr. 2129
PG	Migne, ed., *Patrologia Graeca*, 162 vols., 1857–86
PW	Pauly and Wissowa, eds., *Realencyclopädie*, 83 vols., 1893–1982
Ref.	*Refutation of All Heresies*
RHT	Festugière, *La Révélation d'Hermès Trismégiste*, 4 vols., 2nd edn., 1949–54
SC	Sources Chrétiennes
Scarpi	Scarpi, ed., *La Rivelazione segreta di Ermete Trismegisto*, 2 vols., 2009–11
SH	Stobaean Hermetic Excerpts
SVF	Von Arnim, ed., *Stoicorum Veterum Fragmenta*
TH	Hermetic Testimonies
VC	*Vigiliae Christianae*
VH	Vienna Hermetic Fragments

General Introduction

There are five groups of philosophical Hermetic writings that do not appear in Brian P. Copenhaver's 1992 English translation entitled *Hermetica: The Greek "Corpus Hermeticum" and the Latin "Asclepius"*.[1] The first is the large group of Hermetic excerpts from Stobaeus, an early fifth-century CE anthologist. The second is the Coptic Hermetica (discovered in 1945) featuring two excerpts of previously known writings in addition to a formerly unknown Hermetic tractate (the *Discourse on the Eighth and Ninth*). The third group is the collection of Hermetic *Definitions*, a set of maxims extant in Greek fragments but preserved only fully in Armenian. The fourth is the previously known set of diverse fragments quoted by various (largely Christian) authors in Late Antiquity. The fifth comprises recently discovered Hermetic fragments currently preserved in Vienna and Oxford.

The Coptic Hermetica are widely available in English translations of the Nag Hammadi library.[2] The *Definitions* are now conveniently accessible in English thanks to the work of Jean-Pierre Mahé.[3] What remains to be translated are the fragments from Stobaeus, the fragments and testimonies from various authors, and the fragments from the newly discovered papyri.

[1] Copenhaver's introduction to CH and *Ascl.* remain relevant (Copenhaver, xxxii–xlv). See also Peter Kingsley, "An Introduction to the Hermetica: Approaching Ancient Esoteric Tradition," in Roelof van den Broek and Cis van Heertum, eds., *From Poimandres to Jacob Böhme: Gnosis: Hermetism and the Christian Tradition* (Amsterdam: In de Pelikaan, 2000), 17–40.

[2] See Marvin Meyer, ed., *Nag Hammadi Scriptures: The International Edition* (New York: HarperOne, 2008), 409–36. Introductions to the Coptic Hermetica can be found in *ibid.*, 409–12; 419–21; 425–29; Mahé, *HHE*, 1.31–51, 137–55; 2.47–144; Hans-Martin Schenke, Hans-Gebhard Bethge, and Ursula Ulrike Kaiser, eds., *Nag Hammadi Deutsch: Studienausgabe* (Berlin: de Gruyter, 2007), 359–60; 367–68; 370–71.

[3] Mahé's translation can be found in Clement Salaman and others, trans., *The Way of Hermes: New Translations of "The Corpus Hermeticum" and "The Definitions of Hermes Trismegistus to Asclepius"* (Rochester, VT: Inner Traditions, 2000), 109–22. Mahé introduces the Armenian *Definitions* in *ibid.*, 101–8.

It is high time to present a new translation and annotation of these (chiefly philosophical) Hermetica to the English-speaking world.

Hermes-Thoth

Nothing binds together the multifarious Hermetic fragments beyond their ascription to Hermes Thrice Great. Hermes Thrice Great is a fictional character. Yet for many in the ancient world that fiction was history. If we call Hermes Thrice Great a "myth," we thereby recognize that he is greater and more significant than any one historical figure. How do we introduce a figure that appears in so many different ages in so many different guises? If there was an "original" Hermes Thrice Great, we are obliged to pick up the thread at significant points of reception.

Iamblichus (about 245–325 CE) commences his book (later called *On the Mysteries*) with the following flourish:

> Hermes, the deity who presides over rational discourses, has long and rightly been considered common to all who practice the sacred arts. He who presides over true science concerning gods is one and the same throughout the universe. It is to him that our ancestors dedicated the discoveries of their wisdom, attributing all their own writings to Hermes.[4]

Important here is the frank acknowledgement that many authors wrote under the name of Hermes. The practice of pseudepigraphy was logical for devotees of Hermes.[5] True wisdom and learning merited ascription to the lord of all learning. This is why many Egyptian scholars attributed their writings to Hermes. Iamblichus, himself writing under a false name ("Abammon," an Egyptian priest), calls these writers his "ancestors." These "ancestors" were probably Hellenized Egyptian scribes and priests who lived not very long before Iamblichus himself.

Later, Iamblichus gives a taste of how many persons were writing under the name of Hermes. In *On the Mysteries* 8.1, he passes on the report of a certain Seleucus, who attributed to Hermes a total of 20,000 books. A better-known source, the Egyptian priest and historian Manetho, nearly

[4] Iamblichus, *On the Mysteries*, 1.1.

[5] On Hermetic pseudepigraphy, see Anthony Grafton, *Forgers and Critics: Creativity and Duplicity in Western Scholarship* (Princeton: Princeton University Press, 1990), 85–98; and more generally, Bart D. Ehrman, *Forgery and Counterforgery: The Use of Literary Deceit in Early Christian Polemics* (Oxford: Oxford University Press, 2013), 11–145; 534–48.

doubled this number, crediting Hermes with 36,525 volumes (or 100 volumes for each single day in a 4-year period).[6] So many books would easily fill the shelves of a large temple library (the Egyptian "House of Life"). Perhaps this is the point – all the wisdom of the Egyptian sacred priesthood ultimately reverts to Hermes.

According to Iamblichus, Hermes wrote hundreds of tomes on specialized topics like "the gods in the fiery zone," "the gods in the aether," and "the gods in the heavens."[7] Hermes was the ultimate theologian, yet the scope of his expertise was in fact more vast. There are existing treatises on astrology, the virtues of stones, the principles of creation, the origin and nature of the soul, alchemical practices, Fate, the effects of climate on intelligence, healing, and even why children resemble their parents – all ascribed to Hermes.[8]

The many genres of Hermetic learning are well illustrated by a passage in Clement of Alexandria. This Christian writer around 200 CE describes a procession of Egyptian officials in which forty-two fundamental writings of Hermes were displayed (the number of Egypt's districts or "nomes"). The highest-ranking priest, whom the Greeks called "Prophet," carried the ten "hieratic" books on laws, the gods, and the training of priests. The Stole-keeper presented ten books on education and sacrifice. The Sacred Scribe held up a decade of books on hieroglyphs, geography, and the temples. Then came the Astrologer, who showed four books on astronomical matters (fixed stars, planets, conjunctions, and the risings of astral bodies). Finally, the Singer held in his hands a songbook and an instruction manual for kings. As a supplement, six books on medical matters (anatomy, medicines, medical instruments, and gynecology) were displayed.[9] All this vast store of knowledge was ascribed to Hermes.

Who was this Hermes? We must first of all distinguish a Greek deity from a significantly different Egyptian one. The Greek Hermes was the "winged son of kindly Maia," racing on the winds as Zeus's crafty herald,

[6] The number has yet deeper significance in Egyptian astrology, as pointed out by Christian H. Bull, "The Tradition of Hermes: The Egyptian Priestly Figure as a Teacher of Hellenized Wisdom" (Ph.D. diss., University of Bergen, 2014), 82–83.

[7] Iamblichus, *On the Mysteries*, 8.1–2.

[8] See, for instance, the small treatises *On Earthquakes* and the *Brontologion* attributed to Hermes Thrice Great in *CCAG* 7.167–71; 226–30.

[9] Clement of Alexandria, *Stromata*, 6.4.35.1–6.4.38.1. On books in temple libraries, see further Serge Sauneron, *The Priests of Ancient Egypt*, new edition, trans. David Lorton (Ithaca, NY: Cornell University Press, 2000), 110–67; Garth Fowden, *The Egyptian Hermes: A Historical Approach to the Late Pagan Mind* (Cambridge: Cambridge University Press, 1996), 57–60; Jan Assmann, *Religion and Cultural Memory: Ten Studies* (Stanford: Stanford University Press, 2006), 75, 135–36, 201 nn.35–36.

helmeted with the cap of invisibility, wielding the twisted caduceus with the power to put even Argus with his hundred eyes to sleep.[10] The Egyptian Hermes, on the other hand, was Thoth, depicted as the ibis-headed scribe of the gods, secretary of Re, giver of oracles, master of magic, lord of the moon often appearing in the form of a dog-faced baboon. When the Greeks dominated Egypt, they identified the Egyptian god Thoth with Hermes. But why? What did they see in these two gods that was similar?

There are several overlaps, yet we will focus on two.[11] First of all, Hermes as *psychopomp*, or escort of the dead, resembled Thoth as seen in the various versions of the Egyptian *Book of the Dead* (or the *Book of Going Forth by Day*), chapter 125. In the Hall of Two Truths, Thoth hears the confession of the deceased person. After the person's heart is weighed against the feather of Maat ("Justice," or "Truth"), Thoth carefully inscribes the result with his tablet and stylus. If the heart is pure, Thoth leads the candidate into the presence of Osiris, the ultimate judge of the dead, and finally into the Field of Reeds.[12] Perhaps the most famous scene of Hermes leading souls is the opening of Homer's *Odyssey*, book 24. In this scene, Hermes guides the freshly slaughtered suitors of Penelope to the netherworld. Mindless, the suitors squeak like bats on their way to the halls of Hades.

Yet there was a more basic similarity between Hermes and Thoth. Hermes is more than a herald or messenger. He is the Logos – the Reason, Speech, or Word of God.[13] The Word devises speech and brings his own interpretation, which the Greeks called *hermeneia*.[14] Thoth is also the god who presides over speech and interpretation. He is called "the heart of Re, the tongue of Atum, the throat of the God whose name is hidden." As

[10] The "winged son of kindly Maia" derives from Horace, *Odes*, 1.3.

[11] Other similarities between Thoth and Hermes are catalogued by Maria-Theresia Derchain-Urtel, *Thot à travers ses épithètes dans les scènes d'offrandes des temples d'époque gréco-romaine* (Brussels: Egyptology Foundation Queen Elizabeth, 1981), 136–46; Andreas Löw, *Hermes Trismegistos als Zeuge der Wahrheit: Die christliche Hermetikrezeption von Athenagoras bis Laktanz*, Theophaneia 36 (Berlin: Philo, 2002), 26–29.

[12] See Raymond O. Faulkner, trans., *The Ancient Egyptian Book of the Dead*, ed. Carol Andrews (London: British Museum, 1985), 28 (spell 30b); C. J. Bleeker, *Hathor and Thoth: Two Key Figures of the Ancient Egyptian Religion* (Leiden: Brill, 1973), 145–50.

[13] For Hermes as Logos (or Word), see *Ref.* 5.7.32; Seneca, *On Benefits* 4.7; Cornutus, *Nature of the Gods* 16; Heraclitus, *Homeric Problems* 72; Acts 14:12; Varro in Augustine, *City of God* 7.14; Justin, *First Apology* 1.22; Plutarch, *Isis and Osiris* 54 (*Moralia* 373b).

[14] For devising speech, see Plato, *Cratylus* 407e–408b; compare Diodorus, *Library of History* 1.16 (τὰ περὶ τὴν ἑρμενείαν).

divine speech personified, Thoth is also a creator. "What bursts from his heart has immediate existence; what he pronounces exists for eternity."[15]

In the Hellenistic period (roughly 323–31 BCE), Greeks living in Egypt and Hellenized Egyptians crafted an amalgam of Thoth and Hermes who was called "the Egyptian Hermes" or later "Hermes Thrice Greatest" (*Trismegistos*, *Termaximus*). This Hermes is superlatively great in a superlative (threefold) way. Following English convention, however, here we call "Thrice Greatest Hermes" simply "Hermes Thrice Great."

Greeks typically conceived of Hermes Thrice Great in a Euhemeristic fashion. That is to say, they often considered him to have been an ancient man – a real scribe of a real Pharaoh, often the first divine Pharaoh called Ammon (the Egyptian god Amun). This scribe, named Thoth or Theuth, invented the alphabet and the art of writing.[16] Ever since, humans have been using writing to preserve the vast array of accumulated knowledge. Thoth was later deified to become a recognized Egyptian god or *daimon* (a kind of mediating deity).[17] Writing was the best-known benefit that Thoth offered to human beings, but it was not the only one.

Greeks attributed to Thoth the invention of a host of other arts. Plato (427–347 BCE) made Thoth the discoverer of mathematics and astronomy.[18] Hecataeus of Abdera (fourth century BCE) ascribed to him the invention of a common language, religious ritual, music, wrestling, dancing, and the culture of the olive.[19] The Jewish writer Artapanus (third

[15] These titles derive from hieroglyphic inscriptions from the temple of Denderah printed in Festugière, *RHT*, 1.69 and Wilhelm Bousset, *Kyrios Christos: A History of the Belief in Christ from the Beginnings of Christianity to Irenaeus*, trans. John E. Steely (Nashville: Abingdon, 1970), 394–95. The temple is dated to the time of Nero (mid first century CE). Compare the inscription on the door of the library of the great temple of Philae: "the glorious Ibis who came forth from the heart of the god [Re]; tongue of Tenen [Ptah] when he gives command, throat of him of the hidden name [Amun]" (quoted in Patrick Boylan, *Thoth, the Hermes of Egypt: A Study of Some Aspects of Theological Thought in Ancient Egypt* [London: Oxford University Press, 1922], 214–15). In the Shabaka text, Thoth functions as creator in the form of Ptah (*ibid.*, 119). According to a fourth-century CE papyrus fragment called the *Strasbourg Cosmogony*, Hermes is depicted as creator of the world. For an introduction see Jean-Marie Flamand, "Cosmogonie de Strasbourg," *DPA* 2.478–80. See further Youri Volokhine, "Le dieu Thot et la parole," *Revue de l'histoire des religions* 221 (2004): 131–56.

[16] For Thoth the inventor of writing, see Philo of Byblos in Eusebius, *Preparation of the Gospel* 1.9.24 (= TH 6a), as well as the writers cited in the next paragraph.

[17] Plato (*Philebus* 18b) expressed uncertainty as to whether Hermes (Thoth) was a god, a *daimon*, or divine man. Perhaps he was a man guided by a *daimon*, as in Ammianus Marcellinus, *Historical Events* 21.14.5 (TH 15). In some Hermetic texts, Hermes Thrice Great is distinguished from his grandfather Thoth (*Ascl.* 37, with Fowden, *Egyptian Hermes*, 174–75). A purely Euhemeristic conception of Hermes Thrice Great is taken up by Christians such as Lactantius, *Wrath of God* 11.12 (with the comments of Löw, *Hermes* 111–13, 140–42), *Institutes* 1.6.3 (= FH 3a); Augustine, *City of God* 18.39 (TH 19b).

[18] Plato, *Phaedrus* 274c–d; 275a.

[19] Diodorus, *Library of History* 1.16.

to second centuries BCE), after identifying Moses with Hermes, makes him the teacher of navigation, devisor of weapons, machines of war, and philosophy.[20] According to the Roman orator Cicero (mid first century BCE), Hermes-Thoth "gave the Egyptians their laws and letters."[21] In the early first century CE, the Roman poet Manilius called Hermes "first founder of this great and holy science" – meaning astrology.[22] The Christian writer Tertullian in the early third century CE dubbed Hermes Thrice Great "teacher of all the natural philosophers."[23] This tradition of philosophy stretched back to Thales in the sixth century BCE. When one reads these testimonies (printed more fully at the end of this volume), one gains a sense of the vast knowledge ascribed to Hermes.[24] There was nary a branch of learning over which the Thrice Great did not preside.

To the question: "Why was the Egyptian Hermes called 'Thrice Great'?" one can answer: triple greatness was the special prerogative of Thoth.[25] A god twice or thrice great was a god supremely great – greater indeed than all his divine competitors (at least in the minds of his devotees).[26] Clay shards in the archive of Hor (around 168 BCE) yield a Greek translation of Thoth's Egyptian epithet: "the greatest, yes, greatest god, great Hermes!"[27] In Egyptian, the repetition likely had a

[20] Eusebius, *Preparation for the Gospel* 9.27.4–6 = frag. 3 in *OTP* 2.898–99. See further Gerard Mussies, "The Interpretatio Judaica of Thot-Hermes," in M. Heerma van Voss, among others, eds., *Studies in Egyptian Religion Dedicated to Professor Jan Zandee* (Leiden: Brill, 1982), 89–120 at 90–108.

[21] Cicero, *Nature of the Gods* 3.56 (= TH 2).

[22] Manilius, *Astronomica* 1.30 (= TH 3).

[23] Tertullian, *Against the Valentinians* 15.1 (= FH 1a). See further Fowden, *Egyptian Hermes*, 198.

[24] See in particular TH 21 from Cyril of Alexandria.

[25] Florian Ebeling notes that, "From the second millennium BCE on, Thoth was revered as the 'twice great,' which was then escalated into 'thrice great,' that is, 'greatest of all'" (*The Secret History of Hermes Trismegistus: Hermeticism from Ancient to Modern Times*, trans. David Lorton [Ithaca, NY: Cornell University Press, 2007], 30).

[26] Erik Hornung, *Conceptions of God in Ancient Egypt: The One and the Many*, trans. John Baines (Ithaca, NY: Cornell University Press, 1982), 185–88. Greek usage is analogous. Plutarch comments that, "We customarily express 'many times' also by 'three times,' just as we say 'thrice blessed'" (*Isis and Osiris* 36 [*Moralia* 365c]).

[27] Mahé, *HHE*, 1 (μέγιστος καὶ μέγιστος θεὸς μέγας Ἑρμῆς). The text is printed in J. D. Ray, *Archive of Hor* (London: Egypt Exploration Society, 1976), 2, 159–60; Maria Totti, *Ausgewählte Texte der Isis- und Sarapis-Religion* (Hildesheim: Georg Olms, 1985), 140–44. Alternatively, we could translate: "the greatest and greatest, the great god Hermes." The exact epithet to which the Greek translation corresponds remains unclear because of the great variation of Thoth's epithets. These variations are summarily listed by Jan Quaegebeur, "Thot-Hermès, le dieu le plus grand!" in Hartwig Altenmüller, ed., *Hommages à François Daumas*, 2 vols. (Montpellier: University of Montpellier, 1986), 2.525–44 at 537–38. See further Jacques Parlebas, "L'origine égyptienne de l'appellation 'Hermès Trismégiste,'" *Göttinger Miszellen* 13 (1974): 25–28 with the correctives of Maria-Theresia and Philippe Derchain, "Noch einmal Hermes Trismegistos," *Göttinger Miszellen* 15 (1975): 7–10; and Bull, "Tradition of Hermes," 35–38.

distributive sense as well: Thoth is great on every occasion, at all times, in every respect.[28]

The earliest that Hermes attains the actual epithet "Thrice Great," it seems, is with Thrasyllus of Alexandria, famous astrologer of the emperor Tiberius (reigned 14–37 CE).[29] In Greek, threeness evokes the notion of perfection and pluri-potentiality. Hermes is the greatest god, and his manifold powers were available in multiple ways. In this respect, Martial's playful line about the gladiator called Hermes ironically sums up the essence of the Greco-Egyptian god: "Hermes – all things in one and thrice unique!"[30]

As the god of human sciences, both esoteric and empirical, Hermes Thrice Great remained a fundamentally Egyptian deity. The Greek Hermes was never really a scholar or patron of scholars until Late Antiquity.[31] Though "an interpreter, a messenger, a thief and a deceiver in words," the Greek Hermes was never a scribe. Yet writing and the scribal wisdom it represents were associated with Thoth centuries before the Homeric Hermes.

The Egyptian character of the Thrice Great is highlighted in the *Greek Magical Papyri* (*PGM*). These papyri are priceless testimonies of Egyptian domestic religion from the first to the fourth centuries CE. In a hymn recorded in *PGM* 5.400–21, Hermes is called, "Ruler of the world," the "circle of Moon," the "founder of the words of speech, pleader of Justice's cause ... eye of the Sun ... founder of full-voiced speech," sender of oracles, universal healer, and the one "who brings full mental powers." In a slightly longer version of the hymn, Hermes is called lord of the elements, helmsman of the world, and the world's very order.[32] The creative role of Hermes is further underscored in *PGM* 7.551–57, where he is, "the one who [made] the four quarters of the heaven and the four foundations of the earth." According to *PGM* 13.270–77, Thoth, much like the Hebrew god, "brings existence out of the nonexistent, and nonexistence from

[28] Quaegebeur, "Thot-Hermès," in Altenmüller, ed., *Hommages à François Daumas*, 2.537. See also H. S. Versnel, *Ter Unus: Isis, Dionysus, and Hermes: Three Studies in Henotheism* (Leiden: Brill, 1990), 237–44.

[29] Thrasyllus (ὁ λεγόμενος Τρισμέγιστος Ἑρμῆς). The fragment comes from Thrasyllus's *Pinax (or Tablet) for Hieroclea* (= TH 4). Later attestations of the "Thrice Great" title occur in the early to mid second century with Philo of Byblos from Eusebius, *Preparation of the Gospel* 1.10.17 (= TH 6); and Athenagoras, *Embassy* 28.3 (= TH 7). See further Fowden, *Egyptian Hermes*, 26, 162, 216–17; Löw, *Hermes*, 41–46; Bull, "Tradition of Hermes," 38–40.

[30] Martial, *Epigrams* 5.24.15 (*Hermes omnia solus et ter unus*). Compare CH 16.3: the Father of the universe is "the all who is one and the one who is all." See further Versnel, *Ter Unus*, 227–51; Löw, *Hermes*, 30–40.

[31] Fowden, *Egyptian Hermes*, 201–2.

[32] *PGM* 17b.15–19; compare *PGM* 7.668–85.

existent things . . . the true sight of whose face none of the gods can endure to see." As universal creator, Hermes is also the universal knower of "the things hidden beneath heaven and earth."[33]

Greek philosophers tapped into the wisdom of Hermes by – according to legend at least – visiting Egypt and sitting at the feet of Hermes's heirs: Egyptian priests. These priests were naturally reluctant to share their sacred wisdom, but their visitors proved persistent.[34] According to tradition, all the greatest philosophers – among them Pythagoras, Solon, Eudoxus, Plato, and Democritus, among many others – came to "study abroad" in Egypt.[35] Even if one grants the historicity of these sojourns, one reasonably doubts that all these Greeks learned the specific wisdom later associated with the Thrice Great. Yet if all Egyptian wisdom ultimately derives from Thoth, then Greece's finest sages could later be viewed as the god's disciples. Only on occasion, however, is the connection between the philosophers and Hermes himself made explicit. According to Tertullian, Plato was especially intimate with the Egyptian Hermes.[36] Iamblichus affirms that Pythagoras and Plato, during their visits to Egypt, carefully studied the stelae (inscribed pillars) of Hermes with the help of native priests.[37]

By Late Antiquity, Hermes the Egyptian was viewed as the supreme philosopher, or rather the one who stood at the head of the Greek philosophical tradition. Hermes was not a historical author, but he did possess an important "author function."[38] His name guaranteed the antiquity and validity of a host of Greco-Egyptian writings that addressed important scientific and philosophical topics of the time.

[33] *PGM* 8.1–52.

[34] See especially the case of Thessalus, discussed by Festugière, *Mystique*, 141–80; Jonathan Z. Smith, "The Temple and the Magician," in *Map is Not Territory: Studies in the History of Religions* (Chicago: Chicago University Press, 1978), 172–89.

[35] For Pythagoras, see Isocrates, *Busiris* 28; for Solon, see Plato, *Timaeus* 21e–22b; Plutarch, *Isis and Osiris* 10 (*Moralia* 354e); for Pythagoras, Plato, and Democritus, see Cicero, *On Ends* 5.87; for Plato and Eudoxus, see Strabo, *Geography* 17.1.29; for Pythagoras and Solon, see Diodorus, *Library of History* 1.69.4; for Solon, Pythagoras, Eudoxus, and Democritus, see *ibid.* 1.96.2; 1.98.2; for Pythagoras, Anaxagoras, Solon, and Plato, see Ammianus Marcellinus, *Historical Events* 22.16.21–22. These and other texts are collected by Heinrich Dörrie, *Der hellenistische Rahmen des kaiserzeitlichen Platonismus Bausteine 36–72: Text Übersetzung, Kommentar*, vol. 2 of *Der Platonismus in der Antike* (Stuttgart-Bad Cannstatt: Friedrich Fromman, 1990), 166–74, with commentary on 425–53. Peter Kingsley argues that Pythagoras's (i.e. Pythagoras's trip) trip to Egypt was historical ("From Pythagoras to the *Turba philosophorum*: Egypt and Pythagorean Tradition," *Journal of the Warburg and Courtland Institutes* 57 [1994]: 1–13 at 1–3). See further Sauneron, *Priests*, 110–15.

[36] Tertullian, *On the Soul* 2.3 (= FH 1b).

[37] Iamblichus, *On the Mysteries* 1.2 (= TH 12).

[38] Michel Foucault, "What is an Author?" in R. C. Davis and R. Scheifer, eds., *Contemporary Literary Criticism*, 3rd edn. (New York: Longman, 1994), 262–75.

Yet Hermes the Egyptian meant more than Hermes the ancient sage. His Egyptian identity guaranteed the importance and prestige of Egypt throughout the Hellenistic world. To the Greeks, Hermes Thrice Great represented the wisdom of Egypt, just as Moses came to symbolize the wisdom of the Jews, Ostanes the wisdom of the Persians, and Dandamis the wisdom of India. In terms of the discursive practices of Late Antiquity, the Hermetic writings were deeply Hellenic in form and language. Nevertheless, Hermes never stopped being Egyptian, and the Hermetic writings never lost their Egyptian roots and local color.

Hermetic Communities?

The Hermetic literature refers to named teachers and disciples like Hermes, Tat, Ammon, Isis, Horus, and so on. Do these literary characters reflect a social reality of Hermetic teaching?[39] If so, what group did Hermetic teachers belong to or represent? Where did this group or groups meet, and what did they do in their meetings? Theories have come and gone. Richard Reitzenstein initially proposed a kind of Hermetic mother church located in Egypt. By contrast, Jean-André Festugière found, "no trace in the Hermetic literature of ceremonies belonging to supposed believers in Hermes, nothing that resembles sacraments ... There is no clergy, no appearance of hierarchical organization, no degrees of initiation ... On the contrary ... Hermeticism forthrightly expresses its loathing for material acts of worship."[40]

After the discovery of the Nag Hammadi Hermetic writings, however, Gilles Quispel could declare that, "It is now completely certain that there existed before and after the beginning of the Christian era in Alexandria [Egypt], a secret society, akin to a Masonic lodge. The members of the group called themselves 'brethren,' were initiated through a baptism of the Spirit, celebrated a sacred meal and read the Hermetic writings as edifying treatises for their spiritual progress."[41] More cautiously, Jean-Pierre Mahé observed that the prayers in the Hermetic corpus "provide evidence that there were communities placed under the patronage of Hermes in

[39] On spiritual teaching in antiquity, see Richard Valantasis, *Spiritual Guides of the Third Century: A Semiotic Study of the Guide-Disciple Relationship in Christianity, Neoplatonism, Hermetism, and Gnosticism* (Minneapolis: Fortress, 1991), 13–62; Anna van den Kerchove, *Le voie d'Hermès: Pratiques rituelles et traits hermétiques* (Leiden: Brill, 2012), 45–183.

[40] Festugière, *RHT*, 1.81–84.

[41] Quoted in Salaman and others, *Way of Hermes*, 10.

which ... prayer, characterized as ... 'sacrifice of speech,' ... could have the place of a true sacrament."[42]

Today, most scholars seem persuaded that references to "pure food,"[43] a ritual embrace,[44] and formal prayers[45] suggest some sort of ritual and community life.[46] Christian H. Bull in part revives the idea of Reitzenstein that Hermetic community leaders were Egyptian priests increasingly detached from temple service and administration.[47] Partial support for this idea comes from the *Book of Thoth*, a book written in an Egyptian priestly language (demotic) which circulated in the first and second centuries CE. In the book, Thoth – or someone who shares his epithets – dialogues with one seeking knowledge. The book emerged from Egyptian priestly circles and deals with native Egyptian lore. Although most of this lore does not overlap with the contents of the philosophical Hermetica, the genre and format of the *Book of Thoth* strongly resembles these writings.[48]

It must be kept in mind, however, that the community life of the Hermetic practitioners is almost entirely reconstructed from the Hermetic texts themselves. External witnesses sometimes refer to Egyptian priests living in temple complexes and passing on their wisdom.[49] None of these,

[42] Quoted in Copenhaver, 123. See further R. van den Broek, "Religious Practices in the Hermetic 'Lodge': New Light from Nag Hammadi," in van den Broek, ed., *From Poimandres*, 77–96.

[43] *The Prayer of Thanksgiving* (NHC VI,7), 65.6.

[44] *Disc. 8–9* (NHC VI,6), 57.26–27; *The Prayer of Thanksgiving* (NHC VI,7), 65.4.

[45] For example, *The Prayer of Thanksgiving* (NHC VI,7), parallel to *Ascl.* 41.

[46] Van den Kerchove concludes that the "way of Hermes" is "a sequence of concrete ritual practices, some regular, some occasional, some temporary, others developing as a consequence of the disciple's formation. Some are a simple gesture, like a kiss. Others combine words and gestures like the rite of absorption or certain prayers. Almost all are based on a performative word, that of the teacher" (*Voie*, 374–75). See further S. Giversen, "Hermetic Communities?" in J. P. Sorensen, ed., *Rethinking Religion: Studies in the Hellenistic Process* (Copenhagen: Museum Tusculanum, 1989), 49–54; Gebhard Löhr, *Verherrlichung Gottes durch Philosophie: Der hermetische Traktat II im Rahmen der antiken Philosophie- und Religionsgeschicthe* (Tübingen: Mohr Siebeck, 1997), 385–97; Matthias Heiduk, "Offene Geheimnisse – Hermetische Texte und verborgenes Wissen in der mittelalterlichen Rezeption von Augustinus bis Albertus Magnus" (Ph.D. diss., Albert-Ludwigs-Universität, 2007), 41–59.

[47] Bull, "Tradition of Hermes," 437–70; see also David Frankfurter, *Religion in Roman Egypt: Assimilation and Resistance* (Princeton: Princeton University Press, 1998), 198–237; Roger S. Bagnall, *Egypt in Late Antiquity* (Princeton: Princeton University Press, 1993), 261–74; Françoise Dunand and Christiane Zivie-Coche, *Gods and Men in Egypt 3000 BCE to 395 CE* (Ithaca, NY: Cornell University Press, 2004), 210–13; Ian S. Moyer, *Egypt and the Limits of Hellenism* (Cambridge: Cambridge University Press, 2011), 264–73.

[48] Richard Jasnow and Karl-Theodor Zauzich, eds., *The Ancient Egyptian Book of Thoth: A Demotic Discourse on Knowledge and Pendant to the Classical Hermetica*, 2 vols. (Wiesbaden: Harrassowitz, 2005), especially 65–70.

[49] See especially Chaeremon, frag. 10 (van der Horst) = Porphyry, *On Abstinence* 4.6.8, also printed in Fowden, *Egyptian Hermes*, 54–55, and discussed by P. W. van der Horst, "The Way of Life of the Egyptian Priests according to Chaeremon," in van Voss, ed., *Studies in Egyptian Religion*, 61–71.

however, refer to what we would call a Hermetic community.[50] One could imagine a Hermetic community as a kind of philosophical discussion group, a school with a master teacher, a loose collection of individuals seeking salvation through initiatory readings – or a fluid blend of all these models.[51] With regard to Late Antiquity, one should take seriously the proposal of Giulia Sfameni Gasparro that what developed was something like a Hermetic "audience cult." Such cults "do not display formal organization or constitute structured groups devoted to a dogmatic creed, but rather participate in a common heritage of knowledge and interest."[52]

The philosophical treatises of Hermes were religious and initiatory, but they came to be read more and more as school exercises. Like Platonic dialogues, Hermetic dialogues were later dissected for the opinions of Hermes. These opinions were then incorporated into doxographies. Johannes Stobaeus, for instance, quoted Hermes as an ancient philosophical authority for the education of his son. Late Antique Christian authors like Lactantius and Cyril quoted Hermes as a theological authority to prove the antiquity of their creeds. The Hermes of Iamblichus was a theosophical expert explaining a universal way of salvation. Naturally, there were no hard and fast distinctions between what we call theosophy, theology, and philosophy in the ancient world. The point is that Hermes had come to represent an ancient authoritative discourse. For the educated elite, the discourse that interested them tended to be philosophical and scientific. Hermes was an authority on philosophy, medicine, and astronomy because his wisdom lay at the root of all these disciplines. The name "Hermes" meant knowledge, both scientific (*epistēmē*) and spiritual (*gnōsis*).[53]

Dating

Since Isaac Casaubon (1559–1614), the treatises in the Byzantine collection called the *Corpus Hermeticum* (CH) have been dated anywhere from the late first to the late third centuries CE. The *Perfect Discourse* (originally composed in Greek but only fully preserved in a periphrastic Latin translation) probably appeared toward the end of this period. In large part,

[50] See further Fowden, *Egyptian Hermes*, 156–95; Bull, "Tradition of Hermes," 4–11.

[51] Heiduk, "Offene," 58.

[52] Giulia Sfameni Gasparro, "*Religio mentis:* The Hermetic Process of Individualization," in Jörg Rüpke, ed., *The Individual in the Religions of the Ancient Mediterranean* (Oxford: Oxford University Press, 2013), 387–434 at 418.

[53] For the later reception history of the Hermetica, see Copenhaver, *Hermetica*, xlv–lxi.

this dating is rooted in internal criteria. Writers of the philosophical Hermetica were conversant with Stoicism and Middle Platonism, but not Neoplatonism (which arose in the mid third century).

External witnesses to Hermetic books begin appearing in the second century.[54] Astrological writings seem to have been ascribed to Hermes as early as the first (some would say second) century BCE. Collections of Hermetic maxims (such as we find in SH 11) may also have appeared around this time.[55] Hermes-Thoth was recognized as an ancient sage from the time of Plato (the fourth century BCE). He begins to be widely recognized as a philosopher by the early third century CE, as witnessed by Tertullian.[56]

There is no overriding reason to date the Stobaean and other Hermetic fragments outside the date range of CH (that is, from the late first to the late third centuries CE). Perhaps more precision can be attained with regard to a peculiar collection of Hermetic treatises in which Isis addresses her son Horus (SH 23–26). Lucian in the mid second century CE refers to sacred books of Horus and Isis in the inner shrines of Egyptian temples.[57] The fact that such books were known in the Greek world made it logical for a Greek-speaking Egyptian to write Hermetic books in the name of Isis.

Walter Scott used external criteria to narrow the date of one particular tractate, namely the *Korē Kosmou* (SH 23). The treatise was written, he proposed, between 263–68 CE since the atrocities spoken of in SH 23.55–61 reflected, according to Scott, the historical calamities in Alexandria between 262–63 CE.[58] As Scott himself admitted, however, matching generalized literary description to specific historical events is precarious. Slightly more secure is the stylistic criteria pointed out by Eduard Norden: "Meyer's law of the accentual clausula is largely, though not invariably, observed in an elevated passage of the *Kore Kosmou*."[59] Thus on the

[54] For instance, Plutarch, *Isis and Osiris* 61 (*Moralia* 375f) (Ἐν δὲ ταῖς Ἑρμοῦ λεγομέναις βίβλοις).

[55] Mahé, *HHE*, 2.278.

[56] Tertullian, *Against the Valentinians* 15.1 (= TH 1a, dated from 207–12 CE). On the dating of the Hermetica see further Fowden, *Egyptian Hermes* 11; van den Kerchove, *Voie*, 5–6.

[57] Lucian, *The Dream, or the Cock* 18: "I [a man reincarnated as a rooster] went to Egypt to commune with the prophets in their wisdom. I even penetrated into their inner sanctuaries and fully learned the books of Horus and Isis."

[58] Scott, *Hermetica*, 3.474–75.

[59] Quoting A. D. Nock, "Diatribe Form in the *Hermetica*," in Zeph Stewart, ed., *Essays on Religion and the Ancient World*, 2 vols. (Cambridge, MA: Harvard University Press, 1972), 1.26–32 at 31. Nock refers to Eduard Norden, *Agnostos Theos: Untersuchungen zur formengeschichte religiöser Rede* (Leipzig: Teubner, 1913), 66, n.1 where Norden demonstrates Meyer's law in a lengthy passage from the *Korē Kosmou*.

"grounds of prose-rhythm," one would place the *Korē Kosmou* not earlier than around 300 CE.[60]

Papyrologists have dated the Vienna papyri to the end of the second or the beginning of the third century CE. The contents of the fragments themselves, however, may be a generation or two earlier. These fragments appear in numbered treatises, indicating that there were collections of Hermetic writings existing as early as the second century CE. Some – or rather most – of these collections did not survive. Johannes Stobaeus made excerpts from some of them around the year 400 CE. Authors like Tertullian, Lactantius, and Cyril were evidently reading and excerpting from other collections of philosophical Hermetica in the third and fourth centuries. Cyril specifically mentions fifteen "Hermaic" books composed in Athens.[61]

By that time, Hermes's reputation as one of the oldest sages was well established. Obviously this Hermes was older than Jesus, and native Egyptians dated Hermes-Thoth long before the time of Moses (excoriated by some Egyptian authors as a leper expelled from Egypt).[62] One Jewish author, as we saw, countered this view by identifying Moses with the Egyptian Hermes (see TH 1). Later Christian authors worked hard to undermine Egyptian chronology such that Hermes was considerably younger than Moses. In the famous panel in the Siena Cathedral (figure 1) a kind of compromise was worked out. The enrobed and bearded Hermes was labeled explicitly as Moses's contemporary (*contemporaneus Moysi*).[63]

As it turns out, there is a complex historical dialectic between Hermes the prophet of Christianity and Hermes's pagan competitor. From Late Antiquity to the Renaissance, Christians tended either to laud Hermes as a precursor or scold him as a sorcerer. The Hermetic fragments and testimonies translated here offer some of the primary sources required to trace this history. In the course of time both Muslims and Christians interested in the sciences of alchemy, astrology, and (natural) magic found ways to integrate Hermes into their sacred histories. Some Christians like

[60] Nock, "Diatribe Form," in *Essays*, 1.31, n.16. [61] See TH 21 (from Cyril).

[62] See the texts cited by John G. Gager, *Moses in Greco-Roman Paganism* (Nashville: Abingdon, 1972), 113–33.

[63] See further Brian P. Copenhaver, *Magic in Western Culture: From Antiquity to the Enlightenment* (Cambridge: Cambridge University Press, 2015), 160–65; Copenhaver, "Hermes Theologus: The Sienese Mercury and Ficino's Hermetic Demons," in John W. O'Malley, Thomas M. Izbicki, and Gerald Christianson, eds., *Humanity and Divinity in Renaissance and Reformation: Essays in Honor of Charles Trinkaus* (Leiden: Brill, 1993), 149–84.

Figure 1

Augustine celebrated the destruction of Egyptian gods in Late Antiquity. Yet the ever-transforming Egyptian Hermes survived his own prophesied apocalypse and greatly influenced the course of both science and spirituality in Late Antiquity and beyond.

A Note on This Translation

The critical edition employed for the SH and most of the FH fragments is contained in the third and fourth volumes of Nock and Festugière, eds., *Corpus Hermeticum: Fragments. Extraits de Stobée, Fragments Divers*, 1954 (= NF). More recent critical editions are used for FH 36–45 and all of the TH material. The new papyrus fragments (OH and VH) stem from the critical editions printed by J.-P. Mahé and J. Paramelle.

When my reading of the Greek text departs from the printed editions, it is flagged in the notes (along with other significant divergences in the manuscripts). As much as possible, I have endeavored to use consistent English words for Hermetic technical terms, preferring, for instance, "energy" for *energeia*, and "consciousness" for *nous*. (In this case, "consciousness" should be understood as spiritual consciousness, the highest form of intellect.) Occasionally, words or phrases are added in parentheses to maximize comprehension and readability.

Generally speaking, I favour a literal translation. Nevertheless, clear and quality English prose often requires the breakup of long and tortuous Greek sentences. Readers should know that the style of the Greek changes, sometimes radically, depending upon the fragment in question. The *Korē Kosmou* (SH 23), for instance, presents a somewhat flowery though elegant prose totally lacking in SH 17–21. These latter fragments feature highly compressed and ultra-technical terminology that makes for difficult reading in any language. Accordingly, changes of style in the translation represent similar shifts in the Greek.

Subtitles in **bold** are original to the ancient manuscripts. Subtitles in ***bold italics*** are added by the translator. Sometimes the names of the dialogue partners are also added in *italics*. In the notes, short quotations of ancient works are provided for ease of reference. The reader is always encouraged, however, to look up the passage cited to know its full context. Translations from CH are taken, with slight modifications, from Copenhaver's *Hermetica* (1992). Translations from DH are taken from Mahé's text in *The Way of Hermes* (1999). All other translations of ancient works in the notes, unless otherwise noted, are my own.

Sigla Adopted for This Translation

Angled brackets < >	enclose an editor's insertion of a word or words into the Greek text
Square brackets [ ]	enclose an editor's deletion of a word or phrase from the Greek text
Pointed brackets { }	enclose a word or words regarded as unintelligible in the Greek text
Parentheses ( )	enclose a word or words added by the translator for clarification or smoother translation
An ellipsis . . .	indicates an actual gap in the Greek text
An ellipsis in angled brackets <. . .>	indicates a suspected gap in the Greek text

Stobaean Hermetica (SH 1–29)

The Author and His Work

Johannes Stobaeus derived his name from Stobi in Macedonia (in northern Greece). In this city during the early fifth century CE, he compiled a vast collection of excerpts for the education of his son Septimius – particularly for fostering his son's memory. The name Johannes (Ἰωάννης) suggests that Stobaeus was a Christian or a man raised in the Christian tradition. His exclusion of Christian writers from his collection, however, may indicate that Stobaeus primarily identified with his Hellenic heritage. The vast cathedral of learning he offered to his son was certainly a masterpiece of Hellenic learning.

Photius the scholarly Patriarch of Constantinople (roughly 820–91 CE) summarized the contents of Stobaeus's work in some detail. Photius called the work *Excerpts, Sayings and Precepts* (Ἐκλογαί ἀποφθέγματα ὑποθῆκαι). During Photius's time, Stobaeus's oeuvre was divided into four books. Later the books came to be grouped under two titles: *Physical and Ethical Excerpts* (books 1–2) and the *Florilegium* (books 3–4). For simplicity, we will refer to Stobaeus's entire work as the *Anthology*.

In the time of Photius, Stobaeus's *Anthology* contained 208 chapters. Some of these chapters, along with the first part of the introduction, have been lost in the process of transmission. Photius relates that Stobaeus's (now mostly missing) introduction began by praising philosophy and surveying the philosophical schools. The remnants of our surviving book 1 exposit topics in ancient physics (the study of the natural world from earth to the stars). Book 2 begins with matters of logic and epistemology. From chapter 7 of book 2 to the end of book 3, chiefly ethical topics are discussed. What remains of book 4 largely treats matters of society, politics, and family.

Stobaeus's collection is structured on several different levels. The organization of the materials shows that Stobaeus made an effort to cover the three main branches of ancient philosophy: physics, logic, and ethics. The individual chapters are organized by theme (for instance, there is a chapter on Providence, War, Marriage, and so on). In each chapter are quotations that usually cite the original authors, though Stobaeus may have derived these quotes second-hand. Stobaeus tended to cite poets first, before turning to famous philosophers, orators, historians, doctors, kings, and generals (not necessarily in that order). Altogether, Stobaeus excerpted over 500 authors from Homer in the late eighth century BCE to Themistius in the fourth century CE (over a 900-year period).[1]

Stobaeus treated Hermes chiefly as a philosopher. He quoted Hermes as an authority equal to the greatest of his philosophical authorities (notably Plato and Pythagoras). Stobaeus had access to what we call the *Corpus Hermeticum* 2, 4, 10, and the *Asclepius.* He also quoted from Hermetic tractates that are otherwise lost. We cannot tell exactly how much of these tractates Stobaeus preserved. Sometimes he quoted a short maxim; at other times he seems to have transcribed virtually the whole text of a Hermetic discourse. For instance, what is classified here as SH 27 is a single sentence. By contrast, SH 23 seems to reproduce nearly an entire Hermetic tractate.[2] Stobaeus probably edited his Hermetic material to increase its intelligibility and to fit the scope of his (mainly philosophical) project.[3] He may also have split up or combined Hermetic excerpts from different treatises. These are normal practices of an ancient excerptor.

Manuscript Tradition

Stobaeus's *Anthology* in the complete form to which Photius had access was abbreviated probably in the tenth or eleventh century by a Byzantine epitomizer. The epitomizer was partial to the Neoplatonic tradition, a fact that probably secured the preservation of many Hermetic excerpts. The

[1] See further R.-M. Piccione, "Sulle fonti e le metodologie compilative di Stobeo," *Eikasmos* 5 (1994): 281–317; G. Reydams-Schils, ed., *Thinking through Excerpts: Studies on Stobaeus* (Turnhout: Brepols, 2011).

[2] For Stobaeus, see further Scarpi, 1.255–66.

[3] Christian Wildberg opines: "The main reason why the Hermetic fragments preserved in his [Stobaeus's] writings read so much more clearly than our manuscripts is not that he had access to an unspoiled tradition, but rather that he doctored, corrected, and emended for the benefit of his own readers, not at all unlike what modern editors have done" ("*Corpus Hermeticum*, Tractate III: The Genesis of a Genesis," in Lance Jenott and Sarit Kattan Gribetz, eds., *Jewish and Christian Cosmogony in Late Antiquity* (Tübingen: Mohr Siebeck, 2013), 139–64 at 149.

modern critical edition of Stobaeus was produced by Curt Wachsmuth and Otto Hense in the late nineteenth and early twentieth centuries. Wachsmuth edited books 1–2 of the *Anthology*, and Hense books 3–4.

Most of the Hermetic excerpts derive from Stobaeus's *Anthology* books 1–2. For these books, Wachsmuth based his text on the fourteenth-century codex Farnesius III D 15 (abbreviated "F") and the fifteenth-century codex Parisinus gr. 2129 (here abbreviated "P"). F is of better quality and more complete than P. Both manuscripts derive from a common archetype, a Byzantine epitome of Stobaeus's *Anthology*. Additional material is preserved in codex Laurentianus VIII, no. 22 (L). Dated to the fourteenth century, L is not a manuscript of Stobaeus's *Anthology*, but another anthology that incorporates material from it. Importantly, L derives from a manuscript written before the *Anthology* was epitomized. Unfortunately, L itself is only partially preserved.

Books 3–4 of the *Anthology* are better attested. Two families of manuscripts have been identified as deriving from a manuscript close to the one described by Photius. The first is represented by the eleventh-century codex Sambucus (S), the extracts in Vossianus gr. O,9, and the collection published by Froben (*Gnomae Frobenii*). The second family is subdivided into two branches. To the first belong codex Parisinus gr. 1985 (A); codex Mendoza (M); the extracts from Stobaeus in the *Corpus Parisinum* (that is, Parisinus gr. 1168); the extracts in M^{d} ("d" standing for the collation of M by Dindorf) as well as those in the *Rosetum* compiled by Macarius Chrysocephalus. The other branch is represented by L and the fourteenth-century *Excerpta Bruxellensia* (or *Brussels Excerpts*).[4]

Organization

We turn to the Hermetic fragments preserved by Stobaeus. Since the edition of Walter Scott in 1924, these fragments have been organized according to their attributions. (Nock and Festugière in volume 3 of their Budé edition followed Scott's ordering with minor modifications.) There are ten discourses of Hermes to Tat (SH 1, 2A, 2B + 11 [counted as one], 4–10), five discourses of Hermes to Ammon (SH 12–16), five discourses of Isis to Horus (SH 23–27), and six discourses ascribed to Hermes alone

[4] On the manuscript tradition, see further NF 3.i–ix; J. Mansfeld and D. T. Runia, *Aëtiana: The Method and Intellectual Context of a Doxographer. Volume 1: The Sources*. Philosophia Antiqua 73 (Leiden: Brill, 1997), 196–271; Denis Michael Searby, "The Intertitles in Stobaeus: Condensing a Culture," in *Thinking through Excerpts*, 23–70.

(SH 3, 17–22). There is a single excerpt from a treatise called *Aphrodite* (SH 22), as well as an astrological poem attributed to Hermes (SH 29). Finally, there are three single-sentence quotations, one attributed to Hermes (SH 28), another to Hermes speaking with Akmon (possibly we should emend to Ammon, SH 13), and the third to an unknown king (perhaps Ammon, SH 27).[5]

Scott's organization of the excerpts is logical enough, though it disrupts the order of the excerpts as they appear in Stobaeus. One must acknowledge that Stobaeus ordered the excerpts according to his own categories. It is just possible, however, that he preserved something of the order of the original Hermetic collections from which he drew, especially when he cited multiple Hermetic excerpts in the same chapter of his *Anthology*. Oftentimes knowing the Stobaean order of the excerpts can aid in the task of interpretation.

Here we offer some indication of the different ordering of Stobaeus and Scott important for interpretation. Stobaeus's *Anthology* 1.5 treats the topic of "Fate and the Good Ordering of Events." In this chapter, Stobaeus quoted three Hermetic excerpts. The first (selection 14 = SH 29) is a hexameter poem describing the seven planets. The second (selection 16 = SH 14) subordinates Fate to Providence and defines Fate as the cause of astral formations. The third (selection 20 = SH 12) calls the stars Fate's "instrument." In this case, Scott's ordering (SH 12, 14, 29) reverses the order in which these excerpts appear in Stobaeus.

Another example: Stobaeus's *Anthology* 1.41, called "On Nature and its Derived Causes," includes a total of seven Hermetic excerpts. The very first selection (= SH 2B) relates how a person can live a devoted life even though nothing on earth is true (or real). Continuous with this selection (with no break in Stobaeus's text) is SH 11, mostly composed of a list of forty-eight maxims formally similar to the Hermetic *Definitions* (DH). As selection 4 (= SH 16), Hermes speaks to Ammon on the relation of soul and body. In selection 6 (= SH 4), Hermes discourses at length with Tat on the topics of animal intelligence and energies. The very next selection (7 = SH 15) presents a complex reflection on the birth of intelligent life. It is immediately followed by selection 8 (= SH 5) on divine and human bodies, with an appendix on sleep. Finally selection 11 (= SH 21) distinguishes the eternal and temporal creators (the Preexistent God and the Sun, respectively). Here again, Stobaeus's ordering (selections 1, 4, 6–8, 11) does not jibe with the re-ordering of Scott. To take them in Stobaeus's

[5] NF 3.i–xiii; Scott, *Hermetica*, 1.82–86; 4.243–46.

order, one must read SH 4 after 16 and SH 5 after 15. Scott also split apart two Hermetic excerpts (separated out as 2B and 11), which Stobaeus seems to have viewed as one.

As a final example, we mention Stobaeus's magisterial chapter (*Anthology* 1.49) entitled "On the Soul." On this topic, Stobaeus found abundant material in the Hermetica worth citing. He included a total of eight Hermetic excerpts, four of them the length of whole tractates. Technically speaking, Stobaeus included nine excerpts, though his selection 1c, which defines the soul in exactly the same terms as the opening line of his selection 6, is not counted as a separate excerpt. In Stobaeus's third selection 3 (= SH 20), Hermes relates the nature of soul and its gift of life to the body. The very next selection (= SH 17) tells how the soul is integrated with the body's drives and desires. The selection immediately following (5 = SH 3) relates the soul to motion and defines three main types of soul. Selection 6 (= SH 19), in turn, speaks of the soul's life apart from the body. These selections follow a certain logical sequence and may even derive from the same Hermetic tractate. If so, their rearrangement by Scott is unfortunate. Note especially how Scott widely separated SH 3 from other excerpts proximate in their original Stobaean context.

Genre and Themes

The genre of most of the Stobaean Hermetica (SH 1–22, 27–28) might be called "technical school treatise in dialogue form." Plato had long established the dialogue as an accepted form of philosophical discourse. The amount of actual back-and-forth conversation varied widely in this genre. Hermetic treatises tended to become monologues – and logically, since the authority and wisdom of Hermes was so great. Unlike Platonic dialogues, Hermetic dialogues presented divinely revealed truths. The setting for these Hermetic dialogues is never made explicit. One might opine that they breathe the air of the classroom. Yet the Hermetic classroom is more like the inner room of a chapel in which secret teachings are disclosed to a select few.

Formally speaking, SH 23–26 are also dialogues, but they are better defined as philosophical myths in dialogue form. Again, Plato set the precedent for telling lengthy philosophical myths in his own dialogues. The myths of the Hermetica are distinctive for their blend of Greek, Jewish, and Egyptian ideas. The only outlier is SH 29, a poem written in epic hexameters inspired by astrological ideas.

If we list the topics dealt with in the twenty-nine excerpts of Stobaeus, not much internal consistency can be detected. There are, however, repeated themes (influenced by Stobaeus's own philosophical interests): the ineffability of God, the nature and destiny of the soul, the unreality of earthly things, the rule of Fate and its relation to God's higher order, the stars and their energies that pervade the cosmos. Stobaeus's interests were broad, and Hermetic learning seemed to have known no bounds. Thus we also find disquisitions on time, matter, sleep, Justice, climate, and familial resemblance – to name just a few. Collectively, Hermetic texts provided something like "a theory of everything" at the risk of great internal tensions.

Here we can only touch on some of the major themes in the Stobaean Hermetica. We commence, as Stobaeus did long ago, with God. The primal, or "preexistent," God is not the cosmos or a deity in the cosmos. He is a supreme, ineffable being who transcends language, bodies, and all perceptible reality (SH 1.1–2; 21.1). The creation of this God is eternal as are the (probably astral) bodies that he makes (SH 2A.1; 5.1). The image of God is not the whole cosmos, but the Sun (SH 21.2). The Sun is the creator of the cosmos and of all bodies that change (SH 2A.14). Yet the Sun is so far below the primal God that his ability to truly imitate him is limited (SH 5.2). The way to God is lived by cultivating devotion and the spiritual senses. Reaching God ultimately involves an ascent beyond the material world.

All changeable bodies on earth exist in a realm of untruth and false appearance (SH 2A; 11.2 §16). Everything in the lower world is an illusion, not a stepping-stone toward higher reality. Science and empiricism are, it seems, not ways to God. The only right response to radical falsehood is radical devotion to the super-cosmic God (SH 2B.2). Life on earth is a battle against the drives and desires of the body. Ultimately, the body must be abandoned before one ascends to God (SH 2B.6–8) and beholds him (SH 6.19).

Body and soul are fundamentally different realities. Bodies are ever-changing and corruptible, therefore "nothing in the realm of body is true" (SH 11.2 §16). The soul is an eternal, bodiless entity. Nevertheless, the soul, while existing in the body, can be negatively affected by the body's motions and energies (SH 3.7). Since energies must exist in bodies, many energies are forces bringing corruption (SH 4.8–16) and – when they stream from the stars – catastrophic destruction (SH 6.7, 12).

The precise relations between Providence, Necessity, and Fate are difficult to reconstruct. As regards Fate, however, the position in the Stobaean Hermetica is clear: Fate has powers over bodies that are born, but not over immortal, incorporeal souls (SH 7.3; 20.7). Fate itself is subject to a higher order, the order of Providence – an order to which the intelligent motion of the soul corresponds. Fate uses the stars as its instrument, but the energies of the stars only affect bodies (SH 12.2). In itself, the soul has the power to choose freely (SH 18.3; 19.3). But when the soul lets itself be dictated by bodily drives and desires, it is drawn into the realm and grip of Fate.

Both cosmology and theology are somewhat different in SH 23–26. In these tractates, a major concern is to explain the divine origin of the soul while maintaining the souls' essential differences in rank. The ranked nature of souls explains for the most part why they enter different bodies – from the bodies of divine kings to brutish animals. Yet in their ranked hierarchies, souls possess a degree of both upward and downward mobility based on their moral actions. Ultimately, the cosmic system is just, though it may at times seem harsh. Souls are not inherently evil, just curious to the point of audacity. Souls in bodies learn to chasten their audacity; the point, however, was never to crush their curiosity. When they keep to their stations, souls are encouraged to wonder at creation and give humble thanks to their creator.

SH 1

The first excerpt from Stobaeus derives from the first chapter of the second book of his *Anthology* (2.1.26). It is entitled, "On the Interpreters of Divine Matters and How the Truth concerning the Essence of Intelligible Realities is Incomprehensible to Human Beings." It is preceded by a selection from a certain Eusebius on the necessity of believing in the gods, and followed by a quote from Plato's *Timaeus* 48b–d.

By virtue of its content, SH 1 rightly stands at the beginning of a Hermetic collection. The decisive question is how a human being, fixed in a time-bound body and equipped with fallible senses, can comprehend the incorporeal and eternal essence of God. Strictly speaking, however, it is not impossible to understand God; it is simply difficult. The difficulty is rooted in the alterity of the divine nature. God is positively defined as perfect, eternal, strong, and beautiful. Negatively, God is characterized as a being without a body, without shape, without matter, and outside of time. The clumsy tool of human language cannot grasp or define such a being. Language is based on the perception of bodies. Perception trades in imperfect images. Since God is imperceptible, God is in fact inexpressible.

Excerpt of a Discourse of Hermes with Tat

1. It is difficult to understand God. Even for the person who can understand, to speak of God is impossible.[1] After all, it is impossible to

[1] This sentence is quoted in the *Exhortation to the Greeks on True Religion* 38.2, a work attributed to Justin Martyr, but probably written by Marcellus of Ancyra in the fourth century CE. The sentence is also quoted without attribution by Gregory of Nazianzus, *Theological Orations* 28.4 (= FH 38). It is quoted in a fuller form by Lactantius, *Epitome of the Divine Institutes* 4.5 (and echoed in his *Divine Institutes* 2.8.68; for which see Antonie Wlosok, *Laktanz und die philosophischen Gnosis: Untersuchungen zu Geschichte und Terminologie der gnostischen Erlösungsvorstellung* [Heidelberg: Carl Winter, 1960], 202–3; Löw, *Hermes*, 184–95). Lactantius called the passage an *exordium*. Possibly, then, it was the first text to stand at the head of an ancient Hermetic collection. The content consists of a Middle Platonic interpretation of Plato, *Timaeus* 28c: "Now to find the Maker

signify with a body what has no body.[2] Likewise, the perfect cannot be comprehended by the imperfect. Moreover, it is grievous for the eternal to have fellowship with the ephemeral.[3] The former lasts forever, while the latter passes away. The one is in truth, while the other is shrouded by appearances. The weaker stands apart from the stronger and the lesser from the greater as much as the mortal is distant from the divine.[4]

2. The intervening distance dims the vision of the Beautiful.[5] Bodies are seen by eyes, and sights are spoken by the tongue. But what is bodiless, invisible, without shape, and not consisting of matter cannot be grasped by our senses.[6] I have this insight, Tat, I have this insight! What cannot be expressed – this is God.[7]

and Father of this universe is quite a task, and even when he is found, it is impossible to declare him to everyone." Indeed, this very passage is quoted by Stobaeus shortly before the present excerpt (*Anthology* 2.1.15) and was often adapted, for instance, by Philo, *Decalogue* 51; Justin, *Dialogue with Trypho* 7.3; 56.1; Julian, *Orations* 4.131d–132a. See further Wlosok, *Laktanz*, 252–56; A. D. Nock, "Exegesis of Timaeus 28c," *VC* 16 (1962): 79–86.

[2] Compare CH 2.4: "the incorporeal is either divine or else it is God."

[3] Compare FH 7: "the mortal cannot approach the immortal, nor the temporal the eternal, nor the corruptible what is incorruptible"; Cyril of Alexandria: "For creator and creature are not to be accounted the same in nature or dignity or worth; one nature is born, the other unborn, one is incorruptible, the other subject to corruption" (*Against Julian* 1.31, Riedweg).

[4] The fourth-century author of *On the Trinity* (formerly ascribed to Didymus the Blind) used a similar phrase: "as much as the immortal is greater than the mortal" (τοσούτῳ κρείττονος, ὅσον τὸ ἀθάνατον τοῦ θνητοῦ) (*PG* 39 776a = Scott, *Hermetica*, 4.175). In FH 25, Cyril of Alexandria quotes SH 1.1 but has a different text of SH 1.2. A form of SH 1.1 is also quoted by Ibn Durayd (died 933 CE) cited by Kevin Van Bladel, *The Arabic Hermes: From Pagan Sage to Prophet of Science* (New York: Oxford University Press, 2009), 198–99.

[5] Compare Plato: "Nor will the Beautiful appear . . . in the guise of a face or hands or anything else that belongs to the body . . . [it is] absolute, pure, unmixed, not polluted by human flesh or colors" (*Symposium* 211a–e). CH 6.4 identifies the substance of God with the Beautiful.

[6] Similar formulas of negative theology occur in Plato: "What is in this place [the region beyond heaven] is without color and without shape and without solidity, a being that really is what it is . . . visible only to consciousness (νοῦς)" (*Phaedrus* 247c). Compare CH 4.9: "the Good is invisible to what can be seen. For the Good has neither shape nor outline. This is why it is like itself but unlike all others, for the bodiless cannot be visible to body"; CH 7.2: "All are sober and gaze with the heart toward one who wishes to be seen, who is neither heard nor spoken of, who is seen not with the eyes but with mind and heart"; SH 2A.9: "truth is . . . the unchangeable Good"; 2A.15: "the primal truth is . . . not made from matter, not embodied, not qualified by color or shape; it is unshifting, unchanging, ever existing."

[7] Compare Apuleius: "Plato . . . most frequently proclaims that this God alone – such is the amazing and ineffable excess of his majesty – cannot be comprehended, even to a limited extent, in any discourses owing to the poverty of human speech, and that even for wise men, when, by vigor of mind they have removed themselves from the body as far as they can, the comprehension of this God is like a bright light fitfully flashing with the swiftest flicker in the deepest darkness, and that only from time to time" (*God of Socrates* 124). On the inexpressibility of God, see further Festugière, *RHT*, 4.70–78.

SH 2A

Excerpt 2A derives from a chapter of Stobaeus (*Anthology* 3.11.31) called "On Truth." It is immediately preceded by a quotation from Eusebius concerning when it is permissible to lie. It is followed by a quote from Homer on truth as the most beautiful reality, even among the gods.

SH 1 declared the inability to know God; SH 2A propounds the inability to know the world – but for a different reason. God as an eternal bodiless entity is above knowing. Reality on earth is, as it were, *below* knowing since it is ever–changing and not consistent with itself. It is not just that statements about objects are untrue. The objects themselves are unreal because nothing on earth is in fact real. To be real, an object must be unchanging; and to be unchanging it must be without a body. Degrees of truth and reality are not acknowledged. This position represents Platonic skepticism in a radical form: nothing is true on earth; it is the cave of shadows.

Some Platonists allowed that human consciousness is an image or spark of reality and so can see what is real. Such a faculty is not admitted here. Humanity is radically imperfect, compounded of different, unreal elements. As a result, it cannot grasp reality. Like all reality on earth, humanity ever changes and is not identical with itself. Logically, then, humanity only produces diverse conceptions and opinions which do not and cannot claim to represent reality. The human ability to grasp the truth is made to depend solely upon God's will. Yet only to a few does God grant a vision of the truth.

To perceive truth, what is needed is a different kind of body – an eternal one. Eternal bodies are composed of eternal matter created by the Forefather. These eternal bodies are the stars, and chief among them is the sun. The sun, as the Craftsman of the world, is the image of the higher Craftsman (evidently the Forefather). Even the sun, however, is not without body or change. Consequently, there must be a higher truth, and a higher God.

Just as birth results in decay, falsity is a parasite on truth. The sheer fact that this world is false indicates that there is a realm of truth. Since false appearances are shadows of truth, truth can employ falsity to lead the human consciousness to a higher vision.

Excerpt from the Discourses of Hermes with Tat

On Truth and Falsity

1. "Concerning truth, Tat, a human being dares not speak.[1] For a human being is an imperfect animal composed of imperfect members, a tent made up of foreign and multiple bodies.[2] Yet what is possible and correct, this I speak: the truth is in eternal bodies alone.[3]

2. Among these eternal bodies, the bodies themselves are true: fire is solely essential fire and nothing else; earth is essential earth and nothing else; air is essential air; water is essential water and nothing else. Yet our bodies are constructed of all these elements. They possess a share of fire, a share of earth, a share of water, and a share of air – though it is not (really) fire or earth or water or air or anything that is true.[4] Now if our frame did not possess truth from the beginning, how can it see or speak the truth? It can understand only if God so wills.[5]

[1] The Greek word ἀλήθεια (translated "truth") has the additional sense of "reality" in this and other Hermetic texts (for instance, CH 7.3, "the fair vision of ἀλήθεια"). For consistency, I have translated it "truth" throughout.

[2] By contrast, the cosmos is a perfect "animal" with perfect members (Plato, *Timaeus* 32d). The body as tent is a common metaphor. See §11 below; SH 26.4 (Nature as tent-maker); CH 13.12: "This tent – from which we also have passed, my child – was constituted from the zodiacal circle"; 13.15: "strike the tent."; Ocellus Lucanus: "the tents of living beings constrain living beings" (*On Law*, cited by Stobaeus, *Anthology* 1.13.2); Pseudo-Plato, *Axiochus* 366a: "Nature has fashioned this tent for suffering"; Wisdom 9:15: "For the corruptible body weighs down the soul, and the earthly tent burdens the much-thinking mind"; 2 Cor 5:4: "We in this tent groan because we are weighed down"; 2 Pet 1:13: "as long as I am in this tent."

[3] Eternal bodies may refer to the bodies of star gods. Compare SH 5.1: "the lord and Craftsman of all" makes eternal bodies that are immortal and need nothing; CH 8.4: "the bodies of heavenly beings have a single order that they got from the father in the beginning"; CH 13.3: "I went out of myself into an immortal body . . . I have been born in Consciousness"; CH 16.9: "in an immortal body the change is without dissolution; in a mortal body there is dissolution."

[4] Compare Plato, *Timaeus* 51c (the eternal form of Fire); Lactantius, *Divine Institutes* 2.12.4–5: "(Hermes Thrice Great) says that our bodies are composed by God from these four elements. They contain something of fire, air, water, and earth which is neither fire, air, water, or earth." Lactantius uses this citation to prove the dual composition of the human body, not the unreality of the elements (Michel Perrin, *L'homme antique et chrétien: l'anthropologie de Lactance 250–325* [Paris: Beauchesne, 1981], 260–62). See further Löw, *Hermes*, 124–25, 157–60.

[5] Here reading νοῆσαι with the MSS.

3. Every reality that is upon earth is not true, Tat. Rather, it is a copy of truth – and not even every truth is a copy, but only a few of them.[6] 4. The others are false and deceiving, Tat. They are illusions consisting of appearances like phantoms. When appearance receives the emanation from on high, it becomes an imitation of reality. Apart from this active power from on high, all that remains is a lie.[7]

It is like the image which displays the body in a painting but, as a visualized appearance, is not itself a body. Though the painting is viewed as having eyes, it sees nothing, <and though it is seen as having ears>, it hears nothing at all. And though the painting has all other parts of the body, they are false and deceive the vision of the viewers. Some of these people believe that they see what is real, though in truth the objects are false.[8]

5. Those who do not see a lie see truth. So if we understand each of these or see them as they are, we both understand and see things that are true, but if we understand or see them apart from what they are, we will neither understand nor know anything true."

6. "Then is there truth, father, upon earth?"

"You err, my child. Truth is hardly upon earth, Tat, nor can it arise there. Few among human beings can grasp anything concerning truth – only those to whom God grants the power of vision."[9]

7. "So there is no truth upon earth?"

"I understand and declare to you: they are all appearances and illusions. I understand and declare what is true."

[6] Compare *Gospel of Truth* (NHC 1,3) 17.20: Error creates "a substitute for truth."

[7] Compare the position attributed to Democritus, Anaxagoras, and Empedocles: "nothing can be cognized, perceived or known; the senses are constricted, minds are feeble, the course of life is brief, and, as Democritus says, truth is submerged in an abyss (*in profundo veritatem esse demersam*) . . . nothing is left for truth, and all things are enveloped in darkness" (Cicero, *Academica* 1.12.44 = LS 68A). Sextus Empiricus noted that the "natural philosopher Anaxagoras, attacking the senses because they are weak, says, 'Owing to their feebleness, we are not able to discern the truth'" (*Against the Mathematicians* 7.90 = Anaxagoras frag. B21, Curd).

[8] Plato observed that a painting imitates appearance, an imitation far removed from truth (*Republic* 10.598b). According to Sextus Empiricus, Anaxarchus and Monimus compared "existing things to stage-painting and took them to be like experiences that occur in sleep or insanity" (*Against the Mathematicians* 7.88 = LS 1D).

[9] Compare SH 7.3: Humans "do not possess the power of seeing the divine"; *Ascl.* 22–23 (few are called); *Ascl.* 29 (divine vision); FH 14: "This contemplation the Thrice Great most justly named 'theoptical'"; FH 16: "the God-seeing soul"; Philo: "Do not suppose that the Existent which truly exists is comprehended by any person; for we have in us no organ by which we can picture it, nor do we have sense perception of it, for the Existent is not sensed, nor do we have the mental capacity" (*Change of Names* 7).

"But at least knowing and speaking true things we should call truth?"[10]

8. "How so? One must know and speak what is real: there is no truth upon earth. This is what is true: the fact that in this realm there is nothing at all true. How could there be, my child? 9. Truth is the most perfect excellence, the undiluted Good itself; it is what is not muddied by matter nor shrouded by body. It is the naked, manifest, unshifting, sacred, and unchangeable Good.[11] The things of this realm, my child, such as you see them, cannot receive this Good.[12] They are corruptible, vulnerable, dissolvable, shifting, and ever-changing from one thing to another. 10. Now things untrue in themselves, how can they be true? Everything changeable is false, not remaining in its nature; as it shifts, it shows us many and various appearances."

11. "Is not even humanity true, father?"

"Humanity as such is not true, my child, for what is true is what maintains its consistency from itself alone and remains what it is in itself. But humanity is compounded from many things and does not remain in itself. Instead, it shifts and changes from one stage of growth to another, from one form to another, and this happens while it is still in this tent.[13] Indeed, many people have not recognized their own children after a short interval of time; and *vice versa*, children have not recognized their parents.

12. So can what changes to the point of being misrecognized, Tat, be true? Is it not rather the reverse, namely falsity that arises in the appearances of changeable phenomena? You, surely, realize that what is in some measure true is permanent and eternal? Humanity does not exist forever, so it is not true. Humanity is an appearance, and appearance is the height of falsehood."[14]

13. "Father, are not even eternal bodies, when they change, true?"

[10] The implicit question may be: if there is no truth on earth, how can Hermes speak it?

[11] Compare the almost identical formulation in CH 13.6.

[12] CH 2.14: "that Good is he [God] alone and none other."

[13] Compare Sextus Empiricus: "humanity is one of those things that, as he [Plato] puts it, are always becoming and never really exist and . . . it is impossible, according to him, to assert and firmly assert anything about that which never really exists" (*Outlines of Pyrrhonism* 2.28).

[14] Compare Plutarch: "It is neither reasonable for a person to undergo different passions without change nor in the midst of change to be the same person. And if one is not the same person, one does not exist, but changes one's very existence as one shifts from one person to another. In our ignorance sense perception falsely represents what appears as belonging to reality" (*On the E at Delphi* 18 [*Moralia* 392e]). Plato speaks of the eternal form of humanity in his *Parmenides* 130c–132d. For the notion of "Humanity itself" (αὐτοάνθρωπος), see Aristotle, *Metaphysics* 1.9.29, 991a.

"Everything able to be born and change is not true. But the beings created by the Forefather can possess true matter.[15] Still, even these beings contain what is false in the process of change. This is because nothing that does not remain in itself is true."

14. "What then, father, would one call true?"

The Sun as Image of Truth

"Only the sun, which is beyond all other things unchanging, remaining in itself, we would call truth. Accordingly, he alone is entrusted with crafting everything in the world, with ruling and making everything. I indeed venerate him and worship his truth. I recognize him as Craftsman subordinate to the One and Primal (Deity)."[16]

15. "What then is the primal truth, father?"

"It is singular and unique, Tat – not made from matter, not embodied, not qualified by color or shape; it is unshifting, unchanging, and ever existing.[17]

[15] The Forefather is also mentioned as the name for the highest deity in SH 2B.3; 23.10, 55. Compare the "preexistent Being" in SH 21.1. Iamblichus asserted that the Egyptians, "prioritize a creator (δημιουργὸν) as Forefather (προπάτορα) of all generated things and they recognize both a vital power prior to the heavens and one in the heavens [the sun]" (*On the Mysteries* 8.4 = TH 12). According to Irenaeus, *Against Heresies* 1.1.1, the Forefather (*Propatora*) is the highest deity in the Valentinian system. Compare *Secret Book of James* (NHC V,3.33–34): "I am from the preexistent Father."

[16] Compare SH 21.2: "the sun is an image of the celestial Craftsman deity"; CH 16.5–9: "the Craftsman (I mean the Sun) binds heaven to earth, sending essence below and raising matter above, attracting everything toward the Sun and around it, offering everything from himself to everything"; CH 11.15 (humanity the image of the sun); *Ascl.* 29: "The Sun is indeed a second god, Asclepius ... governing all things and shedding light on all that are in the world, ensouled and soulless." For Plato, the Sun is the offspring of the Good, and most like it (*Republic* 506e). The Sun's light is the medium in which things are seen, just as the intellectual light is the medium in which truth is seen (*Republic* 507b–509a). Cleanthes the Stoic philosopher viewed the sun as the world's commanding faculty (Diogenes Laertius, *Lives of Philosophers* 7.139). Cicero called the sun "the leader, chief, and regulator of the other lights, the mind and moderator of the universe" (*Dream of Scipio* 4.2 = *Republic* 6.17). Compare Plutarch: "those who know and honor beautiful and wise analogy – such as ... light to truth – relate the sun's power to the nature of Apollo. They declare that the sun is his offspring and child, ever born of the one who ever exists" (*Obsolescence of Oracles* 42 [*Moralia* 433d]); Filastrius: "Hermes ... Thrice Great taught that beyond God Almighty humans ought to adore no other except the Sun himself" (*Diverse Heresies* 10.2 = TH 17); Iamblichus: "the Sun stands over the helm of the whole world" (*On the Mysteries* 7.2); Julian: "There is not a single thing that can come into light and birth apart from the crafting power of the Sun" (*Oration* 4.140d). For Julian, the Sun is also the offspring of a higher deity (in this case Helios).

[17] The description recalls Plato: "What is in this place [the region beyond heaven] is without color and without shape and without solidity, a being that really is what it is ... visible only to intelligence" (*Phaedrus* 247c). Compare CH 4.1: "you should conceive of him [the Craftsman] as present, as always existing, as having made all things"; CH 13.6: "What is true ... [is] unlimited, colorless, figureless"; SH 8.2: The "intelligible is without color, without shape, without body, and drawn from the primal and intelligible reality itself."

16. What is false decays, my child; and Providence from the one who is true has seized, holds, and will hold everything on earth in decay.[18] Apart from decay, birth could not exist. Decay follows every birth, so that it is born again. This is because what is born is born from what is decayed. What is born must decay, so that the birth of entities does not grind to a halt. Decay is the first Craftsman for the birth of beings.[19]

Now what is born from decay is false, since it is born now one thing, now another. Such things cannot be born as the same entities. But what is not itself, how can it be true? 17. We must call these things appearances, my child, if we are to speak correctly. The human is the appearance of Humanity: the child is the appearance of the Child, the young man is the appearance of the Young Man, the man is the appearance of the Man, the elderly man is the appearance of the Elderly Man. So a human is not a human, nor a child a child, nor a young man a young man, nor a man a man, nor an elderly man an elderly man.[20]

18. As these states change, there is falsity, both with respect to what was before and is at present. Yet understand this, my child: even these false activities depend upon the truth itself from above. This being the case, I say that falsity is a product of truth."

[18] Compare Marcus Aurelius: "The parts of the universe, I say, as many as are comprised in the cosmos, must perish by necessity (ἀνάγκη φθείρεσθαι)" (*Meditations* 10.7.1).

[19] Compare SH 11.2, §35: "decay is the beginning of human birth"; SH 14.1: "Fate is the cause of birth and decay in life." Plutarch summarily discussed how elements decay into and thus create other elements (*On the Principle of Cold* 10–13 [*Moralia* 948f–950d]).

[20] Compare Plutarch: "What is born of it [mortal substance] never attains to being, because growth never ceases or stands still, but sperm, ever-changing, makes an embryo, then an infant, then a child, in turn a boy, a young man, then a man, a mature man, an old man, corrupting the first stages of growth and maturity by those which come after" (*On the E at Delphi* 18 [*Moralia* 392c]); DH 7.1: "What is humanity? The immortal species of every human."

SH 2B

Withdrawn from Stobaeus's *Anthology* 1.41.1, SH 2B is the first excerpt in a chapter called "On Nature and its Derived Causes." Tat's initial question, "If there is no truth in this realm . . . ?" seems to presume the content of SH 2A. Logically, these excerpts have been grouped as part of the same tractate.[1] Both texts also use the title "Forefather," which appears elsewhere only in the *Korē Kosmou* (SH 23.10). In Stobaeus's *Anthology*, Excerpt 2A is immediately followed by what is here classified as SH 11.

Jens Holzhausen notices several links between SH 2B and CH 10. Both texts refer to "our forefathers" – named Ouranos and Kronos in CH 10.5 – who attained the truth and the Good. In addition, CH 10.19 speaks of a battle concerning devotion and in 10.20 the punishment of the soul attached to evil deeds is similarly described. The ascent of the soul and its division from bodies and the lower parts of the soul is the theme of CH 10 (§§6–8, 16). Finally, CH 10.19 calls the knower "devout" and emphasizes the connection of knowledge and the praise of God (CH 10.21).[2] Holzhausen concludes that both texts may stem from the same author.

As to SH 2B's content, Tat asks a logical question: if there is no truth in this realm, then how should one live?" Hermes's response is emphatic: "Show devotion!" Hermetic theology is no cold rationalism. Knowing reality reveals one's awesome debts to the creator.

There is a connection between God (here called "the Good") and the soul. The soul who knows the Good loves goodness and begins the ascent back to ultimate Good. But the ascent involves continuous struggle. Two parts of the soul – elsewhere called "drive" and "desire" – oppose the ascending mind and try to drag it down to earth. Minds who do not conquer the lower self are reincarnated. By contrast, those who have learned to fly above this realm of body and appearance wing their way to the upper world.

[1] Scott, *Hermetica*, 3.305–6; NF 3.xviii. [2] Holzhausen, *CH Deutsch*, 2.332.

An Excerpt of a Discourse of Hermes with Tat

1. *Hermes:* "In the first place, my child, I write this treatise both for the sake of my love for humanity and out of my devotion to God.[3] There can be no devotion more just than to understand reality and to give thanks for it to our maker.[4] I will not cease my thanksgiving until the end."

2. *Tat:* "If there is no truth in this realm, what should one do, father, to live one's life well?"

Hermes: "Show devotion, my child! The one who shows devotion has reached the heights of philosophy. Without philosophy, it is impossible to reach the heights of devotion.[5] The one who has learned the nature of reality, how it is ordered, by whom, and for what purpose, will offer thanks for all things to the Creator as to a good father, a kind provider, and a faithful administrator; and the one who gives thanks will show devotion.[6]

3. The one who shows devotion will know the place of truth and its nature. The more one learns, the more devout one will become. Never, my child, has an embodied soul that disburdened itself for the perception of him who is good and true been able to slip back to their opposites.[7] The reason is that the soul who learns about its own Forefather holds fast to passionate love, forgets all its ills, and can no longer stand apart from the Good.[8]

4. Let this, my son, be the goal of devotion. Arriving at this goal, you will live well and die blessed, since your soul is not ignorant of where it

[3] "In the first place" can also be translated "first" (πρῶτον). The language may indicate that this is the original prologue to SH 2A–B (NF 3.xvii–xx).

[4] CH 1.3: "I wish to learn about the things that are, to understand their nature and to know God"; CH 1.29 (hymn of gratitude).

[5] On devotion (εὐσέβεια), compare CH 1.27: "I began proclaiming to humankind the beauty of devotion and knowledge"; CH 4.7: "Choosing the stronger ... shows devotion toward God"; CH 6.5: "Only one road travels from here to the beautiful – devotion combined with knowledge"; CH 9.4: "devotion is knowledge of God, and one who has come to know God ... has thoughts that are divine"; *Ascl.* 29: "every good person is enlightened by fidelity, devotion, wisdom, worship, and respect for God." Note also Philo, *Decalogue* 52 (the greatest virtue is devotion) with the comments of Gregory E. Sterling, "'The Queen of the Virtues': Piety in Philo of Alexandria," *Studia Philonica Annual* 18 (2006): 103–23.

[6] On giving thanks, see *Ascl.* 41, which is roughly equivalent to NCH VI,7, *The Prayer of Thanksgiving*.

[7] Here reading ὄντος ἀγαθοῦ with FP. God alone is good and true, as in CH 2.15–16: "This is the good; this is God ... The good is what is inalienable and inseparable from God, since it is God himself"; compare SH 2A.15 (the description of the primal truth).

[8] For the role of passionate love (ἔρως) in the ascent to heaven, see Plato, *Phaedrus* 244a–252b, *Symposium* 206a–212a.

should wing its upward flight.[9] 5. This alone, my child, is the way toward truth which our ancestors trod and having trod it, attained the Good. This way is venerable and smooth, though it is difficult for a soul to travel on it while still in the body.[10]

The Battle within the Soul

6. The reason is, first of all, that the soul must battle with itself, make a violent separation, and be taken advantage of by one part.[11] The battle is of one against two.[12] The one flees, while the others drag it down. Strife and manifold conflicts occur among them – the one part desires to flee, while the others eagerly hold it down.[13]

7. The victory of each part is not the same. The one rushes toward the Good, the others reside with evils. The one yearns to be free, but the others are content with slavery. If the two parts are conquered, they stick to their own affairs, deprived of their ruler. But if the one part is conquered, it is driven by the two and conveyed as a punishment to life in this realm.[14]

9 For the soul's ascent, compare Plato: "the soul is released in a natural way and finds it pleasant to take its flight" (*Timaeus* 81d); Maximus of Tyre: "Pythagoras of Samos was the first among the Greeks to dare to say that his body would die, but that his soul would up and fly away, ageless and immortal" (*Oration* 10.2); CH 4.11: "you will discover the road that leads above"; CH 5.5: "Would that you could grow wings and fly up into the air"; CH 10.15: "For humankind this is the only deliverance: the knowledge of God. It is ascent to Olympus."

10 Compare CH 4.8–9: "do you not see how many bodies we must pass through, my child . . . So let us seize this beginning and travel with all speed, for the path is very crooked that leaves familiar things of the present to return to primordial things of old"; CH 11.21: "To be ignorant of the divine is the ultimate vice, but to be able to know, to will and to hope is the easy way leading to the good. As you journey, the good will meet you everywhere and will be seen everywhere, where and when you least expect it"; Matt 7:14: "the road is hard that leads to life"; Porphyry: "difficulty is proper to the ascent" (*To Marcella* 6).

11 The separation is probably that of soul and body, which can begin in this life (Plato, *Phaedo* 64c–69d).

12 Namely, consciousness (νοῦς) against drive (θυμός) and desire (ἐπιθυμία). Compare the chariot image in Plato, *Phaedrus* 246a–248b; CH 16.15: "The daimones on duty at the exact moment of birth . . . take possession of each of us as we come into being and receive a soul . . . Those that enter through the body into the two parts of the soul twist the soul about . . . But the rational part of the soul stands unmastered by the daimones, suitable as a receptacle for God."

13 Compare Plato: "a man should make all haste to escape from earth to heaven" (*Theaetetus* 176b); CH 7.3: "Such is the odious tunic you have put on. It strangles you and drags you down with it so that you will not hate its viciousness."

14 Compare Plato: "If [the chariot of the soul] . . . does not see anything true . . . and by some accident takes on a burden of forgetfulness and wrongdoing, then it is weighed down, sheds its wings and falls to earth" (*Phaedrus* 248c).

8. This discourse, my child, is the guide of the path to the upper world.[15] Before you reach the goal, you must, my child, first abandon your body, conquer this life of struggle, and after conquering, ascend!"[16]

[15] Compare CH 4.11: "the road that leads above . . . the image itself will show you the way." Here the "image" appears to refer to the Hermetic treatise itself (NF 3.xxii).

[16] Compare CH 7.2: "first you must rip off the tunic [body] that you wear"; CH 10.19: "Knowing the divine and doing wrong to no person is the fight of devotion"; CH 5.5: "Would that you could grow wings and fly up into the air!"; CH 11.19: "Command it [your soul] even to fly up to heaven"; Philo: some souls "are lifted on light wings to the aether to tread the heights forever" (*On Dreams* 1.139); Seneca: "When souls are quickly dismissed from human dealings . . . they fly back more easily to their origin" (*Consolation to Marcia* 23.1).

SH 3

Stobaeus transmitted the following excerpt (from his *Anthology* 1.49.5) in a chapter called "On the Soul" (the same chapter as SH 17, 19–20, and 23–26). It is immediately preceded by what is here classified as SH 17. It is directly followed by what appears below as SH 19. Scott removed SH 3 from its context in Stobaeus's *Anthology* because its definition of a non-rational animal (3.8) was linked with the definition in SH 4.1. SH 4 is addressed to Tat, whereas SH 17 and 19 are addressed to Ammon. The best placement of SH 3 is still open to debate.

SH 3 begins with a Platonic affirmation of the soul's immortality based upon its continual motion. Motion is of two types: motion from bodies and motion from energies. Bodily motions can only affect bodies. Evidently, then, soul motion is the motion of energies. This theory is in some tension with what we find in SH 4, where the soul is strictly distinguished from an energy (4.8–10, 21–23).

At any rate, SH 3 rephrases the two motions in terms of soul and body motion. Beings on earth are affected by the motions of both bodies and souls. The motion of bodies tends toward decay and dissolution. Soul motion is eternal because motion is its own proper activity.

There are four kinds of souls. The divine soul works in a divine body, such as a star. The human soul is in fact a divine soul which, when separated from drive and desire, goes to inhabit a star body. A non-rational soul only possesses drive and desire. A fourth type of soul is added as something of an appendix. It is the soul which moves inanimate bodies outside of it by a kind of accessory motion. Here again there is some tension with SH 4, in which inanimate beings are explicitly said to be moved by energies (4.12).

From the Same Author[1]

The Soul Ever-moving

1. Every soul is immortal and ever-moving.[2] We were saying in the General Discourses that motions were of two types: those propelled by energies and those propelled by bodies.[3]

2. We declare that the soul comes from a reality that is not material since the soul is without body and from a substance that is itself without body. This is based on the general principle that everything born must be born from something.[4]

3. Now beings in the world of birth are affected by decay and must be affected by two motions: the motion of the soul by which it is moved, and the motion of the body by which it grows and withers. This latter kind of motion is undone when the body itself is undone. I call this "the motion of decaying bodies."

4. The soul is ever-moving because the soul always moves itself and energizes the motion in other beings.[5] According to this definition, every soul is immortal and ever-moving because it possesses motion as its proper activity.

Kinds of Souls

5. These are the kinds of souls: divine, human, and non-rational. The divine soul is the energy that propels its divine body, for it moves by itself in its body and also moves its body. 6. When the soul of mortal animals separates from its non-rational parts, it goes off into the divine body which

[1] In the context of Stobaeus's *Anthology*, the author is Hermes.

[2] Compare Plato: "Every soul is immortal. That is because whatever is always in motion is immortal" (*Phaedrus* 245c); *Ascl.* 2: "Every human soul is immortal"; SH 16.1: "The soul is a bodiless reality . . . it is always moving by nature"; DH 10.7 (= SH 19.1): "Therefore soul is an immortal essence, eternal, intellective, having as an intellectual (thought) its reason endowed with consciousness"; OH 1.2 (the soul is unborn and self-moved).

[3] The General Discourses are also referred to in SH 6.1; CH 10.1, 7; 13.1. Christian Wildberg argues that these discourses were oral ("The General Discourses of Hermes Trismegistus," an unpublished paper available at princeton.academia.edu/ChristianWildberg). Evidently the soul is equated with an energy. The topic of energies recurs in SH 4.6–16.

[4] Scott argues that this paragraph (§2) interrupts the flow of thought from §1 to §3 (the two motions) (*Hermetica*, 3.346). Yet the two kinds of motion in §1 and §3 are different. The non-material substance from which soul comes could be νοῦς ("consciousness"), which proceeds from God (CH 12.1).

[5] Compare DH 2.1: "soul (is) a necessary movement adjusted to every (kind of) body."

is ever-moving and moved in itself. In this way, the soul circles round the universe.[6]

7. The human soul has a portion of the divine. Yet non-rational elements, namely drive and desire, are attached to it.[7] Drive and desire are also immortal inasmuch as they are energies, the energies of mortal bodies. These energies are far from the divine part when the soul inhabits the divine body. But when this divine part enters a mortal body, drive and desire travel round with it; with them present, a human soul is always the result.[8]

8. The soul of non-rational animals is composed of drive and desire. Accordingly, these animals are called "non-rational," since their souls lack reason.[9]

9. Consider the fourth type of soul to be the moving agent of inanimate beings. This soul, since it is outside bodies, moves them by force. This would include the soul active in the divine body, moving other bodies by a kind of accessory motion.[10]

[6] The divine body is apparently a star body or the vehicle of the preexistent soul (Plato, *Timaeus* 41d–e) to which the soul returns after death (*Timaeus* 42b). Compare CH 10.16: "consciousness, since it is divine by nature, becomes purified of its garments and takes on a fiery body, ranging about everywhere."

[7] For drive and desire, see Plato, *Republic* 588b–89a (the image of the tripartite soul); SH 2B.6–7. The portion of the divine in the soul is what other Hermetists call consciousness (νοῦς).

[8] Compare Plato, *Timaeus* 41e–42a.

[9] Compare CH 12.4; SH 4.1 (non-human animals lack reason).

[10] Inanimate things within the outer circle of heaven are moved in the whirl of heaven by a kind of accessory motion. This kind of motion is different from energies inhabiting sticks and stones (SH 4.12).

SH 4

Selected from Stobaeus's *Anthology* 1.41.6, SH 4 belongs to a chapter called "On Nature and its Derived Causes" (the same chapter as SH 2B, 5, 11, 15, 16, and 21). It is preceded by an excerpt from Pseudo-Archytas's *On the First Principle* and is immediately followed by what is classified here as SH 15.

SH 4 commences with the question of animal intelligence. Some nonrational creatures seem by observation to act rationally. Nevertheless, Hermes insists that these animals act by instinct and not by intelligence. The sign of instinct is that the seemingly intelligent behavior of animals requires no instruction.

The discussion then shifts to the topic of energies. SH 4 presents the longest discussion of energies in the Hermetic fragments. Energies fill the cosmos. In themselves, energies are bodiless, but they can only work in bodies. Unlike souls, then, energies cannot be independent of bodies. Both souls and energies, as bodiless, are immortal. Yet since energies only work in bodies, bodies too must be collectively immortal, though individually they dissolve. Energies always create new bodies. In this way, all events in the cosmos rest on immortal and eternal energies that cycle in the vast wheel of growth and decay.

There are different kinds of energies. The higher energies are active in souls; lower energies are active in bodies. The purest energies work in eternal bodies, but there are specialized energies that work in all sorts of bodies, including wood and stone. Energies are even at work in dead bodies to break them down. General energies are involved in basic life functions such as motion and sensation; special energies are involved in the acts of higher intelligence.

As a final topic, the author turns to sensation. Like energies, sensations are connected with bodies. Sensations, however, are connected with lower, animal bodies. Energies come from higher, divine bodies such as the stars. But energies and sensations are connected. Sensations are the effects of energies and manifest the energies.

There are different kinds of sensation, depending on whether the animal is rational, non-rational, or inanimate. If the being is inanimate, sensation is not connected to consciousness, but reduced to factors like growth and decay. Ensouled and especially rational beings experience the sensations of pain and pleasure. Both pain and pleasure are harmful because they jolt and disturb consciousness and incite attachment to bodies.

Pain and pleasure are sensations, but they are also called energies. This point leads to a subtle disquisition. If sensations are in bodies (like energies), are sensations also bodiless (like energies)? Hermes clarifies that although both sensations and energies are connected to bodies, energies are bodiless whereas sensation is a type of body. Thus the bodiless soul somewhat surprisingly has no sense perception in itself.

Excerpt from the Discourses of Hermes with Tat

Animals Lack Reason

1. *Tat:* "Rightly you demonstrated this, father; yet teach me still more. You said at one point that knowledge and skill are activities of the rational part. Now you say that non-rational animals are called non-rational through lack of reason.[1] It is necessary, by this reasoning, that non-rational animals do not share in knowledge or skill, given that they lack rationality."

2. *Hermes:* "Necessarily, my child."

Tat: "How then, father, do we observe some non-rational animals using knowledge and skill? For instance, ants store up food for the winter;

[1] Tat's point seems to pick up from SH 3.8: "Accordingly, these animals are called 'non-rational,' since their souls lack reason." Compare CH 12.1: "In animals without reason, there is natural impulse"; CH 12.6: "In humans, mind is one thing, but it is another in unreasoning animals"; VH 1: "animals . . . were ordained to be unreasoning"; SH 23.39 ("irrational beasts"). A passage ascribed to Aristotle: "animals too have some small sparks of reason and understanding (λόγου γὰρ καὶ φρονήσεως), but are entirely deprived of contemplative wisdom (σοφίας θεωρητικῆς)" (from Iamblichus, *Protrepticus* 36.7–13 [Pistelli]), if genuine, would grant animals a measure of rationality. Aristotle also granted some animals the ability to learn (*Metaphysics* 1.1, 980a27–69). In general, however, Aristotle denied that animals had reason or λόγος (*On the Soul* 3.3, 428a24; *Eudemian Ethics* 2.8, 1224a27; *Politics* 7.13, 1332b5). See further Liliane Bodson, "Attitudes toward Animals in Greco-Roman Antiquity," *International Journal for the Study of Animal Problems* 4 (1983): 312–20; Richard Sorabji, *Animal Minds and Human Morals: The Origins of the Western Debate* (Ithaca, NY: Cornell University Press, 1993), 7–16; Ingvild Saelid Gilhus, *Animals, Gods and Humans: Changing Attitudes to Animals in Greek, Roman and Early Christian Ideas* (London: Routledge, 2006), 37–63; Catherine Osborne, *Dumb Beasts and Dead Philosophers: Humanity and the Humane in Ancient Philosophy and Literature* (Oxford: Clarendon Press, 2007), 63–97.

air-borne animals, likewise, make nests; and four-footed animals recognize their own dens."[2]

3. *Hermes:* "They do these things, my child, not by knowledge or skill, but by instinct.[3] The reason is that knowledge and skill are taught, but no non-rational animal teaches anything.[4] The things that come about by instinct come about by a universal practice; but the things that come about by knowledge and skill arise secondarily in intelligent animals, though not all of them.[5]

What arises <for all> animals is activated by nature. 4. For example, human beings look upwards, but not all human beings are musicians or archers or hunters, and so on.[6] Rather, some of them learned something by the operation of knowledge and skill. 5. In the same way, if some ants performed this activity while others did not, you would rightly say that they did this by knowledge and gathered their food by skill. Yet if all are

[2] For a general defense of animal reason, see Philo, *On Animals* 10–71. Plutarch argued that every animal that has sensation has a measure of intelligence (*Whether Land or Sea Animals Are Cleverer* 3 [*Moralia* 961b]; compare his *Beasts Are Rational* 9 [*Moralia* 991e–92c]). Porphyry argued that animals have reason (λόγος) by virtue of their meaningful utterances as well as their ability to perceive, remember, and learn (*On Abstinence* 3.1–19). For canine reasoning, see Sextus Empiricus, *Outlines of Pyrrhonism* 1.14.69–72. For ant intelligence, see Philo, *On Animals*, 42; Plutarch, *Whether Land or Sea Animals Are Cleverer* 11 (*Moralia* 967d–968b); Celsus in Origen, *Against Celsus* 4.81–85. See further Sherwood Owen Dickerman, "Some Stock Examples of Animal Intelligence in Greek Psychology," *Transactions of the American Philological Association* 42 (1911): 123–30.

[3] Alcmeon of Croton (around 460 BCE) asserted that humans alone understand whereas animals perceive but do not understand (in Theophrastus, *On the Senses* 25.1–6 = DK 24 A5). Aristotle, *Physics* 2.8, 199a20–30. On animal instinct, compare Seneca: "Don't you see the massive subtlety (*subtilitas*) in bees for constructing their little houses . . . how the weaving of a spider has no mortal imitation? . . . This art is born not taught (*nascitur ars ista, non discitur*), and for this reason no animal is more learned (*doctius*) than any other . . . Whatever art passes on is uncertain and uneven (*inaequabile*); but what nature assigns is uniform (*ex aequo venit*)" (*Epistles* 121.22–23); Galen: "Hippocrates says that the instincts of animals are untaught. So it seems to me that the other animals acquire their skills by instinct rather than by reason; bees, for example, molding their wax, ants working at their treasuries and labyrinths, and spiders spinning and weaving. I judge from the fact that they are untaught" (*Use of Parts* 1.3, trans. Margaret Tallmadge May, modified).

[4] Porphyry disagreed, arguing that nightingales teach their chicks to sing, grooms teach their horses to be ridden, and hunters teach their dogs to track and catch prey (*On Abstinence* 3.6.5–6; compare 3.15.1–2). See also the *Book of Thoth* 172.6–7 (Jasnow and Zauzich): "The sacred beasts and the birds, teaching comes about for them, (but) what is the book chapter which they have read?"

[5] Compare Philo: "For since art is an acquired skill, what accomplishment is there when there has been no previously acquired knowledge which is the basis of the arts? Now for example, birds fly, aquatics swim, and terrestrials walk. Is this done by learning? Certainly not. Each of the above-mentioned creatures does it by its nature" (*On Animals* 77–78, trans. Abraham Terian). In CH 12.10, non-rational animals are granted consciousness (νοῦς), but it is reduced to natural impulse, joined with instinct. Contrast "Pythagoras" who inferred that, "as everything comes to rational creatures by teaching, it must be so also for wild creatures which are believed to be rational" (Iamblichus, *Pythagorean Way of Life* 60). The intelligence of animals is also a theme in Pliny, *Natural History* 8–9.

[6] Compare *Ascl.* 6: "he [a human being] looks up to heaven."

driven to this same activity by nature and without their will, it is clear that they do not act by knowledge or skill.

On Energies

6. There are energies, Tat, which in themselves are bodiless but dwell in bodies and work through them. For this reason, Tat, inasmuch as they are bodiless, I say that they are immortal. Yet inasmuch as they cannot work apart from bodies, I say that they are always in a body. 7. For entities born by Providence and Necessity for some purpose or reason cannot always remain inactive with respect to their own activity. For what is will always be – for this constant activity is its selfhood and life.

According to this reasoning, it follows that bodies also exist forever. Consequently, I say that the production of bodies itself is an eternal activity. This is the reasoning: if earthly bodies break apart, and if it is necessary for bodies to exist as places and instruments of the energies, and if the energies are immortal, and if what is immortal always exists, then the making of bodies is an energy, given that it always exists.

Kinds of Energies

8. Energies do not all attend the soul all at once. Rather, some of them are activated with the non-rational parts of the soul when the person is born. The other, purer energies cooperate with the rational part of the soul at each stage of maturity. 9. These energies are dependent upon bodies. The body-making energies come from divine bodies into mortal ones.[7] Each of them energizes either the bodily elements or those related to the soul. Even in the soul itself energies do <not> arise apart from a body. After all, the energies are eternal, but the soul is not always in a mortal body. The soul can exist apart from the body, but the energies cannot exist apart from bodies.

10. This is a sacred teaching, my child. A body cannot exist apart from the soul, yet it can continue to exist as follows."[8]

Tat: "How, father?"

Hermes: "Consider it this way, Tat. When the soul departs from the body, the body itself remains. This body, while it remains, is acted upon by being

[7] Compare *Ascl.* 3: "a continuous influence carries through the world and through the soul of all kinds and all forms throughout nature"; SH 11.2 §40: "The energies are not borne upwards, but downwards."

[8] Reading τὸ δὲ εἶναι δύναται ("it can continue to exist") with F.

broken down and losing its form. The body could not suffer these things apart from energy. Thus energy persists in the body when the soul has departed.

11. This is the difference between an immortal and a mortal body. The immortal body is made from a single material, while the other is not.[9] The one acts, while the other is acted upon. Everything active rules, while what is acted upon is ruled. The ruling part leads like a free commander while the subject part is borne about as a slave.

12. Now the energies do not only energize bodies with souls, but also those lacking souls: trees, stones, and the like.[10] Energies cause these bodies to grow, bear fruit, ripen, rot, waste away, become fetid, break down – performing like actions that bodies without souls undergo. Energy, my child, has been called this very thing: anything brought into being.

13. There must always be birth for the majority of – or rather all – beings. For the world is never widowed of any being. It bears all in itself and conceives entities that are never free from its decay.[11] 14. Think of every energy as eternal and immortal in whatever body it finds itself.

15. Among energies, some belong to divine bodies, some to decaying bodies; some are general, others special; some apply to whole species, others to single members.[12] The divine energies are those active in eternal bodies. These are perfect, as they exist in perfect bodies. Particular energies operate in each animal species. Special energies operate in each individual.

16. The conclusion of this teaching is this, my child: all things are full of energies![13] For if it is necessary that energies be in bodies, and there are many bodies in the world, I profess that there are more energies than there are bodies. For oftentimes in a single body there are one, two, or three energies apart from the attending general energies. By general energies I mean the truly bodily ones which arise through sensations and motions.

[9] If the immortal bodies are the elements, they consist of a single homogenous material: either fire, air, water, or earth.

[10] The energies here seem to function as what Aristotle called the nutritive soul (*On the Soul* 2.4, 415a23–27; 3.12, 434a22–26). Compare *Ascl.* 6: "living things without soul"; CH 2.9 (sticks and stones are soulless things); *Ref.* 5.7.10: "Even the stones, he [the Naassene writer] says, are ensouled, for they have the ability to grow." Albert the Great reported that, "Democritus and others say that the elements have souls and are themselves the causes of stones' coming into being, consequently he says that there is a soul in a stone just as in any other generative seed" (*On Minerals* 1.1.4 = Democritus frag. 161, Taylor); Plotinus, *Enneads* 6.7.11.24: "One must suppose that the growth and molding of stones . . . takes place because an ensouled crafting principle is working within them and giving them form" (trans. Armstrong).

[11] Reading, with F, αὐτοῦ ("*its* decay").

[12] Compare CH 10.22: "Energies work through the cosmos and upon humankind through the natural rays of the cosmos."

[13] Compare Thales: "All things are full of gods!" (reported by Aristotle, *On the Soul* 1.5, 411a7–8 = Thales frag. 32, Wöhrle and McKirahan).

Apart from these energies, the body cannot exist. Yet there are other particular energies in the souls of humans that arise through skill, sciences, occupations, and activities.

Sensations

17. Sensations, too, attend the energies; or rather the sensations are the effects of the energies. 18. Now understand, my child, the difference between energies <and sensations. The energy> is sent from the heavenly bodies, while sensation dwells in the body and has its substance from it. When sensation receives the energy, it manifests it, as if embodying it. Thus I call the senses bodily and mortal, since they exist insofar as the body exists. In fact, senses are born and die with the body.[14]

19. The immortal bodies themselves, however, do not have sensation, since they exist from an immortal substance.[15] For sense perception is nothing but a faculty <that signals> the harm or good added to or removed from the body.[16] Nothing is added to or removed from eternal bodies, thus sensation is not produced in them.[17]

20. *Tat:* "Is sensation at work in all bodies?"[18]

Hermes: "Yes, my child, and in all of them energies are at work."

Tat: "Even in beings without soul, father?"

Hermes: "Even in these, my child. Yet there are different kinds of sensation. Some belong to rational beings and arise with reason. Others belong to non-rational beings and are solely bodily. There are sensations of beings without soul; but they are only able to passively experience growth and decrease. This is because passive experience and perception depend upon a single source and are conveyed to the same goal by the energies.[19]

[14] Both energies and sensations exist in and with the body, but energies do not die.

[15] Contrast CH 9.5–6, 9: "the cosmos has its own sensation . . . far stronger and simpler. The sole sensation and understanding in the cosmos is to make all things and unmake them into itself again . . . God is not without sensation and understanding." Compare DH 8.2: "Divine bodies do not have access paths for sensations, for they have sensations within themselves, and (what is more) they are themselves their own sensations." Compare Macrobius, *Saturnalia* 7.9.16 (no divine body possesses sensation whereas the soul is itself more divine than any body, even if the body is a god's).

[16] The word σημαντική (here: "that signals") is an emendation of Desroussaux. FP reads σωματική ("bodily").

[17] Though the heavenly bodies lack sensation, "they possess a higher sort of consciousness." Humans have both sensation and intelligence (νόησις); the heavenly bodies have νόησις alone (Scott, *Hermetica*, 3.338).

[18] Evidently Tat refers to mortal bodies, since divine bodies do not have sensation.

[19] On kinds of sensation, compare CH 9.2: "Apparently there is a difference between sensation and understanding, the former being material and the latter essential . . . Both sensation and

Pain and Pleasure

21. There are two other energies of ensouled animals that attend senses and experiences, namely pain and pleasure. Apart from these, an ensouled animal and especially a rational one cannot perceive. Thus I call them types of energies that prevail mostly in rational animals.[20]

22. Pain and pleasure, as bodily entities, are stirred up by the irrational parts of the soul. Therefore I call both harmful.[21] The reason is this: though joy provides a pleasurable sensation, it becomes the source of much harm to the one who experiences it. Pain, likewise, affords sufferings and powerful sorrows. So logically both are harmful."[22]

23. *Tat:* "Is sensation of soul and body the same, father?"

Hermes: "What do you understand, my child, by 'sensation of soul'? Isn't the soul bodiless and sensation a body?"[23]

Tat: "Is sensation a <body>, father, because it is in a body?"

Hermes: "If we posit that sensation is something <bodiless> in a body, my child, we make it the same thing as soul or the energies, for we say that these are bodiless entities in bodies. Yet sensation is neither an energy, nor soul, nor bodiless, nor anything else bodiless beyond what was already mentioned. Thus it is not bodiless; and if it is not bodiless, it is a body. This is because entities are always either bodies or bodiless."[24]

understanding flow together into humans, intertwined with one another ... At any rate <sensation> is distributed to body and to soul, and, when both these parts of sensation are in harmony with one another, then there is an utterance of understanding, engendered by mind."

20 NF delete the sentence that follows: "Energies energize, whereas sensations manifest the energies" (αἱ μὲν ἐνέργειαι ἐνεργοῦσιν, αἱ δὲ αἰσθήσεις τὰ ἐνεργείας ἀναφαίνουσιν).

21 Compare CH 12.2: "Every soul, as soon as it has come to be in the body, is depraved by pain and pleasure."

22 Compare Pseudo-Plato, *Definitions* 9.4: "Soul's illness: sadness and joy." See further Plato, *Republic* 402e–403a; 583e, 586b; *Phaedo* 60b–c, 83d; and especially *Timaeus* 86b–c.

23 Compare CH 9.2: "<sensation> is distributed to body and to soul."

24 Reading ἀεί ("always") with FP. Sensation as a body approaches a Stoic view, wherein sensation is made possible by bodily breath (πνεῦμα). Compare SH 19.5: "sensate breath judges apparent phenomena." Contrast Plato, who "declares that sensation is the shared product (κοινωνίαν) of soul and body toward things outside; for the power of sensation belongs to the soul, but the instrument of sensation belongs to the body" (Pseudo-Plutarch, *Opinions of the Philosophers* 4.8.3 [899e]); Aristotle: "The most important characteristics of animals ... are those shared (κοινά) by both soul and body, like sensation" (*On Sense* 1,436a7–10); "the use of sensation is not the distinctive property of either soul or body, for its potentiality and actuality belong to the same subject, and what is called sensation, as an actuality, is a movement of the soul through the body" (Aristotle, *On Sleep* 1,454a7–12).

SH 5

In the context of Stobaeus's *Anthology* (1.41.8), SH 5 belongs to a chapter called "On Nature and its Derived Causes" (the same chapter as SH 2B, 4, 11, 15, 16, and 21). It is immediately preceded by what is here classified as SH 15. It is followed by a selection from Plato's dialogue *Cratylus*.

According to this excerpt, there are two creations executed by two Craftsmen. The primal, unnamed Craftsman creates the eternal bodies of the stars and enters into permanent rest. In turn, the Second Craftsman, or Sun, creates mortal bodies that dissolve and die. The Sun imitates the primal Craftsman as creator; but the Sun cannot imitate the primal Craftsman by creating eternal bodies. Eternal bodies like the stars are self-sufficient, requiring no energy from outside. They are also immortal, as they are composed of a single element, namely fire. By contrast, mortal bodies are made up of many different elements, and so in the whirr of existence eventually suffer dissolution.

Dissolution would more rapidly occur were it not for the gift of sleep. The stars, which revolve in an unbroken circle around the sky, do not rest, nor do they require it. Mortal animals, on the other hand, need a period of repose in which the body is renewed and nourishment integrated. Sleep counteracts the constant motion of the soul by allowing the body to be still. The body thus enjoys sleep and spends half or even more of its time in repose.

The division between the higher Craftsman who creates the eternal star gods and the lower Craftsman (in fact, the star gods themselves) who create mortal lifeforms goes back to Plato's *Timaeus* 41b–c. Hermes, however, puts the focus on one particular star god – the Sun – who serves as the lower Craftsman. Hermes also makes explicit that the higher Craftsman, like the God of Genesis, ceases from his labors.

Excerpt from the Discourses of Hermes with [Ammon] Tat

The Primal Craftsman

1. Moreover, the lord and Craftsman of all eternal bodies, Tat, once he created, ceased creating, and does not create at present. After entrusting these (creative energies) to these very (bodies), he joined them together as one and left them to proceed on their course.[1] They need nothing, since they are eternal. If they need anything at all, it is each other. Yet they need no contribution from the outside, since they are immortal. It was necessary that bodies that came into being through the primal Craftsman also possess an immortal nature.

The Second Craftsman

2. Yet our Craftsman, who is embodied, created us, ever continues to create, and will continue to create bodies that dissolve and die.[2] It is not lawful for him to imitate his own Craftsman – not least because it is impossible. For the primal Craftsman created from primal, bodiless substance, but our Craftsman made us from a bodily material that itself came into being. 3. Logically, then, if we reason correctly, those bodies arising from bodiless substance are immortal, while ours dissolve and die, since our material consists of bodies.[3]

The Weakness of the Body

4. Since our bodies are weak, they are in need of much assistance. To be sure, how would the connecting link of our bodies resist even occasional harm if it did not maintain the ingestion of foodstuffs made from the same elements which daily reinforce our bodies? Indeed, an influx of earth, water, fire, and air flows into us which renews our bodies and holds

[1] In this context, the eternal bodies probably designate the stars. Compare the immortal bodies in SH 4.11, 19.

[2] "Our Craftsman" is the Sun. Compare CH 16.5: "the craftsman – I mean the Sun – binds heaven to earth, sending essence below and raising matter above, attracting everything toward the Sun and around it, offering everything from himself to everything"; CH 16.18: "Therefore the father of all is God; their craftsman is the Sun; and the cosmos is the instrument of his craftsmanship"; SH 2A.14 (the Sun crafts everything in the world); SH 21.2 (the Sun is image of the celestial craftsman deity).

[3] Plato spoke of different deities creating the eternal and mortal parts of creation (*Timaeus* 40d–41d). The assignment of mortal creation to the Sun is distinctly Hermetic.

together this tent.[4] 5. Consequently, in the face of commotions, we are incredibly frail and cannot bear them for a single day.

On Sleep

You well know, my child, that if we did not rest our bodies at night, we could not withstand a single day. For this reason, the good Craftsman who foreknows all things, created sleep for the continuance of living creatures, which is the greatest <cessation> from the fatigue of motion.[5] Moreover, he ordered an equal measure of time for each state – or rather, he allotted more time to repose.

6. Understand, my child, the magnificent activity of sleep; it is opposed to the activity of the soul, but not inferior to it. Just as the soul is an activity of motion, in the same way, too, bodies cannot live without sleep; for there is a relaxing and loosening of the connected limbs.[6]

7. Sleep operates within, making ingested matter into bodies, distributing the proper elements to each bodily part: water to blood, earth to bones and marrow, air to nerves and veins, and fire to vision.[7] Accordingly, the body intensely enjoys sleep since it activates this pleasure (of the body's reconstitution).

[4] For the tent image, see SH 2A.1, with note 2 there.

[5] The good Craftsman echoes Plato, "Now why did he who framed this whole universe of becoming frame it? . . . He was good" (*Timaeus* 29d–e). Compare "the Good who makes all things" (CH 5.11).

[6] Compare Tertullian, *On the Soul* 43.7 (sleep is the re-fashioner of bodies, the re-integrator of strength).

[7] Compare Aristotle, *On Sleeping and Waking* 1, 455a1–3 (animals absorb more nourishment during sleep); Tertullian, *On the Soul* 43.3 (food is dispersed in sleep). On vision as using fire, compare Empedocles, who taught that the pupil enclosed "primeval fire" (ὠγύγιον πῦρ) (in Aristotle, *On Senses* 2, 438b32 = Empedocles frag. 103.8, Inwood). Note also Plato: "Now the pure fire inside us, cousin to that [gentle] fire, they [the young gods] made to flow through the eyes" (*Timaeus* 45b); Alcinous: "Having placed upon the face the light-bearing eyes, the gods enclosed in them the luminous aspect of fire, which, since it is smooth and dense, they considered would be akin to the light of day" (*Handbook of Platonism* 18.1, trans. John Dillon).

SH 6

Excerpt 6 appears to be from a Hermetic treatise on the heavenly bodies. Extracted from Stobaeus's *Anthology* 1.21.9, it is the last excerpt in a chapter called "On the Cosmos: Whether it Has a Soul, is Administered by Providence, the Location of its Ruling Faculty, and its Source of Nourishment." It appears after several excerpts attributed to Philolaus, a Pythagorean philosopher who wrote a work *On the Cosmos.*

The main topic of SH 6 is the thirty-six decans, or the astral bodies who each govern ten degrees of the zodiac. In ancient Egypt, the decans were symbols of regeneration. In the first millennium BCE, they were depicted as animal-human hybrid deities who protected the deceased.[1] In the present tractate, the decans are the uppermost heavenly bodies, guardians located between the outer circle of the universe and the band of stars that contain the zodiac. They control and coordinate the speeds of the circles of the universe. They send their energies coursing through all the lower stars. These energies govern and hold the entire universe together.

The decans rule especially over the planets and through them exercise direct influence on earth. Yet they do not suffer from the limitations of the planets such as retrograde motion and the influence of the sun. Through the workings of the planets, the decans are responsible for world-shaking events such as coups, famine, draught, earthquakes and the like.

The children of the decans are popularly called "daimones." These daimones are the energies of the decans. The energies sow the seeds of both health and destruction on earth. The assistants of the daimones fill up the whole region of the aether and are endowed with a peculiar energy. These lesser lords are associated with more negative effects like plague and death.

The rest of the treatise is a kind of star catalogue, detailing the different kinds of heavenly bodies. The central axis of the universe runs through the

[1] Ebeling, *Secret History*, 30–31.

Bear constellations (Ursa Maior balanced by Ursa Minor). Around them are the unnamed fixed stars. Exhalations from the earth form meteors which move sluggishly and break apart below the circle of the moon. Comets soar in the higher circle of the sun. Unlike meteors, they do not dissolve. They are always present, though most often hidden by the rays of the sun. Comets appear specifically as signs of global significance.

Although this treatise treats theoretical astrology, there is little here that would qualify as practical technique. Hermes is engaged in the cosmological task of explaining the astral bodies, not with horoscopes per se. The purpose is not divination via the stars, but the vision of God. As with Plato, knowledge about the stars teaches one not to locate beauty in the shifting forms and colors of objects here below. Beauty, like God, lies above bodies. Beauty is God, or the unknown being beyond God. The praise of this deity is the aim of Hermetic astrology.

Excerpt of a Discourse of Hermes with Tat

On Decans

1. *Tat:* "Since in previous General Discourses you promised to explain to me about the thirty-six decans, explain them now, along with their energies."[2]

[2] On General Discourses, see SH 3.1, note 3. The star gods called decans are named for presiding over ten (δέκα)-day weeks in the Egyptian calendar. They came to preside over ten degrees of the 360-degree zodiac. Hence there are three decans for each zodiacal sign and thirty-six for the entire circle. In *Ascl.* 19, they are called "hour watchers." They are associated with (the healing of) individual body parts (Origen, *Against Celsus* 8.58). Compare the originally Greek tractate ascribed to Hermes, *On the Thirty-six Decans* 1.1–39, 16.2 in Scarpi, 2.174–85, 236 with the comments of Wilhelm Gundel, *Neue astrologische Texte des Hermes Trismegistos: Funde und Forschungen auf dem Gebiet der antiken Astronomie und Astrologie* (Munich: Bavarian Academy of Sciences, 1936), 7.115–23. C. E. Ruelle published a separate *Holy Book of Hermes to Asclepius* on the topic of decans ("Hermès Trismégiste: Le livre sacré sur les decans," *Revue de Philologie* 32 [1908]: 247–77). Other relevant *comparanda* include *Testament of Solomon* 18 (*OTP* 1.977–81); Manilius, *Astronomica* 4.294–407; Firmicus Maternus, *Mathesis* 2.4.1–3; 4.22.2–3. See further Wilhelm Gundel, *Dekane und Dekansternbilder: Ein Beitrag zur Geschichte der Sternbilder der Kulturvölker* (Hamburg: J. J. Augustin, 1936), 234–37, 341–425 (a collection of ancient sources on the decans); O. Neugebauer and H. B. Van Hoesen, *Greek Horoscopes* (Philadelphia: American Philosophical Society, 1959), 5–6. On the original role of decans in Egyptian astronomy see O. Neugebauer and Richard A. Parker, *Egyptian Astronomical Texts 1. The Early Decans* (Providence: Brown University Press, 1960), 95–121; Neugebauer and Parker, *Egyptian Astronomical Texts III. Decans, Planets, Constellations and Zodiacs* (Providence: Brown University Press, 1969), 105–74; Dorian Gieseler Greenbaum, *The Daimon in Hellenistic Astrology: Origins and Influence* (Leiden: Brill, 2016), 223–35.

Hermes: "I do not begrudge you this, Tat. This may indeed be my principal teaching, the crown of them all.

Consider it this way. 2. We spoke with you about the circle of the zodiac – the band of stars featuring animal-like shapes – and the circles of the five planets plus sun and moon."

Tat: "So you spoke, Thrice Great."

Hermes: "In this way I want you also to understand the thirty-six decans, and remember them so that this teaching about them might be well-known to you as well."

Tat: "It is as good as memorized, father."

3. *Hermes:* "We said at one point, my child, that there is a body that encompasses all things. Think of it as circular in shape, for such is the shape of the universe."[3]

Tat: "I envision it so, father."

Hermes: "Underneath the circle of this body are arranged the thirty-six decans, in between the circle of the universe <and> that of the zodiac, dividing both circles. They buoy up, as it were, the circle of the universe, and define the shape of the zodiac.

4. The decans travel along with the planets.[4] They are equal in power to the seven planets as they alternate with them in the rushing motion of the universe. Moreover, they slow the motion of the enveloping body. This is the outermost body in the rushing motion, due to the fact that it contains the universe by its own power. On the other hand, the decans accelerate the movement of the seven other circles because they move slower than the circle of the universe. Working as a kind of necessity, the decans move the planetary circles and <the> circle of the universe.

5. Let us consider that the decans preside as guardians over the circle of the seven planets and the circle as a whole, or rather over all things in the cosmos. They hold all things together and maintain the good order of all things."[5]

Tat: "I consider it as you say, father."

[3] The body is the outermost heavenly sphere. Compare Plato, *Timaeus* 33b; [Aristotle], *On the Cosmos* 2, 391b19–20 (the whole heaven and cosmos are spherical and moving).

[4] Bouché-Leclercq suggested that they travel around with the fixed stars, emending πλάνησι to ἀπλανέσι (*L'astrologie grecque* [Paris: E. Leroux, 1899], 223, n.3).

[5] Compare the thirty (possibly one should read thirty-six) counselor gods in Diodorus, *Library of History* 2.30.6: "of these one half oversee the regions above the earth and the other half those beneath the earth, having under their purview the affairs of humankind and those of the heavens."

6. *Hermes:* "Consider still more, Tat, that the decans are unaffected by what other planets undergo. When checked in their course, they do not halt, nor when hindered do they undergo retrograde motion. Nor indeed are they covered by the light of the sun, which affects the other planets. The decans are free, above all things, serving as exacting guardians and overseers of the universe, surrounding it during the entire diurnal cycle."

The Energies of the Decans

7. *Tat:* "So then, father, do the decans exert an energy toward us?"

Hermes: "The greatest energy, my child! For if they exert their energies on the planets, how not on us as well, both as individuals and in common? 8. The energy emitted from the decans – pay close attention! – drives all general events on earth: overthrows of kings, uprisings in cities, famines, plagues, tsunamis, and earthquakes. None of these occur, my child, without the energies of the decans.[6]

9. Consider this too. If the decans preside over the planets and we are under the power of the seven planets, do you not suppose that some of the decans' energy extends to us, whether in the form of the decans' children, or through them?"

10. *Tat:* "What then, father, would be the bodily form of these children?"

Hermes: "The common crowd calls them 'daimones.' Yet there is no particular class of daimones, nor do they have other bodies from a special kind of matter, nor are they moved by a soul like us. Rather, they are energies of these thirty-six deities.[7]

11. Consider too the product of their energy, Tat. They sow into the earth emanations called *tanai.*[8] Some of these bring health, while others are destructive.

[6] On general astrology, compare Ptolemy: "some things happen to people through more general circumstances and not as the result of an individual's own natural propensities – for example, when people perish in multitudes by conflagration or pestilence or cataclysms" (*Tetrabiblos* 1.3.11–12). Such natural and social disasters are attributed to daimones in CH 16.10, 14: "What the gods enjoin them they effect through torrents, hurricanes, thunderstorms, fiery alterations and earthquakes; with famines and wars, moreover, they repay irreverence."

[7] Compare CH 16.13: "for energy is the essence of a daimon." The traditional Platonic position on daimones is that they are divine intermediaries between gods and human beings (Plato, *Symposium* 202d–203a). Compare Plutarch, *Obsolescence of Oracles* 10–15 (*Moralia* 415b–418d); Maximus of Tyre, *Discourses* 8–9; Plotinus *Enneads* 3.4.3–6. See further Greenbaum, *Daimon*, 221.

[8] Festugière derived *tanai* from the Greek verb τείνω ("to stretch, reach"). They are the stretched-out rays of the decans (NF 3.lvii).

Assistants or Liturgi

12. As the decans move, in heaven they engender heavenly bodies as assistants, which they have as servants and soldiers.[9] These servants, mixed by the decans, are borne aloft in the aether, filling up its whole space so that no place above is void of heavenly bodies.[10] Together, they adorn the universe, each possessing its own energy, an energy in subjection to the energy of the thirty-six decans. They cause destructions of other ensouled animals and they cause the swarms of animals that decimate harvests.[11]

Ursa Maior

13. Underneath the decans is the so-called Bear (Ursa Maior), located at the center of the zodiac and consisting of seven stars.[12] Over its head it has another Bear (Ursa Minor) serving as a counter-weight. The function of this (Great) Bear is analogous to that of an axis, never setting nor rising, remaining in the same spot wheeling round the same point, energizing the <revolution> of the zodiacal circle, handing on this universe from night to day <and> from day to night.[13]

[9] The assistants "seem to be those fixed stars which are within the domain of one or other of the decans, or which rise at the same time as they" (Clark, Dillion, and Hershbell, *Iamblichus On the Mysteries*, 327, n.458). Firmicus Maternus apportioned 3 assistants to each decan, 9 to a sign, thus 108 in all (*Mathesis* 2.4.4). Martianus Capella (*Marriage of Philology* §200) mentioned 84 attendants alongside the decans. In *Pistis Sophia* 3.132 (Schmidt-MacDermot, 342), there are 365 assistants involved in the process of human formation in the womb. See further Greenbaum, *Daimon*, 251.

[10] Compare CH 9.3 (no part of the cosmos is void of daimones).

[11] Compare Firmicus Maternus, *Mathesis* 2.4.5: "by these [assistants] they say are decreed sudden accidents, pains, sicknesses, chills, fevers, and everything that happens unexpectedly."

[12] Compare Aratus, *Phaenomena* 26–44 with the comments of *Ref.* 4.48.7–9. Scott understands this to mean that Ursa Maior "is at the apex of a cone, the base of which is the zodiacal circle" (*Hermetica*, 3.377). In this way, Ursa Maior would be at the center of the Zodiac, though far above it. The cosmic pole or axis runs down from Ursa Maior through the center of the universe. See further Greenbaum, *Daimon*, 252.

[13] Compare Pseudo-Aristotle: "The whole heaven and the cosmos is spherical and continuously moved . . . but there are two points opposite each other that are necessarily unmoved . . . around which the entire mass is turned in a circle. They are called 'poles.' If we think of a straight line joining them together (which some call the axis), this will be the diameter of the universe . . . One of these unmoved poles is always visible over our heads at the northern latitude, called arctic [the 'bear' pole]" (*On the Cosmos* 2, 391b20–392a5). For Ursa Maior as a cosmic steering wheel, perpetually rotating the universe on its central axis, compare CH 5.4: "Who owns this instrument, this Bear, the one that turns around itself and carries the whole cosmos with it?"; *PGM* 7.686–702: "Bear, Bear, you who rule the heaven, the stars, and the whole world; you who make the axis turn and control the whole cosmic system by force and compulsion."

14. Beyond the Bear constellation is another chorus of heavenly bodies that we have not deemed worthy of name. Yet those who come after us, acting in imitation, will give them names.[14]

Meteors

15. Below the moon, there are other heavenly bodies that deteriorate, move sluggishly, and exist for a short time. They consist of exhalations from the earth itself into the air above the earth. We even see them break apart. Their natures resemble those of useless animals on earth. They are born only to destroy, like the race of flies, fleas, worms, and the like. Such animals, Tat, are useful neither to us nor to the cosmos; just the reverse: they cause sorrow and trouble. They are nature's byproducts, existing as the result of excess. In the same way, these heavenly bodies exhaled from the earth do not attain the higher realm, and are unable because they rose from below. They contain much that is heavy, dragged below by their own matter. They quickly melt, dissolve, and fall back again to earth, doing nothing except disturbing the air over the earth.[15]

Comets

16. There is another kind of heavenly body, Tat. It is called the comet, occasionally appearing and again disappearing after a short time. They neither rise, set, nor break apart. Comets are appointed to become manifest as messengers and heralds of events with world-wide significance. They occupy the place below the circle of the sun. They appear when something is about to happen in the cosmos. After appearing for a few days, they return again below the circle of the sun and remain

[14] In this prophecy *ex eventu*, Hermes refers to the constellations of fixed stars. Compare *Ref.* 4.6.3, itself dependent on Sextus Empiricus, *Against the Mathematicians* 5.97–98. It seems odd, in light of this passage (SH 6.14), that Filastrius accused Hermes Thrice Great of introducing names for the stars beyond what is found in the Bible (*Diverse Heresies* 75).

[15] For an explanation of earthly exhalation leading to meteor formation, see Aristotle, *Meteorology* 1.4, 341b1–342a33; Seneca, *Natural Questions* 1.1.7–9; 1.14–15 and 7.23 (end).

invisible. Some appear in the east, some in the north, some in the west, and some in the south. We call them "foretellers of the future."[16]

Such is the nature of the heavenly bodies.

Constellations

17. Heavenly bodies differ from constellations. Heavenly bodies are borne aloft in the heaven, while constellations lie within the body of heaven and revolve in it.[17] From the constellations, we name the twelve signs of the zodiac.

The Vision of God

18. The one not ignorant of these matters can accurately conceive of God.[18] If one must speak boldly, one sees God face to face, beholding and being beheld so as to attain blessedness."[19]

Tat: "Truly blessed, father, is the one who has beheld God."

Hermes: "Yet it is impossible, my child, for one in the body to obtain this boon.[20] One must exercise one's soul down here first to arrive up there where it can behold and not slip from the path. 19. All human beings who

[16] Comets are the stars with long hair (κομήτης from κόμη, hair). For a more detailed and technical discussion of comets, see Aristotle, *Meteorology* 1.3, 342b25–344a4; Pseudo-Aristotle, *On the Cosmos* 4, 392b3–5; 395b4–17; Seneca, *Natural Questions* 7.1.5: "there is no lack of people who create terror and predict dire meanings of it [the comet]"; 7.11.1: "they are seen as much in the east as in the west"; 7.20.4: "We do not see many comets because they are obscured by the rays of the sun"; 7.23.3: "The comet is not extinguished, but simply departs." A comet or long-haired star was said to foretell the significance of king Mithridates VI Eupator (Justin, *Epitome of Trogus* 37.2.1–3). Origen, *Against Celsus* 1.58–59 (the star of Bethlehem can be classed as a comet, but in this case a harbinger of good).

[17] The body of heaven is the outermost circle of the universe. The constellations are stenciled, as it were, on the outer circle. Macrobius makes a different kind of distinction between planets (*stellae*) and stars in constellations (*sidera*), which he relates to the distinction between ἀστήρ (a single star) and ἄστρον (a constellation) (*Commentary on the Dream of Scipio* 1.14.21).

[18] On astronomy as preparation for divine vision, see Plato, *Republic* 528e–530c.

[19] The combination of a God beyond name with whom one can have intimate communion is distinctive to Hermetic thought. According to Philo, the great Moses who reportedly saw God "face to face" (Exod 33:11) could actually only see God's Logos (*Allegorical Interpretation* 3.97–103; *Confusion of Tongues* 95–97).

[20] Compare CH 10.6 (a soul cannot be deified while in a human body). Contrast *Ascl.* 41: "we rejoice that, even though we are in these molded bodies you have deified us by the knowledge of yourself."

love bodies can never behold the sight of the Beautiful and Good.[21] Its beauty is such, my child, that it contains neither shape nor color nor body."[22]

Tat: "Is there a beauty apart from these things, father?"

Hermes: "It is God alone, my child, or rather the name greater than God."[23]

[21] Compare CH 11.21: "While you are . . . a lover of the body, you can understand none of the things that are beautiful and good."

[22] Plato: "How would it be, in our view, if someone got to see the Beautiful itself, absolute, pure, unmixed, not polluted by human flesh or colors or any other great nonsense of mortality, but if he could see the divine Beauty itself in its one Form" (*Symposium* 211d–e). Compare FH 25.2 (from Cyril): "If there is an incorporeal eye, let it go out from the body to the vision of the Beautiful, fly up and soar on high, seeking to behold not a shape nor a body, nor forms."

[23] Namelessness is a native Egyptian way to express transcendence. Erik Hornung (*The Secret Lore of Egypt: Its Impact on the West*, trans. David Lorton [Ithaca: Cornell University Press, 2001], 18) quotes Papyrus Leiden 1.350 (chapter 200): "No god can call him [Amun] by his name"; CH 5.10: "This is the God who is greater than any name"; *Ascl.* 20: "God, Father, Master of all, whatever name people use to call him something holier or more reverent, a name that should be sacred among us because of the understanding we have"; FH 3a: "God is one. He who is one has need of no name"; VH 2: "the one God requires no name"; *Sentences of Sextus* 28: "Do not seek God's name, for you will not find it."

SH 7

In Stobaeus's *Anthology* 1.3.52, SH 7 appears in a chapter entitled, "On Justice, Punisher of Errors, Arrayed alongside God to Oversee Human Deeds on Earth." It is sandwiched between quotes from Herodotus and Hierocles on divine punishment.

The main character of the excerpt is, naturally, Justice, known to the Greeks as *Dikē*. As in the famous philosophical poem of Parmenides, Justice is called a "daimon." By the Hellenistic period, a daimon no longer meant a fully-fledged deity, but typically a mediating deity subordinate to a higher God. According to Hermes, just as Providence and Necessity are appointed over the divine order, Justice is appointed over human beings on earth. Her task is to oversee human life and punish wrongdoing.

From a Treatise of Hermes

On Justice

1. The greatest female daimon who wheels round the center of the universe has been appointed, my child, to observe everything that happens on earth at the hands of human beings.[1] Just as Providence and Necessity

[1] For daimones as watchers or guardians, see Hesiod, *Works and Days* 123–25, 252–55. Compare Parmenides: "in the midst of these [cosmic rings] is a female daimon who steers all things" (frag. 12, lines 3–4, Gallop). Justice (*Dikē*) appears in Hesiod as the daughter of Zeus and Themis (*Theogony* 902). When she is wronged, she sits beside her father and reports the wrong (*Works and Days* 220–24, 256–61). According to the poet Aratus, *Dikē* lived with the men of the Golden Age, put up with the Silver race, and finally fled earth at the start of the Bronze Age (*Phaenomena* 96–136, compare Vergil, *Eclogues* 4.6; Ovid, *Metamorphoses* 1.149–50; Pseudo-Eratosthenes, *Constellations* 9; Hyginus, *Astronomy* 2.25). In her present state, *Dikē* is often said to sit by Zeus, keeping a record of human wrongdoing. Philo, who calls *Dikē* God's assessor (*Joseph* 48), depicts her as taking vengeance on the builders of Babel's Tower (*Confusion of Tongues* 118). According to 4 Maccabees 18:22: "Divine Justice pursued and will pursue the plagued tyrant [Antiochus Epiphanes]." Justice also appears in Acts 28:4: "This man [Paul] must be a murderer . . . Justice has not allowed him to live." In an Orphic fragment, *Dikē* is said to sit by the throne of Zeus and watch over all the deeds of

are appointed over the divine order, in the same way, Justice has been appointed over human beings – and she performs the same activity as Providence and Necessity do.[2] 2. For she controls the order of existing beings inasmuch as they are divine, do not wish to err, and cannot. Indeed, it is impossible for the divine to go astray – hence its infallibility.

Now Justice is appointed to be punisher of human beings who err upon the earth.[3] 3. Humanity is an <errant> race, inasmuch as it is mortal and composed from base matter. They are especially prone to slip since they do not possess the power of seeing the divine. Justice especially holds sway over these people.[4]

Humans are subject to Fate due to the energies operative in their nativity; and they are subject to Justice due to their mistakes during this life.[5]

human beings (πάντα τὰ τῶν ἀνθρώπων ἐφορᾶν) (Bernabé *OF* 33 = Pseudo-Demosthenes, *Oration* 25.11). See further Hugh Lloyd-Jones, *The Justice of Zeus* (Berkeley: University of California Press, 1971), 35–36, 86–87, 99–101.

[2] Namely overseeing and keeping good order. For doctrines of Providence in antiquity, see Myrto Dragona-Monachou, "Divine Providence in the Philosophy of the Empire," *ANRW* II.36.7, ed. Wolfgang Haase (Berlin: de Gruyter, 1994), 4461–90.

[3] Plato specifically called Justice an "avenger" (τιμωρός) (*Laws* 716a); and in an Orphic poem she is called "much-punishing" (πολύποινος) (Proclus, *Commentary on Plato's Republic* 2.145.3, Kroll).

[4] Compare *Ascl.* 28: "When soul withdraws from the body, it passes to the jurisdiction of the chief daimon who weighs and judges its merit, and if he finds it faithful and upright, he lets it stay in places suitable to it. But if he sees the soul smeared with the stains of wrongdoing and dirtied with vice, he sends it tumbling down from on high to the depths below and consigns it to the storms and whirlpools of air, fire and water in their ceaseless clashing."

[5] Fate does not remove moral responsibility. Compare SH 20.6 (when the soul takes a body it comes under Fate).

SH 8

SH 8 (Stobaeus, *Anthology* 1.4.8) comes from a chapter called "On <Divine> Necessity, by which things Planned by God Inevitably Occur." It is preceded by what appears below as SH 13 (*Anthology* 1.4.7^{b}) which gives the opinion of Hermes on Necessity. Hermes's view is then complemented by the views of other famous philosophers on the same topic (*Anthology* 1.4.7^{c}). Jean-André Festugière understood SH 8 to be part of the same treatise as SH 7 on the topic of Providence, Necessity, and Fate.[1] Based strictly on its content, however, SH 8 might better be read (and indeed placed) among SH 12–14.

After an introductory formula, Tat asks Hermes to distinguish the forces of Providence, Necessity, and Fate. Hermes answers the question in a roundabout way by distinguishing three kinds of bodiless entities separately governed by these three forces. Providence governs intellectual reality (elsewhere called *nous*); Necessity governs non-rational forces (like drive and desire), and Fate governs the incidental properties of bodies (qualities like shape, color, place, and time).

Nous is free from the forces of Necessity and Fate when in direct relation to God. When separated from God, *nous* falls into a body according to the will of Providence. *Nous* is then joined to the non-rational parts of the soul (namely, drive and desire) which are subject to Necessity. Insofar as *nous* is joined with these lower parts of the soul, it falls under the power of Necessity. When the human *nous* turns toward God, however, it can both save the lower soul and transcend the power of Necessity.

[1] NF 3.lxi–lxii.

Excerpt of a Discourse of Hermes with His Son

1. *Tat:* "Rightly you relate to me all things, father. Yet remind me still more about matters governed by Providence, Necessity, and Fate."[2]

Three Kinds of Bodiless Entities

2. *Hermes:* "As I said, Tat, within us there are three kinds of bodiless entities. The first is intelligible. It is without color, without shape, without body, and drawn from the primal and intelligible reality itself.[3]

3. Yet there are also within us formations opposed (to intellect), although they receive (intellect).[4] That is to say, what is moved by intelligible reality according to reasoning immediately changes into another (rational) form of motion.[5] This process is a reflection of the Craftsman's intellect.

4. The third form of bodiless entity is the coincidental property of bodies; for example: place, time, motion, shape, surface area, size, and generic type.[6] There are two sorts of coincidental properties: intrinsic

[2] A distinction between these forces is not always made. Chrysippus said, "what comes about by Fate also comes about by Providence (*quae secundum fatum sunt etiam ex providentia sint*)." His successor Cleanthes distinguished Providence and Fate, since not everything that comes about accords with the divine will (both views are transmitted by Calcidius, printed in LS 54U). Pseudo-Plutarch is one of the few authors clearly to distinguish three levels of Providence (*On Fate* 572f–573a). Compare Apuleius, *On Plato* 1.12. See further Michael A. Williams, "Higher Providence, Lower Providences and Fate in Gnosticism and Middle Platonism," in Richard T. Wallis and Jay Bregman, eds., *Neoplatonism and Gnosticism* (Albany: SUNY Press, 1992), 483–508.

[3] Hermes apparently refers to consciousness (νοῦς), but avoids the term. Compare CH 12.1: "Consciousness, O Tat, comes from the very essence of God"; Plato: "What is in this place [the region beyond heaven] is without color and without shape, an intangible reality, truly existing, observable by the soul's guiding mind alone" (*Phaedrus* 247c).

[4] The two "formations" (σχηματότητες) are drive (θυμός) and desire (ἐπιθυμία). Accepted here is Nock's conjecture τούτου ὑποδεκτικαί (here: "although they receive intellect"). In the next sentence καὶ ὑποδεχθέν, which appears to be superfluous, is not translated.

[5] Compare SH 17.7: "Drive and desire are harmonized with reasoning . . . and draw within themselves intelligence as it spins round."

[6] "Aristotle supposed that the elements of all things are substance and incidental properties. The underlying substance is one for all things, whereas the incidental properties are nine: quantity, quality, relation, location, time, possession, position, activity, and passivity" (*Ref.* 1.20.1). Compare Aristotle, *Categories* 4.1b25–2a4. See further Jaap Mansfeld, *Heresiography in Context: Hippolytus' Elenchos as a Source for Greek Philosophy* (Leiden: Brill, 1992), 59–62.

qualities, and the qualities that characterize a body.[7] Intrinsic qualities include shape, color, form, place, time, and motion. The qualities that characterize a body include the instantiated shape, the instantiated color, the instantiated form, the surface area, and the size. These latter types do not participate in the former.[8]

5. The intelligible reality, when in direct relation to God, has power over itself. In the act of preserving something else, it preserves itself, since its actual substance is not subject to Necessity. When taken leave of by God, the intelligible reality chooses a bodily nature according to Providence, and is born as an entity of this world.[9]

6. Everything non-rational is moved by a certain rationality. 7. What is rational moves according to Providence, what is non-rational by Necessity, and coincidental properties related to the body are moved by Fate."[10]

This is the discourse about matters governed by Providence, Necessity, and Fate.[11]

[7] The distinction between intrinsic and supervening qualities can be traced to the Stoics (Plutarch, *Common Notions* 36 [*Moralia* 1077d]). Intrinsic qualities are essential and inseparable qualities that inhere in a thing or person. Chrysippus argued that a thing or object could not have more than one intrinsic quality (Philo, *On the Eternity of the World* 48). Alcinous argued for the incorporeal nature of qualities in his *Handbook of Platonism* 11.1–2. Porphyry distinguished between separable and inseparable coincidental properties: sleeping is separable; but for a raven being black is inseparable (*Introduction* §5, Barnes).

[8] Coincidental properties do not participate in consciousness or the lower parts of the soul. By contrast, the lower parts of the soul can participate in consciousness or reason. On the philosophical notion of quality, see further Myrto Hatzimichali, *Potamo of Alexandria and the Emergence of Eclecticism in Late Hellenistic Philosophy* (Cambridge: Cambridge University Press, 2011), 113–17.

[9] The Hermetic writer lacks a doctrine of the soul's fall. Compare Empedocles frag. 11 (Inwood): "There is an oracle of Necessity, an ancient decree of the gods . . . whenever one by wrongdoing defiles his dear limbs with blood . . . (I speak of) the daimones who are allotted long-lasting life, this one wanders for thrice ten thousand seasons away from the blessed ones, growing to be all sorts of forms of mortal beings"; Plato, *Phaedrus* 248c (the soul that takes on a burden of forgetfulness and wrongdoing is weighed down, sheds its wings and falls to earth); *Republic* 617d–e (the soul chooses its life on earth). In SH 23.25, 30: God punishes souls by having them assigned to bodies.

[10] For distinct levels of causality, see Denzey Lewis, *Cosmology and Fate*, 119–21.

[11] Possibly this sentence is a scribal gloss.

SH 9

Taken from Stobaeus's *Anthology* 1.11.2, SH 9 is part of a chapter called "On Matter." It is preceded and followed by quotations from Aëtius's *Opinions of the Philosophers* on matter as the substrate undergoing all kinds of transformations.

It was a debated question in antiquity whether matter always existed or came into being. In this excerpt, "Hermes" attempts a both/and approach. In its unformed state, matter is eternal. When unformed matter receives the seed of becoming, it comes into being. Specifically, the female Craftsman, possibly to be identified with Nature, forms matter according to preexistent Ideas. Matter formed according to the Ideas is actualized into existence. There is a kind of double entendre here. Non-existence is not only sheer lack of being but also formlessness. When matter receives form, therefore, it is said to come into being.

An Excerpt of Hermes from His Discourses with Tat

On Matter

1. Matter has come into being, my child, though it preexisted. Matter is the vessel of becoming.[1] Becoming is the sphere of activity for the unborn and preexistent being, namely God.[2] Now matter received the seed of becoming and has come into existence. 2. It was changeable and, when formed, assumed shapes. As matter itself was transformed, the female Artificer presided over the Ideas of matter's transformations.[3] The formlessness of matter was equivalent to non-existence. The activation of matter is its birth.

[1] Plato, *Timaeus* 49a: matter is "the receptacle of all becoming, its wet-nurse."

[2] Reading τόπος (here: "sphere of activity") with FP. For the preexistent being, compare SH 21.1: "Now there is a preexistent being over all existing beings."

[3] Compare CH 1.14, where Nature enfolds the intelligible Human.

SH 10

Taken from Stobaeus's *Anthology* 1.8.41, SH 10 appears in a chapter called "On the Nature and Divisions of Time, and the Extent of its Causation." It is sandwiched between quotations from Zeno the Stoic and Apollodorus's *Natural Art* on the definition of time.

Both SH 9 and 10 present a similar tendency: they attempt to hold two conflicting viewpoints in paradoxical harmony. SH 9 posits that matter is both born and unborn. SH 10 argues that time is something both disjointed and continuous. In its disjointed state, even the existence of time comes into question. Three times (or tenses) are distinguished: past, present, and future. It is not clear how or when the future becomes present and the present becomes past. Moreover, none of these times appears to exist on its own, since the past is gone, the future has not come, and the present is unstable.

An Excerpt from the Discourses of Hermes with Tat

Three Divisions of Time

1. As to what we can discover about the three times, they are neither completely independent nor joined as one; conversely, they are joined as one yet independent.[1] 2. If you suppose that the present exists without the past, the present cannot actually exist unless the past also exists. Logically, the present arises from the past and the future comes from the present.

3. If one must examine the matter further, let us reason in this way: past time proceeds into a condition in which it is no longer itself; future time does not exist since it is not yet present; but even the present is not present

[1] The three "times" or tenses refer to past, present, and future.

since it does not remain.[2] For what cannot stand still an instant or for a single point in time – how can this unstable entity be called "present"?[3]

4. Conversely, the past joined to the present, and the present with the future makes a single time. By virtue of their identity, unity, and continuity, they do not exist apart from one another. 5. In this way, time is both connected and disjointed, though it is one and the same thing.

[2] Compare Numenius: "But the time past we ought to consider altogether gone, already so gone and escaped as to exist no longer; on the other hand, future time is not, but professes to be able at some future time to come into being" (frag 5, des Places from Eusebius, *Preparation for the Gospel* 11.10.2). These reflections are probably based on Plato, *Timaeus* 38b: "we also say things like these: that what has come to be *is* what has come to be, that what is coming to be *is* what is coming to be, and also that what will come to be *is* what will come to be ... None of these expressions of ours is accurate."

[3] Compare Aristotle: "One might suppose that there is no such thing as time or only in some virtual or obscure sense. Some of time is past and does not exist; some of it is future and does not yet exist; and from past and future infinite, ever-grasping time consists. But what consists of non-existents cannot be thought to share in reality. In addition, if something exists, necessarily its whole is divisible; when it exists, either all its parts exist or some of them. When it comes to time, however, some of it is past and some of it is future. None of it exists when divided up. The present moment is not a part. A part measures something, and the whole consists of parts. But time does not consist of the present moment" (*Physics* 4.10, 217b32–218a30). The Stoics in particular developed these reflections. Chrysippus affirmed that "no time is wholly present (οὐθεὶς ὅλως ἐνίσταται χρόνος). For since continuous things are infinitely divisible, on the basis of this division every time too is infinitely divisible. Consequently no time is present exactly (μηθένα κατ' ἀπαρτισμὸν ἐνεστάναι χρόνον), but is broadly said to be so" (Stobaeus, *Anthology* 1.8.42 = LS 51B). Plutarch observed: "time is something moved (κινητόν) ... ever flowing ... The familiar 'later,' 'earlier,' 'will be' and 'has been,' when they are uttered, are of themselves an admission of nonexistence (τοῦ μὴ ὄντος). For to speak of what has not yet occurred or has ceased to exist as if it existed is naïve and absurd" (*On the E at Delphi* 19 [*Moralia* 392f]). Against the Stoics, Plutarch wrote: "It is contrary to the [common] conception to hold that future and past time exist while present time does not ... Yet this is the result for the Stoics, who do not admit a minimal time or wish the present to be indivisible but claim that whatever one thinks one has grasped and is considering as present is in part future and in part past. Consequently no part of a present time corresponding to the present moment remains or is left, if the time said to be present is distributed into parts that are future and parts that are past" (*Common Notions* 41 [*Moralia* 1081c–e]). Proclus similarly noted that the "Stoics make it [time] a mere thought (κατ' ἐπίνοιαν ψιλήν), fleeting (ἀμενηνόν), virtually nonexistent (ἔγγιστα τοῦ μὴ ὄντος)" (*On Plato's Timaeus* 271d = LS 51F). Sextus Empiricus uses Stoic reflections on time to support philosophical skepticism (*Outlines of Pyrrhonism* 3.19.144–46; *Against the Mathematicians* 10.169–247). For a Christian adaptation, see Augustine, *Confessions* 11.17–38.

SH 11

The eleventh excerpt is transmitted by Stobaeus (*Anthology* 1.41.1, lines 44–142) immediately after SH 2B, with no break in Stobaeus's text. It makes up the latter half of the first excerpt in a chapter called "On Nature and its Derived Causes." Following it is a quotation from Pseudo-Archytas's *On the First Principle.*

The heart of SH 11 is a collection of Hermetic teachings in forty-eight maxims. They are presented as starting points for further oral teaching. In terms of genre, one can compare Epicurus's *Principal Doctrines*, the *Sentences of Sextus*, and the pithy maxims of Egyptian wisdom literature. The latter literature may indeed have inspired or shaped the present collection of maxims. In turn, the maxims may have served as the basis for longer Hermetic dialogues. The maxims would have been useful for the beginner, since they lack the tensions and paradoxes of the more advanced dialogues.

The maxims of SH 11 are paradoxical and exist in no clear order. Thematically speaking, they regularly contrast heavenly and immortal things versus earthly and mortal things. Heavenly realities like star gods came into being once, do not break down, are unchanging and eternal. Earthly realities like human bodies are subject to constant birth, dissolution, change, and corruption. Knowledge of heavenly matters is possible (for they do not change), while knowledge of earthly appearances is impossible. Goodness exists above, while evil dwells on earth. Freedom reigns on high, and Fate below. Good energies travels down from heaven, but evil on earth does not ascend. Due to the communication of heavenly things with earthly things, the contrast (or dualism) between them is not absolute. The Hermetic universe remains single and connected.

By way of conclusion, Hermes admonishes that his teachings be kept from the crowds. The danger is that morally corrupt people will use Hermes's teachings to justify their own wicked behavior. If they learn of earth's contingency, they will despise the world. If they know that the earth is governed by Fate, they will inevitably use this knowledge an excuse for vice.

The Principles of Reality

1. "Now, my child, I will discuss what is real in summary points. You will understand what I say if you remember what you hear.[1]

2.

1. All existing things move, only what does not exist is immovable.
2. Every body is changeable, but not every body can be broken down.[2] [Some bodies can be broken down.]
3. Not every lifeform is mortal; not every lifeform is immortal.
4. What can be broken down decays. What remains unchanging is eternal.
5. What is ever born, ever decays. What is born once never decays or becomes something else.[3]
6. God is first, the cosmos second, and humanity third.[4]
7. The cosmos is made for humanity, and humanity for God.[5]
8. The perceptible part of the soul is mortal, the rational part is immortal.
9. Every substance is eternal, every substance is changeable.
10. Everything that exists is double. No existing thing stands firm.
11. Not everything is moved by soul, but soul moves all that exists.[6]

[1] The memorization of short maxims prepared the way for more in-depth instruction. On the literary genre of the maxim or γνώμη, see Mahé, *HHE*, 2.407–16.

[2] The body is made up of elements, but individual elements cannot be further broken down. Compare CH 16.9: "the permanence of every body is change: in an immortal body the change is without dissolution."

[3] Compare Plato, *Timaeus* 38c (the world as a whole came into being and by divine decree will never perish); CH 8.2 (the cosmos is immortal); SH 5.1 (on eternal bodies).

[4] Compare CH 8.2–3, 5: "God is in reality the first of all entities . . . But by his agency a second god came to be in his image . . . the cosmos . . . According to the Father's will, and unlike other living things on earth, humankind, the third living thing, came to be in the image of the cosmos"; CH 10.12, 14: "the cosmos is first, but after the cosmos the second living thing is the human, who is first of mortal beings and like other living things has ensoulment . . . there are these three, then: God the Father and the good; the cosmos; and the human"; *Ascl.* 10: "The master of eternity is the first God, the world is second, humankind is third."

[5] Compare DH 9.1: "Humanity [exists] for the sake of God; all things for the sake of humanity."

[6] Not everything that exists is moved by soul, since there is a being beyond existence (ἐπεκεινα τῆς οὐσίας, Plato, *Republic* 509b). Compare Plato, *Phaedrus* 245c (there is a self-mover who is the source of motion); CH 2.8: "all motion is moved in immobility and by immobility. And it happens that the motion of the cosmos and of every living thing made of matter is produced not by things outside the body but by those within it acting upon the outside, by intelligible entities, either soul or spirit or something else incorporeal."

12. <Not> everything that undergoes experience has sensation; everything that has sensation undergoes experience.[7]
13. Everything that feels pain feels pleasure [the mortal animal], but not everything pleasurable is painful [the eternal animal].[8]
14. Not every body grows sick, but every body that does grow sick breaks down.
15. Consciousness is in God, rationality is in humanity, rationality is in consciousness, consciousness cannot suffer.[9]
16. Nothing in the realm of the body is true; everything in the realm of the bodiless is without falsehood.[10]
17. Everything born can change, but not everything born decays.[11]
18. There is no good upon earth, there is no evil in heaven.
19. God is good and humanity evil.[12]
20. The good is freely chosen, evil is not freely chosen.[13]

[7] Adding a negation to the first clause seems necessary (Holzhausen, *CH Deutsch*, 369, n.132). Compare SH 4.19 (immortal bodies do not have sensation); Aristotle, *On the Soul* 2.5, 416b33–36; 2.11, 424a1–2 (sense perception [αἰσθάνεσθαι] is undergoing experience [πάσχειν]), repeated by Tertullian, *On the Soul* 12.4.

[8] Compare Plato: "Take note of pleasures that don't emerge from pains lest perchance you suppose at present that pleasure is by nature the cessation of pain ... Think about the pleasures of smell which suddenly become extraordinarily great even to one not in pain, and when they cease they leave no pain behind" (*Republic* 584b). For more examples of painless pleasures, see his *Philebus* 51a–52b.

[9] For "rationality is in consciousness" (ὁ λογισμὸς ἐν τῷ νοΐ), compare CH 12.13: "consciousness is in soul and reason [*or*: speech] is in consciousness" (λόγον δὲ ἐν τῷ νῷ). Contrast CH 10.13: "consciousness is in the reason" (ὁ νοῦς ἐν τῷ λόγῳ).

[10] Compare SH 2A (entire). [11] Compare SH 2A.13 on eternal bodies.

[12] Compare the *Instruction of Amenemope* 18: "God is ever in his perfection, man is ever in his failure" (Lichtheim, *Ancient Egyptian Literature* 2.157, cited by Bull, "Tradition of Hermes," 222, n.838); CH 6.6: "a human cannot see nor even dream of what the good might be. Humankind has been overrun by every evil, and he believes that evil is good." According to Gilles Quispel ("Hermes Trismegistus and Tertullian," *VC* 49 [1989]: 188–90 [189]), the maxim in SH 11.2 §19 was the starting point for Tertullian's reflection: "God is good (*Deus bonus*) ... but humankind is evil (*sed homo malus*)" (*Testimony of the Soul* 2.2). Tertullian cites these phrases as common expressions which support the idea that every soul contains an idea of God. See further van den Kerchove, *Voie*, 150–51.

[13] Compare Plato: "none of the wise men thinks that any human being willingly makes a mistake or willingly does anything wrong or bad" (*Protagoras* 345e; 358d); "Every unjust man is unjust against his will. No man on earth would ever deliberately embrace any of the supreme evils, least of all in the most precious parts of himself – and as we said, the truth is that the most precious part of every man is his soul" (*Laws* 731c); "No one is willfully evil. A man becomes evil, rather, as a result of one or another corrupt condition of his body and an uneducated upbringing. No one who incurs these pernicious conditions would will to have them" (*Timaeus* 86e). For doctrinal summaries of Plato's position, see Alcinous, *Handbook of Platonism* 31.1–2; Apuleius, *Plato* 2.11; *Ref.* 1.19.20). Note also Marcus Aurelius: "no one does the wrong thing deliberately" (*Meditations* 4.3).

21. The gods choose goods as they are.[14]
22. {Good order is good order of what is great. The law is good order.}[15]
23. {Time is divine; law is human.}[16]
24. The vice of the world is luxury, the time of humanity is decay.
25. Everything in heaven cannot be altered; everything on earth can be altered.
26. Nothing in heaven is enslaved, and nothing on earth is free.
27. There is nothing unknown in heaven, and nothing known upon earth.[17]
28. Nothing <in heaven communicates with things on earth, but> things on earth <communicate> with things in heaven.
29. Everything in heaven is blameless, everything on earth is blameworthy.
30. The immortal is not mortal, the mortal is not immortal.[18]
31. Everything sown is not born, but everything born is also sown.
32. There are two periods of a dissolvable body: the period from sowing to birth, and the period from birth to death. An eternal body has only a period from birth.[19]
33. Bodies that break down grow and diminish.
34. Matter that breaks down changes into its opposite. [Destruction and birth.] Matter that is eternal changes into itself or into something similar.[20]
35. Birth is the beginning of human decay, decay is the beginning of human birth.

[14] Possibly the antithetical colon has dropped out. Meineke would supplement: "Humans choose evil since they view it as good" (apparatus *ad loc.* in NF 3.55).

[15] This maxim is corrupt. Theiler rewrites: "Good order is with consciousness, lack of order is without consciousness" (ἡ εὐνομία μετὰ νοῦ, ἡ ἀνομία ἄνευ νοῦ) (apparatus *ad loc.* in NF 3.55).

[16] Another corrupt maxim. Nock, following Theiler, suggests "eternity is divine law; time is human law" (αἰὼν νόμος θεῖος, χρόνος νόμος ἀνθρώπινος) (apparatus *ad loc.* in NF 3.55). In *Ascl.* 30, divine law frames the movements of the stars which inform time.

[17] Nothing is known on earth because it is the realm of appearances (SH 2A); all is known in heaven because there one is free from bodily sensations and mere appearances.

[18] A possible polemic against a saying of Heraclitus: "Immortal mortals, mortal immortals: the one living their death, the other dying their life" (in *Ref.* 9.10.6). (Familiarity with Heraclitus is presumed in CH 10.25 = 12:1: "Agathos Daimon has said that gods are immortal <humans> and humans are mortal gods"). Compare §38 below.

[19] Star gods are born, but by God's will do not die.

[20] The mortal combinations of matter break down into the immortal elements that can be exchanged but not further broken down.

36. What goes out of existence <comes into existence; what comes into existence also> goes out of it.[21]
37. Of existing things, some are in bodies, some in ideal forms, and some in energies. A body is in an ideal form;[22] both ideal forms and energies are in bodies.[23]
38. What is immortal does not share what is mortal, but the mortal shares the immortal.[24]
39. A mortal body does not come into an immortal one, but an immortal body can arrive in a mortal one.[25]
40. The energies are not borne upwards, but downwards.[26]
41. Nothing in earth benefits what is in heaven; everything in heaven benefits things on earth.
42. Heaven receives eternal bodies, the earth receives decaying bodies.[27]
43. The earth is non-rational, while heaven is rational.[28]
44. Heavenly things are subject <to Providence>; earthly things [in earth] are subject <to Necessity>.[29]

[21] Contrast sayings §§5, 32 (eternal bodies need not die or go out of existence). For §§30–36, compare DH 10.4, 6: "Evil is a deficiency of good, good (is) fullness of itself . . . Providence and Necessity (are), in the mortal, birth and death, and in God, unbegotten (essence). The immortal (beings) agree with one another and the mortal envy one another with jealousy because evil envy arises due to knowing death in advance. The immortal does what he always does, but the mortal does what he has never done. Death, if understood, is immortality; if not, understood death. They assume that the mortal (beings) of this (world) have fallen under (the dominion) of the immortal, but (in reality) the immortal are servants of the mortal of this (world)."

[22] One expects here that the body is *not* in an ideal form. Holzhausen daggers this clause as corrupt (*CH Deutsch*, 2.371–72).

[23] For energies in bodies, see SH 4.6.

[24] Compare sayings §§28, 41; DH 10.4: "The immortal nature (is) the movement of the mortal nature . . . The immortal came into being because of the mortal, but the mortal comes into being by means of the immortal."

[25] Compare Philo, *Embassy to Gaius* 118: "Sooner could God transform into a human than a human into God": John 1:14: "The Logos became flesh." In the present Hermetic maxim, the immortal in the mortal may refer to divine consciousness in the body. Compare SH 3.7 (a divine part enters the mortal body).

[26] The energies may be astral energies (from the decans or their offspring). Compare SH 4.18: "<energy> is sent from the heavenly bodies"; CH 10.22: "Energies work through the cosmos and upon humankind through the natural rays of the cosmos"; *Ascl.* 2: "From the heavens all things come into earth and water and air . . . whatever descends from on high is a breeder."

[27] Compare DH 10.4: "[as to] mortality, earth is its grave; [and] heaven [is] the place of the immortal."

[28] Compare CH 1.10–11: the heavy elements of earth are bereft of reason; the craftsman-mind rationally moves the heavens.

[29] Followed here are Scott's emendations: τὰ ἐν οὐρανῷ <προνοίᾳ> ὑπόκειται· τὰ ἐπὶ γῆς [τῇ γῇ] <ἀνάγκῃ> ὑπόκειται (Scott, *Hermetica*, 1.432, apparatus *ad loc.*; 3.418); compare saying §46 below.

45. Heaven was the first element and earth the last.
46. Providence is divine order; Necessity is Providence's maidservant.[30]
47. Chance is an unordered impulse, an image of activity, a false vision.[31]
48. What is God? Unchanging good. What is humanity? Changing evil.[32]

3. If you remember these chief points, you will easily recall the points I discuss at greater length. For the main points are summaries of the explained teachings.

Secrecy

4. But shun conversations with the common crowd.[33] I do not want you to begrudge people; but to the common crowd you will appear ridiculous.[34] Like is received by like, and unlike things are never friends. These teachings convince precious few listeners, or perhaps it will convince not even a few.

5. These teachings contain something peculiar. They incite evil people toward evil. Therefore these teachings must be kept from the common crowd who do not understand the excellence of what is said."[35]

Tat: "What do you mean, father?"

Hermes: "Let me explain, my child. The human animal taken as a whole is starkly inclined toward evil. It grows up and is nurtured by it. As a result,

[30] Compare SH 7–8; 12.1. Bull regards this maxim as a summary of SH 7 ("Tradition of Hermes," 221).

[31] Compare the definition of chance in Pseudo-Plato, *Definitions* 411b "a motion moving from the unmanifest to the unmanifest" (φορὰ ἐξ ἀδήλου εἰς ἄδηλον).

[32] Compare maxim §19 above; CH 10.12: "the human is not only not good, but because he is mortal he is evil as well."

[33] Compare CH 13.22: "reveal the tradition of rebirth to no one lest we be accounted its betrayers"; *Ascl.* 32: "hide these divine mysteries among the secrets of your heart and shield them with silence."

[34] Compare Iamblichus, *Life of Pythagoras* 104: The Pythagoreans spoke to each other in symbols which appear "laughable and trival to ordinary persons, full of nonsense and rambling."

[35] Compare CH 9.4: "one who has come to know God . . . has thoughts that are divine and not like those of the multitude. This is why those who are in knowledge do not please the multitude, nor does the multitude please them. They appear to be mad, and they bring ridicule on themselves. They are hated and scorned, and perhaps they may even be murdered"; Matt 7:6: "Do not give what is holy to dogs or cast your pearls before swine lest they trample them with their feet and turn to tear you to pieces." See further Albert de Jong, "Secrecy I: Antiquity," *DGWE* 1050–54; Kocku von Stuckrad, "Secrecy as Social Capital," in Andreas B. Kilcher, ed., *Constructing Tradition: Means and Myths of Transmission in Western Esotericism* (Leiden: Brill, 2010), 239–52.

it takes pleasure in it. So if this animal learns that the world is born, that all things arise by Providence and Necessity under the rule of Fate – will it not be far worse than at present? Despising the universe as something born, and referring the causes of evil to Fate, the human species will never relinquish any evil act.[36] So the teaching must be kept from them, so that, held in ignorance, they may be less evil through fear of what is uncertain."

[36] On the rule of Fate, see SH 12.2: "One can neither escape Fate nor protect oneself from the powerful influence of the stars"; SH 14.2: "Fate is the cause of astral formations. Such is the inescapable law that orders all things." Plato likewise believed that his teachings, if read by the common crowd, would lead to either disdain or foolish elation (*Letter* 7.341d–e). Compare *Disc. 8–9* (NHC VI,6) 62.22–28: "Write an oath in the book, lest those who read the book bring the language into abuse, or oppose the acts of Fate." Compare CH 12.5–7: "If it is absolutely fated for some individual to commit adultery or sacrilege or to do some other evil, how is such a person still to be punished . . . ?" Zeno the Stoic "whipped a slave caught stealing. When the slave said, 'I was fated to steal!' Zeno said, 'And to be thrashed!'" (Diogenes Laertius, *Lives of Philosophers* 7.23).

SH 12

Taken from Stobaeus's *Anthology* 1.5.20, SH 12 comes from a chapter called "On Fate and the Good Ordering of Events." It is immediately preceded by an excerpt from Plutarch's work *Whether Knowledge of the Future is Beneficial*; it is followed by the famous passage in Plato's *Republic* in which souls choose their fate (620d–621a).

As a group, SH 12–17 are addressed to Ammon. The first three probably belong to a single treatise and treat the subject of Fate. In fact, it is tempting to insert SH 13 directly into SH 12 (see the notes). SH 12 and 14 derive from the same chapter in Stobaeus. Logically, SH 14 might better be placed before SH 12.

SH 12 strongly asserts the rule of Fate, a teaching noted in passing at the end of SH 11. Yet in SH 12, Fate is put in relation to two higher forces: Providence and Necessity. Fate is a power of Providence, the perfect Reason (*logos*) of God. Fate, however, operates through the stars and affects earthly things below. The influence of the stars is powerful and inescapable. Nevertheless, since Providence reigns supreme, Fate is the tool of the divine will.

Excerpt from the Writings of Hermes to Ammon

Providence, Necessity, and the Rule of Fate

1. Everything comes to pass by nature and by Fate, and there is no region bereft of Providence.[1] Providence is the reason of the celestial God that is perfect in itself. Providence has two powers generated from its own

[1] Here nature does not seem to be personified (though compare SH 15.5). On the mutual relations of Providence, Necessity, and Fate, see SH 8, 11.2, §46. *Ascl.* 39–40 (Fate, Necessity, and Order).

nature: Necessity and Fate.[2] Fate serves Providence and Necessity.[3] 2. The stars serve Fate. One can neither escape Fate nor protect oneself from the powerful influence of the stars. The stars are the instrument of Fate. By Fate's decree, all things reach their intended end in nature and among human beings.[4]

[2] Here one is tempted to insert the one-line SH 13 ("Necessity is a firm judgment and an unbending power of Providence"), so that Providence, Necessity, and Fate are all spoken of in due order (Scott, *Hermetica*, 3.425).

[3] Compare Posidonius: Fate is "third from Zeus; for first there is Zeus, second Nature, and third Fate" (frag. 103, Kidd); Epictetus, *Discourses* 1.6.

[4] Fate seems all-powerful, but only because it is servant to Providence. For the distinct levels of cosmic causality, see Denzey Lewis, *Cosmology and Fate*, 119–21.

SH 13

SH 13 (from Stobaeus, *Anthology* 1.4.7b) appears in a chapter called "On <Divine> Necessity by which things Planned by God Inevitably Occur." The excerpt is directly joined to what precedes: "Thales was asked, what is strongest? He answered: Necessity, since it rules over all" (*Anthology* 1.4.7a). If one observes the similar structure of SH 28, SH 13 could have been introduced as: "Hermes was asked what Necessity is. He answered: . . ."

The quotations following SH 13 give the opinions of other famous philosophers (namely Pythagoras, Parmenides, Leucippus, Plato, and Empedocles) about Necessity. The quotation that follows these views is SH 8, which seems to introduce a treatise on Providence, Necessity, and Fate. SH 13 reinforces the idea that Necessity is subject to Providence, a view stated in slightly different terms in SH 11.2 §46 ("Necessity is Providence's maidservant").

Excerpt from the Writings of Hermes to <Ammon>[1]

Necessity is a firm judgment and an unbending power of Providence.

[1] Manuscript F reads (in translation): "An Excerpt from the Writings of Plato" with a marginal note "from Akmon the Pythagorean." In P, the marginal note has worked its way into the text. In scholia, Akmon appears as the father of Ouranos or sometimes as a name for Ouranos himself. A figure called Ἄκμωνός appears in the fourth-century CE *Exhortation to the Greeks on True Religion* 36e–b (= Scott, *Hermetica*, 4.6–7). In Hesychius (*s.v.* Ἀκμονίδης), an aphorism is ascribed to Ἄκμων, who is identified with Ouranos and Kronos. See further Hoefer in *PW* 1.1 col. 1173–74, under the word "Akmon." Scott suggested that Ἄκμωνα be emended to Ἀγαθοῦ δαίμονος ("Agathos Daimon," *Hermetica* 4.7, n.1). Here I follow the majority of editors by emending Ἄκμωνα to Ἄμμων (Ammon).

SH 14

SH 14 appears in a chapter of Stobaeus's *Anthology* (1.5.16) named "On Fate and the Good Ordering of Events." It is immediately preceded by a section of Aëtius's *Opinions of the Philosophers* wherein well-known sages define the nature of Fate. It is followed by a quotation of Iamblichus's *Letter to Macedonius* on the chain of causes. Two excerpts prior to SH 14 is a poem on the seven planets ascribed to Hermes (appearing below as SH 29).

SH 14 defines the overlapping roles of Providence, Necessity, and Fate. Fate is particularly active in the earthly sphere of birth and decay. It is the cause of astral formations and the cosmic whirl. Providence belongs to a higher order. By itself, Fate is not ineluctable law; what is ineluctable is that Fate fulfills the design of Providence.

On the Government of the Universe. An Excerpt from the Writings of Hermes to <Ammon>[1]

1. Now Providence firmly governs the whole world, Necessity constrains and contains it, and Fate drives and drives round all things by force. Indeed, its nature is to use force. Fate is the cause of birth and decay during the time of life.

2. The universe experiences the work of Providence first, for it is the first to receive its influence. Providence is spread out in heaven because gods too revolve in heaven and are moved with a tireless and ceaseless motion.[2]

[1] Here the form of Ammon is written Amun (Ἀμοῦν), the supreme deity worshiped especially in Egyptian Thebes (modern Luxor). Herodotus, along with most later Greeks, believed Amun to be a form of Zeus (*Histories* 2.42.5). Plutarch rightly understood Amun (Ἀμοῦν) and Ammon (Ἄμμωνα) to be variants of the same name (*Isis and Osiris* 9 [*Moralia* 354c]). See further Copenhaver, 200–1.

[2] The "gods" refer to the fixed stars and other heavenly bodies. For the divinity of the stars, compare Apuleius: "neither Greek nor barbarian would readily hesitate to call either the sun or the moon gods. Nor indeed is it just these that have been called gods . . . but also the five stars commonly called

Fate (also) is spread out because it is moved by Necessity.[3] Whereas Providence provides order, Fate is the cause of astral formations.[4] Such is the inescapable law that orders all things.[5]

'wandering' [the planets] . . . If you share Plato's view, then place the remaining stars too in the same class of visible gods" (*God of Socrates* 119–20). For a similar but expanded discussion of the relation of Providence to Fate, see Boethius, *Consolation of Philosophy* 4.6.

[3] The clipped sentence εἱμαρμένη δέ, διότι καὶ ἀνάγκῃ can be variously construed. On the relation of Fate and Necessity, see further *Ascl.* 39–40.

[4] Fate is not identical to the stars or their formations. Compare SH 12.2: "The stars serve Fate"; Bardaisan: "Fate does not have power over everything. For that which is called Fate is really the fixed course determined by God for the Rulers and guiding signs" (*Book of the Laws of Countries*, trans. Drijvers, 33). A somewhat different view is expressed by Sallustius, *Concerning the Gods and the Universe* 9: "It is reasonable and true to believe that not only the gods but also the divine (heavenly) bodies administer human affairs, and in particular our bodily nature." See further Denzey Lewis, *Cosmology and Fate*, 123.

[5] The inescapable law is apparently Providence and Fate working together. Compare the "inviolate law" of SH 24.1.

SH 15

Taken from Stobaeus's *Anthology* 1.41.7, SH 15 belongs to a chapter called "On Nature and its Derived Causes" (the same chapter as SH 2B, 4, 5, 11, 16, and 21). It is immediately preceded by what appears above as SH 4. It is immediately followed by SH 5. To preserve the order of Stobaeus, therefore, one must read SH 4, 15, and 5 in sequence. The fact that SH 4 is addressed to Tat and SH 15 to Ammon does not necessarily indicate that they belonged to a separate collection or that they were not at one time juxtaposed. The *Corpus Hermeticum* (CH) is a single collection addressed to multiple recipients (CH 2 to Asclepius, CH 4–5 to Tat, CH 11 to Hermes, CH 16 to Ammon).

SH 15 focuses on the power of Nature (*physis*) which we might also translate "Growth." It relates in brief compass a story both of the birth of the cosmos (cosmogony) and the birth of intelligent human life (anthropogony). In the cosmogony section, the focus is on how the four elements emerge. These elements (earth, air, fire, and water) give way to the creation of life-breath (*pneuma*) which is active in male semen.

The mention of human seed leads abruptly to the anthropogony. In the womb, the life-breath in semen provides for the growth of the fetus. The fetus is not yet intelligent, but since it has the life-breath (*pneuma*), it is receptive to intelligent life. Once the fetus is born, it can then receive intelligent life by the infusion of soul. Although there is no natural connection between soul and body, they are acclimatized to each other and joined by the decree of Fate.

Excerpt from the Discourses of Hermes with Ammon

Motion and Nature

1. What is moved is moved by the energy of the movement that moves the universe. The nature of the universe affords (two) motions to the universe, one motion according to nature's potentiality, and another

according to its actuality.[1] The former pervades the whole cosmos and provides it with cohesion from within, the latter is coextensive with the cosmos and envelops it from without. Both kinds of motion travel back and forth through all things in common.

2. Now universal Nature makes all creatures grow, provides growth to what is growing, sows its own seeds of generation,[2] and controls movable matter.

The Origin of the Elements

When Nature stirs, it grows warm and matter arises in the form of fire and water. Fire is vigorous and strong; water is receptive.[3] Fire, when it opposed water, dried a part of it so that <earth> arose, borne upon the water.[4] When the water completely dried out around it, a vapor arose from these three elements – namely, water, earth, and fire. As a result, air was born.[5]

3. These elements combined in harmonious proportion. Heat was in proportion to cold, and dryness to wetness. From the combined wafting of the air, life-breath and seed came into being in harmonious proportion to the atmospheric life-breath.[6]

Production of Offspring

4. This life-breath, injected into the womb, was not barren in the seed.[7] As a productive force, life-breath begins the work of transformation. When the seed is transformed, it becomes capable of growth and mass.

[1] Potentiality and actuality are originally Aristotelian distinctions (for example, Aristotle, *Physics* 8.4, 255a30–b32). On the two movements, compare *Ascl.* 30: "The world's motion is a twofold activity: eternity enlivens the world from without, and the world enlivens all within it."

[2] Here reading γενέσεως ("of generation") instead of γένεσις (following Holzhausen, *CH Deutsch*, 2.380, n.163).

[3] CH 1.5 (fire leaps up to heaven from the watery nature below); CH 1.17: "Water did the fertilizing. Fire was the maturing force [for the first human beings]."

[4] In Heliopolitan mythology, earth rises as a primeval mound, a small pyramid (the *Benben* stone) from the waters of Nun. Compare CH 3.2 ("moist sand"); FH 31 (from Cyril).

[5] Compare Philo: "When the World-shaper began to form the unordered substance . . . he rooted earth and water in the middle and drew up the 'trees' of air and fire to the heights and he fortified the aetherial region in a circle as a boundary and guardian of what lay within" (*Noah's Work as a Planter* 3).

[6] Compare Aristotle, *Generation of Animals* 2.3, 736b36–38 (semen contains life-breath, or πνεῦμα, analogous to aether in the stars).

[7] Compare Chrysippus in Diogenes Laertius, *Lives of Philosophers* 7.159 (semen is life-breath); Zeno reported by Eusebius, *Preparation of the Gospel* 15.20.1 (sperm as life-breath plus moisture combines with female life-breath in the womb). See further the texts cited in NF 3.lxxxviii–xcvii.

The formed image is drawn in the mass that is shaped. The generic form is conveyed in the figure. This generic form is the means through which the (fetal) form is formed.[8]

5. Since, then, the life-breath does not possess vital motion in the womb, but only the motion that provides initial growth, Nature harmoniously fitted this latter motion (of growth) to serve as a receptacle of intelligent life.[9] Intelligent life is without parts, immutable, and never removed from immutability. Nature, serving as midwife, brings to birth what is in the womb, (and brings it) into the outside air according to fixed measurements (of time).[10]

6. Moreover, the most proximate soul is acclimated (to the body), not because these (two) share a natural kinship, but because this is what is fated.[11] The soul has no natural urge to be with a body.[12] 7. For this reason, by Fate Nature provides what is born with intelligent motion and intelligent reality in which its life consists. For intelligent motion steals within the seed by means of life-breath and moves with the vigor of life.[13]

[8] Compare OH 5.8–9 below.

[9] Compare SH 8.3: "what is moved by intelligible reality according to reasoning immediately changes into another (rational) form of motion." The Hermetic writer distinguishes between the spermatic breath, principle of vegetative life, and the intellective soul, principal of intelligent ("true") life. Apparently, the latter does not enter the body until birth. Compare Iamblichus: "concerning the intellect, many Peripatetics posit one intellect from seed and from the natural world, which arises immediately at the first generation. They add that a second intellect, which they call separate and external, comes into being along with it but arises late, when the potential intellect is actualized and participates appropriately in actual intellection" (*On the Soul* 15, trans. Dillon and Finamore, modified).

[10] For fixed measurements, compare the *Pythagorean Notes* in Diogenes Laertius, *Lives of Philosophers* 8.29: "First taking solid shape in about forty days, the infant is completed and born according to harmonic ratios in seven, nine or at most ten months." See also Diocles of Carystus, frags. 44–46 (van der Eijk).

[11] Here reading οἰκειότητα ("kinship") with V, not ἰδιότητα with P. Contrast SH 8.5, where the soul chooses a body depending on Providence.

[12] For the soul unwillingly entering the body, compare SH 23.33–34; DH 7.4: "The soul goes into the body by necessity (κατ' ἀνάγκην)." The soul rather has a "natural urge" (ἔρως) for intelligent reality (SH 19.4).

[13] Compare CH 10.17: "mind cannot seat itself alone and naked in an earthy body . . . Mind, therefore, has taken the soul as a shroud, and the soul, which is itself something divine, uses the breath as a sort of armoring-servant." For "stealing in" (παρεισέρπει), compare Aristotle, *Generation of Animals* 2.3, 736b27–28 (divine mind enters [ἐπεισιέναι] the soul from outside). According to Iamblichus, Hermetic lore teaches two souls, one from the highest God and the other from the circuit of the heavenly bodies "into which slinks (ἐπεισέρπει) the God-seeing soul" (*On the Mysteries* 8.6 = FH 16). According to Macrobius, the soul "does not suddenly assume a defiled body out of a state of complete incorporeality, but, gradually sustaining imperceptible losses and departing farther from its simple and absolutely pure state, it swells out with certain increases of a planetary body: in each of the spheres that lie below the sky it puts on another ethereal envelope, so that by these steps it is gradually prepared for assuming this earthly dress" (*Commentary on the Dream of Scipio*, 1.11.12).

SH 16

In the context of Stobaeus's *Anthology* (1.41.4), SH 16 belongs to a chapter called "On Nature and its Derived Causes" (the same chapter as SH 2B, 4, 5, 11, 15, and 21). It is preceded by an excerpt from Porphyry's *Starting Points toward the Intelligibles.* It is followed by a selection from Pseudo-Archytas, *On the First Principle.*

SH 16 explains the different natures of soul and body. In itself, the soul is bodiless. When the soul enters the body it does not lose its incorporeal nature. Since the soul is superior to the body, it does not have to live in and for the body or in relation to any bodily form. It is independent and stands in relation to nothing outside itself. It is prior to the body and for this reason not subject to it. The essential characteristic of the soul is thinking.

The body, by contrast, is not independent, but entirely depends on bodiless things external to itself. The body is always in time, space, and subject to external motions (the principle of growth). It is always related to a particular shape or structure. It is always meant for something else, notably the soul. In relation to these three dependencies, the body undergoes constant change (growth and decay). The essential property of the body is change. Yet even in the process of change, the body always remains a body. It is only the constitution of the body that changes. Bodies always change into different bodies.

A brief appendix on three incorporeal entities – space, time, and natural motion – closes the excerpt.

Excerpt from the Discourses of Hermes with Ammon

Soul in Relation to Body

1. The soul is a bodiless reality. Though it is in a body, it does not lose its own essential principle.[1] This is because it is always moving by nature and self-moved by thought.[2] It is not moved in anything or in relation to anything or for anything. It is first in power, and what is first does not need what comes later.

2. By "in something," then, I mean <in> space, time, and nature. By "in relation to something," I mean <in relation to> harmony, shape, and figure. By "for something," I mean <for> the body.[3]

3. Time, space, and nature are made for the body. These participate in each other by means of their congenital affinity. Logically, then, the body required space – for it is impossible for a body to exist without space. Without time and natural motion, it cannot undergo natural changes; nor, apart from harmony, can it attain bodily structure.[4]

4. Thus space exists for the sake of the body. It receives the changes of the body and does not allow what is changed to be destroyed. As a body changes from one thing to another, it loses and is deprived of its condition, but it never stops being a body. As it changes into another body, it takes on the condition of the other body. For the body, as body, remains a body. Yet the manner of its constitution is not stable. So the body changes according to its constitution.

5. Furthermore, space, time, and natural movement are bodiless.[5]

[1] SH 15.4–7 tells how the intelligent soul is introduced into the body. The present excerpt picks up with the soul in the body. By "soul" here, the higher soul or consciousness (νοῦς) seems to be in view. The word οὐσιότης (here: "essential principle") recurs in CH 12.1, 22, where it refers to the superior reality of God. Compare Alcinous: "the primary god is . . . essentiality" (*Handbook of Platonism* 10.3). Οὐσιότης also occurs in SH 21.1 ("universal essentiality"); and FH 18 (translated "principle of being").

[2] Compare SH 3.1 (soul ever-moving), a standard doctrine of Plato: "Every soul is immortal. That is because whatever is always in motion is immortal" (*Phaedrus* 245c).

[3] Compare *Ascl.* 15: "'Place' I call that in which all things are, for none of them could have been, lacking a place to keep them all (a place must be provided for everything that is to be); the fact is, that if things were nowhere, one could not distinguish their qualities, quantities, positions, or effects." Sextus Empiricus, *Against the Mathematicians* 10.10. For the philosophical notion of place or space, see Hatzimichali, *Potamo*, 117–21; Richard Sorabji, *Matter, Space and Motion: Theories in Antiquity and their Sequel* (Ithaca: Cornell University Press, 1988), 125–218.

[4] At the beginning of the sentence, reading ἐπεὶ τοίνυν ("Logically, then") with FP.

[5] On bodiless entities, compare SH 8.4.

6. Each of these has its own peculiar property. The property of space is receptivity;[6] the property of time is interval and number;[7] the property of nature is motion; the property of harmony is friendship; the property of body is change; the property of soul is its natural intellectual ability.

[6] Compare Aristotle, *Physics* 4.1–5.

[7] Compare Aristotle: "time is the number (ἀριθμός) of motion relative to what proceeds and comes after" (*Physics* 4.11, 219b1–2). Simplicius reports that, "Among the Stoics, Zeno said that time is the interval of all motion plain and simple (πάσης ἁπλῶς κινήσεως διάστημα); Chrysippus said that time was the interval of the motion of the cosmos" (*SVF* 2.510; repeated by Philo in his *On the Creation* 26).

SH 17

In his *Anthology* (1.49.4), Stobaeus transmitted SH 17 in a chapter called "On the Soul" (the same chapter as SH 3, 19, 20, 23–26). It is immediately preceded by what is here classified as SH 20. It is immediately followed by what appears above as SH 3.

The central point of the excerpt is how the cardinal virtues (justice, self-control, courage, and wisdom) are produced. There are three faculties in the soul: rationality, drive, and desire. Drive conformed to rationality produces courage, desire conformed to rationality produces self-control, and the rational balance of drive and desire produces the virtue of justice. Wisdom is apparently produced by the rational faculty itself.

At the end of the excerpt, there is an effort to distinguish a higher and a lower rationality. Higher rationality is intelligent reality (elsewhere called consciousness or *nous*), while lower rationality is the calculating faculty (*logos*). Intelligent substance is the ruler; the calculating faculty is the counselor. Intelligent substance moves in a circle and has no direct contact with drive and desire. Rationality is linear and has direct contact with drive and desire. Nevertheless, drive and desire – when turned to rationality – conform to the motions of higher intelligence.

Excerpt from a Writing of the Same Author[1]

1. Thus the soul, Ammon, is a reality perfect in itself. In the beginning, soul chose a life according to Fate and drew to itself a rationality adapted to matter. (The soul) had in its control both drive and desire.[2]

[1] In the context of Stobaeus's *Anthology*, the author is Hermes.

[2] The soul is rational, but it must assume a lower rationality that can mix with drive and desire (see §7 below). For drive and desire, see SH 2B.6–7. Compare SH 8.5 (soul chooses a bodily nature); SH 15.6 (the adaptation of the soul). For the soul choosing its life according to Fate, see Plato, *Republic* 617e–619a.

The Production of Virtues

2. Indeed, drive exists as matter. If drive generates a disposition fitted to the soul's intellect, it becomes courage and does not fade away under fear.[3] Desire, for its part, affords the same possibility. If it is produced as a disposition conforming to the rationality of the soul, it becomes self-control and is not stirred by pleasure.[4] 3. Reasoning fills up the insufficiency of desire. The virtue of justice is born under three conditions: when both drive and desire agree, when they produce a balanced state, and when they are controlled by the soul's rationality. Their balanced state removes the excessiveness of drive and compensates for the insufficiency of desire.[5]

4. The ruler of both drive and desire is intelligent reality, possessing itself as itself, existing in its own intelligizing reason, and controlling it. 5. This intelligent reality rules and governs as a ruler while its reason serves as counselor.[6]

6. The discursive reason of reality, then, is knowledge of calculations that bestows a faded image of rationality in what is non-rational.[7] In relation to (true) rationality, the image is dim. Yet in relation to the non-rational, discursive reason serves as reasoning like an echo in relation to a voice, and the light of the moon compared with the light of the sun.[8]

7. Drive and desire are tuned to a certain rationality.[9] They balance each other and draw within themselves the intelligence that revolves as a sphere.[10]

[3] Compare Plato: "the part of the mortal soul that exhibits manliness and spirit [= drive], the ambitious part, they [the young gods] settled near the head ... so that it might listen to reason and together with it restrain by force the part consisting of appetites" (*Timaeus* 70a); Aristotle: "actions should accord with correct reason (ὀρθὸν λόγον) (*Nicomachean Ethics* 2.2, 1103b31–32); "virtue is the state in accord with correct reason" (*ibid.*, 6.12, 1144b21–22).

[4] Plato does not admit that desire or the desiring part can conform to reason (*Timaeus* 70e–71a).

[5] For Plato, the virtue of justice is the rule of reason over drive and desire (*Republic* 4.443d). Drive and desire are like two horses pulling a chariot with reason as the driver (*Phaedrus* 246a–b). The horses must be of equal condition and disposition for the chariot to drive well. In SH 17, the virtues are called enduring attitudes (ἕξεις), following Aristotle (for example, *Nicomachean Ethics* 2.4, 1106a11–12). The doctrine of the golden mean is also Aristotelian: "we must choose the intermediate condition, not the excess or the deficiency, and the intermediate condition is as right reason dictates" (*ibid.*, 6.1, 1138b18–21).

[6] Compare SH 19.1: "Now the soul is an eternal intelligent reality, employing intelligence as its own rational faculty. While united <to a body> it draws to itself discursive thought."

[7] Here περινοητικὸς λόγος ("discursive reason") is taken to be roughly equivalent to διανοητικός λόγος in SH 18.5.

[8] Higher intelligence is consciousness or νοῦς, which is distinct from lower rationality or λόγος.

[9] That is, they are attuned to the lower rationality of discursive reason.

[10] The mention of circular thoughts recalls Plato, *Timaeus* 90d where a person has the task of bringing into order the disordered motions of the soul through knowledge of the harmonic rotations of heaven.

SH 18

Taken from Stobaeus's *Anthology* 2.8.31, SH 18 derives from a chapter called "On What is in Our Power" (roughly, "Free Will"). It is immediately preceded by a quotation from a certain Rufus who himself made a selection from Epictetus's treatise *On Friendship*. It is followed by a quotation from Plutarch's treatise *On Friendship*. SH 18 is, along with SH 1, the only excerpt to come from the second book of Stobaeus's *Anthology*.

The first part of the excerpt does not focus on human choice, but on the four grades of intelligence. These four grades of intelligence are all interwoven and come to make up the form of the human soul. The lower faculties of soul like opinion and sensation are only in contact with a lower grade of intelligence (discursive thought). In themselves, opinion and sensation vary and mislead. Yet when they are governed by discursive thought, they result in valid judgments.

Abruptly the excerpt turns to human choice. Free choice is the birthright of the soul because intelligence in soul is not subject to Fate. Only bodies are subject to Fate. Thus it is only when human choosing is dictated by bodily desires and lusts that the soul subjects itself to Fate.

Textual corruptions on the final paragraph (§5) make it difficult to interpret. The basic point seems to be that intelligent reality, when it assimilates discursive reason according to the will of God, accepts the plan of God that it is to be embodied. Yet in its embodied state, human intelligence remains in principle separate from the body and thus free from Fate.

Discourse of Hermes

The Components of Soul

1. So there is (intellectual) reality, reason, intellect, and discursive thought. Opinion and sensation are oriented toward discursive thought. Reason surges toward (intellectual) reality, while intellect surges through it

and is interwoven with discursive thought. These four interpenetrate each other and become a single form: the form of soul.[1]

Opinion and Sensation

Opinion and sensation are oriented toward the soul's discursive thought, but they do not remain in the same (state).[2] 2. As a result, they experience excess, deficiency, and non-identity. They become inferior when drawn away from discursive thought. Yet when they follow and obey discursive thought, they share in intelligizing reason through instruction.[3]

The Power to Choose

3. We have the power to choose. To choose the better is up to us. By the same principle, choosing the worse is unwilled.[4] Choosing, when dictated by vices, draws near to bodily nature. For this reason, Fate still dominates the one who chooses.[5] 4. Since, then, intelligent reality or all-intelligent reason in us has free choice, Fate does not control it. This intelligent reality is always self-consistent and self-identical.

5. When intelligent reality takes along[6] the primal discursive reason from the primal deity, it accepts the entire rational operation that Nature arranged for creatures. The soul, when it shares with these creatures, shares in their fates, though it does not participate in the nature of created beings.[7]

[1] Four different mental operations connect hierarchically like a chain. For discursive thought (διάνοια) as subordinate to intellect (νοῦς), compare Plato, *Republic* 509d–11d (the line image).

[2] Compare Plato: "opinion involves unreasoning sense perception" (*Timaeus* 28a). For a fuller discussion, see Plato, *Republic* 476c–80a.

[3] Compare SH 8.3 (in humans there are "formations" that receive intellect); Aristotle, *Nicomachean Ethics* 1.13.15–19, 1102b14–1103a4 (the non-rational part of the soul sometimes obeys the rational).

[4] The choice of evil is involuntary because it is dictated by the body and Fate. Compare SH 11.2 §20, with note.

[5] When one chooses according to bodily desires, one remains under the power of Fate. See further Porphyry, *On What is in our Power* (Wilberding).

[6] Here reading παραθεῖσα with FP.

[7] The reference here is to the higher soul or consciousness. The soul might not participate in the physical body, as in SH 19.4, but it can still be implicated in the body's fate.

SH 19

In his *Anthology* 1.49.6, Stobaeus transmits this excerpt in a chapter called "On the Soul" (the same chapter as SH 3, 17, 20, and 23–26). It is immediately preceded by what is here classified as SH 3. It is immediately followed by selections from Aëtius's *Opinions of the Philosophers* concerning the nature of the soul.

SH 19 continues to sketch the differences between the intellectual properties of the soul in contrast to the properties of the body. The distinction of three different grades of intelligence in the soul (the highest intelligence, reason, and discursive thought) is reminiscent of SH 18.1. The basic principle in SH 19 is that soul shapes and enlivens the body by its intellectual powers. Body participates in soul as something lesser, but soul does not participate in body. Just as heaven influences earth and not *vice versa*, the body cannot impact the higher intelligent soul. The higher soul can live completely independent of the body.

One must therefore distinguish two kinds of life and movement. The first kind is that of the higher intelligent soul; this sort of life and movement is universal, independent, and free. The second kind of life and movement belongs to the body: it is particular, dependent, and subject to necessity. Only when intelligent reality is united to a body does the body begin to participate in the higher (universal and free) life, also identified with real being.

There are two cognitive and critical faculties in the human person. The first is reason, which appreciates heavenly beauty. The second is breath (*pneuma*), which judges the sensible objects on earth. According to Stoic physiology, the senses operate by channels of breath running from the heart to the sense organs. The judgments produced by breath-operated sensation amount only to opinion, since they deal with the changing phenomena of this world. The judgments of reason, by contrast, since they deal with unchangeable heavenly realities, produce knowledge.

From a Writing of the Same Author

The Soul in and out of the Body

1. Now the soul is an eternal intelligent reality, employing intelligence as its own rational faculty. Contemplating its own thought, it becomes cognizant of harmony.[1] When it sheds the physical body, it remains self-determined and self-identical in the intelligible world.[2]

Intelligent reality is master of its own reason, bringing to the body that begins life a movement similar to its own thought.[3] The thought is called life. 2. This is the distinctive trait of the soul: it provides to other beings something like its own distinctive nature.[4]

3. Now there are two kinds of life and motion (in the soul): one is in accordance with (intellectual) reality, the other in accordance with the natural body. The former is universal, <the latter particular>. The life in accordance with (intellectual) reality has free will; the other is constrained by necessity, for everything moved by necessity is subordinate to the constraint of what moves it.[5]

4. The movement that moves <soul> is inseparably linked to the passionate desire for intelligent reality. Assuming that the soul is not a body, it does not participate in the physical body.[6] For if it is a body, it has neither reason nor intelligence, since all body lacks intellect. When a breathing animal participates in intellectual reality, it has attained (true) existence.[7]

Reason and Life-breath

5. Breath belongs to the body, and reason to (the) reality (of soul). Reason contemplates beauty, while sensate breath judges apparent

[1] Here reading συννοοῦσα with F (supported by the Armenian) and ἐπίσταται (also supported by the Armenian) instead of ἐπισπᾶται. See further Jean-Pierre Mahé, "Stobaei Hermetica XIX,1 et les *Définitions* hermétiques Arméniennes," *Revue des Études Grecques* 94 (1981): 523–25.

[2] The first paragraph of SH 19 appears somewhat differently in DH 10.7. For comparison, see Mahé, *HHE*, 2.329, 400–3.

[3] Compare SH 17.4: intelligent reality exists in its own intelligizing reason and controls it.

[4] That is, the soul provides the body with the life and movement that are distinctive to the soul.

[5] Compare Iamblichus: "The soul has a double life, the one with the body, the other apart from all body" (*On the Mysteries* 3.3).

[6] Compare SH 18.5 (ἀμέτοχος).

[7] That is, the body attains the life of the soul that is intelligent, universal, and free. Here there are close connections to SH 15.5–6, where the soul grants the body – which only has vegetative life through breath – intellectual movement and life in a higher sense. See also SH 20.3: "By 'existence,' here I mean being endowed with reason and sharing in intellectual life."

phenomena. It is distributed throughout the sense organs and is parceled out into breath-vision, breath-hearing, smelling, tasting, and touching. Breath, analogous to thought, judges what is perceived. Without it, there are only illusory images.[8]

6. Breath belongs to the body and receives all things. Reason only belongs to (intellectual) reality and (serves as) the faculty of wisdom. Knowledge of what is honorable coexists with reason. Opinion coexists with breath. 7. Breath has its energy from the surrounding cosmos. The soul is self-energized.

[8] The theory of breath (πνεῦμα) here resembles Stoic teachings. According to Chrysippus: "The soul is found to be natural breath . . . The soul's parts flow from their seat in the heart, as if from the source of a spring, and spread through the whole body . . . The soul as a whole dispatches the senses . . . like branches from the trunk-like commanding faculty to be reporters of what they sense" (reported by Calcidius, LS 53G). Compare Philo: "Our command center resembles a spring (ἐοικὸς πηγῇ) gushing many powers like (water) through the veins of earth. These powers it sends to the sense organs – eyes, ears, nostrils, and so on – which, for every animal, is in the region of the head and face. So just as from a spring the face, command center of the body, is watered from the soul's command center which stretches out the visual breath to the eye, the acoustic breath to the ear, the breath of smelling to the nose, the breath of tasting to the mouth, and the breath of touch to the whole surface (of the body)" (*Flight and Finding* 182); Pseudo-Plutarch: "From the commanding faculty there are seven parts of the soul which grow out and stretch out into the body like the tentacles of an octopus. Five of these are the senses, sight, smell, hearing, taste, and touch" (*Opinions of the Philosophers* 4.21 [903b] = LS 53H). Similar teaching appears in Diogenes Laertius, *Lives of Philosophers* 7.52; Iamblichus in Stobaeus, *Anthology* 1.49.33 = LS 53K); Pseudo-Galen, *Medical Definitions* 116–21 cited on NF 3.cxiv; Galen, *Doctrines of Hippocrates and Plato* 3.1.9–11 (reporting the views of Chrysippus).

SH 20

Stobaeus (*Anthology* 1.49.3) transmitted this excerpt in a chapter called "On the Soul" (the same chapter as SH 3, 17, 19, and 23–26). It is preceded by a quote from Plato's *Phaedrus*. It is immediately followed by what is here classified as SH 17.

SH 20 contrasts the properties of body and soul. The immortal soul cannot be a body because bodies change, decay, and break down. A body depends on a preexistent soul for its existence and life. What is meant by "life" here is the life of the soul, or intellectual life. A human body is not just a lifeform, it is a rational lifeform, endowed with true intellectual existence.

Not all animals are able to receive intellectual life. If an animal's temperament is too hot, it will be flighty like a bird. Conversely, if an animal's temperament is too cold, it will be sluggish like a turtle. Nature had to mix the human body into a well-balanced temperament – one "just right" to receive intelligence. Nature mixes the particular temperament of the body with the temperament of a particular (zodiacal) constellation. This particular constellation is the one that rises at each person's birth. As a result, the human body is peculiarly influenced by the energies and qualities of that constellation.

A Discourse of Hermes

Soul is Bodiless and Prior to Body

1. Now the soul is a bodiless reality.[1] For if it consisted of a body, it would not preserve itself.[2] Every body is in need of existence and the life

[1] SH 16 begins with virtually the same sentence. Compare also SH 19.4.

[2] Bodies naturally break down. Compare SH 8.5 (intelligible substance preserves itself and something else); Porphyry, *Sentences* 17: "The soul is an essence . . . which has come to exist in a state of life which holds its living from itself" (trans. John Dillon).

which follows it. 2. This is because everything that has birth must experience change. What comes into being is born in a particular size and needs growth. Everything that experiences growth also experiences diminishment, and with diminishment comes decay. 3. When the body participates in the form of "Life" it lives and participates in existence on account of the soul. Soul, as the cause of existence for something else, is thereby prior.[3]

Soul Provides Intelligent Life

By "existence," here I mean being endowed with reason and sharing in intellectual life. Soul provides intellectual life. 4. A being is called a "lifeform" because it has life; it is called "rational" due to consciousness, and "mortal" because of the body.

So the soul is without body and wields an infallible power. For how can one call something a "lifeform" if it does not have the reality that provides life? What's more, one could not call it rational without there being a reflective reality that provides intelligent life.[4]

Intellectual Life and Bodily Composition

5. Yet intellect does not extend to all lifeforms due to the varied temperament of the body's tempered composition.[5] For if the composition contains excessive heat, the lifeform becomes airy and hot; if it contains excessive cold, it becomes heavy and sluggish. Now Nature tempers the composition of the body to accord with its temperament. 6. There are three kinds of temperament: according to heat, cold, and what lies in between. Nature tempers (bodies) according to the dominant planet of a conjunction of stars.[6]

A soul receives <a body> as it has been fashioned,[7] and provides this work of nature with life. 7. Meanwhile, Nature adapts the temperament of the body to the conjunction of stars and unites the motley blend

[3] Compare Plato, *Phaedo* 105c–d (the soul makes the body alive).
[4] Intelligent life is true life and true existence.
[5] Compare SH 4.1–5 (intellect not in animals); SH 26.5–6, 14–24 (the elemental blend of animals).
[6] The conjunction of stars may refer to a zodiacal constellation or other fixed stars. Compare Ptolemy, *Tetrabiblos* 2.8.83.
[7] Here reading εἴργασται with FP.

of the body to the temperament of the stars with the result that they have a mutual influence on each other. The purpose of the temperament of the stars is to engender mutual influence in accord with the fate of bodies.[8]

[8] Compare SH 29 (lines 9–10): "From their [the planets'] influence we are allotted to draw from the aetherial breath: Tears, laughter, rage, reproduction, reason, sleep, and desire."

SH 21

In the context of Stobaeus's *Anthology* (1.41.11), SH 21 is the last selection in a chapter called "On Nature and its Derived Causes" (the same chapter as SH 2B, 4, 5, 11, 15–16). It is immediately preceded by an excerpt from Plutarch on how Homer terminologically refers to living and dead bodies.

SH 21 distinguishes two kinds of being. The first is universal being in itself characteristic of the unnamed and unnamable preexistent deity. The second type of being is individuated and perceptible being characteristic of lifeforms on earth. In between both earthly lifeforms and the Preexistent are the intelligible and perceptible gods. The intelligible gods probably refer to the Forms and the perceptible gods are most likely the stars. The stars share in the reality of the intelligible Forms and imitate them. The act of imitation is best illustrated by the Sun (or chief star god) who in his work of creation imitates the preexistent God.

A Discourse of Hermes

The Chain of Being

1. Now there is a preexistent Being over all existing beings and over all those who truly exist. It is preexistent by virtue of the fact that its so-called universal essentiality is common to beings that truly exist and those that are conceived of in themselves.[1] The opposite sorts of beings, *vice versa*, have an individuated nature. They (consist of) perceptible reality that contains in itself all things perceptible.

Between these two types of being are intelligible and perceptible deities. The <intelligible ones> share in intelligible realities; the <perceptible ones> in apparent realities. <The perceptible gods> share in the

[1] Truly existent beings may refer to Platonic Forms or intelligences not connected with bodies. In this sentence, κοινή is taken as a predicate and νοητῶν in FP (replaced by νοεῖται in NF) is removed.

intelligible gods.[2] 2. These latter are images of the intelligible, like the Sun is an image of the celestial Craftsman deity.[3] For just as he fashioned the universe, so the Sun fashions animals, produces plants, and presides over winds.[4]

[2] On the relation of intelligible and sensible gods, see *Ascl.* 19.

[3] Compare SH 2A.14 with note and SH 5.1–2, where the primal Craftsman and "our Craftsman" (the Sun) are distinguished. Note also Plotinus, *Enneads* 5.3.9 (the light of the Sun shines from Intellect or divine Consciousness), 5.5.8 (the Sun as an image of Intellect).

[4] "Winds" (πνευμάτων) could also be translated "spirits."

SH 22

Stobaeus transmitted this excerpt in a chapter that treats conception and birth (*Anthology* 1.42.7). It deals with a question standard in both philosophical and medical schools of thought, namely, "How Resemblances from Parents and Ancestors Are Transmitted." The subsection that precedes it dealt with prodigious births; what follows is a subsection on why some children fail to resemble their parents.

The Hermetic treatise from which SH 22 was drawn was called *Aphrodite*. Possibly it dealt with matters of sex and love. Aphrodite is not a birth goddess, but she may have been thought to have jurisdiction over how traits are passed on through sexual intercourse.

The Hermetic explanation of resemblance is distinctive if derivative in its components. Both mother and father are thought to have semen that develops as the excrescence of blood coursing throughout their bodies. The semen contains, as it were, a miniscule replication of the parent. If the semen of the father dominates, his traits are passed on, and *vice versa* for the mother. The author also allows for individual traits to predominate in some cases. Both astrology and physiology combine to explain the body and character of the child. The final sentence indicates either that the father can play the role of a decan or that the decan dominating the horoscope of an ancestor can reproduce traits of a distant ancestor.

Excerpt from a Treatise of Hermes Entitled *Aphrodite*

Family Resemblance

I will account for why babies are similar to their parents or assigned to their families. When nourishing blood <foams up> and the genitals store away the seed, it somehow happens that a certain substance is breathed out from all parts of the body by divine operation – as if the same person were replicated.[1] It is likely that the same thing occurs in the case of women.

When what flows from the male prevails and remains intact, the baby will be produced resembling the father. In the same fashion, *vice versa,* the baby will resemble the mother. Yet if a single trait (of the parent) predominates, the baby resembles that trait.[2]

There are occasions when for many generations, an infant exhibits the form of its ancestor, since his decan has the greater influence at the moment when the woman conceives.[3]

[1] "Foams up" (ἐξαφρουμένου) is Usener's emendation of ἐξαφεδρουμένου ("is secreted") in FP. The seed is, as in Aristotle, the secreted excess of nourishing blood (περίττωμα αἱματικῆς τροφῆς, *Generation of Animals* 1.19, 726b9). The Stoic philosopher Sphaerus maintained that semen is derived from the whole body (Diogenes Laertius, *Lives of Philosophers* 7.159). A similar view is affirmed by Hippocrates: "a man's seed comes from all the moisture in his body, and is the excretion of its most powerful part" (*On Generation* 1.1, trans. Paul Potter).

[2] Compare Lactantius: "[Varro and Aristotle] suppose that resemblances arise in the bodies of children as follows: when seeds mixed together combine, if the male seed dominates, the child – whether male or female – comes out like the father. If female seed prevails, the offspring of either sex corresponds to the mother's image. The seed will prevail which is more plentiful from the two (parents), for the more plentiful seed embraces in a certain fashion and includes the other (seed). From this cause it happens that (the child) shows the features of one (parent)" (*Workmanship of God* 12.8–9). This account of resemblance is close to Lucretius, *Nature of Things* 4.1208–32. Note also Pseudo-Plutarch: "The Stoics say that seeds are carried from the whole body and soul and that traits and marks of resemblance are produced from the same types (of seed) like a painter (paints) the picture of the model from like colors. Women also emit sperm. If the woman's sperm dominates, the child is like the mother; if the man's sperm dominates, the child is like the father" (*Opinions of the Philosophers* 5.11 [906d]). According to Hippocrates, "In the uterus the seed of both the woman and the man comes from their whole body ... so that the child must be formed accordingly. Wherever more of the man's body enters the seed than of the woman's, in that part the child will look more closely like its father, whereas wherever more comes from the woman's body, in that part of its body the child will look more closely like its mother. It is not possible for a child to look like its mother in all its features and like its father in none, nor the opposite of this, nor to look like neither parent in anything; rather there is a necessity to look like both parents in something, if sperm passes into the child from both of their bodies. Whichever parent contributes more to the resemblance and from more parts of their body, that parent the child will resemble in more of its features" (*Generation* 8, trans. Paul Potter); Hippocrates: "If the secretion from the man be male and that of the woman female, should the male gain the mastery, the weaker soul combines with the stronger, since there is nothing more congenial present to which it can go. For the small goes to the greater and the greater to the less, and united they master the available matter" (*Regimen* 2.28, trans. W. H. S. Jones). Galen strove to explain how offspring resembled different features of their parents (*On Semen* 2.5.1–6, De Lacy). Other theories of resemblance are reviewed by Aristotle, *Generation of Animals* 4.3, 769a1–b2; Censorinus, *Birthday Book* 6.5–10.

[3] The decan is similar to the daimon in CH 16.15: "The daimones on duty at the exact moment of generation, arrayed under each of the stars, take possession of each of us as we come into being and receive a soul." Contrast the translation of Festugière (NF 4.92): "It happens that even over the long course of generations the child resembles the form of the father who plays the role of the decan in the hour when the woman conceives." Compare also TH 29b (from Michael Psellus).

SH 23

In Stobaeus's *Anthology*, SH 23 comes toward the end of a long chapter called "On the Soul" (1.49.44). It is immediately preceded by several long excerpts of Iamblichus's work *On the Soul*. It is followed by SH 24, which belonged to the same Hermetic treatise or collection. In fact, SH 23–27 all likely derive from the same Hermetic collection.

In this collection, the goddess Isis addresses her son Horus. Yet Isis is not the source of the teaching; she is the medium of a greater authority who is none other than Hermes himself. According to some Greek traditions, Isis is depicted as Hermes's student;[1] in other sources, she is his daughter.[2] Yet these different relations may in fact express the same idea: an intimate disciple is kin.[3]

The line of Hermetic teaching thus travels from Hermes to Isis to Horus. Horus, physical son of Isis and Osiris, is apparently considered to be Egypt's second king (after Osiris). Diodorus of Sicily (a first-century BCE historian) also represents Isis as the teacher of her son Horus. After resurrecting Horus with the elixir of immortality, Isis teaches him both medicine and prophecy.[4] In alchemical literature, moreover, Isis reveals to Horus the secrets of metals.

To the Greeks of the Hellenistic and Roman periods (roughly from 300 BCE to 300 CE), Isis was depicted as a culture heroine. She taught human beings how to grow food, make medicines, and in general how to live a civilized life. The view of Isis as a civilizer (along with her husband Osiris)

[1] "I am Isis . . . taught by Hermes" (Diodorus, *Library of History* 1.27.4). Isis also claims to be "taught by Hermes" in line 3b of the Cyme aretalogy (Louis V. Žabkar, *Hymns to Isis in Her Temple at Philae* [Hanover: University Press of New England, 1988], 140). See further Anne Burton, *Diodorus Siculus Book 1. Commentary* (Leiden: Brill, 1972), 114–16.

[2] Plutarch, *Isis and Osiris* 3 (*Moralia* 352a). In *PGM* 4.2290, Hermes says: "I am the father of Isis" (Ἴσιδος πατὴρ ἐγώ).

[3] Compare 1 Corinthians 4:17 (Timothy is Paul's son "in the Lord"); Philemon 16 (a Christian slave becomes a "brother").

[4] Diodorus, *Library of History* 1.25.6–7.

is beautifully expressed at the end of this excerpt (§§65–68). This material may derive from popular hymns that laud the virtues of the gods (called "aretalogies").

SH 23 is entitled "An Excerpt of Hermes Trismegistus from the Holy Book entitled *Korē Kosmou.*" In Greek, *korē* means both "maiden" and "pupil (of the eye)." Plutarch, transmitting Egyptian tradition, associates Egypt with the "black part of the eye," or pupil.[5] Perhaps Egypt is itself the cosmic pupil, the center point or heart of the world (as in SH 24.13). In this respect, we might compare Deuteronomy 32:10, wherein Israel is the apple (that is, pupil) of Yahweh's eye.

It is likely, however, that Isis herself is (or is also) the cosmic pupil.[6] According to native Egyptian tradition, the eye of the cosmos is the sun (thought of as Atum or Re), whose pupil is Isis.[7] In our very treatise, sun, moon, and stars are called "the eyes of God" (§34). According to Diodorus, Osiris and Isis were identified with sun and moon. "It is from sun and moon," he remarks, "that the whole body of the physical universe is made complete."[8] It could be that Isis as world pupil is the moon and Osiris the sun. Yet the prominence of Isis is so salient in our treatise, it is right to think of her (perhaps united with Osiris) as the Sun's pupil, the apple of God's eye, the light of this world.[9] As the solar pupil, or its effluence (*aporrhoia*), Isis is rightly associated with the maintenance of justice on earth (§62).

[5] Plutarch, *Isis and Osiris* 33 (*Moralia* 364c). Horapollo says that, "Only the land of Egypt, since it is in the middle of the earth, just as the so-called pupil is in the eye, causes the rise of the Nile in summer" (*Hieroglyphics* 1.21).

[6] Isis was identified with the power of the land of Egypt (Porphyry in Eusebius, *Preparation for the Gospel* 3.11.49; see further Jean Hani, *La religion Égyptienne dans la pensée de Plutarque* [Paris: Belles Lettres, 1967], 146).

[7] Howard Jackson, "Κόρη Κόσμου: Isis, Pupil of the Eye of the World," *Chronique d'Égypte* 61 (1986): 116–35 at 128–31. In a hymn to Isis at her temple in Philae, Isis is called "Eye of Re" (Žabkar, *Hymns*, 107, 145). In an aretalogy to Isis from Oxyrhynchus, Isis is the "eye of the Sun" (text in Totti, *Ausgewählte*, 68, lines 112–13).

[8] Diodorus, *Library of History* 1.11.1–2, 6; Diogenes Laertius, *Lives of Philosophers* Prologue §10.

[9] Compare Jesus in John 8:12: "I am the light of the world." In SH 23.62, Isis, along with Osiris, is called the effluence (ἀπόρροια in the singular) of the supreme creator God. They both come to the world as an "unbribable judge" (again, singular), and the Sun – according to both Egyptians and Greeks – was the eye of justice. If in the author's source Osiris alone was depicted as the sun-like effluence, he has modified the tradition to include Isis (§64). As a Hellenistic goddess, Isis was characterized by her universal power and loving care for individual worshipers. In this regard see Apuleius, *Metamorphoses* 11.1–7. See further Giulia Sfameni Gasparro, "The Hellenistic face of Isis: Cosmic and Saviour Goddess," in Laurent Bricault, Miguel John Versluys, and Paul G. P. Meyboom, eds., *Nile into Tiber. Egypt in the Roman World: Proceedings of the IIIrd International Conference of Isis Studies, Faculty of Archaeology, Leiden University, May 11–14 2005* (Leiden: Brill, 2007), 40–72.

The *Korē Kosmou* was likely constructed from several different sources. The narrative is episodic and contains overlapping material that generates internal tensions (two stories of creation, two reasons why human souls are embodied, and so on). Nevertheless, maximalist source criticism – breaking up the document into stand-alone units representing "sources" that derive from distinct intellectual milieus – is precarious and often insensitive to a developing narrative logic.[10] The author (or editor) of this text used different sources to construct what becomes a new narrative.

The story frame presents a dialogue between Isis and Horus. In the dialogue, Isis speaks to Horus in fifteen distinct passages with Horus interrupting only once (§22). A genuine exchange between the interlocutors only occurs at the end of the treatise (§§64–70).

Isis begins the conversation by pouring a draught of ambrosia (the deathless drink of the gods) for her son Horus. If there was a longer introduction preceding this act, Stobaeus has omitted it.

Immediately the reader is thrust into the first creation story. The order of the stars and planets (the upper world) is assumed to already exist. The lower world is alive, but in disarray. Somehow conscious, the lower world fears being ordered by the superior powers called "mysteries" (§§2–4).

Suddenly Hermes makes his debut. He is introduced as neither divine nor human, but as one whose soul understands God and all things. On a sojourn to the unordered earth, he partially reveals his knowledge to his disciples Tat and Asclepius. After prayer, Hermes ascends to heaven, possibly as the planet Mercury.

In heaven, Hermes defends himself for not having revealed all knowledge to his pupils. He points out their youth and tells how he deposited his knowledge, written in sacred letters, near the secret objects of Osiris (§§5–8).

Presumably Isis and Osiris later find these books and transmit their civilizing knowledge to human beings (§66). Perhaps Isis herself reads from these books as she unveils the creation of the world. In §25, Isis says that the words she gives to her son are those of Hermes (compare §§27, 29). Then in §§26, 30, 48–50 Hermes narrates in the first person his deeds regarding the creation of human beings.

Hermetic tradition is thus split into two streams: on the one hand, Tat and Asclepius hand on their direct knowledge of Hermes's teaching

[10] For maximalist source criticism, see Richard Reitzenstein, *Die Göttin Psyche in der hellenistischen und frühchristlichen Literatur* (Heidelberg: Carl Winters, 1917), 70–84.

(represented in CH); on the other hand, Isis hands on her knowledge derived from Hermes's works. In §32, we also learn that Isis preserves lore from her forefather Kamephis – an ancient, self-generated god. This is not an independent stream of tradition, since Kamephis was also taught directly by Hermes. Perhaps the author(s) of SH 23–26 was competing with or trying to supplement other Hermetic traditions such as those given to Tat and Asclepius.

In §§9–13, God creates Nature who with her child Invention begin the process of ordering the lower world. Heaven, air, and aether (the upper layers of the cosmos) are filled with astral beings over whom Invention presides. Land creatures, including humans, are ready to emerge in the lower world. Nevertheless, the consummate event of the story must first be described.

The center of the *Korē Kosmou* is occupied by a myth of human souls: how they were created, how they fell, and how they can ascend to heaven again (§§14–42). God makes the original soul mixture from his own substance, called "breath" or "spirit" (*pneuma*). To this substance, he adds fire, air, and other unknown elements. Like an alchemist standing over his gleaming brew, God pronounces secret formulas. He vigorously mixes the materials and forms the souls from the brew's sparkling froth. The multifarious grades of froth produce sixty different grades of souls. Regardless of their rank, all souls are eternal and divine, since they originate from God's essence. God places the souls according to their rank in distinct heavenly realms. He bids them to turn heaven's gigantic axle and warns them not to neglect their stations (§§14–17).

At this point, God mixes the remaining soul stuff with the heavier elements of water and earth. Over the mixture he again speaks secret formulas and stirs. From this lesser-grade material, he creates the human-shaped signs of the zodiac. These signs will be models for later human bodies. Then he creates the animal signs of the zodiac as models for animals on earth. He gives the souls the rest of the mixture and bids them to make physical animals. The souls need only make the animals once, since God bestows on them the power to reproduce (§§18–22).

The souls are innately curious, a quality that – blended with presumption – leads to their downfall. Before they make animals, they seek to find the origin of the soul mixture from which they were made. This mixture is their own substance – and so they seek knowledge of themselves and their own origins. Since their origins are in God, by examining the mixture they pry into God's nature. Now apprehensive, the souls turn to create animals using successively lesser grades of the soul mixture.

Proud of their powers, the souls abandon their assigned realms. Naturally inquisitive like children, they soar here and there as natural – if naughty – explorers. The supreme God takes immediate notice of the commotion. He calls a council of the heavenly deities – Sun, Moon, and the other Planets (§27). Each of these gods promise to influence in some way the human body that Hermes will produce (§§28–29). Human bodies are designed as prisons for souls. Souls will be placed on earth in bodies to praise God and the star deities. Human existence thus has a dual purpose: rebellious souls are chastened and given an opportunity to know and praise the divine.

Hermes makes human bodies out of the now dried-out soul stuff. He softens the mixture by over-saturating it. The watery nature of the mix guarantees that the human body will be weak. Despite its frailty, the body is not evil, but a work worthy of God's own admiration (§30). Souls only experience the body as a prison because their true nature is purer, dryer, swifter, and more powerful.

Knowing their fate, the souls howl in lament. Amidst the din, the story focalizes on the dirge of a single soul (§§31–37). This soul especially bewails the fact that embodied humans will only be able to see a small portion of heaven (the souls' home). The pious petition of this soul moves God to pity. He ensures that enough of heaven will be clear for embodied souls to find their purpose and origin in the coursing "mysteries" of the stars.

God announces that Eros and Necessity will be lords over souls. As divine forces, Eros will propel the souls toward God; Necessity, in turn, will limit them. The Hermetic God is stern; yet he is also the loving Father of souls, teaching them to learn their limits and rediscover their true home (§§38).

In a solemn council, God lists four fates for souls. First, souls who obey God's orders will return to their heavenly home. Graciously, the same fate is reserved for souls whose mistakes are minor. Conversely, souls with serious crimes return to human bodies. Finally, those with yet more heinous faults are born as animals. The system is one of karma: deeds determine fate. The implied reader hopes that most souls will find their way back home. Yet it is possible for some to degrade still further (§§39–42).

Suddenly the spirit of Blame rears his ugly head. He recommends additional chastening for embodied humans (§§43–47). He advises that they be inflicted with inflated desires and deceitful hopes. These traits will guarantee human failure – the only way to tame their ambition.

The mechanism of Fate, personally put in motion by Hermes, is the final and most efficient chastener. Human bodies can travel only so far as their nature and the astral powers allow (§48–49).

In preparation for human embodiment, a second creation story is told (§§50–52). According to this account, God calls a (second) council of star gods. As they once provided their gifts to humankind, so now they offer their products to the world. The mist and dark chaos that is lower earth is immediately ordered and made visible to the heavens above. God himself directly provides all the products of nature to the world system. The earth is ready to receive the host of souls.

Locked up in mortal bodies, the souls prove utterly rebellious and barbarous. Remembering their noble birth, humans impiously assault the star gods. On earth, the strong ruthlessly oppress the weak. Temples are polluted with the bodies of the butchered. There are no laws and no fear of punishment (§§53–54).

Four figures rise to call a halt to human savagery. They are the elements: Fire, Air, Water, and Earth. Lamenting their defilement, the elements petition the supreme God to send a subordinate god to civilize the world (§§55–61). The high God responds by sending his own emanation in the form of Isis and Osiris. When they arrive on earth, they fill it with the blessings of law, art, and religious rites. They discover and ensure the preservation of Hermes's ancient wisdom. After prayer, Isis and Osiris re-ascend – like Hermes of old – to their heavenly home.

With their return journey complete, the tractate comes to a close. Isis herself guarantees that true knowledge of creation will persist on earth by passing it on to her son Horus – and hence to all future readers of Hermetic lore.

What the Hermetic reader must remember is that despite their savagery and capacity to degrade, humans are essentially divine. They come from the realm of the stars. Their souls are of varying quality, but none of them lacks divinity. All they need is a guide to bring them the culture and education that will allow them to remember who they are.

Earlier interpreters who championed the influence of Jewish myth (in particular, the fallen angel myth of 1 Enoch) emphasized the theme of forbidden knowledge.[11] Yet knowledge is never actually forbidden in the *Korē Kosmou*. It is God who invites the lower world to search for and find him. God wills to bring order out of disorder, and the creation of souls is

[11] See the summary of Ferguson, *Hermetica*, 4.xxxiv–xlii, who discusses Wilhelm Bousset and other earlier interpreters.

part of that plan. Human souls are born curious, but curiosity is not in itself a sin. Souls are not punished with bodies by a jealous God in a world that is a tragic mistake. Rather, souls are chastened so that they are ready for the knowledge that God is ready to give through his chosen intermediaries. The *Korē Kosmou* is itself a gift of divine knowledge given through the cosmic queen.

An Excerpt of Hermes Trismegistus from the Holy Book Entitled *The Pupil of the Cosmos*

1. When she said these things, Isis poured for Horus the first sweet draught of ambrosia which the souls of gods are accustomed to receive.[12] So doing, Isis began her most sacred discourse.

2. *Isis:* "Since, Horus my child, the many-wreathed heaven lies over every being below and is in no region deprived of the things which the whole world now contains, there was every need that all underlying nature be ordered and brought to fulfillment by the beings above.[13]

Naturally, beings below cannot order those of the higher array. Thus it was necessary that the lesser mysteries give way to the greater.[14] The order of the higher beings is indeed superior to that of those below; it is stable in every way and not subject to mortal thought.[15]

[12] The word ἀπό ("*from* [the gods]") is omitted here. Ambrosia was the food (or in this case drink) of the gods. According to legend, Isis resurrected and immortalized Horus by granting him the "drug of immortality" (τὸ τῆς ἀθανασίας φάρμακον). In our passage, however, the deification of Horus by imbibing ambrosia is not in view. Compare CH 1.29, where ambrosial water is parallel to words of wisdom. An epigram attributed to Ptolemy the astronomer reads: "when the revolving spirals of the stars in mind I trace ... I am filled with ambrosia." Ambrosia here may be a metaphor for "intelligence and pure knowledge" (Plato, *Phaedrus* 247d). On souls receiving divine food, see further Thomas McAllister Scott, "Egyptian Elements in Hermetic Literature" (Ph.D. diss., Harvard Divinity School, 1987), 119–21.

[13] The heaven is wreathed or crowned with the concentric circles of planets and stars. It is not said how the "beings above" (star gods) are formed, but compare CH 3.2: "While all was unlimited and unformed, light elements were set apart to the heights and the heavy elements were grounded in the moist sand, the whole of them delimited by fire and raised aloft, to be carried by spirit. The heavens appeared in seven circles, the gods became visible in the shapes of the stars and all their constellations."

[14] In the Eleusinian mysteries, a person had to be initiated into the Lesser Mysteries before initiation into the Greater. Here the "greater mysteries" probably refer to the orderly courses of the stars (compare §§3, 51 below). The lesser mysteries may refer to the physical laws of the world below the moon.

[15] On the relation of superior to inferior, Iamblichus observes: "higher beings, serving as models, guide lesser beings, and the superior supplies existence and form to the inferior" (*On the Mysteries* 1.8). This was a general Platonic principle. Compare [Timaeus Locrus]: "Since the elder is superior to the younger and the ordered is prior to the disordered, the God who is good and who saw matter receiving the idea and being changed in all kinds of ways but in a disordered manner, wanted to put

3. Then the beings below groaned, seized with panic in the face of the great beauty and eternal stability of higher realities. It was worth investigation and agony to see the beauty of heaven manifesting God (who was yet unknown), as well as the rich sanctity of the night. The night offers a light which – though less than that of the sun – still dazzles. There is also the light of the other mysteries moved in heaven, each in its turn, by the ordered motions and revolutions of time. Through their secret effluences, they jointly order things below and cause them to grow. In this state of affairs, there was unbroken panic and searchings without end.[16]

4. As long as the Architect of all so resolved, ignorance controlled all things. Yet when he decided to unveil his identity, he inspired the (star) gods with the desires of love. He bestowed on their thoughts the manifold sparkle of his heart so that first they might will to seek, then desire to find, and finally be able to succeed.[17]

All-knowing Hermes

5. This, my wondrous child Horus, could not be accomplished by mortal seed – which did not yet exist – but by a soul corresponding to the heavenly mysteries. This was the soul of all-knowing Hermes.[18] He saw everything. When he saw, he understood, and when he understood, he had strength to disclose and to divulge it. What he understood, he inscribed; and when he inscribed it, he hid it, keeping most of it in unbroken silence rather than declaring it so that every future generation born into the world might seek it.[19] 6. This done, he ascended to the stars to accompany the gods who were his kin.[20]

His son Tat, however, was his successor. He was both Hermes's son and the possessor of his teachings. Not long afterwards, there was Asclepius Imhotep by the counsels of Ptah or Hephaestus – and as many others who,

matter in order and to bring it from a condition of indefinite change into a state with a definite pattern of change" (*On the Nature of the World and the Soul* 7 [94c], trans. Tobin).

16 Reading, with the corrector of P, ἄληκτοι ("without end") instead of ἄλεκτοι ("untold") in FP.

17 "Sparkle," representing αὐγήν, is Canter's correction of αὐτήν in FP.

18 Possibly a reference to the elder Hermes, called the "recorder of all deeds" in §32. On Hermes-Thoth as all-knowing, see Scott, "Egyptian Elements," 97–98.

19 According to (Pseudo?) Manetho (reported by George Syncellus, *Chronological Excerpts* 72 = TH 10b), the first Hermes, or Thoth, wrote inscriptions in hieroglyphics later translated and set in books. On the dynamics of passing on Hermetic lore, see Van Bladel, *Arabic Hermes*, 134–35, 137; Bull, "Tradition of Hermes," 21–28.

20 "Accompany" (δορυφορεῖν) has the additional sense of "escort," or "attend as a bodyguard." Hermes's divine family may refer to star gods or planets.

by the will of Providence Queen of all, would investigate precisely the deposit of heavenly teaching.[21]

7. Now indeed Hermes defended himself to the ambient since he had not entrusted the complete teaching to his son because of his young age.[22] At the rising of the sun, Hermes scanned the regions of the dawn with his all-seeing eyes, and perceived something indistinct. As he looked on, accurate realization slowly dawned upon him. He was to deposit the sacred symbols of the cosmic elements near the hidden objects of Osiris, and then, after praying the following words, return to heaven.[23]

8. It is unfitting for me to leave this report incomplete, my child. I must tell what Hermes said when he deposited the books. He proclaimed the following:

O sacred books prepared by my imperishable hands! I anoint you with the unguent of incorruption and clasp you tight. Remain undecayed for all eternity and incorruptible throughout time, unseen and undiscovered to all who travel the fields of earth until Heaven in his old age fathers formations worthy of you, which the Craftsman called souls.[24]

[21] Ptah (Πτανὸς) is Reitzenstein's correction for σπανὸς in FP. See further Festugière, "Le Style de la '*Korē Kosmou*,'" *Vivre et Penser* 2 (1942): 15–57 at 53–57. On Ptah as universal creator, see "The Theology of Memphis," *ANET*^{3}, 4–6. According to Manetho, Ptah was the first king (frag. 3, Waddell). Iamblichus spoke of Ptah as the creative Consciousness (or demiurgic mind) (*On the Mysteries* 8.3). The Greeks identified Imhotep (Imouthes), a (later deified) doctor and architect in the time of Pharaoh Djoser (ruled 2687–2668 BCE) with Asclepius. In the New Kingdom (about 1550–1077 BCE), Imhotep was venerated as the patron of scribes, and in the Turin Papyri as the son of Ptah, chief god of Memphis (see further Manetho frags. 11–12, Waddell; Hornung, *Secret Lore*, 48–51; Dietrich Wildung, *Imhotep und Amenhotep. Gottwerdung im alten Ägypten* [Munich: Deutscher Kunstverlag, 1977], 88–109; Lichtheim, *Ancient Egyptian Literature*, 3.104–7; David Klotz, *Caesar in the City of Amun: Egyptian Temple Construction and Theology in Roman Thebes* [Turnhout: Brepols, 2012)], 119–21). An aretalogy survives to Asclepius-Imhotep (see E. J. and L. Edelstein, *Asclepius: A Collection and Interpretation of the Testimonies*, 2 vols. [Baltimore: Johns Hopkins University Press, 1945], 1, §331). See further Copenhaver, 124–25. Hermetic lore is passed on through succession, an idea common at this time (compare apostolic and rabbinic succession in early Christianity and Judaism, respectively). The learning of Tat and Asclepius is representative of CH, but it does not represent the fullness of Hermetic wisdom.

[22] The "ambient" (translating ὁ περιέχων here and below) is taken to refer to the atmosphere or surrounding sky, as in astrology.

[23] In terms of chronology, Osiris's arrival is still in the future (§66). Presumably, all-knowing Hermes knows ahead of time the location of his hidden objects, probably a reference to his true mummified remains (Plutarch, *Isis and Osiris* 18 [358a–b], Iamblichus, *On the Mysteries* 6.5) possibly to be located in Abydos (*PGM* 4.106–8). Isis and Osiris will discover Hermes's books in §66. Compare the "archives of Hermes" in *PGM* 24a.1. See further Scott, "Egyptian Elements," 98–100.

[24] For the apocalyptic motif of hiding imperishable books or tablets (later rediscovered), compare TH 10b, Josephus, *Antiquities* 1.71; Philo of Byblos in Eusebius, *Preparation for the Gospel* 1.9.26; *Apocalypse of Paul* (NHC V,2) 2–3; *Disc. 8–9* (NHC VI,6) 62.1–27. See further Dylan M. Burns, *Apocalypse of the Alien God: Platonism and the Exile of Sethian Gnosticism* (Philadelphia: University of Pennsylvania Press, 2014), 55–57.

When he spoke over the books, praying for his own works, he entered the sacred precinct of his own spheres.[25]

The First Creation Story

9. The intervening time of inactivity was long <and> hidden. Nature, my child, was barren until those the King, the God of all, already ordered to whirl round heaven came to him and announced the inactivity of reality.[26] They said that it is necessary to arrange the universe, and that this was no one else's task but his. 'We entreat you,' they said, 'to take thought for the beings that exist now and what they have need of in the future.'

10. At these words, God smiled and said, 'Let Nature exist!'[27] From his voice a wondrous female being came forth, a sight which stunned the deities who beheld her.[28] The forefather God honored her with the name 'Nature' and bade her be productive.[29]

11. Meanwhile, fixing his eyes on the ambient, he uttered, 'Let heaven, air, and aether be filled to the full!' God spoke and it came to be.[30] 12. Nature spoke within herself and knew that she must not disobey the command of her father. 13. Coupling with Labor, she produced a lovely daughter whom she called 'Invention.' God granted her existence. After granting this gift, he divided the beings that already existed, filled them with mysteries, and granted Invention leadership over each of them.

[25] Hermes ascends to heaven, apparently to the sphere of Mercury (see §29 below). For Hermes as Mercury, compare the Hermetic *Disc. 8–9* (NHC VI,6) 62.16–20. Hermes's ascent apparently repeats and expands the one mentioned in §6.

[26] The creation story picks up where it left off in §4 where God inspires the star gods to seek him. On the title "the king, the God of all," see Scott, "Egyptian Elements," 58–62. On creation in SH 23, see Mahé, "La création," 43–46.

[27] For God creating by word alone, compare FH 32a, 33; the Memphite Theology: "the Ennead (of Ptah) . . . is the teeth and lips in his mouth, which pronounced the name of everything, from which Shu (Air) and Tefnut (Moisture) came forth, and which was the fashioner of the Ennead (or nine primeval gods)" (*ANET*[3], 5); Genesis 1:3: "And God said, Let there be . . .". For God creating by laughter, see *PGM* 13.161–95, 472–531. See further Siegfried Morenz, *Egyptian Religion*, trans. Ann E. Keep (Ithaca: Cornell University Press, 1973), 163–66.

[28] Compare Sirach 24:3 (Wisdom comes from the mouth of the Most High).

[29] The title "Forefather" is also used in SH 2A.13 (see note there); SH 2B.3; and §55 below.

[30] Compare Genesis 1:20: "God spoke . . . and so it was"; 1:22, 28 (animals fill seas and earth); [Longinus], *On the Sublime* 9.9 (the Jewish account of creation).

The Birth of Souls

14. No longer did God will the upper world to be inert. He decided to fill it with living breaths so that its parts would not remain immobile and inactive. So, to this end, he began his work of art, using sacred substances for the generation of his distinctive work. He took a sufficient amount of breath from himself and, by an act of intellect, mixed it with fire.[31] He blended this with other materials in an unknown way.[32] He unified each of these materials with each other via secret formulas. Meanwhile he vigorously stirred the whole blend until a very subtle material in the mixture began to sparkle.[33] It became purer and clearer than the materials from which it derived. It was transparent in itself, and the Artificer alone beheld it.[34]

15. This material, since it was made from fire, did not melt when burned; and since it was perfected from warm breath, did not grow cold. Rather, it was unique and akin to the compound of the blend, one of a kind and peculiar in its composition. God called the compound 'animatrix' by virtue of its auspicious name and because its activity resembled its name.[35]

From the condensed froth, he generated souls ten thousand strong, orderly and measuredly shaping the efflorescence from his contribution to the blend deliberately, skillfully, and with fitting design. 16. Consequently, individual souls did not differ from each other any <more than> was necessary.

The efflorescence that distilled like vapor by divine activity was not homogenous. Rather, the first layer of the efflorescence was superior, denser, and in every way purer than the second. The second was as inferior

[31] According to Diodorus, Egyptians call breath or spirit "Zeus," the high God, since he is the cause of life for all beings (*Library of History* 1.12.2). The high God in CH 1.12 gives birth to Humanity (Ἄνθρωπος) directly. According to Numenius, the Primal God is "the seed of all soul who sows it in all things that partake of himself" (frag. 13, des Places, from Eusebius, *Preparation for the Gospel* 11.18.13–14).

[32] Here reading ἀγνώστως with FP. No one knows the precise recipe for making souls.

[33] More literally: "until a certain material in the mixture laughed." Compare the smile of God in §10 above. The author of *Ref.* says that Plato imagined the soul "in a mixing bowl with a gleaming body" (*Ref.* 1.19.10). The mixing bowl image recurs in CH 4.4; FH 22 (Ephrem); TH 29h (Michael Psellus).

[34] Compare Plato, *Timaeus* 41a–44d. Festugière compared God's activity here (SH 23.14) to the making of philosophical mercury – the material of all metals and the stuff of life (*Mystique*, 233–40).

[35] Animatrix (ψύχωσις) is the stuff of souls. Its activity is to give the souls life, since "soul" in Greek (ψυχή) also means "life."

to the first as much as it was superior to the third. Consequently there were completely crafted sixty different grades of soul.[36]

Still, the Craftsman legislated that all souls be eternal, since they were from the same substance which he alone knew how to perfect. He appointed for them districts and chambers in the heights of nature above, so that they could revolve the cosmic axis in due order and efficiency to their father's delight.[37]

17. This done, the Father stood on the gilded pedestal of the aether and summoned the now existing natures. 'O souls consisting of my breath and the product of my care!' he said. 'Lovely children whom I, with my own hands, have brought to birth and now consecrate for my universe – hear my words as though they were laws and touch no place except the one assigned to you by my judgment. To those of you who remain in place, heaven will likewise remain, along with your assigned constellation and thrones full of excellence.[38] Yet if you revolt against my decrees, I swear by my sacred breath in you, by the blend from which I fathered you, and by my soul-creating hands, that for you I will quickly forge a chain with chastisements.'

18. When God who is also my lord finished his speech, he mixed in the remaining elements akin to each other, namely water and earth. He likewise pronounced sacred words over this new blend. These words were powerful, yet not like the first. Then he vigorously stirred it and inspired it with life. When froth of the right color and consistency gathered on the surface as before, he took a portion and from it formed the human-shaped signs of the zodiac.[39]

19. The remainder of the mixture he gave to the souls, now called sacred divinities, who had already advanced into the regions of the gods and into

[36] Compare SH 25.11 (sixty air strata) and the sixty treasuries of the *First Book of Jeu* 38, 40 (Schmidt and MacDermot). See further Erin Evans, *The Books of Jeu and the Pistis Sophia as Handbooks to Eternity: Exploring the Gnostic Mysteries of the Ineffable* (Leiden: Brill, 2016), 16–17, 21–23, 27.

[37] The cosmic axis is the pole running through the center of the universe, which can be turned like a rotor. Plato depicts the cosmic axis as the spindle of Necessity in *Republic* 10.616c–17b.

[38] Compare 1 Enoch 108:12: "I will seat each one (the souls of the pious) on the throne of his honor." See further Gallusz Laszlo, *The Throne Motif in the Book of Revelation* (London: Bloomsbury, 2014).

[39] Possibly the Greek simply means that God fashioned the animals that were similar to human form (τὰ ἀνθρωποειδῆ τῶν ζῴων), but §20 below suggests an astral interpretation. The human signs of the zodiac are Virgo, Sagittarius, Aquarius and Gemini. The zodiac signs have a less pure substance than the souls, composed of divine breath and fire plus water and earth – the same substances of which human bodies consist. Thus the zodiac only has an influence on the human body. The human soul is higher and essentially independent of the zodiac (and thus Fate). The zodiac serves as the connecting link between higher and lower reality.

places near the stars. God addressed them: 'O children and offspring of my own nature, do the work of molding! Take the remainder of what my art has made and let each soul form something like its own nature. I will present for you these models.'[40]

20. He took a portion of the blend and with skill and beauty ordered the zodiacal heaven in tune with the movements of the souls.[41] To the human-shaped signs of the zodiac, he fitted the animal signs in order. On these signs, God bestowed powers to do all things. He also gave them the all-creating breath that produces all future general events for all time.[42]

21. God withdrew with the promise to yoke his invisible breath to the souls' visible creations.[43] He also promised to give to each of their creations a mode of being that can reproduce itself so that they would in turn produce other beings like themselves. As a result, the souls would have no need to make anything <beyond> what they first produced."

The Creation of Animals

22. *Horus:* "What then, mother, did the souls create?"

Isis replied: "They received, Horus my child, what had been blended of the material. They first thoughtfully considered the blended mixture of the father, paid it reverence, then investigated the sources of its composition. This was not easy for them to discover. On account of this deed, and because they pried into the matter, they feared that they might succumb to the father's wrath; and so they turned to perform his commands.

23. Then the souls skillfully crafted the race of birds from the upper layer of the material, made of exceedingly subtle froth. As the process continued, the blend became semi-congealed and then took on a fully solid consistency. From this consistency, they formed the race of four-footed creatures – hardly a nimble breed. Then they formed the race of fish,

[40] For creation by modeling, compare the work of the Craftsman in Plato, *Timaeus* 29a. In *ibid.*, 41b–c, the Craftsman entrusts the star gods with the creation of mortal lifeforms (compare Philo, *On the Creation* 72–75). Here the role of the star gods is assumed by the souls.

[41] Made of the same (soul) substance, even if with different ingredients, the souls and the zodiac are attuned.

[42] General astrology covers worldwide events like earthquakes, famine, pestilence, and war. The place of the event is in part determined by the parts of the zodiac which stand over certain regions of the earth (Ptolemy, *Tetrabiblos* 2.7).

[43] The souls create animals, though the earth remains uncreated. For God's withdrawal, compare SH 5.1 (the supreme God ceased to create).

which needed a foreign moisture in which to swim. From the cold residue and dregs, the souls devised the nature of reptiles.[44]

Audacity and Punishment

24. As they worked, my child, already the souls armed themselves for overly inquisitive daring.[45] They performed acts beyond what was commanded, quitting their ranks and stations so that no one stayed put in one place any longer. Ever agitated, they considered ever remaining in a single station equivalent to death.[46]

25. 'And so,' Hermes said – saying what I say to you, my child – 'what they performed did not escape the attention of the Lord and God of the universe. He investigated what chastisement and chain they would miserably endure. Thus the Commander and Master of all decided to craft the physical formations of human beings and by this means forever punish the race of souls.

26. Then he summoned me,' Hermes said, 'and spoke: "O soul of my soul and sacred consciousness of my consciousness, 27. how long is this hated nature of lower beings to be viewed? How long are the beings now born to remain inactive and without praise?[47] Come, gather all the gods in heaven this instant."' So God spoke, my child, as Hermes reports.[48]

[44] In Plato's *Timaeus* (91d–92b), the creation of animals occurs considerably later from the degraded souls of humans. Compare SH 26.19–22 (the elemental composition of various animals).

[45] Plotinus (204–70 CE) attributed the fall of souls to "daring" (τόλμα, *Enneads* 5.1.1.4), the same word that is used here.

[46] The wording is reminiscent of a saying of Heraclitus: "for them to stay put is a toilsome burden, but to change brings rest" (reported in Iamblichus, *On the Soul*, 27, Dillon and Finamore). The fall of souls is because of their curiosity and disobedience. Contrast the view of Origen, who depicted souls as cooling in their love for God, resulting in the loss of their fiery nature and their fall into bodies (*On First Principles* 2.8.3).

[47] In Egyptian theology, Thoth is the "heart of Re," the heart being the seat of understanding (Boylan, *Thoth*, 114, 180). In the Strasbourg Cosmogony, "ancestral Hermes" is apparently the consciousness of the high God (Νόος ἐστὶν ἐμός, Piccardi, *La 'Cosmogonia di Strasburgo*,' 67, 89–91). Compare Macrobius: "the physical scientists say that Dionysus is 'the mind of Zeus,' claiming that the sun is the mind of the cosmic order" (*Saturnalia* 1.18.15). Hermes is the sun (*Saturnalia* 1.19.8–9), parallel to the Sun or image of God in SH 2A.14. See further Peter Kingsley, "Poimandres: The Etymology of the Name and the Origins of the Hermetica," in van den Broek, ed., *From Poimandres*, 41–76. The inactivity of beings (evidently not a reference to souls) is strange, though the language is similar to SH 23.9 and 50.

[48] In this tractate, the gods of heaven (or star gods) appear to be the only gods alongside the Craftsman. Compare the first-century CE Alexandrian philosopher Chaeremon (frag. 5, van der Horst).

All the gods came as ordered. God addressed them, 'Cast your eyes on the earth and everything on the ground.'[49] They saw and swiftly conceived what their Commander willed. As he spoke about creating humanity, they commonly perceived his intent for each god to provide, as each was capable, something to those who would be born.[50]

The Gifts of the Planets

28. The Sun spoke: 'I will shine all the more.'[51]

Moon promised to light up her course in Sun's wake. She added that she had already engendered Fear, Silence, Sleep, and Memory that would be useful to human beings.[52]

Saturn announced that he was already the father of Justice and Necessity.

Jupiter spoke: 'So that the future race might not totally devote themselves to war, I have already fathered for their benefit Fortune, Hope and Peace.'

Mars said that he was already the father of Struggle, Wrath, and Strife.

Venus asserted without hesitation: 'To them, Master, I will yoke Desire, Pleasure, and Laughter so that the souls akin to me, who suffer the most horrid condemnation, might not be punished beyond measure.'

God was greatly pleased, my child, when Venus said this.[53]

29. 'And I will make human nature,' Mercury said, 'and entrust to them Wisdom, Moderation, Persuasion, and Truth.[54] I will not cease to join with Invention.[55] Moreover, I will forever benefit the mortal life of future humans born under my zodiacal signs.[56] The signs that the father and Craftsman entrusted to me are wise and intelligent. I will benefit the race all the more when the movement of the stars that overlie them are in harmony with the natural energy of each individual.'

[49] Technically the earth is not created (or congealed) until §51.

[50] For each of the gods bestowing a gift upon humanity, compare the story of Pandora in Hesiod, *Works and Days* 69–82.

[51] Compare CH 16.5: "he [the Sun] gives freely of his ungrudging light. For it is the sun whence good energies reach."

[52] Reading, with Holzhausen (*CH Deutsch*, 2.429, n.290), ἂν ὠφελῆ. FP reads ἀνωφελῆ, or "useless."

[53] The gifts of the planets are both good and evil, unlike the solely negative influences in CH 1.25. Compare SH 29 below, with notes.

[54] "Mercury" is used instead of Hermes to highlight his planetary nature. In the Greek he is simply Ἑρμῆς (Hermes). Excluded here is the redundant ἔφη ("he said").

[55] For Invention daughter of Nature, see §13. Possibly a sexual sense of joining (συνών) is meant here.

[56] Hermes refers to Virgo and Gemini, two human-shaped signs of the zodiac.

God, the Master of the world, rejoiced when he heard this speech and ordered that the tribe of humans be made.

The Creation of Human Bodies

30. 'Now,' said Hermes, 'I was looking for the material necessary to use in this case, and I entreated the sole Ruler for help.[57] He ordered the souls to relinquish the remainder of the soul mixture. When I receive it, I found it completely dried up. Then I used much more water than was necessary for the mixture to refresh the composition of the material. As a result, what I formed was entirely dissolvable, weak, and powerless. This was so that the human race, in addition to being intelligent, might not enjoy the fullness of power.[58] I shaped it, and it began to be beautiful. Upon inspection, I was pleased with my work and called down the sole Ruler to examine it. He saw it and rejoiced.[59] Then he commanded that the souls be embodied.[60]

The Souls' Lament

31. When the souls learned of their condemnation, they were at first plunged into gloom. 32. I indeed marveled at their speeches.'

Isis: Pay attention, my son Horus, for you listen to a hidden teaching, which my ancestor Kamephis chanced to hear from Hermes the recorder of all deeds.[61] <I in turn> received the tradition from Kamephis, ancestor

[57] On the title "sole Ruler," see Scott, "Egyptian Elements," 68–71.

[58] Hermes takes the role of the star gods in Plato, *Timaeus* 42e–43a. In SH 23, the mixture from which human bodies are made is looser (thus weaker) than the bodies of animals.

[59] Compare the Memphite Theology: "Thus Ptah was satisfied after he had made all things" (*ANET*[3], 5); Genesis 1:31: "God saw everything that he had made, and indeed, it was very good."

[60] Striking here is that the human body and soul, though different compounds and mixtures, are made from the same original substance. Humans are not made from clay, as in Genesis 2:7 and in the myth of Prometheus (Pseudo-Apollodorus, *Library*, 1.7.1).

[61] Kamephis (Egyptian *Km-atef*) is variously spelled in Greek sources. According to Plutarch, "Kneph" was honored in Egyptian Thebes (Luxor) as an "unborn and immortal" god (*Isis and Osiris* 21 [*Moralia* 359d]). The Hellenistic *Oracle of the Potter* identifies "Knephis" with Agathos Daimon (a serpent deity of Alexandria) (translation in Fowden, *Egyptian Hermes*, 21–22; compare CH 10.23). Philo of Byblos claimed that the Phoenicians identify the Egyptian "Kneph" with Agathos Daimon. He is the first and most divine being, in snake form with the head of a hawk. When he opens his eyes, he fills the universe with light. He is depicted as stretched across the middle of a circle, which represents the world or primordial ocean (Eusebius, *Preparation of the Gospel* 1.10.48–49). *PGM* 3.141–44 similarly refers to Kmeph as "the brilliant Sun who shines through the whole inhabited world, who rides upon the ocean." Porphyry called "Kneph" the Craftsman who appears in human form holding a scepter and a belt (or possibly the *ankh* sign of life) (in Eusebius, *Preparation of the*

of all, when he honored me with the perfect black (land).[62] Now you hear it from me.

33. When, you wondrous and glorious child, the souls were about to be shut up in bodies, some of them simply lamented their imprisonment. They growled like wild animals born free but about to be cruelly enslaved and already pulled from their accustomed and beloved haunts. Other souls fought and were in open revolt. They would not act in accord with those who took hold of them. If they escaped, they would surely have delivered their attackers to death. Other souls hissed like ancient asps.

34. Another soul piercingly shrieked and wept for a long time before speaking, often turning above and below what served as its eyes.[63] 'O heaven,' it said, 'source of our generation, you aether and air – hands of the sole-ruling God – sacred breath, you brilliant stars, the eyes of God, and you tireless light of Sun and Moon, reared with us from our birth – from all of you we are dragged and suffer agonies![64] We suffer all the more, since we who are from vast and luminous realms, from the sacred spreading aether, from the riches of heaven's pole and – still more – from the blessed commonwealth of the gods, will be shut up in dishonorable and lowly tents![65]

Gospel 3.11.45). Iamblichus (assuming Gale's correction of ἠμήφ to Κμήφ) named Kmeph "leader of the celestial gods . . . an intellect thinking himself" (*On the Mysteries* 8.3). Compare Damascius, *Problems and Solutions Concerning First Principles* 125.4. For further sources and discussion, see NF 3.clxiii–clxvi; Griffiths, *Iside*, 374; Heinz J. Thissen, "ΚΜΗΦ – Ein Verkannter Gott," *Zeitschrift für Papyrologie und Epigraphik* 112 (1996): 153–60; Klotz, *Caesar*, 133–42.

62 Egypt is the black land (*Chemia*, compare חם in Hebrew). Plutarch explained that Egypt "has the blackest of soils." Thus the Egyptians call it "by the same name as the black portion of the eye [or pupil], *Chemia*, and compare it to a heart" (*Isis and Osiris* 33 [*Mor.* 364c]). Vergil (*Georgics* 4.291) knew that the Nile fertilizes Egypt with its "black sands." In a prayer to Isis from *PGM* 7.492–93, we read: "I call on you, Lady Isis, whom Agathos Daimon permitted to rule in the entire black [land]." Isis also wore a black garment (Plutarch, *Isis and Osiris* 52 [*Moralia* 372d]); Apuleius, *Metamorphoses* 11.3, *Ref.* 5.7.23; and is called "wearer of the black stole" in hymns (e.g., *Orphic Hymns* 42.9). The idea that the "perfect black" refers to Egypt does not exclude the idea that it refers to alchemy as well. See further Griffiths, *Iside*, 425–26; David Bain, "Μελανῖτις Γῆ: An Unnoticed Greek Name for Egypt: New Evidence for the Origins and Etymology of Alchemy?" in David R. Jordan, Hugo Montgomery, and Einar Thomassen, eds., *The World of Ancient Magic: Papers from the First International Samson Eitrem Seminar at the Norwegian Institute at Athens, 4–8 May 1997* (Bergen: John Grieg AS, 1999), 205–26.

63 The soul is not yet embodied so it does not have physical eyes. Compare the "superior eye of the soul" (ψυχῆς ὄμμα φέριστον) in *Chaldean Oracles* frag. 213 (Majercik); and the "incorporeal eye" in FH 25.

64 Compare Pseudo-Plato, *Axiochus* 366a: "the soul in pain yearns for its native heavenly aither"; Euripides, *Electra* 59: "I send shrieks to my father in the vast aether!" (γόους τ' ἀφίημ' αἰθέρ' ἐς μέγαν πατρί).

65 On tent imagery for the body, see SH 2A.1 with note 2 there.

35. What did we wretched souls do that was so improper? What was worthy of these punishments? How many failures await our miserable selves? What acts will we perform because of our wicked hopes so as to furnish the necessities to a waterlogged body so quickly dissolved?

36. The eyes of souls who have ceased to belong to God can see little. Ceaselessly will we groan, since our watery pupils can only see an infinitesimally small part of heaven, our ancestor – and there will be a time when we will not see it at all![66] As wretches we have been condemned. Direct sight has not been given to us, because sight apart from light has not been granted. These (physical) eyes are not eyes, but hollow spaces. When we hear our brother spirits blowing in the air, we will endure it with pain, since we will not breathe along with them.[67] Our home, instead of the aerial world, will be the tiny hovel of a human heart.[68] 37. Grieving will only end when we are released from such (shells) into which we have come.[69] Master, father, maker, if you so quickly neglect your works, set limits to our suffering! Count us worthy of a response, even if brief, while we still have power to see across this vast and brilliant universe!'

[66] The soul is the pupil designed to see God. But the watery pupil can only behold a narrow band of fiery heaven. Placed immediately after this sentence is a gloss: "From this comes Orpheus's saying 'We see by means of light; with our eyes we see nothing'" (Bernabé *OF* 161). Compare Bernabé *OF* 377, lines 15–17: "in all mortals there are mortal pupils in their eyes, small . . . and weak to see the One ruling through the universe."

[67] The correlation between breath, wind, and soul was well known in antiquity. "In the so-called Orphic epics . . . the soul comes in from the respiration of the universe, brought by the winds" (Aristotle, *On the Soul* 1.5, 410b27–31 = Orphic frag. 421, Bernabé). The natural philosopher Anaximenes stated that the soul is air, "for it holds us together" (in Eusebius, *Preparation for the Gospel* 14.14.3). In the second century CE, the astrologer Vettius Valens quoted "the most divine Orpheus" as saying that "drawing the air we pluck a divine soul" and "the soul in humans is rooted from the aether" (*Anthology* 8.1.12–14 = Bernabé *OF* 422 and 436). See further Carlos Megino, "Presence in Stoicism of an Orphic Doctrine of the Soul quoted by Aristotle (*De Anima* 410b 27 = *OF* 421)," in *Tracing Orpheus: Studies of Orphic Fragments in Honour of Alberto Bernabé*, ed. Miguel Herrero de Jáuregui (Berlin: de Gruyter, 2011), 139–46.

[68] Intentional alliteration between "hovel" (οἶκος) and "heart" (ὄγκος), also played upon by Philo, *Allegorical Interpretation* 2.77. A closer parallel is *idem, The Worse is Wont to Attack the Better* 90: "How then is it likely that human consciousness, as small as it is, and locked up in the tiny lumps (βραχέσιν ὄγκοις) of the (cranial) membrane or the heart, has room for so great a magnitude of heaven and the cosmos if it is not an inseparable fragment of that divine and blessed soul?" See further Marc Philonenko, "La plainte des âmes dans la *Koré Kosmou*," *Proceedings of the International colloquium on Gnosticism, Stockholm, August 20–25, 1973* (Stockholm: Almqvist & Wiksell International, 1977), 153–56 at 155.

[69] Compare Empedocles (DK 31 B119 = Inwood 114) cited by *Ref.* 5.7.30: "from what magnificent honor and what great beatitude [souls have fallen]!"

The Fate of Souls

38. The souls, Horus my son, succeeded in their petition. The sole Ruler came, sat on the throne of truth, and answered their supplications.[70] 'O souls, Eros and Necessity will be your masters, for they, after me, are the masters and chief directors of all.[71] As for you souls who serve my ageless royal scepter, know that as long as you do not err, you will dwell in heavenly realms. Yet if blame attaches to one of you, you will dwell condemned in mortal guts as your allotted realm. 39. Those of you whose blame is not severe will break free of the baleful bond of flesh and once again, without groans, greet your own heaven. Yet if you are workers of greater sins, you will not advance from the molded body when your due service is paid. You will not dwell in heaven, nor even in human bodies. You will complete the rest of your lives wandering in the bodies of non-reasoning beasts.'[72]

40. This was his decree, Horus my son. He bestowed breaths on all the souls.[73] Once again he pronounced: 'Not at random or by chance have I lawfully determined your transformations. If you practice what is shameful, you will be transformed into something worse. Likewise, if you resolve to do something worthy of your origin, you will rise to a better state. Now I and no other will be your supervisor and overseer.[74] Know well, then,

[70] Inserted into FP here is the subtitle λόγοι τοῦ θεοῦ ("God's Decrees").

[71] Eros rules the soul, Necessity the body. They are the gifts of Venus and Saturn, respectively (§28). For the bestowal of Necessity, compare FH 34. Note also Macrobius: "The Egyptians . . . say that four gods attend a human being as it is born: Deity, Chance, Eros, and Necessity . . . Eros is signified by a kiss, Necessity by a knot" (*Saturnalia* 1.19.17).

[72] Tertullian mentioned Albinus (a mid second-century Platonist) as making the Egyptian Hermes the source and origin of the doctrine of transmigration (*On the Soul* 28.1 = FH 1c). According to Diodorus, Pythagoras learned the doctrine of transmigration from the Egyptians (*Library of History* 1.98.2). Compare *Ascl.* 12: "a vile migration unworthy of a holy soul puts them in other bodies." Contrast CH 10.20: "Do you, too, believe what they all think, my son, that the soul which has left the body becomes an animal? This is a great error." The basis for bestial reincarnation appears to be Plato: if a soul continues to live wickedly, it will be born "into some wild animal that resembled its wicked character" (*Timaeus* 42b, summarized in Alcinous, *Handbook of Platonism* 16.2 and adapted by [Timaeus Locrus], *On the Nature of the World and the Soul* 86 [104e]). Origen observed that, "It is a mark of extreme negligence and sloth for any soul to descend and to lose its own nature so completely as to be bound, in consequence of its vices, to the gross body of one of the irrational animals" (*On First Principles* 1.4.1). See further Osborne, *Dumb Beasts*, 43–62.

[73] The souls are already composed of divine breath (πνεῦμα, §14). The breaths received here likely serve as coverings or "membranes" for the souls that will adapt them to bodily life. Compare CH 10.17: "the soul, which is itself something divine, uses the breath as a sort of armoring-servant." See further SH 24.10 with note 16.

[74] Compare *Ascl.* 27: "God is everywhere and surveys everything all around"; *Strasbourg Cosmogony*, recto, lines 6–8 (Piccardi, *Cosmogonia*, 67): Zeus sits in a place of vantage and watches over the creative work of his son Hermes.

that it is due to your former deeds that you endure the punishment of embodiment.

41. The variation in your rebirth, as I said, will consist in the variation of your bodies; and the dissolution of the body will be a benefit and a return to your former blessedness. If you plan to do anything unworthy of me, your mind will be blinded.[75] As a result, you will think wrong-headedly, endure your punishment as if it were a boon, and consider promotion a dishonor and an outrage.

42. You souls who are more just and who are able to receive transformation into divinity will enter humans as just kings, genuine philosophers, founders of cities, lawgivers, true seers, genuine root-cutters, most excellent prophets of the gods, experienced musicians, intelligent astronomers, wise augurs, accurate sacrificers, and whatever other noble vocations there are of which you are worthy.[76]

If you enter into birds, you will become eagles.[77] The reason is that eagles neither screech at their brother birds nor feast upon them, nor does it let its animal neighbors attack another weaker animal. The eagle, truly just in nature, will pursue (the attacker).[78]

If you enter into four-footed animals, you will become lions. The lion is powerful and endowed with a virtually unsleeping nature, it exercises an immortal nature in a corruptible body – for lions neither grow weary nor sleep.[79]

[75] Compare DH 7.3: "a soul which has no intellect [νοῦς] is blind."

[76] These are chiefly Egyptian priestly professions (Bull, "Tradition of Hermes," 173–76), but the idea of reincarnation into people of high status has a Greek pedigree. Compare Empedocles frag. 136 (Inwood = DK 31 B146): "And finally they [embodied daimones] become prophets and singers and doctors / and leaders among earth-dwelling people; / and from these states they sprout up as gods, first in honors." On this passage, see Günther Zuntz, *Persephone: Three Essays on Religion and Thought in Magna Graecia* (Oxford: Clarendon Press, 1971), 232–34; Peter Kingsley, *Ancient Philosophy, Mystery and Magic* (Oxford: Clarendon Press, 1995), 344–45. Note also the ranked professions in Plato, *Phaedrus* 248d–e: "the soul that has seen the most [of the divine world] will be planted into a man who will become a lover of wisdom or of beauty, or who will be cultivated in the arts and prone to erotic love. The second sort of soul will be put into someone who will be a lawful king or warlike commander; the third, a statesman, a manager of a household, or a financier; the fourth will be a trainer who loves exercise or a doctor who cures the body; the fifth will lead the life of a prophet or priest of the mysteries. To the sixth the life of a poet or some other representational artist is properly assigned."

[77] On reincarnation into animals, see Plato, *Timaeus* 42b–c; 90e–92c; Plotinus, *Enneads* 3.4.2. See further Osborne, *Dumb Beasts*, 43–62.

[78] Compare Porphyry: "the falcon . . . pities humans, laments over a corpse, and scatters earth on its eyes" (*On Abstinence* 4.9.7).

[79] For reincarnation into a lion, compare Empedocles DK 31 B127 (Inwood 135): "Among beasts they [will be] mountain-lying lions sleeping on the ground." The tradition that the lion does not sleep may go back to Manetho (οὐδέποτε καθεύδει ὁ λέων, frag. 88 Waddell). Compare Aelian: "Even when asleep, the lion moves his tail, showing, as you might expect, that he is not altogether

If you enter into reptiles, you will become snakes. This animal is powerful because it is long-lived. It is also harmless and in some ways friendly to humans. It will be tamed and non-venomous.[80] The snake will become young when old, just like the nature of gods.[81]

If you enter a swimming creature, you will become dolphins, for they take pity on those thrown into the sea, and convey them while still breathing to land.[82] They will never touch those who have perished at sea, though marine animals are the most voracious.'[83]

When God spoke these things, he morphed into incorruptible Consciousness.[84]

The Speech of Blame

43. After these things happened, my son Horus, a most powerful spirit rose from the earth, incomprehensible in its bodily extent and in the power of its thinking. Its body was of human form, handsome and dignified, though extremely savage and full of terror.[85] This spirit, though it knew of

quiescent, and that, although sleep has enveloped and enfolded him, it has not subdued him as it does all other animals. The Egyptians, they say, claim to have observed in him something of this kind, asserting that the lion is superior to sleep and forever awake" (*Characteristics of Animals* 5.39); Plutarch: the lion sleeps only for a moment with eyes that gleam (*Table Talk* 4.5.2 [*Moralia* 670c]); Macrobius: "The lion is also seen to have wide-open, fiery eyes, as the sun looks upon the earth with its open, fiery eye in one long, untiring gaze" (*Saturnalia* 1.21.17). In Plato's Myth of Er, the soul of Ajax chooses to be a lion and that of Agamemnon chooses to be an eagle (*Republic* 10.620a–c).

80 Aelian: "They say that the asp to which the Egyptians have given the name *Thermuthis* is sacred, and the people of the country worship it, and bind it, as though it was a royal headdress, about the statues of Isis. They deny that it was born to destroy or injure human beings . . . And the Egyptians assert that the Thermuthis alone among asps is immortal" (*Characteristics of Animals* 10.31). Compare Pliny, *Natural History* 29.67.

81 Compare Aristotle, *History of Animals* 7.17, 600b15–17 (casting off "old age"); Philo of Byblos in Eusebius, *Preparation of the Gospel* 1.10.47: the snake is the "most long-lived, and its nature is to put off its old skin . . . to grow young again."

82 Compare the story of Arion variously reported in Herodotus, *Histories* 1.23; Dio Chrysostom, *Orations* 37.2–4; Plutarch, *Cleverness of Animals* 36 (*Moralia* 984a–985c). The fish that Empedocles becomes in DK 31 B117 (Inwood 111) is probably the dolphin (Zuntz, *Persephone*, 199).

83 On the voraciousness of marine animals, compare Aristotle, *History of Animals* 7.2, 591b29–30. Oppian likewise presented the eagle, lion, dolphin, and snake as the lords of their respective domains (*Halieutica* 2.539–42).

84 The high God is Consciousness (νοῦς) in CH 1.6, 12; 13.9; In CH 2.14, however, he is the cause of Consciousness.

85 The spirit here is personified Blame, the fault-finding god. Blame also played a role in the lost Homeric epic *Cypria*. He advised Zeus to beget a beautiful daughter so that many men would die fighting over her at Troy (West, *Greek Epic Fragments*, frag. 1). Compare Hesiod, *Theogony* 214, where Night independently gives birth to Blame. Lucian depicted Blame as faulting Hephaestus for not making human words and thoughts more transparent (*Hermotimus* 20, compare Babrius, *Fable* §59). See further Jacques Schwartz, "La *Korē Kosmou* et Lucien de Samosate (a propos de Momus et de la creation de l'homme)," *Le Monde Grec: pensée, littérature, histoire, documents. Hommages à*

what it asked and beheld the souls swiftly entering molded bodies, still inquired: 44. 'Hermes, scribe of the gods, what are these called?'

Hermes answered, 'Human beings.'

Blame: 'You speak, O Hermes, of a daring work, this making of humanity.[86] This species is curious of eye and loquacious of tongue; it will hear what is none of its business, will be greedy to sniff and destined to mishandle all that can be touched. Have you, its father, determined to leave this species carefree, a species that will behold with brazen face the beautiful mysteries of nature? Do you wish that this species be without sorrow, a species that will launch its designs to the ends of the earth?

45. Human beings will dig up the roots of plants and test the properties of their sap. They will investigate the nature of stones, dissect animals down the middle – not only unreasoning animals, but even themselves – in their desire to discover how they are formed. They will stretch out audacious hands as far as the sea, chopping down naturally growing forests to ferry themselves to the lands beyond. They will investigate what objects exist deep within temple shrines. They will hunt as far as heaven, wanting to observe the movement established there.[87]

I mention only their moderate endeavors! Nothing will remain any more except the remotest regions of earth. Yet the blackest nights of these places, too, they will explore in their lust.[88] 46. They will have no hindrance, but initiated into the richness of a life without grief, and not pricked by the painful goads of fear, they will luxuriously enjoy a carefree existence. Will they not arm themselves as far as heaven with overcurious audacity? Will they not stretch their carefree souls to the stars?[89]

Claire Préaux, ed. J. Bingen (Brussels: University of Brussels, 1975), 223–33. Lucian's Blame is a comic figure. In the *Korē Kosmou*, Horus weeps rather than laughs (§47).

[86] An ironic comment, since it was daring that caused human souls to fall.

[87] "Heaven" (οὐρανοῦ) is Canter's correction for οὖν in FP. Originally the souls, who turned heaven's axle, were the cause of this motion (§16 above).

[88] Here reading τουτῶν with F. In ancient topography, the earth was divided into five zones, with the two extreme southern and northern zones plunged in night and "perpetual mist" (Pliny, *Natural History* 2.172).

[89] For polemics against human technology and audacity, compare Sophocles: "Many things are formidable, and none more formidable than man! He crosses the gray sea beneath the winter wind, passing beneath the surges that surround him; and he wears away the highest of the gods, Earth ... Skillful beyond hope is the contrivance of his art, and he advances sometimes to evil, at other times to good" (*Antigone* 332–75); Horace: "All to no avail did God deliberately separate countries by the divisive ocean if, in spite of that, impious boats go skipping over the seas that were meant to remain inviolate. The human species, audacious enough to endure anything, plunges into forbidden sacrilege ... In our folly we aspire to the sky itself" (*Odes* 1.3.21–40); Philo: "Love of learning is by nature curious and inquisitive, not hesitating to bend its steps in all directions, prying into everything, reluctant to leave anything that exists unexplored, whether material or immaterial. It has an extraordinary appetite for all that there is to be seen and heard, and, not content with what

Teach them, then, to have a passion for their projects so that they fear the bleakness of failure, so that they are tamed by biting grief when they fail to obtain their hopes. Let the niggling curiosity of their souls be cut down by lusts, fears, waves of grief, and deceitful hopes. Let continual love affairs take vengeance upon their souls, along with varied hopes, and desires sometimes fulfilled, sometimes shattered so that the sweet bait of success becomes a striving for more perfect evils. Let them be weighted down with fevers, so that they, when they lose heart, chastise their desire.'[90]

47. *Isis:* Are you sad, Horus my son, as your mother interprets these things for you? Do you not wonder or stand dumbfounded when you see pitiful humanity weighed down? Hear now what is more terrible![91]

48. Hermes took pleasure in the speech of Blame – for he spoke what suited him. He performed exactly what Blame had advised, remarking, 'Very well, Blame, the all-encompassing nature of divine breath will no longer be clearly visible.[92] After all, the Master of all has declared that I be steward and foreseer. The sharp-sighted goddess Nemesis will be appointed as overseer of the universe.[93] As for me, I will devise a secret mechanism maintaining unerring and inviolable scrutiny. To it all things on earth will necessarily be enslaved from birth to their final decay. This mechanism maintains the fixity of what must be completed. All other things on earth will obey it.[94]

it finds in its own country, it is bent on seeking what is in foreign parts" (*Migration of Abraham* 216; compare Philo, *Every Good Man is Free* 65–66, a polemic against mining and sea-diving); 1 Enoch 8 (fallen angels teach humans the arts of mining and root-cutting). In other Hermetic tractates, humankind's bold explorations are cause for celebration, as in CH 10.25: "the human rises up to heaven and takes its measure and knows what is in its heights and its depths, and he understands all else exactly."

90 Compare Aeschylus: "Zeus . . . has established as a fixed law that 'wisdom comes by suffering.' But even as trouble, bringing memory of pain, drips over the mind in sleep, so wisdom comes to men, whether they want it or not" (*Agamemnon* 177–80).

91 Compare *Ascl.* 25, where Hermes asks, "Asclepius, why do you weep? There are matters much worse."

92 Hermes appears to refer to aether, substrate of the stars. The invisibility of the true heaven was already mentioned (§36). Here I accept Scott's emendation οὐκέτ' ἀργή for ἐναργῆ in FP (*Hermetica*, 3.542).

93 Adrasteia or Nemesis is the inescapable goddess of vengeance who punishes arrogant and unbridled speech and behavior.

94 Compare SH 12.2 (the instrument of Fate), 14.2: "Fate is spread out [in heaven], and . . . is the cause of astral formations. Such is the inescapable law that orders all things."

I, Hermes, spoke these things to Blame and immediately the mechanism was set in motion.[95] 49. When this occurred, and the souls were embodied, I won praise for what was accomplished.'[96]

A Second Creation Story

50. Again the sole Ruler convened a plenary assembly of the gods. The gods arrived and again God addressed them: 'Ye elite deities, endowed with an imperishable nature, allotted to ever administer this vast universe, for you all (elements) will never tire exchanging themselves for themselves.[97] How long will we be lords of this government that none recognize? How long will these sights be unseen by sun and moon? Let each one of us be productive in ourselves. By our power let us wipe away this still inert structure. Let chaos be considered a tall tale to those who will later be born.[98] Take hold of great deeds! I myself shall make a beginning.'

He spoke and immediately there came to be an ordered division in the still dark amalgam. 51. Then heaven appeared, ordered and adorned with all its mysteries. The earth was still quivering as it was congealed by the shining sun.[99] It appeared fully adorned with all its blessings. For even what mortals consider foul is good in God's sight because it is made to serve God's laws. God rejoiced to see his works already set in motion.[100]

52. Having filled his hands – which stretched as wide as the ambient – with the products of Nature, he strongly squeezed the contents in his hands and said, 'Receive, O sacred land, receive, you who are

[95] Hermes the Word has the power of creating by word alone. Compare FH 32a, 33 (from Cyril).

[96] "Embodied" (ἐνεσωματίσθησαν) is Canter's emendation; P reads ἐνεσηματίσθησαν ("entombed"). Perhaps P's reading should be retained, since the putatively Orphic saying "the body is a tomb" (σῶμα σῆμα) was well known (Philolaus DK 44 B14; Plato, *Cratylus* 400c; *Gorgias* 493a; *Phaedrus* 250c). See further Pierre Courcelle, "Le corps-tombeau," *Revue des études anciennes* 78 (1966): 101–22.

[97] Plato, likely dependent upon Empedocles, asserted that the elements can change into each other (*Timaeus* 53e, 54b).

[98] With the creation of Nature and Invention in §§10–11, one would think that chaos had already gone. Yet here the chaos seems to refer to chaos on earth, a region not explicitly said to be ordered.

[99] Bousset compared the evident separation of heaven and earth with the separation of Geb (Earth) and Nut (Heaven) by Shu (Air) in Egyptian mythology (*PW* 11.2, col. 1389, under the word "Korē Kosmou"). This episode prepares for the souls' exile on earth (even though previous episodes assume the existence of earth). Earth is apparently separated from the *lower* heaven (or atmosphere), since the cosmic heavens (the circles of planets and stars) have already been established. Compare FH 31; Diodorus, *Library of History* 1.7.1–7 (who also mentions the sun's rays compacting the earth).

[100] Compare Plato, *Timaeus* 37c: "Now when the engendering Father observed the ornament of the eternal gods set in motion and alive, he was pleased."

extraordinarily honored to be the mother of all![101] From now on, consider that you lack nothing!' God spoke, opened his hands – the kind of hands fit for a deity – and released all things into the structure of reality.

Primitive Barbarism

53. At first, ignorance was everywhere.[102] Souls had only recently been shut up in bodies. They, not tolerating their dishonor, vied with the gods in heaven. They strongly maintained and laid claim to their noble birth, asserting that they also were offspring of the same Craftsman. They were in open revolt. Using the weaker people who remained as tools, they made them attack, oppose, and battle one another. In this way, power mastered weakness. The strong burned and butchered the powerless. They butchered the living all around temples, and threw their dead bodies into the inner shrines.[103]

The Plea of the Elements

54. This violence went on until the Elements, deeply disturbed, saw fit to entreat the sole-ruling God concerning humans' savage way of life. When much evil had already been done, the Elements approached God their maker, addressing him with speeches of blame.[104]

55. Fire had the right to speak first. 'Master and Craftsman of this new world,' he said. 'Name hidden among gods, sacrosanct among all humans to the present day.[105] How long, O Divinity, will you be resolved to let the

[101] For Nature, see §§10–13 above.

[102] In §4 above, ignorance (or lack of knowledge) controlled the cosmos. Here human ignorance is in view.

[103] Reading κατὰ τῶν ἀδύτων with the MSS. Technically these shrines ought only to exist after the advent of Osiris and Isis (§ 65). Yet they have a proleptic existence already in §7. The bestial life of primitive humanity was a common theme in poetry and history. See, for instance, Diodorus, *Library of History* 1.90: "When people, they say, first ceased living a bestial life and gathered into groups, at the outset they cannibalized and battled against each other, the stronger ever dominating the weaker"; Sextus Empiricus, *Against the Mathematicians* 9.16 (citing an Orphic poem): "When mortals took a flesh-eating life from one another / And the stronger tore up the weaker"; 54 (citing Critias, contemporary of Plato): "There was a time when the life of humans was without order, / Beastlike and subject to force, / When neither the good had any reward / Nor did the bad receive any punishment." Compare the apocalyptic scenario in *Ascl.* 25 (baleful angels will drive humans "to every outrageous crime – war, looting, trickery").

[104] Empedocles viewed the elements as divine (DK 31 B6 = frag. 17, Inwood). Note in this regard Kingsley, *Ancient Philosophy*, 301, n.37. Compare the intercession of the four great angels in 1 Enoch 9. See further Wilhelm Bousset, "Zur Dämonologie der späteren Antike," *Archiv für Religionswissenschaft* 18 (1915): 134–72 at 167–68.

[105] Compare the "secret name" of God in 1 Enoch 69:14.

life of mortals be godless? 56. Rouse yourself, offer an oracle to the world, and initiate the savagery of life into the rites of peace. Grant laws to human life, grant oracles at night. Fill all with good hopes! Let humans fear vengeance from the gods and let no one persist in stubbornness. If they pay back due wages for sins, the rest will keep themselves from injustice. They will fear oaths and not a single person will any more ponder sacrilege.

Let them learn, when benefited, to give thanks so that fire, rejoicing in libations, can perform its service – so that I can send fragrant mists to you from altar hearths. Up to the present moment I am defiled, master, and am forced by the godless daring of human creatures to melt fleshly bodies.[106] They do not allow my nature to remain as it is, and indecently debase what is incorruptible!'

57. Then air spoke up: 'I too am polluted, master. From the smoke of dead bodies I am diseased and no longer wholesome. I behold from above what is unlawful to see.'[107]

58. Water had authority to speak next, my magnanimous child. It declared: 'Father and wondrous maker of all, self-born Divinity and maker of nature who is ever-productive by your power – order now at last, O Divinity, that my ever-flowing streams be pure. For shame! Rivers and seas wash the hands of murderers or receive the bodies of those murdered!'

59. Earth was standing by, deeply sullen. I will set forth the <substance> of her speech, my great and glorious child. She began as follows: 'King, presider, and master of the heavenly rings, leader and father of us elements who stand before you! From us elements all things commence to grow and diminish, and into us again when a creature ceases, it must find its end.

O God who are greatly honored, an irrational and godless chorus of inhuman creatures has risen up against me! I make space to hold the nature of all beings – for it is I, as you ordered, who bear all things and receive the bodies of those slain. 60. Now I am dishonored! Your earthly world is full of all things, but has no god. Humans act lawlessly with respect to everything, since what they should fear they do not. Into the ridges of my back they drill with every wicked device. I am entirely drenched and corrupted with the pus of corpses!

[106] "Defiled" (μιαίνομαι) is Canter's correction for μαίνομαι ("I am out of my mind") in FP. Fire refers to his role in cremation.

[107] Compare *Pseudo-Clementine Homilies* 8.17.1: "By the outpouring of much blood, the pure air will be defiled by impure exhalation and the sickened air will cause diseases among those who breathe it."

61. Henceforth, lord, and because I am forced to make a place for the unworthy, in addition to all I bear – I want to make room for a god. Grant to the earth, if not yourself – for I could not endure you – then some part of your sacred effluence.[108] Transform the earth by making her more honored than the other elements. To her alone of your creations is it right to speak boldly, since she provides all things.'[109]

62. So spoke the elements. Then God filled the universe with his sacred voice: 'Go forth, sacred and worthy children of a great Father, and do not attempt to rebel in any way, nor leave my world bereft of your services. Among you already is another effluence of my nature who will be the holy overseer of deeds, an unbribable judge of the living, a lord not only frightening, but the punisher of those under the earth.[110] To each human being through the generations a fitting reward will follow.'[111]

63. At the master's bidding, the elements ceased their entreaty, and grew silent. Each element ruled and was master over its own sphere of authority."

Isis and Osiris

64. After this, Horus asked: "Mother, how then did earth obtain the effluence of God?"

[108] CH 2.14 (all beings are incapable of containing the nature of the Good). Wisdom is God's effluence in Wisdom 7:25.

[109] Compare the apocryphal *Apocalypse of Paul* 6: "Sometimes the waters have also protested against the children of humanity, saying: O Lord God Almighty, the children of humanity have all defiled your holy name . . . Often also the earth cried out unto the Lord against the children of humanity, saying: O Lord God Almighty, I suffer hurt more than all your creation, bearing the fornications, adulteries, murders, thefts, perjuries, sorceries, and witchcrafts of human beings, and all the evils that they do, so that the father rises up against son, and the son against father, the stranger against the stranger, every one to defile his neighbor's wife . . . Therefore I suffer hurt more than the whole creation, and I would not yield my wealth and fruits to the children of men."

[110] Although originally the judge may have referred solely to Osiris, in context Isis is also in view. Compare Isidorus: "You [Isis] . . . look down on the manifold / deeds of impious men and observe those of the pious" (*Hymn* 3.26–27 [Vanderlip, *Four Greek Hymns*, 4–6]); Andros aretalogy lines 42–43: "I [Isis] make threats even as far as the graves of bellowing Hades" (Totti, *Ausgewählte*, 6).

[111] Holzhausen (followed here) modifies δ' into τ' to preserve the οὐ μόνον – ἀλλὰ καί construction. For Osiris as judge of the dead, see Spell 125 in the *Book of Going Forth by Day* (*Book of the Dead*), in William Kelly Simpson, ed., *The Literature of Ancient Egypt: An Anthology of Stories, Instructions, Stelae, Autobiographies, and Poetry*, 3rd edn. (New Haven: Yale University Press, 2003), 267–77. See further John Gwyn Griffiths, *The Divine Verdict: A Study of Divine Judgment in the Ancient Religions*, Studies in the History of Religions 52 (Leiden: Brill, 1991), 201–36.

Isis replied: "I refrain from speaking about his birth, since it is not lawful to recite the source of your sowing, Horus of immense strength.[112] I refrain for fear that in the future the birth of immortal gods becomes known among human beings. I will say only this: the sole-ruling God, the world-maker and Craftsman of all things, bestowed for a short time your supremely great father Osiris and the supremely great goddess Isis as helpers in a world in need of all things.

65. They filled life with the goods of life.

They put a stop to the savagery of mutual killing.[113]

They consecrated precincts and sacrifices for the ancestral gods.[114]

They bestowed laws, food, and protection on mortals.[115]

66. 'They will come to know and discern the secrets of my writings,' says Hermes, 'even if they withhold some of them.[116] Yet those that extend benefits to mortals, they will inscribe on steles and obelisks.'

67. They first revealed law courts and filled all things with good order and justice.[117]

They were the founders of covenants and loyalty and introduced the great god Oath into human life.[118]

They taught people how to enwrap (bodies), as one ought, for those who ceased to live.[119]

After they investigated the cruel fact of death, they learned that the spirit was fond of returning from outside into human formations. If the spirit is

[112] For the story of Horus's birth, see Coffin Text 148 printed in Simpson, *Literature*, 263–65.

[113] Compare: "I [Isis] put a stop to murders" (Cyme aretalogy, line 26 in Žabkar, *Hymns*, 141).

[114] Compare: "I [Isis] established sacred precincts of the gods" (Cyme aretalogy line 24 in Žabkar, *Hymns*, 141, 152). On the founding of precincts (or temples), see Scott, "Egyptian Elements," 104–6. On the establishment of sacrifice, see van den Kerchove, *Voie*, 224–32.

[115] For the benefactions of Isis and Osiris, see Diodorus, *Library of History* 1.14.1–4; 1.27.4; Plutarch, *Isis and Osiris* 13 (*Moralia* 356a–b). Compare "I [Isis] gave laws to humankind . . . I am the one who discovered grain" (Cyme aretalogy, lines 4 and 7 in Žabkar, *Hymns*, 140); Porphyry: "It is Isis who nourishes and raises up the fruits of the earth, and Osiris represents among the Egyptians the fertilizing power" (in Eusebius, *Preparation of the Gospel* 3.11.50); Isidorus: "You [Isis] revealed customs for the existence of justice . . . and you discovered the flourishing growth of all grains" (*Hymn* 1.6, 8 in Vanderlip, *Four Greek Hymns*, 18; compare 2.3 in *ibid.* 35).

[116] Compare §8; Andros aretalogy: "From the tablets of sagacious Hermes I learned secret symbols" (line 10 in Totti, *Ausgewählte*, 5).

[117] Compare the Andros aretalogy: "I [Isis] am giver of sacred laws for articulate peoples . . . I am the one who offers strong provision for the administering of justice" (lines 20, 35 in Totti, *Ausgewählte*, 6); "I am called lawgiver" (Cyme hymn, line 52 in Žabkar, *Hymns*, 141). Further Egyptian parallels in Scott, "Egyptian Elements," 110–19.

[118] For Oath son of Strife, see Hesiod, *Theogony* 231; see also *Works and Days* 219, 804; Sophocles, *Oedipus at Colonus* 1767 (Oath, associated with Zeus, is all-seeing). In the Cyme aretalogy, Isis says: "I made nothing more frightening than an oath" (line 33 in Žabkar, *Hymns*, 141).

[119] περιστέλλειν has a more general sense of "bury," but in an Egyptian context, mummification seems to be in view. On Egyptian burial customs, see Diodorus, *Library of History* 1.91–94.

ever absent, it produces a swoon from which there is no recovery.[120] If the bodily formation is ever lacking, the soul who cannot retake it loses heart.

After they learned from Hermes that the ambient was full of divinities, they inscribed it on hidden steles.[121]

68. They (Isis and Osiris) alone, after learning from Hermes the secrets of divine legislation, became initiators and legislators of the arts, sciences, and all occupations.

They learned from Hermes how lower things were arranged by the creator to correspond with things above, and they set up on earth the sacred procedures vertically aligned with the mysteries in heaven.[122]

They, recognizing the corruption of bodies, ingeniously devised a perfect remedy in (the persons of) all of their prophets.[123] Their purpose was that no future prophet who raised his hands to the gods would ever be ignorant of what exists, that philosophy and magic would nourish the soul, and that medicine would preserve the body when sick.[124]

69. All these things, my child, Osiris and I performed. When we saw the world completely full, we were from that time recalled by the dwellers of

[120] In rare cases, such as that of Hermotimus of Clazomenae, a soul could leave the body and return to it (Pliny *Natural History* 7.174; Lucian, *Fly* 7).

[121] In the *Pythagorean Notebooks* (second to first century BCE), there is reference to all the souls of the dead filling the air as heroes and divinities (= daimones) (Diogenes, *Lives of Philosophers* 8.32). Compare CH 9.3: "no part of the cosmos is without a daimon that steals into the mind to sow the seed of its own energy"; CH 16.10: "around the sun are many troops of daimones looking like battalions in changing array."

[122] Compare SH 20.7: "Nature adapts the temperament of the body to the conjunction of stars and unites the motley blend of the body to the temperament of the stars with the result that they have a mutual influence on each other"; Philo: "in accordance with a certain natural sympathy the things of the earth depend on the things of heaven" (*On the Creation* 117).

[123] The "prophet" may correspond to the *hem netcher* (servant of God) priest who cared for the materials used in the daily offering for the gods. Here he combines ritual, medical, and philosophical knowledge. Porphyry, dependent on Chaeremon, says that in Egypt of old, "true philosophy was practiced by prophets" (*On Abstinence* 4.8.5); compare Clement of Alexandria, *Stromata* 1.15.71.3 (the Egyptian prophets excelled in philosophy). Iamblichus calls Bitys a "prophet," that is an interpreter of sacred lore (*On the Mysteries* 8.4). Clement of Alexandria described an Egyptian prophet who was "prime minister of the sanctuary" and in control of revenue (*Stromata* 6.4.37.1). The prophet Pachrates of Heliopolis showed the emperor Hadrian all "the truth of his magic" (*PGM* 4.2443–2455). The speaker in CH 17 is called a "prophet"; see the note of Copenhaver, 208–9. See further Sauneron, *Priests*, 5–109, Jacco Dieleman, *Priests, Tongues, and Rites: The London-Leiden Magical Manuscripts and Translation in Egyptian Ritual (100–300 CE)* (Leiden: Brill, 2005), 185–284; Emily Teeter, *Religion and Ritual in Ancient Egypt* (Cambridge: Cambridge University Press, 2011), 16–38.

[124] Narratively speaking, it is odd that Isis refers to herself in the third person. One suspects here that the author of this text has integrated a preexisting hymn of praise to Isis and Osiris which referred to these deities in the third person. See further NF 3.cxlvii–cxlix. Isis was known for discovering health-giving drugs and being versed in the science of healing (Diodorus, *Library of History* 1.25.2). For Egyptian magic and medicine, see Teeter, *Religion*, 171–77.

heaven. Yet it was not possible to ascend without first invoking the sole ruler, so that the ambient be full of this knowledge and so that we obtain a welcome ascent.[125] God, after all, rejoices in hymns."[126]

70. "Mother," said Horus, "grant knowledge of this hymn to me also, so that I not be unlearned."[127]

Isis replied: "Listen closely, my child! . . ."

[125] The activity of Isis and Osiris is parallel to that of Hermes in §§5–8: inscribing knowledge, passing it on, ascending after prayer. The ascent of Isis and Osiris also foreshadows the ascent of righteous souls.

[126] Compare *Ascl.* 9: "Rightly the supreme divinity sent the chorus of Muses down to meet humankind lest the earthly world lack sweet melody"; instead, with songs set to music, humans praised and glorified him who alone is all and is Father of all, and thus, owing to their praise of heaven, earth has not been devoid of the charms of harmony." For hymns that serve as the culmination of Hermetic treatises, compare CH 1.31; *Ascl.* 41.

[127] Compare CH 13.15–20: "'Father, I would like to hear the praise in the hymn which you said I should hear from the powers once I had entered the Ogdoad.' . . . 'Be still, my child; now hear a well-tuned hymn of praise, the hymn of rebirth. To divulge it was no easy choice for me except that I do it for you, at the end of everything.'"

SH 24

Stobaeus transmits the following excerpt as the forty-fifth selection in his long chapter "On the Soul" (*Anthology* 1.49, the same chapter as SH 3, 17, 19–20, 23, 25–26). It is immediately preceded by what appears above as SH 23 (the *Korē Kosmou*). It is followed by an oracle concerning the activity of souls after their exodus from the body. Stobaeus indicated that SH 24 comes from the same book or collection of treatises as the *Korē Kosmou*. The title *Korē Kosmou* may have applied to a single book in the collection or to the collection as a whole.

SH 23 and 24 are both conceptually and stylistically akin. In the latter excerpt, however, Horus more actively sets the agenda by posing additional questions. There are, moreover, some points of tension. The *Korē Kosmou*, for instance, narrates how all souls transgressed and were bound to bodies as a punishment. In SH 24, some souls, namely royal ones, transgressed only slightly and, though they fall into bodies, do not suffer embodiment as a punishment (§4).

As background to the incarnation of royal souls, Isis unveils the order of the cosmos (§§1–3). It has four regions, each ruled by an appropriate king. The divine Craftsman rules the gods in heaven; the Sun rules the stars in the aether, the Moon rules the souls in the air, while the human king rules people on earth. All kings are emanations of the highest king (the Craftsman). The theory represents the principle of correspondence: "as above, so below."

The human king on earth is a virtual god – an idea with a long pedigree in Egyptian royal theology. There are two types of kings, distinguished according to the dignity of their soul. One kind of royal soul leads a blameless life and is destined to be deified. The other kind is already fully divine and is incarnated specifically to rule on earth (§4). In both cases, embodiment is not a punishment but a service.

Surprisingly, the character of royal souls is determined less by their innate qualities than by their retinue. Practically speaking, ancient peoples would have normally dealt with a king's subordinates (who could be blamed in case of maladministration). The retinue of royal souls are angels (divine messengers) and daimones (lesser divinities), though these two types of being are not strongly differentiated. The incarnated king, according to the character of his escort, makes war or peace, legislates, makes music, or practices philosophy (§§5–6).

Horus then asks why certain souls are nobler than others. The tractate preceding SH 24 speaks of sixty different soul grades (SH 23.15–16). The tractate following it (SH 25.13) tells of sixty different soul regions. SH 24 states that royal souls descend from a higher level (§3) and that there are more glorious regions from which nobler souls descend as well (§7).

The author seems to assume that nobler souls are born as males. He admits that the distinction between male and female only makes sense when souls are embodied (§8). Nevertheless, the nobility of a soul seems to be expressed by its being born in a male body. In section 9, the author appeals to physiological distinctions among male and female bodies to naturalize their putative differences in character.

Horus then asks how intelligent souls arise. Isis responds by comparing the soul to the eye. The eye has the innate power of sight, just as the soul has the power of intelligence. Nevertheless, the aerial membranes of the soul – just as the membranes of the eye – can cloud the power of intellect (§10). The soul requires these aerial membranes, apparently, in order to inhabit a body.

Intelligence is also affected by climate. Egypt, as it turns out, has the best climate for producing intelligent souls. Egypt's temperate climate depends on its central location on the earth's surface. A vivid image illustrates this centrality (§§11–12). Earth is imagined as a woman lying on her back. Her head is Ethiopia, her buttocks and thighs constitute Greece, and her calves and feet are spread out as northern Europe. This leaves the region of her chest or heart aligned directly over Egypt. The Egyptians and Stoics agreed that the heart was the location of human intelligence and the command center for the entire body. Thus all the bodily virtues in which other ethnicities excel Egyptians excel in too – with the addition of a keener intelligence.

It remains to discuss chronic illnesses that lead to dumbness and dementia (considered to be diseases of the soul). Isis explains these illnesses by her theory of elements. Creatures are naturally adapted toward some elements and repelled by others. So also with the divine soul. It prefers and rejects some elements, but is at home in none. Thus it must struggle continually against bodily ailments. If the body has a bad mixture of elements, the soul also suffers (§§16–18). In this passage, we are perhaps not far from modern theories of chemical imbalance which can dramatically affect psychological states.

From the Same (Book)

1. *Isis:* "As for you, my great-souled son, if you desire something else, make your request."

Horus replied: "O richly honored mother, I want to know how royal souls are born."

The Embodiment of Royal Souls

Isis answered: "My child Horus, the difference that distinguishes royal souls can be described as follows. There are four places in the universe subject to inviolate law and authority – namely heaven, aether, air, and most sacred earth. Gods, my child, dwell above in heaven. They are ruled, along with all the others, by the Craftsman of all. In the aether dwell the stars.[1] Their ruler is the great light-giver, the Sun. In the air, souls dwell by themselves, ruled by the Moon.[2] On earth dwell humans and the other animals, ruled by the current king. Gods, my child, give birth to kings worthy of being their offspring on earth.[3]

2. Rulers are emanations of the king, and the one nearest the king is more kingly than the others.[4] Hence the Sun, inasmuch as he is nearer to God, is greater than the Moon and more powerful. The Moon takes second place to the Sun in rank and power.

3. The king is last in the rank of the other gods, but premier among human beings.[5] As long as he dwells on earth he is divorced from true

[1] The aether is the upper, purer atmosphere not affected by clouds and mist. The gods of heaven in SH 23 appear to be star gods (including the planets).

[2] Here reading μόναι ("alone") with P. Compare SH 25.9: "The region from the moon to us, my son, is the dwelling place of souls"; Philo: "The air is the dwelling of bodiless souls" (*On Dreams* 1.135). Plutarch, following Empedocles, calls purified souls "daimones" (*Face of the Moon* 30 [*Moralia* 944c]).

[3] Ancient Egyptian kings enthroned were considered to be manifestations of Horus, son of the divine Osiris. See further Scott, "Egyptian Elements," 80–85.

[4] "Rulers" suggests a large administration of governors under the sole king or emperor, as in the Roman Empire.

[5] The divinity of kings is an idea native to Egypt (Ph. Derchain, "L'authenticité de la inspiration égyptienne dans la Corpus Hermeticum," *Revue de l'Histoire des Religions* 161 [1962]: 175–98 at 183–86; David P. Silverman, "Divinity and Deities in Ancient Egypt," in Byron E. Shafer, ed., *Religion in Ancient Egypt: Gods, Myths, and Personal Practice* [Ithaca: Cornell University Press, 1991], 9–87 at 58–87), but basic to Roman imperial theology as well. Firmicus Maternus, for instance,

divinity. Yet he possesses a quality superior to other human beings – an element like unto God. This is because the soul sent down into him is from that realm higher than the one from which other people are sent.[6]

4. Souls are sent down from that realm to rule for two reasons, my child. Some souls, destined to be deified, run through their own lifetime nobly and blamelessly so that, by ruling, they train to hold authority among the gods. The other group of souls are already divine and veer only slightly from the divinely inspired ordinance. They are sent into kings so as not to endure embodiment as a punishment. On account of their dignity and nature, they suffer nothing like the others in their embodiment. Rather, what they had when free (of the body) they possess while bound to it.[7]

The Character of Kings

5. Now the character differences that develop among kings are distinguished not by a distinction in their soul. All royal souls are divine. The differences arise by virtue of the soul's angelic and daimonic retinue during its installation. For such great souls descending to such great tasks do not descend apart from an advance parade and military escort. For Justice on high knows how to apportion dignity to each soul, even though they are pushed from the placid realm.[8]

observes that the emperor "is also considered among the number of the gods whom the Supreme Power has set up to create and conserve all things" (*Mathesis* 2.30.5). There was often a dialectic between the divine office of the king and the human office-holder. What may be implied here is that the king stands on the borderline between humanity and divinity and would thus qualify as a "divine human" (θεῖος ἄνθρωπος, as in Plato, *Sophist* 216b).

[6] Compare SH 26.2, 8, 10: "Those sent down to rule, Horus my child, are sent down from the upper zones . . . Some leap down from the royal stratum whence the souls have the disposition to rule . . . Now the one who rules all, my child, is from the upper realms"; Cicero: "The governors and protectors of these [commonwealths] proceed from here [heaven] and return there (after death)" (*Dream of Scipio* 3.1); Vergil, *Eclogues* 4.7: the divine child is sent down to rule from high heaven (*caelo demittitur alto*). Manilius refers to "royal souls" (*regales animos*) who touch the summits of the world bordering on heaven (*Astronomica* 1.42 with the comments of Bull, "Tradition of Hermes," 151–55; Ecphantus the Pythagorean: "the king is an alien and foreign thing which has come down from heaven" (quoted in Stobaeus, *Anthology* 4.7.64 [Hense 4.275, lines 1–3]).

[7] Iamblichus conceived of some souls as making a pure descent to help in the administration of worldly affairs. "The soul that descends for the salvation, purification, and perfection of this realm makes even its descent in an undefiled way. The soul, on the other hand, that interacts with bodies for the exercise and correction of its own character is not entirely free of passions and was not sent away unburdened in itself" (*On the Soul* 29, Dillon and Finamore). See further John F. Finamore, *Iamblichus and the Theory of the Vehicle of the Soul* (Chico, CA: Scholars Press, 1985), 96–101.

[8] For the king's retinue, see Scott, "Egyptian Elements," 85–96.

6. Whenever the angels and daimones escorting the soul downwards are warlike, Horus my child, then the soul has the ability to take over their disposition. This soul is oblivious of its own deeds, or rather it remembers them up until it is joined by a different escort. Conversely, when the angels and daimones are peaceful, then the soul runs through the course of its own life doing the works of peace. When they practice the art of justice, then the soul also exercises justice. When they are musical, then the soul also sings. When they love the truth, then the soul also practices philosophy.

Thus it is by necessity that these souls take over the disposition of those who escort them. They fall into humanity oblivious of their own nature – all the more when greatly separated from it. Yet they recall the character of those who shut them up (in the body)."

Noble Souls

7. *Horus:* "You relate all things to me well, Mother," said Horus. "You have not yet told me how noble souls are born."

Isis: "As on earth, Horus my child, there are different ways of life, so it is in the case of souls.[9] Souls also have realms from which they spring, and the soul from the more glorious realm is nobler than those not of the same condition. Just as among people, the free person is thought nobler than the slave, for what is superior and royal in souls necessarily enslaves the inferior. 8. In this way, male and female souls are born.

"The souls, my child Horus, are of like nature to each other, inasmuch as they are from a single locale where the Craftsman shaped them. They are neither male nor female. Sexual differentiation occurs in bodies and does not apply to bodiless beings.[10] 9. The difference between the fiercer souls and the gentle ones is the air, my child Horus, in which all things are born.[11] Air is the very body of the soul and its covering.[12]

The body is a molded composition of the elements earth, water, air, and fire.[13] Now since the female composite has more of the wet and cold, it

[9] Here reading πολιτεῖαι ("ways of life") with FP.

[10] Compare Clement of Alexandria: "against the one who divides male and female, the soul makes them one, since the soul is of neither gender" (*Stromata* 3.13.93.3). Compare Athenagoras, *On the Resurrection* 23.4: "there is not in them [i.e. souls] the differentiation of male and female."

[11] Holzhausen takes this sentence as a gloss (*CH Deutsch*, 2.454, n. 370).

[12] Compare the vapor in SH 26.13, 25.

[13] For the body as made of four elements, compare Plato: The young gods "borrowed parts of fire, earth, water and air from the world . . . and bonded together into a unity the parts they had taken [to create the human body]" (*Timaeus* 42e–43a); Philo: "Every person . . . in the structure of the

lacks the dry and warm. For this reason, the soul shut up in this sort of molded body becomes moist and dainty. The reverse is found in the case of the males. In them, there is more dryness and heat, with a deficit of the cold and moist. For this reason, the souls in these kinds of bodies are rougher and more active."[14]

Climate and Intelligence

10. *Horus:* "How do intelligent souls arise, mother?"

Isis replied: "The seeing eye, my child, is covered by membranes.[15] When these membranes are thick and dense, the eye does <not> see well; whereas if they are thin and light, then sight is most keen.[16] The same applies to the soul. It has its own incorporeal envelopes, just as the soul itself is incorporeal. These envelopes are the air layers in us.[17] When they are light, thin, and transparent, then the soul is intelligent. When, conversely, they are thick, dense, and clouded, then the soul does not see far – as in stormy weather – but only what lies at its feet."[18]

11. Horus asked: "For what reason, mother, are the people outside our most sacred land not truly wise in their deliberations like our people?"

body is adapted to all the world, for he is a blend of the same things, namely earth, water, air, and fire" (*On the Creation* 146–47). Alcinous: "The gods molded humanity primarily out of earth, fire, air, and water" (*Handbook of Platonism* 17.1); *Ref.* 33.7 (humanity constructed from every substance); Firmicus Maternus, *Mathesis* 3, proem §2: "God the creator, copying nature, has made man in the image of the universe, a mixture of four elements" (trans. Jean Rhys Bram).

[14] Compare Aristotle: "females are weaker and colder in their nature" (*Generation of Animals* 4.6, 775a14). In Macrobius, *Saturnalia* 7.7.2–7.7.7, however, the Egyptian scholar Horus tries to prove that female nature is warmer than that of males.

[15] Compare *Ref.* 8.10.4: "We only see the eyelids, the whites of the eye, the membranes, the iris with its many folds and fibers, the cornea, and underneath it the pupil, the choroid membrane, the retina, the lens – and any other membranes for the light of the eye that enrobe and conceal it."

[16] Compare Aristotle, *Generation of Animals* 5.1, 780a25–29: "the nature of the skin over the so-called pupil must be translucent, and (this layer) must be thin and white and even."

[17] Air is incorporeal in the sense that it is a subtle body, not thick and dense like flesh. On the airy or pneumatic garment of the soul, see CH 10.13: "the soul is in the breath"; SH 23.40: God "bestowed breaths on all the souls." Compare the "murky and moist breath" mentioned by Iamblichus, *On the Mysteries* 4.13. Plotinus conceived of the soul as riding on πνεῦμα, a πνεῦμα that can be polluted based on bodily habits (*Enneads* 3.6.5.24). He referred to a πνεῦμα around the soul in *Enneads* 2.2.2.21. See further E. R. Dodds, *Proclus. Elements of Theology*, 2nd edn. (Oxford: Clarendon Press, 1963), 313–21, esp. 317; Finamore, *Iamblichus and the Theory*, 1–32.

[18] Porphyry described the pneumatic membrane as becoming dark by attracting humid exhalations (*Sentences* 29). See the comments of Luc Brisson in *Porphyre. Sentences*, 2 vols. (Paris: J. Vrin, 2005), 2.593–96.

Isis replied: "The earth in the center of the universe lies on its back like a person viewing the sky.[19] She is divided into as many limbs as the human body possesses. She looks up into the sky as to her own father so that by his transformations she can coordinate the transformation of her own properties. Her head lies toward the southern portion of the universe, her right shoulder to the east, <her left shoulder toward the west,> her feet are under the Bear constellations in the north, <her right foot under its tail>, her left foot under the Bear's head.[20] Her thighs, in turn, are in the regions that come before the Bear, and the center of her body under the central regions of the sky.[21]

12. The sign of this is that people in the southern areas who dwell on the crown of the head have fine heads and lovely hair.[22] Those in the east have a penchant for fighting and archery – for their right arm is their *raison d'être*.[23] Those in the west are secure in the face of danger. In accordance with their geographical position, they mostly fight with the left hand. To the degree that other people are active on the right side, these people incline to the left. Those under the Bear have <forward-springing> feet and especially strong calves.[24] Those who live a short distance before them [along the latitude of what is now Italy and Greece] are all endowed with fine thighs and beards.[25] As a result of the extraordinary beauty of their thighs, men there stoop to sexual intercourse with other men.[26] 13. Since all these limbs of earth's body are inactive with regard to the other parts of the body, they make the people who live in those regions inactive.

[19] The Egyptian god Geb (Earth) was imagined as a man lying on his back facing the sky. For Greeks, however, Earth (Γῆ) was feminine.

[20] The Bear referred to here is the constellation Ursa Maior. Compare SH 6.13–14.

[21] On Egyptocentrism, see Morenz, *Egyptian Religion*, 42–49; Ph. Derchain, "L'authenticité," 182. Compare the topographical human of Hippocrates, who depicts the head and face as the Peloponnese, the Bosporus as the feet, and Egypt as the belly (*On Hebdomads* 11).

[22] Those living south of Egypt under the direct sun are depicted with thick woolly hair by Ptolemy (*Tetrabiblos* 2.2), Vitruvius (*Architecture* 6.1.4), and Strabo (*Geography* 2.2.3).

[23] One might also understand the text (τοξιανούς) to say that these people are "born under Sagittarius." Sometimes certain nations are said to be under particular signs of the zodiac as in Ptolemy, *Tetrabiblos* 2.3.

[24] "Forward-springing" translates προτενεῖς, the emendation of Desrousseaux. Ferguson suggests παχυσκελεῖς (thick-legged, *Hermetica*, 4.468). The MSS read πρός τινα.

[25] Here reading εὐπωγονότεροι (well-bearded) with FP. The phrase in brackets was probably a marginal gloss.

[26] Here reading μηρῶν ("thighs") with FP. For same-sex relations linked to astrology, compare Ptolemy, *Tetrabiblos* 2.3: "because of the occidental aspect of Jupiter and Mars, and furthermore because the first parts of the aforesaid triangle are masculine and the later parts feminine, they [Europeans] are without passion for women ... but are better satisfied with and more desirous of associations with men" (trans. F. E. Robbins).

Since the most sacred land of our ancestors lies in the center of the earth, and the center of the human body is the precinct of the single heart, and the heart is the headquarters of the soul, for this reason, my child, people in this region possess these other fine qualities no less than all other people.[27] In distinction to all others, however, they have a superior intelligence and moderation as those born and raised in the region of the world's heart.[28]

14. The southernmost region is especially <sluggish>, my son, since it is susceptible to clouds condensed from the surrounding air.[29] They say that our river flows from the precipitation of the clouds formed there during the ice melt.[30] Whenever a cloud descends, it turns the air around it into mist, and saturates it so that it has the appearance of smoke.[31] Smoke and mist is not only an impediment to the eyes, but to consciousness as well.

The eastern region, high-famed Horus, is disturbed by the intensity of the rising sun and is extremely hot. Likewise, the opposite western region shares the same problems when the sun sets. These regions cause a complete lack of focused attention among the peoples born there. The northernmost region numbs by its whistling cold both the bodies and consciousness of those born under its power.[32]

[27] According to the Egyptian "expounders of sacred truths," the heart is the dwelling of the soul (Tertullian, *On the Soul* 15.5). This view was generally associated with the Stoics. Compare Pseudo-Hippocrates: "for human intelligence grows by nature in the left chamber [of the heart] and rules over the rest of the soul" (*The Heart* 10); Lucretius *On the Nature of Things* 3.136–40. The heart, as the body's control center, experiences all the strengths of the body as a whole.

[28] For Egypt as the heart, see Plutarch, *Isis and Osiris* 33 (*Moralia* 364c). Compare *Ascl.* 24: Egypt is "the temple of the whole world." Greek authors agreed about the effects of climate on intelligence, but naturally preferred their own regions. See, for instance, Plato, *Timaeus* 24c: "the goddess established your State [Athens], choosing the spot wherein you were born since she perceived in it the temperate blend of the seasons, and that it would bring forth men most intelligent" (compare Pseudo-Plato, *Epinomis* 987d); Aristotle, *Politics* 7.6.1, 1327b20–34: "The nations who live in cold places and in [northern] Europe are full of drive, but lacking in intelligence and skill . . . The nations of Asia are intelligent and inventive in soul, but lack drive and so continue to be subjugated and enslaved. But the Hellenic race, situated in the middle regions, participates in both. That is, it is both driven and intelligent." Vitruvius made similar claims about Italy: "within the space of the whole world and the regions of the earth, the Roman people possess the territory at the very middle. For in Italy the people are best balanced in both the members of their body and the aspects of their mind" (*Architecture* 6.1.10–11). See further, Bruce Lincoln, *Theorizing Myth: Narrative, Ideology, Scholarship* (Chicago: Chicago University Press, 1999), 114–18.

[29] "Sluggish" (νωθρός) is Theiler's addition.

[30] "Our river" is the Nile. For theories on the origin of the Nile flood, see Seneca, *Natural Questions* 4A; Aelius Aristides, *Orations* 36; Ammianus Marcellinus, *Historical Events* 22.15.4–8.

[31] Here reading γενομένων with P.

[32] Compare Servius: "He [Vergil] says that the dissimilarity exists not in souls but in bodies, inasmuch as they are lively or sluggish and accordingly make souls either lively or sluggish . . . Hence we see that Africans are cunning, Greeks fickle, and Gauls rather sluggish in mind because nature produces

15. The central region, however, is separate from these ailments and untroubled. It is superior in itself and by virtue of all its inhabitants. In unremitting serenity it generates, adorns, and instructs. Only with those in need of instruction does it quarrel and claim the victory. Although set in charge of them, it even lavishes, like a good satrap, its own victory upon the vanquished."[33]

Diseases of Soul

16. *Horus:* "Explain this also to me, my queenly Mother. For what reason is human speech and reasoning itself and the very soul sometimes beset with chronic diseases while people are still alive?"

Isis answered: "Among living beings, my child, some feel at home in the fire, some in the water, some in the air, and some on earth; some feel at home in two or three elements and some in all of them. Conversely, some living things are estranged from fire, some from water, some from earth, some from air, some from two elements, some from three, and some from them all.

17. For example, the cricket and all flies, my child, flee fire. The eagle, hawk, and all birds that soar on high avoid water. Fish avoid air and earth. The snake spurns the pure air. Snakes and all reptiles love the earth, and creatures that swim love the water. Creatures that fly love the air in which they live, all that soar high and <are> near to air by virtue of their mode of life.[34] There are also certain animals that love fire. Salamanders, for instance, even lurk in the fire.[35]

their climate ... Ptolemy says that a person transferred to another climate in part changes his nature" (*Commentary on the Aeneid* 6.724). Compare Posidonius, who "says that in different localities men's characters exhibit no small differences in cowardice and daring, in love of pleasure and of toil, the supposition being that the affective movements of the soul in every case follow the physical state, which is altered in no small degree by the mixture (of elements) in the environment" (Galen, *Doctrines of Hippocrates and Plato* 5.5.23, trans. Phillip de Lacy).

[33] The satrap analogy of cosmic administration is developed by Pseudo-Aristotle, *On the Cosmos* 398a27–398b27; Philo, *Decalogue* 61; *Ref.* 5.26.3; Philostratus, *Life of Apollonius* 1.27; Origen, *Against Celsus* 8.35.

[34] Here adding ἔχει after ἐγγύς.

[35] Compare Philo: "Animals attached themselves to the large-scale divisions of the universe: land animals to earth, swimmers to water, winged creatures to air and the fire-born to fire" (*Noah's Work as a Planter* 12). Aristotle said that the salamander walks through fire and extinguishes it (*History of Animals* 5.19, 552b15–17; compare Aelian, *On Animals* 2.31); Pliny that salamanders can extinguish fires (*Natural History* 10.188). Compare Cicero: "There are some beasts that are even thought to be born in fire and often appear flying in burning furnaces" (*Nature of the Gods* 1.103).

18. Each of these elements serve as a covering for these bodies. Every soul in the body is weighed down and oppressed by these four elements. Accordingly, it is natural that the soul likes some elements and dislikes others. For this reason, the soul does not enjoy the height of its happiness. Rather, because the soul is divine by nature, it struggles amidst these elements. The soul has understanding, to be sure, but does not understand the things it would if untethered from bodies. Whenever bodies experience restlessness and turmoil, whether from disease or fear, then the soul itself is heaved by waves – like a person in the open sea – and produces nothing stable."[36]

[36] For the wave image, compare Plato: "The [embodied] souls, then, being thus bound within a mighty river neither mastered it nor were mastered, but with violence they rolled along" (*Timaeus* 43b); Philo: "The other souls descending into the body as though into a stream have sometimes been caught in the swirl of its rushing torrent and swallowed up in it" (*Giants* 13).

SH 25

Stobaeus transmits the following excerpt toward the end of his long chapter "On the Soul" (the same chapter as SH 3, 17, 19, 20, 23–24, and 26). It is immediately preceded by selections from Iamblichus's treatise *On the Soul.* It is directly followed by what appears below as SH 26.

SH 25 seems to assume, and perhaps originally followed, SH 23 (the *Korē Kosmou*). The heart of the *Korē Kosmou* tells the story of the souls' creation and embodiment. Accordingly, Horus first thanks Isis for telling him about the souls' embodiment (SH 25.1). He wants to know what happens immediately after souls depart from their bodies.

Strongly rejected here is the Epicurean idea that souls are dispersed like smoke. Dispersal is impossible, given that the soul is simple (made up of a single substance), immortal, and divine. In addition, although the soul was made from divine breath, it exists as something qualitatively different than air. Thus it retains its integrity as it soars through the air, just like water runs over oil.

The more precise question, then, is what realm or realms souls occupy after death. As it turns out, the soul occupies one of the levels of air that exist between the moon and earth. It naturally ascends to its own level, just as creatures of sky, water, and land seek their own natural element. There are sixty distinct levels of air, just as there are sixty grades of souls in the *Korē Kosmou* (23.16). The air strata have four main divisions in which there are four, eight, sixteen, and thirty-two subdivisions as one ascends higher (§§11–13). The height to which the soul ascends depends on the soul's nobility. This nobility hinges, at least in part, on the soul's choices during bodily life.

An Excerpt of Hermes: A Discourse of Isis with Horus

1. *Horus:* "Wonderfully have you told me in detail, Isis my supremely powerful mother, about God's wondrous creation of souls – and I persist

in wonder. Still, you have not yet declared to me where the souls go when freed from their bodies. Thus I desire, after having become an initiate in this vision as well, to bestow thanks on you alone, immortal mother."[1]

2. Isis replied: "Pay close attention, my son, for this inquiry is utterly indispensable. 3. Well then, here my teaching shall begin.

The Destiny of Souls after Death

What subsists and does not pass away occupies a realm. For souls released from bodies do not pour forth in a jumbled heap into the air, my wondrously great child of a great father Osiris, dispersed amidst all the remaining boundless breath.[2] In this case, these souls would no longer be able to go back into bodies with their identities preserved. Nor would they return any more to that realm from where they came at first. In the same way, water received from uplifted jars cannot flow back to the same place from which it was taken.[3] Nor does water occupy its own place after being taken and poured out. Rather, it is mixed with the confused mass of liquid.

4. The release of souls is not like this, high-minded Horus. Now as an initiate of immortal Nature, and as one who has traversed the Plain of Truth, I will relate to you the actual realities in each single detail.[4]

This I will say first, that water is a body lacking reason, compressed from many compounds into a confused mass of liquid. The soul, by contrast, is

[1] For the metaphor of initiation, compare §4 below. For the language of mysteries, compare §11 below with SH 23.2–5, 44, 68. See further Christian H. Bull, "The Notion of Mysteries in the Formation of the Hermetic Tradition," in *Mystery and Secrecy in the Nag Hammadi Collection: Ideas and Practices. Studies for Einar Thomassen at Sixty*, ed. Einar Thomassen and others (Leiden: Brill, 2012), 399–425.

[2] Isis alludes to Epicurean views wherein souls are "dispersed like smoke when released from bodies" (Sextus Empiricus, *Against the Mathematicians* 9.72). Compare Lucretius, *Nature of Things* 3.434–39: "Now therefore, when you observe … how cloud and smoke disperse in the air, believe that the soul too is dispersed much more swiftly and is rapidly dissolved into the elements immediately upon leaving and receding from human limbs." The language goes back to Plato, and indeed to Homer. Plato says that people fear that when the soul leaves the body "straightaway it flies away and is no longer anywhere, scattering like a breath or smoke" (*Phaedo* 70a). The soul of Patroclus is depicted as going under the earth like smoke (Homer, *Iliad* 23.100–1). For boundless breath, compare the "aetherial breath" in SH 29.8.

[3] Here reading ἄνω ("uplifted") not κάτω as in FP.

[4] For the Plain of Truth, compare Plato, *Phaedrus* 248b (fitting pasturage for the best part of the soul is in the Plain of Truth); Pseudo-Plato, *Axiochus* 371c (Minos and Rhadamanthys judge the dead in the Plain of Truth); Plutarch: the Plain of Truth is where "the forms and the patterns of all things that have come to pass and of all that shall come to pass rest undisturbed" (*Obsolescence of Oracles* 22 [*Moralia* 422b]).

its own proper entity, my child – something royal, a work of the hands and consciousness of God – a work that by itself is guided into consciousness.[5]

Now something that arises from a single substance and not from another cannot be blended with something else.[6] For this reason, it is necessary that the soul's adaptive connection to its body come about by divine compulsion.[7] 5. The soul does not proceed toward its same and single realm diffused, haphazardly, and by chance. Rather, each soul is sent up to its own proper region. This point is clear from the pains that the soul – coarsened contrary to its own nature – suffers while still in the molded body.[8]

Natural Habitats

6. Now pay attention, dearest Horus, to my reiterated comparison. Imagine that into one and the same cage are enclosed humans, eagles, doves, swans, hawks, swallows, sparrows, flies, snakes, lions, leopards, wolves, dogs, rabbits, cows, sheep, and other animals that hold both water and land in common – such as seals, water serpents, turtles, and our crocodiles.[9] Then imagine that in a single instant these animals are released from their cage.

7. Will not all the people make their way to the markets and houses? Will not the eagle make its way into the aether, the place of his natural domain? Will not the doves dwell in the air nearest the earth and the hawks above them? Will not the swallows dwell where people do and the sparrows around fruit-bearing trees? Will not the swans dwell where they can sing? Will not the flies dwell close to earth itself, keeping apart from it only so far as they can rise to the smell of human beings – for the fly, my child, is both peculiarly greedy for human flesh and flying near the ground. Will not the lions and leopards dwell in the mountains and the

[5] For God's creation of souls, compare SH 23.14–15.

[6] The soul is composed from fire, breath (πνεῦμα), and certain unknown materials (SH 23.14).

[7] The soul is not blended with, but adapted to the body. Compare SH 15.6: "The soul has no natural urge to be with a body"; DH 7.4: "The soul goes into the body by necessity (κατ' ἀνάγκην)." The soul does not go into a body willingly, as is vividly depicted in SH 23.33–34.

[8] The soul adapted by the body is affected by the body's pains and passions. Compare Plato: the bad soul is "interpenetrated with the corporeal which intercourse and communion with the body have made a part of its nature" (*Phaedo* 81c).

[9] Nock adds ὕδατος καὶ γῆς ("water and land," NF 4.69, apparatus *ad loc.*). The crocodiles highlight the Egyptian local color of the dialogue.

wolves in deserted places? Will not the dogs follow human footsteps, the rabbits hop into the brush, cattle lumber to stables and fields, and sheep walk to their pastures? Will not snakes dwell in the crevices of the earth? Will not seals and turtles with their like dwell in the lowlands and streams so that they are not deprived of level ground or removed from their congenial water? Will not each creature turn to its own place by its own inner decision?[10]

8. In this way, each soul incarnated as human or dwelling on earth in some other form knows where it must go – unless some follower of Typhon were to step forth and tell us that a bull can live its life in the depths of the sea or a tortoise in the air![11] Now if the souls plunged in flesh and blood do not transgress order even when punished – and embodiment is their punishment – how much more will they enjoy their own proper freedom when <they are freed> from the punishment of being plunged in the body?[12]

[10] Compare the Greek legend of Tefnut: "Hermes says . . . 'All things that exist prefer nothing more than the place of their birth. Each is strong, well-adapted, and prosperous in its own ancestral territory" (printed in Stephanie West, "The Greek Version of the Legend of Tefnut," *Journal of Egyptian Archaeology* 55 [1969]: 161–83 at 166–67). Similarly Pseudo-Aristotle: "if one held in the folds of one's cloak an aquatic animal, a land animal, and a winged animal, and then threw them out all together, clearly the animal that swims will leap into its own habitat and swim away, the land animal will crawl off to its own customary pursuits and pastures, and the winged creature will rise from the ground and fly away high in the air; a single cause has restored to all of them the freedom to move, each in the manner of its species. So too in the case of the cosmos" (*On the Cosmos* 398b30–399a1, trans. D. J. Furley); Galen: "If you raise each one of them [an eagle, a duck and a snake] in the same house, then release them outside, the eagle will soar up to the heights, the duck will fly down into a pond, and the snake will crawl into the earth" (*Use of Parts* 1.3.7; similarly Philo, *Who is the Heir* 237–38).

[11] Seth-Typhon, the brother and murderer of Osiris, came to represent confusion and irrationality. Plutarch describes Typhon in *Isis and Osiris* 27 (*Moralia* 361d): "through envy and spite he wrought terrible deeds and, producing confusion everywhere, filled the whole earth and sea with evils." A follower of Typhon (literally "someone Typhonic") was thus someone who introduced confusion and disorder. In Plato, *Phaedrus* 230a, Socrates examines whether he is himself a "tangled Typhon." See further H. te Velde, *Seth, God of Confusion* (Leiden: Brill, 1967).

[12] Wachsmuth adds ἀπολυθεῖσαι (here: "they are freed"). On the body as punishment, compare SH 23.25–41. The idea goes back to Pythagorean and Orphic teaching. See, for instance, Empedocles frag. 11 (Inwood = DK 31 B115): "There is an oracle of Necessity, an ancient decree of the gods . . . whenever one by wrongdoing defiles his dear limbs with blood . . . [I speak of] the daimones who are allotted long-lasting life, this one wanders for thrice ten thousand seasons away from the blessed ones, growing to be all sorts of forms of mortal beings through time, interchanging the painful paths of life." Compare Athenaeus: "Euxitheus the Pythagorean used to say that all people's souls are bound to the body and the present life in order to punish them, and that God has announced that if they do not remain in their bodies until he wills to release them, they will be afflicted with more and greater outrages" (*Learned Banqueters* 4.157c).

The Cosmic Order of Souls

9. The most sacred ordering (of heavenly realms) is as follows. Look up already, my magnificently noble son, at the ordered arrays of souls! From the pinnacle of heaven to the moon is the place reserved for gods, stars, and the other Providence.[13] The region from the moon to us, my son, is the dwelling place of souls.[14]

10. Now the great mass of air contains a current which we are accustomed to call "wind." It is the peculiar layer in which air is moved for the refreshment of earthly beings – a point to which I shall return.[15] Yet in no way is this recycled air a hindrance to souls. For even when the wind moves, souls can fly up and down without hindrance wherever chance may lead. They flow through the wind without mixing or fusing with it, as water flows over oil.[16]

11. This mediating region of the air, Horus my son, has four main divisions and sixty separate strata.[17] The first main division contains four strata. It proceeds from the ground and stretches as far as the hills and ridges. Above these heights it does not have the nature to exceed in altitude.

From this point, the second main division contains eight strata in which wind currents arise. Pay attention, my son, for you listen to the secret mysteries of earth and heaven and all the sacred breath in between![18] Where there are wind currents, there birds can fly. Above this point, air can neither move nor support an animal. This air has the ability to cycle through its own eight regions and – against its nature – the four regions of the earth together with the animals contained in it. Yet the (strata of the) earth can <not> rise to the eight strata of the wind.

[13] A different, slightly more complex, partition is present in SH 24.1. The "other" (ἄλλῃ) Providence may designate the higher Providence (SH 26.2) as opposed to the lower, which in Hermetic thought would be Necessity. "According to Aristotle, the world is divided into many different parts. Our part of the world, which extends from the earth to the moon, lacks providential care and direction. It is self-sufficient by virtue of its own nature alone. In contrast, the part from the moon until the outer surface of heaven is ordered with all providential care and direction" (*Ref.* 7.19.2). Compare Theophrastos, frag. 162 (FHSG 1:326–27). See further Robert W. Sharples, "Aristotelian Theology after Aristotle," in Frede and Laks, eds., *Traditions of Theology*, 1–40 (22–26).

[14] The dwelling place of souls is the air, as made clear in §11. Section 10, something of an interlude, discusses the nature of air. Compare Plutarch: "All soul, whether without mind or with it, when it has issued from the body is destined to wander in the region between earth and moon" (*Face in the Moon* 28 [*Moralia* 943c]).

[15] See §11 below. [16] For souls dwelling in the air, compare SH 23.11; 24.1.

[17] Compare the sixty classes of souls in SH 23.16.

[18] Compare the similar exhortation in SH 23.32.

12. The third main division comprises sixteen strata full of air that is subtle and pure.

The fourth main division comprises thirty-two strata in which there is the most subtle, pure, and translucent air. This air makes its upper limit the higher, naturally fiery heavens.

13. Now this arrangement of strata proceeds in a straight line from above to below, with there naturally being no fusing of the different strata. Consequently, there are four main divisions, twelve intermediate divisions, and sixty strata.[19]

In these sixty strata dwell the souls, each one according to its proper nature. The souls are of one and the same constitution, but not of the same rank.[20] For as much as each stratum is higher than the one closer to earth, so much do the souls contained in the higher levels surpass those in the lower. Each region and soul, my child, falls short of those of higher dignity. 14. Which souls are released into the higher and lower realms I will commence to tell you in turn, greatly renowned Horus, starting from those above to those nearest earth."[21]

[19] Theiler suggested that the original number of intermediate regions was fifteen (ιε') since the four main divisions stand in a relation of 1:2:4:8, which adds to fifteen. Perhaps the twelve regions should be emended to "winds" (for twelve winds, see Pliny, *Natural History* 2.119; Seneca, *Natural Questions* 5.16.3–5.17.4).

[20] In SH 24.8 souls are said to be of "like nature."

[21] If Isis begins from the top, then she would start with the return of royal souls to their heavenly homes. The embodiment of royal souls is the subject of SH 24. See also SH 26.8–11.

SH 26

Stobaeus transmits this excerpt as the last of his long chapter called "On the Soul" (the same chapter as SH 3, 17, 20, 19, and 23–25). It is immediately preceded by what is classified here as SH 25.

Although the tractate is labeled "On the Incarnation and Reincarnation of Souls," it is more concerned with the question of why souls are qualitatively different.[1] Initially the difference seems to be based on the hierarchical placement of the soul in heaven. But this ranking is in turn influenced by the soul's moral decisions. Virtue leads to promotion and vice to demotion. At the end of the tractate, it is explained how the vapor that surrounds the embodied soul also has an effect on the soul's character.

As if picking up the thread from SH 25, SH 26 begins to speak of the layered regions in which disembodied souls dwell. Yet the conception of these regions is different and they are not numbered at sixty. What is important in SH 26 is the hierarchical arrangement of souls. Souls of the highest quality (namely, royal souls) dwell in the highest regions; souls of the lowest quality inhabit the lowest regions.

Yet based on its deeds during bodily life, a soul can be promoted or demoted in the heavenly hierarchy. Providence manages the promotions and demotions. She has two ministers: a Steward and Escort of souls. The Steward protects the disembodied souls, and the Escort assigns them to bodies.

Down below, Nature crafts the bodies (called "tents") that serve as receptacles for souls. Nature likewise has two ministers: Memory and Experience. Memory records the character of the soul when it enters and exits the body so that the soul can be accurately judged; Experience adapts bodies so that they fit the character of the descending soul. Animal souls

[1] Scott, *Hermetica*, 3.598.

are penned up in animal bodies. Only an intelligent soul enters a human body. Yet simply because a soul fits its body does not mean that all souls obey their nature.

All sorts of souls descend, including many kinds of royal souls. Royal souls do not simply become kings, but any persons at the top of their class or profession. Thus the leaders in philosophy, medicine, and literature all possess types of royal soul. Royal souls come from the fieriest regions above. Souls that come from more airy and humid regions take up more technical occupations.

The character of persons and animals is also determined by the mix of elements in their bodies. Each body has an elemental mixture. This mixture exudes a kind of vapor which surrounds and qualifies the soul. Animals have a different elemental mixture than humans. In humans, there is an excess of fire which is converted into intelligence. Maintaining the peculiar balance of one's elemental mixture is the key to health and wellbeing for all creatures.

On the Incarnation and Reincarnation of Souls

1. *Isis:* "The region between earth and heaven is divided, my child Horus, according to measure and harmony. Our ancestors sometimes called these regions 'zones,' sometimes 'solid plates,' and sometimes 'ribbons.'[2] Among these regions, the souls released from bodies roam along with those that have not yet been embodied. Each of these souls, my child, has its own rank and realm. As a result, the divine and royal souls dwell in the highest region of all, while the base souls of least rank dwell in the lowest region of all, and the intermediate souls dwell in the intermediate region.

2. Those sent down to rule, Horus my child, are sent from the upper zones. When released, they return to the same regions or ascend even higher unless some of them did something <against> the dignity of their own nature and the precept of divine law. The higher Providence exiles these souls among the lower regions according to the degree of their errors,

[2] The zones refer to the planetary zones, or the spheres governed by the seven planets, as in CH 1.25. Compare Pseudo-Plutarch: "Thales, Pythagoras, and the Pythagoreans divide the sphere of the entire heaven into five circles which they call zones" (*Opinions of the Philosophers* 2.12 [888c]). "Plates" (στερεώατα) can also be translated "firmaments." The Jewish deity creates a single "firmament" (στερέωμα) in Genesis 1:6. The use of "ribbons" (πτυχαί) is poetic, as in Euripides, *Phoenician Women* 84: "O Zeus who lives in heaven's shining ribbons"; compare his *Orestes* 1636.

just as she raises those of lesser power and rank from the lower realms to those higher and more honorable.[3]

3. On high, general Providence has <two> ministers. One of them serves as Steward of souls and the other as their Escort. Now the Steward of souls <watches over unembodied souls>, and the Escort is the sender and assigner of embodied souls. The first watches over the souls while the second dispatches them according to the judgment of God.[4]

4. By analogy, my son, Nature on earth conforms to this alternation of affairs on high. She is the molder and tent-maker of the vessels <into which> souls are thrown.[5] Two active Powers attend her as well, namely Memory and Experience. The work of Memory is this: that Nature observe and hold firmly (in mind) the type of each individual originally thrown down as well as the composition of each individual who arrives above.[6]

Experience has the task of making the bodily formation suitable for each of the souls descending into bodies. She makes those swift in their soul swift in body, and those slow in soul slow in body. She grants active bodies to active souls, sluggish bodies to sluggish souls, strong bodies to strong souls, furtive bodies to furtive souls. In a word, she grants (a body) fitting to each soul.[7]

5. Not without purpose did Nature furnish birds with feathers and adorn rational creatures with heightened and more precise powers of perception.[8] Not without purpose did she fortify some four-footed animals

[3] Compare SH 23.38–41. The thought stems from Plato: "Since a soul is ever coordinated with different bodies at different times and undergoes all sorts of transformations for its own sake or that of another soul, no task remained to the divine Chess-player except to transfer the better character to a better place, and the worse character to a worse place, as was fit for each of the souls so that they receive their appropriate fate" (*Laws* 903d).

[4] The role of the Soul Steward and the Soul Escort recall the roles of Osiris and Anubis, respectively, in Egyptian mythology. They also resemble Plato's *daimones*, as in *Phaedo* 107e: "when each person dies their daimon whom they acquired in life leads them by the hand to a certain place where those gathered must be judged and proceed to Hades with their leader whose task is to lead them there. When they have ... stayed the necessary time, another guide conveys them back here (to earth) again after much time and long revolutions." In Greek mythology, Hermes was widely known as the "Soul Escort" (ψυχοπομπός) (Homer, *Odyssey* 24.1–12; Vergil, *Aeneid* 4.242; *Ref.* 5.7.30–41). Discussing Pythagorean lore, Diogenes Laertius explains: "Hermes is the steward of souls (ταμίαν τῶν ψυχῶν), and for that reason is called 'Hermes the Escort' (πομπαῖον) ... since it is he who brings in the souls from their bodies from both land and sea" (*Lives of Philosophers* 8.31).

[5] Here reading ἀγγείων with FP. For the body as tent, compare Excerpt 2A.1 with note 2 there.

[6] The composition (φύραμα) may refer to the original composition of the souls mixed by God as in SH 23.14–16 or their composition before their embodiment (assuming that past embodiments have already occurred).

[7] Compare Galen: "Nature prepares the body to suit the soul's traits of character and powers" (*On Semen* 2.2.5, trans. De Lacy).

[8] Stoics credited humans (rational animals) with keener senses, as in Cicero, *Nature of the Gods* 2.145.

with horns, some with teeth, and others with claws and bodily armor. She softened reptiles with sleek and supple bodies; and in order that they not remain excessively weak due to the moistness of their bodies, she lined the mouths of some with rows of sharp teeth and clothed others with power by sharpening their bulky bodies with spikes. In this way, these animals by their cautionary behavior in the face of death end up stronger than others.[9]

To skittish creatures of the sea, Nature granted to live in the element in which light has no ability to activate either of its powers. That is to say, while in water, fire neither shines nor burns. Each individual sea creature flees wherever it wants by swimming with the help of scales and spines. They are suited in the armor of their own fear, using water as a means of protection to avoid being seen.

6. In each of these bodies, a corresponding soul was penned. Accordingly, souls that make judgments go into human beings, souls that avoid humans go into birds, souls without the power of judgment go into four-footed creatures – since sheer strength is their mode of operation. Deceitful souls go into reptiles since none of them attack people directly, but strike only in ambush. Fearful souls go into sea creatures and whatever souls are unworthy to enjoy the other elements.[10]

7. It so happens that in each <species> an animal can be found not behaving according to its own nature."

"What do you mean, mother?" asked Horus.

Isis replied: "A human does not behave according to its nature, my child, when it transgresses its faculty of judgment. A four-footed animal does not live according to nature when it bucks constraint. A reptile does not live according to nature when it loses its deviousness. A fish does not live according to nature when it discounts fear. Finally, a bird does not live according to nature when it fails to avoid human beings.

[9] Similar observations about animals are provided by Minucius Felix, *Octavius* 17.10: "Why speak about the various means of defense animals possess against each other? Some are armed with horns, some fenced with teeth, shod with hoofs, and spiked with stings, while others enjoy their freedom because of the swiftness of their feet or soaring wings"; Lactantius, *Workmanship of God* 2.1–4: "To each individual species God made their particular protection to repel external attacks, so that the stronger can fight back with natural weapons, and the weaker withdraw from danger by nimble flight, and so that those that lack both strength and speed might protect themselves by cunning or fence themselves in dens."

[10] Compare Plato, *Timaeus* 91e–92c. According to [Timaeus Locrus], the souls of "lightheaded and thoughtless" humans are clothed in the bodies of birds; the idle, ignorant, and foolish are clothed in the shape of water creatures (*On the Nature of the World and the Soul* 86 [104e]).

Enough, then, about the order of the souls above, their descent, and the making of their bodies.

Royal Souls

8. Now it happens, my child, that in each species and genus of the aforementioned animals, royal souls are found. All sorts of other souls descend as well. Some are fiery, some are cold, some are arrogant, others meek, <some are noble,> others perform menial tasks, some are experienced, others untried, some are sluggish, others energetic, some have this quality, and some another. This happens according to their position in the hierarchy of regions, regions from which souls are thrown down to be embodied.[11] Some spring down from the royal zone whence the souls have the disposition to rule.

9. There are many types of royalty. Some are royal in soul, others in body, others in artistry, others in science, and others in various occupations."

"What do you mean by this?" asked Horus.

"For example, Horus my child, Osiris your father is the king of souls already departed. The king of bodies is the leader of each nation. The king of wise counsel is the father and guide of all, Hermes Thrice Great. Asclepius son of Hephaestus is king of medicine. Osiris, once again, is the king of power and might, and you are second to him. Arnebeschenis is the king of philosophy.[12] Asclepius Imhotep, once again, is king of creative literature.[13] In general, my child, if you examine it, you will discover that there are many and various rulers and kings over many and various things.

10. Now the one who rules all, my child, is from the upper realms. But the one who rules over what is partial retains the <rank> of his place of origin. <The souls from the kingly> zone have a more kingly rank. 11. <Those from the fiery zone> become blacksmiths and cooks. Those from the watery zone live their lives on the water. Those from the zone of

[11] Reading καταβάλλονται ("are thrown down") with P²; P reads καὶ βάλλονται ("and are thrown"); F καὶ θάλλονται ("flourish").

[12] Har-neb-eschenis (Hellenized as Arnebeschenis) was Horus of Letopolis on the Nile delta. He was a god associated with magic and worshiped in the Greco-Roman period at Achmim and Kom Ombo.

[13] Asclepius Imhotep is apparently not different than Asclepius son of Hephaestus/Ptah. Compare *Ascl.* 37. The deified Imhotep was associated with scribal culture and was the reputed author of wisdom literature. See further SH 23.6, n.21.

science and craftsmanship spend their time in sciences and crafts. Those from the inactive zone live inactively and aimlessly.

Heavenly Influences

Up above there are springs for all the things that we do and say on earth. These springs pour down their essences upon us by measure and weight. There is not anything that has not descended from above. 12. In turn, what ascends does so in order to descend."[14]

Horus: "What do you mean, mother? Show me."

Isis explained again: "Most sacred Nature has placed this in animals as a clear sign of their return course: the breath that we draw from the air above. This we send up again so that we can receive it again.[15] Moreover, in us there are a pair of bellows that do the work of respiration.[16] When these bellows close their breath-receiving valves, then we no longer exist here, but have risen above.[17]

Elemental Blends

13. There are other things as well, my most famous son, that come from the equilibrium of our (body's) composition."[18]

"What is our (body's) composition, mother?" Horus asked.

Isis: "It is the assembly and blend of the four elements. From this blend and assembly, a vapor is exuded. This vapor wraps itself round the soul and runs through the body. To both – I mean body and soul – it bestows its own quality. In this way, arise the different variations that occur in souls and bodies.[19]

[14] Compare SH 11.2 §40: "The energies are not borne upwards, but downwards." But here (SH 26.12) Isis seems to refer to human souls that go up only to be reincarnated below.

[15] Compare the theory of respiration in Plato, *Timaeus* 79a–e. [16] Isis refers to the lungs.

[17] Compare SH 23.67: "If the breath is ever lacking, it produces a swoon from which there is no recovery."

[18] Compare Philo: "Now the composition (φύραμα) is literally we ourselves, composed and blended of many essences to reach completion. The creator of life mixed and blended opposing qualities: the cold with the hot, the dry with the moist, to make each of us a single compound from all qualities. Hence we are called a composition (φύραμα)" (*Sacrifices of Abel and Cain* 108).

[19] The vapor is a kind of substrate for the soul, but the substrate is not composed of breath or air (as in SH 24.9). It arises from the compositional blend of the four elements. Compare the vapor (ἀτμίς) exuded from the body's internal juices that can mix with the motion of the soul in Plato, *Timaeus* 87a. Note also the breath or spirit that surrounds the soul in CH 10.16. The idea may be traced back to Stoic conceptions in which the perceptive soul is produced by the evaporation of moisture from the body (blood) (Arius Didymus 39.2 quoted in H. Diels, *Doxographi Graeci*, 4th edn. [Berlin: de Gruyter, 1965], 470–71).

14. If fire predominates in the bodily frame, then the soul, already naturally hot, receives additional heat, becomes more enflamed, and produces an active and vigorous animal whose body is keen and agile. 15. If air predominates, then the animal will be light, springy, and unstable in soul and body. 16. If water predominates, then the animal will be easy-going, good-natured, and diffuse in its soul, able to associate with others and be joined to them due to water's cohesive and uniting quality.[20]

Water spreads over all things. When in large volumes, it surrounds and dissolves everything into itself. In small, reduced quantities, it becomes one with what it seeps into. The bodies in which water prevails, however, are not firmly entwined due to their moistness and porousness. Rather, by reason of a slight malady, these bodies are dissolved and gradually lose their own cohesion.[21]

17. If the earthly element predominates, then the soul of the animal is dull. Its body lacks supple tenuousness and the means to spring forth since its sensory organs are swollen. Within, the soul remains by itself chained down by weight and bulk. The body is solid but inactive, heavy, and moved by willpower only by force.

18. If the state of all the elements is balanced, then the animal is constructed as heated for action, light for movement, well-tempered for touch, and nobly fortified.

19. By this reasoning, those that share in abundant fire and breath are turned into birds and live on high among other elements from which they were born.

20. Those who share in abundant fire, a small amount of breath, and an equal measure of water and earth become human beings. In the human animal, the excess of heat is turned into intelligence. Consciousness in us is something warm. It cannot burn up, but pervades and presides over all things.[22]

[20] Compare Lucretius, *Nature of Things* 3.288–306 (the quality of internal air has an effect on temperament).

[21] Compare SH 23.30, 35.

[22] The Stoic Chrysippus explained that "there are two kind of fire, the one uncreative and converting fuel into itself; the other creative, able to produce growth ... like the fire in plants and animals" (Stobaeus, *Anthology* 1.25.3); Cleanthes, his successor, observed: "Now our ordinary fire that serves the needs of daily life is destructive, consuming everything ... Conversely, the bodily fire is life-giving and healthful; it preserves all, grows it, sustains it, and supplies it with sensation" (in Cicero, *Nature of the Gods* 2.41). The all-pervading mind (or consciousness) is a teaching ascribed to Anaxagoras in Plato, *Cratylus* 413c.

21. Those that share abundant water and earth with a moderate amount of breath and a small amount of fire become beasts. Some beasts become braver than other animals by the presence of heat.

22. Those that receive an equal portion of earth and water will turn into reptiles. By lacking fire, they are born wary and skittish; by sharing in water, they are cold; by sharing in earth they are heavy and sluggish; and by sharing in breath they are agile if they so choose.

23. The bodies that receive a greater amount of moisture and a small amount of dryness become fish. By the lack of heat and air, they also are timid. By virtue of their excess moisture and earthy material, they live in elements familiar to them, namely mud and water.

24. Their bodies mature in size according to the share of each element and the extent of each share. The remaining animals are measured according to a smaller measurement, according to an application that is appropriate for each of the elements.[23]

25. Once again, my dearly desired child, I say that from this (original) constitution the blending according to the first conjunction (of elements) and the vapor from this exhalation preserves its own character as much as it can. As a result, if the (creature's own) heat does not receive an alien influx of heat and the airy element does not receive an alien breath nor the moist element an alien moisture nor the earthy element an alien density, then the animal will be healthy.

But if (the animal's composition) does not remain in this state, my child, then the animal becomes sick. In this case, it does not preserve its original quantities of elements. Rather, the elements either increase <or decrease>. (Increase and decrease occur) not by extent or by growth of the animal species or individual animal bodies, but by a fluctuation in the aforementioned systemic blend of the elements. As a result, the hot excessively increases or decreases, and likewise with the other elements.[24]

26. When the hot and airy (elements) – those constant companions of the soul – are disposed (to increase within) the animal, then it succumbs to bizarre cries and spastic behavior. These (hot and airy) elements are condensed, and by their condensation the (animals') bodies break down.

27. The earthly element itself is the body's solidity, the moist element is what is spread out in the body for its cohesion, the airy element is what drives us, and the fire is the stimulating drive of all the elements.

[23] The "remaining animals" would seem to refer to smaller creatures such as insects and worms.

[24] A similar, if somewhat simpler, theory is proposed by Plato, *Timaeus* 81e.

28. So a vapor or, as it were, an act of combustion or exhalation – whatever exactly it is – arises from the first meeting and blending of the elements. This vapor blends with the soul and conforms it to its own nature – whether this nature be noble or not.[25]

29. The soul, by virtue of retaining its original kinship and shared communion with fiery breath, preserves its rank. Yet when a portion greater than what was designed is externally added either to the entire blend or to its parts or to a single part, at that moment the fluctuating vapor changes either the condition of the soul or that of the body. 30. For fire and breath, naturally rising, rush to the soul that belongs to the same (upper) region. Conversely, the moist and earthly elements, naturally descending, take up residence in the body that belongs to the same environment."[26]

[25] A somewhat similar notion appears in Plato: "When any of a man's acid and briny phlegm or any bitter and bilious humors wander up and down his body without finding a vent to the outside . . . they mix the vapor that they give off with the motion of the soul and so are confounded with it. So they produce all sorts of diseases of the soul" (*Timaeus* 87a).

[26] Experience, servant of Nature (§4), originally makes the elemental blend of bodies balanced to receive the appropriate soul. The elemental blend can be thrown out of balance, however, by the increase of elements that are attracted to either soul or body.

SH 27

SH 27 derives from a chapter in Stobaeus' *Anthology* (3.13.65) called "On Bold Speech." It is immediately preceded by several quotations attributed to Socrates and followed by a quotation of Pythagoras.

The excerpt is a single-line maxim stating the role of philosophical refutation. Plato spoke of refutation as a cleansing agent that removes false and inconsistent opinions (*Sophist* 230c–d). Ideally, the recognition of ignorance and accompanying feeling of shame leads to a desire for knowledge and a consequent search for it (*Meno* 84c). Refutation, in this sense, is the beginning of knowledge.

This teaching is attributed to Isis and bestowed upon Horus, who is here christened with the title "greatest of kings." Normally one would expect such a title to be reserved for Osiris, king of power and might (SH 26.9). Yet Horus logically inherits his father's rule.

Hermes: An Excerpt from a Discourse of Isis to Horus

A refutation recognized, O greatest of kings, drives the one refuted to desire things formerly unknown.[1]

[1] In SH 23.4, ignorance rules first, then God supplies the will to search and the desire for knowledge. Compare Plato, *Meno* 84c: "Do you think that before he would have tried to find out that which he thought he knew ... before he fell into perplexity and realized he did not know and longed to know?" For Hermetic discourses addressed to a king, see CH 16.1 (to king Ammon); CH 17 (to an unnamed king).

SH 28

Taken from Stobaeus's *Anthology* 1.1.29a, SH 28 comes from a chapter entitled "God is Craftsman of Existing Things and Pervades the Universe with his Design of Providence." It follows a long quote of unknown Platonists and precedes a doxographical passage from Aëtius's *Opinions of the Philosophers.* Both passages deal with the nature and identity of God.

"What is God?" (*ti theos*) was a standard philosophical question in antiquity. In the present excerpt, Hermes rubs shoulders with the oldest natural philosopher as well as the most famous dialectician – Thales (approximately 624–546 BCE) and Socrates (470–399 BCE), respectively. Hermes's answer to the question "What is God?" introduces two new ideas: God is a Craftsman (or creator) and God is Consciousness or Mind. The latter idea was associated with Anaxagoras of Clazomenae (approximately 500–428 BCE) and the former with Plato's *Timaeus.* Despite this philosophical pedigree, Hermetic devotees claimed these two fundamental notions for their own master, Hermes.

Hermes on God

When Thales was asked, "What is the most ancient of all existing things?" He replied: "God; for God is unborn."[1]

When Socrates was asked, "What is God?" he said, "What is undying and eternal."[2]

[1] Compare Diogenes Laertius, *Lives of Philosophers* 1.35, and the nearly identical answer of Solon in Plutarch, *Banquet of the Seven Sages* (*Moralia* 153c–d).

[2] Compare Aristides of Athens frag. 1.3.2: "I call God . . . he who is without beginning and eternal (ἀΐδιον), immortal (ἀθάνατον) and in need of nothing"; "God is not born, not made; a constant nature, without beginning and without end; immortal, complete, and incomprehensible" (Greek text in J. Rendel Harris and J. Armitage Robinson, *The Apology of Aristides on behalf of the Christians* [Cambridge: Cambridge University Press, 1891], 100).

When Hermes was asked, "What is God?" he said, "The Craftsman of the universe, a Consciousness most wise and eternal."[3]

[3] "Hermes" was not entirely original. "Anaxagoras says that God is mind, the maker of the cosmos" (Anaxagoras testimony A48, Curd). Compare Anaxagoras frag. B12 (Curd): "Consciousness (Νοῦς) controlled the whole revolution [of the cosmos], so that it started to revolve in the beginning" (from Simplicius, *Commentary on Aristotle's Physics* 156.13). Plato likewise reported that for Anaxagoras "Consciousness is the arranger and reason for everything" (*Phaedo* 97b). According to Aristotle, Anaxagoras "above all makes Consciousness (Νοῦς) the principal of all things" (*On the Soul* 1.2, 405a15). As stated by Pseudo-Plutarch, Thales and Democritus identified God with consciousness (νοῦς) as well (*Opinions of the Philosophers* 1.7 [881d]). See further TH 32 from the *Book of Twenty-four Philosophers*.

SH 29

Taken from Stobaeus's *Anthology* 1.5.14, SH 29 appears in a chapter called "On Fate and the Good Ordering of Events." Unlike all other Stobaean excerpts, SH 29 is a poem written in hexameters. It has a total of fourteen lines (twice the number of the seven planets). The text is preceded by a quote from Sophocles's *Phaedra* and is followed by a section of Aëtius's *Opinions of the Philosophers* in which various authors define the nature of Fate.

The poem is itself entitled "On Fate," apparently because Fate is the government of the seven planets (CH 1.9). The content of the poem, however, depicts the planets affording their own distinctive traits on human beings. Humans are not allotted a planet. Instead, the planets are allotted to human beings. The medium of planetary influence is the "aetherial breath," the pure upper air of the cosmos. The gifts of the planets are not entirely good or bad. All the planets bring something necessary to make the experience of being human complete.

The same poem is also transmitted in certain astrological manuscripts of the fifteenth century CE.[1] In several manuscripts, the poem is left anonymous or attributed to the Sicilian philosopher Empedocles (about 490–430 BCE).[2] Although the poem has some overlap with Hermetic lore (note especially the gifts of the planets in SH 23.28), there seems to be nothing about it distinctly Hermetic. Naturally, Hermes is mentioned in his role as the planet Mercury, but the assigning of the poem to Hermes seems secondary.

On Fate. An Extract from Hermes

Seven much-wandering stars turn round the Olympian threshold,
And with them time ever travels:

[1] NF 4.98 n. 1. [2] NF 4.99, apparatus.

Moon shining in the night, sullen Saturn, sweet Sun,
The Paphian[3] who bears the bridal bed, violent Mars, well-winged Mercury,
And Jupiter the progenitor, origin of nature's bloom.
These same stars have obtained by lot the race of mortals. Among us there are
Moon, Jupiter, Mars, the Paphian, Saturn, Sun, and Mercury.[4]
From their influence, we are allotted to draw from the aetherial breath[5]
Tears, laughter, rage, reproduction, reason, sleep, and desire.
The tears are Saturn,[6] Zeus is reproduction,[7] Mercury is reason,[8]
Anger is Mars,[9] Moon is sleep,[10] Cytheria desire,[11]
Sun is laughter – for by him all mortal intelligence
Rightly laughs together with the infinite cosmos.[12]

[3] A name for Aphrodite, or the planet Venus, based on her cult site in Paphos, Cyprus.

[4] In the *Palatine Anthology* (9.491) this line with slight changes is attributed to the mathematician and astronomer Theon of Alexandria (335–405 CE). See John Malalas, *Chronography* 13.36, quoted below in the Addendum: The Reception of Hermetic Fragments from Cyril.

[5] Aether is the fiery medium in which the fixed stars and planets run their course (Zeno in Diogenes Laertius, *Lives of Philosophers* 7.137).

[6] Saturn "makes tears (δάκρυα)" (Vettius Valens, *Anthology* 1.8).

[7] "Reproduction" (γένεσις) could also be translated "birth" or "generation." According to Vettius Valens, Jupiter signifies "having children" (τέκνωσιν), offspring, or the act of generation (γονήν) (*Anthology* 1.17).

[8] Vettius Valens agrees that Hermes signifies "reason" (λόγον); he is also the "giver of discursive thought and wisdom" (δοτὴρ καὶ διανοίας καὶ φρονήσεως) (*Anthology* 1.37–38). Compare SH 19.1: "While united <to a body> it [the soul] draws to itself discursive thought characteristic of the (planetary) harmony."

[9] According to Vettius Valens, Mars represents "force, wars, seizures, shouts, outrages ... wrath, battle, foul speech, enmity" (*Anthology* 1.21); Macrobius makes Mars the source of "fiery spirit" (*animositatis ardorem*) (*Commentary on the Dream of Scipio* 1.12.14).

[10] Naturally people sleep at night under the influence of the shining moon. In some writers, it may be suggested that the Moon (Selene) put her lover Endymion to sleep, for instance Ovid: "See how the moon does her Endymion keep / In night concealed, and drowned in dewy sleep" (*Amores* 1.13; compare Cicero, *Tusculan Disputations* 1.92).

[11] Cytheria is one of Venus's names (Vergil, *Aeneid* 1.257) derived, according to John Lydus, from her powers of conception (τὸ κύειν, *On Months* 4.64 printed in Scott, *Hermetica*, 4.231). According to Vettius Valens: "Venus is desire (ἐπιθυμία) and erotic love"; she also gives "laughter and joy" (*Anthology* 1.28, 31). Servius on *Aeneid* 6.714 makes her bestow *libido* and desires (*cupiditates*, 11.51). According to Macrobius, Venus gives the impulse of passion (*desiderii ... motum*) (*Commentary on the Dream of Scipio* 1.12.14).

[12] Compare the planetary vices in CH 1.25 and their gifts in SH 23.28–29. Note also Servius, *Commentary on Aeneid* 6.714: "when souls descend, they drag with them sluggishness from Saturn, wrath from Mars, sexual desire from Venus, love of money from Mercury, desire to rule from Jupiter"; *ibid.*, 11.51: "as the natural philosophers say, when we are first born we are allotted breath from the sun, a body from the moon, blood from Mars, innate talent from Mercury, desire for honor from Jupiter, erotic desires from Venus and moisture from Saturn"; Isidore of Seville, *On the Nature of Things* 3.4: "The pagans ... say that they have spirit from the sun, body from the moon, language and wisdom from Mercury, pleasure from Venus, fervor from Mars, temperance from Jupiter, and sluggishness from Saturn" (trans. Kendall and Wallis). On planetary influences, see further Tamsyn Barton, *Ancient Astrology* (London: Routledge, 1994), 102–13; Roger Beck, *A Brief History of Ancient Astrology* (Malden: Blackwell, 2007), 70–82.

Oxford Hermetica (OH 1–5)

Introduction

In 1991, J. Paramelle and Jean-Pierre Mahé published Hermetic fragments from a manuscript housed in the Bodleian Library at Oxford.[1] The manuscript, called codex Clarkianus gr. 11, is dated to the thirteenth or fourteenth century. The Hermetic excerpts are located on pages 79–82 of the manuscript. They are preceded by a thirty-seven-page anonymous anthology containing quotations from classical but mostly Christian (patristic) authors. They are followed by two exegetical scholia on Exodus 20:5 ("punishing children for the iniquity of parents, to the third and the fourth generation") and Genesis 6:15–16 (the dimensions of Noah's ark).

On pages 79–80 of the codex there are fragments of CH 12.1–2, 3, 4, 6, 10, 11, 13, 14, 21; 13.7; 14.6 and 7. On pages 80–81 there are excerpts of the *Definitions of Hermes Trismegistus to Asclepius* that correspond to DH 4.1; 5.1; 6.1–3; 7.2–3; 8.3, 7; 9.1–3, 5.[2] On page 81 there is a line from CH 16.4 ("fire, water, and earth depend on a single root"). Finally, on pages 81–82 there are Hermetic fragments previously unknown. These fragments, called here the "Oxford Hermetica" (OH) are translated below.

The Oxford Hermetica deal with diverse topics: the soul, the senses, law, psychology, and embryology. They do not seem to have originally been part of the same Hermetic collection. Instead, the excerpts were anthologized by an unknown author at an unknown time. In terms of content, the OH fragments resemble SH 8, 15–20, and especially 15–17, which are addressed to Ammon.

Festugière detected in SH 15, 19 (for him the continuation of 17), and 22 the influence of the pneumatic medical school, and specifically the

[1] Joseph Paramelle and Jean-Pierre Mahé, "Extraits hermétiques inédits dans un manuscrit d'Oxford," *Revue des Études Grecques* 104 (1991): 109–39. The translation of OH below is based on their text.

[2] For these excerpts, see J. Paramelle and J.-P. Mahé, "Nouveaux parallèles grecs aux Définitions Hermétiques arméniennes," *Revue des Études Arméniennes* 22 (1990–91): 115–34.

Medical Definitions of Pseudo-Galen. Although the pneumatic school arose in the first century CE, the *Medical Definitions* date to the third century CE. Within these limits, one can reasonably date OH 5, though a date in the late second or early third century seems preferred. The other Oxford fragments, because of their similarity with SH and lack of Neoplatonic thought, can be dated to roughly the same time period.

OH 1

On the Soul

1. <. . .> Therefore the soul as bodiless, without shape, without parts and opposed to the incidental traits of the body such as shape, color, and the very alienation that affects bodies, <is a being that is> always stable and permanent. By virtue of a single (factor), it maintains its own immortality since it always belongs to itself.[1]

The soul does not need anything else to preserve itself, and shares in neither movement nor birth.[2] 2. An entity of this kind does not have birth; what is not born does not grow; what does not grow is not diminished; what is not diminished is not corrupted; what is not corrupted is without change;[3] what does not change is stable; what is stable is unmoved by bodily change and efflux; what is unmoved is self-moved by nature; what is self-moved is immortal and intellectual because of intellect – and this would be the power of intelligent reality.[4]

[1] For the soul as bodiless, compare SH 16.1; SH 20.1. The incorporeal soul is therefore like both God (SH 1.2) and truth (SH 2A.15). On the incidental traits (or accidents) of the body, compare SH 8.4. Permanent stability is attributed to intelligent reality in SH 18.4. The immortality of the soul is because of its rational part (SH 11.2, §8).

[2] Here reading αὑτήν ("preserves *itself*") with Paramelle and Mahé ("Extraits hermétiques," 131) not the αὐτήν of the MS. Compare SH 8.5: "The intelligible reality, when in direct relation to God, has power over itself. In the act of preserving something else, it preserves itself, since its very substance is not subject to necessity"; SH 18.5: "The soul . . . does not participate in the nature of created beings" including the body, as in SH 19.4. The soul without movement may refer only to erratic bodily motions (the motion of soul and body are distinguished in SH 3.2–3). The soul is itself ever-moving (SH 3.1; 16.1).

[3] Compare SH 20.2: "For everything that has birth must experience change. What comes into being is born in a particular size and needs growth. Everything that experiences growth also experiences diminishment, and with diminishment comes decay"; SH 2A.16: "Decay follows every birth"; Excerpt 11.2 §5: "What is ever born ever decays. What is born once never decays or becomes something else."

[4] One could also translate: "and this would be the faculty (δύναμις) of intellectual reality." This statement shows that we are dealing with the soul in its essential (intellectual) purity apart from drive and desire. Compare DH 10.7 (= SH 19.1): "Now the soul is an eternal intelligent reality, employing intelligence as its own rational faculty." For intellectual reality (νοητὴ οὐσία), compare SH 8.5.

OH 2

Senses and Elements

1. In the eye is the power of seeing, <in the ears the power of hearing, in the nostrils the power of smelling, and> in the tongue is the power of taste.[1] 2. Each of these has its counterpart in the four elements: sight aligns with fire, hearing with air, smell with water, and taste with earth.

[1] Power (δύναμις) seems to be the word linking OH 1 and 2. They may or may not come from the same treatise. I follow Paramelle and Mahé by supplementing in angled brackets <ἐν δὲ ὠσὶ δύναμις ἀκουστική, ἐν δὲ ῥισὶ δύναμις ὀσφρητική> ("Extraits hermétiques," 132).

OH 3

Laws without Justice

1 <. . .> By opinion human beings laid down a law that serves as a guide to those who judge lawsuits because they have abandoned the true Justice, and the eternal soul joined with a body.[1] 2. They accuse each other and are accused, practicing mutual hatred rather than mutual affection, hatred of humanity rather than human kindness, ignorance instead of knowledge.[2] Through their ignorance they draw to themselves misfortunes and bouts of distress, the condition of their stupidity.[3] Inexperienced in truth, they abound with clever tricks. 3. For this reason, heaven is pure of such laws.[4]

[1] The soul eternally joined to its body could be the souls in the stars, the soul in the Sun, or the World Soul in the cosmos. Compare SH 3.5: "The divine soul is the energy which propels its divine body." Compare the law of human necessity in DH 8.1: "there is a law which is in heaven above destiny, and there is a destiny which has come into being according to a just necessity; there is a law which has come into being according to the necessity of humans." For the figure of Justice, compare SH 7.1 below.

[2] Compare DH 10.6: "The immortal (beings) agree with one another and the mortal envy one another with jealousy, because evil envy arises due to knowing death in advance." For criticism against litigiousness, compare 1 Corinthians 6:1–11.

[3] Unhappiness is caused by the failure to recognize reality as it is. Compare CH 10.8: "the vice of the soul is ignorance."

[4] Compare SH 11.2 §18: "There is no good upon earth; there is no evil in heaven"; SH 11.2 §29: "Everything in heaven is blameless; everything on earth is blameworthy"; SH 11.2 §43: "The earth is non-rational, while heaven is rational."

OH 4

Reason versus Drive and Desire

1. Whenever the power of human drive is pulled away from reasoning, it becomes the mother of audacity. Audacity becomes a varied vice, and so hatred is rife among the wicked.[1] 2. Whenever desire is pulled away from reasoning, it gives birth to pleasure. Then desire, in a state of rebellion, invents a twisted mass of misfortunes and is for all time walled up in human life.[2]

3. Pleasure, impending and impinging upon vision, gives birth to madness. It fires (the body) for immoderation and by this means joins it to sacrilegious intercourse; it invents horrible utterances, sacrilegious audacity, and excessive impiety, all the while producing a twisted mass of maladies.[3] <. . .>

4. For between consciousness and reason there is reasoning that <follows> consciousness.[4] Whenever the non-rational is dragged away from reasoning, ignorance and audacity are born.[5] But when reasoning

[1] Audacity caused the fall of souls (SH 23.24). Nevertheless, when drive conforms to reason, it becomes courage (SH 17.2).

[2] Conversely, when desire is conformed to reason, it becomes self-control (SH 17.2). Compare CH 4.5: "these people [who did not receive the gift of consciousness] have sensations much like those of unreasoning animals and, since their temperament is willful and angry, they feel no awe of things that deserve to be admired; they divert their attention to the pleasures and appetites of their bodies; and they believe that humankind came to be for such purposes."

[3] Similar heinous sins are attributed to daimones in CH 9.3.

[4] Paramelle and Mahé emend ἐπίμονος in the MS to ἑπόμενος ("following"). If we retain the manuscript reading, we could translate: "For between consciousness and reason there is reasoning that *remains* with consciousness." Compare SH 11.2 §15: "rationality is in consciousness." On the diverse types of rationality, see SH 18.1: "Reason surges toward (intellectual) reality," and SH 19.1: "Intelligent reality is the master of its own reason."

[5] Compare *Ascl.* 12: "For in this bodily life the pleasure one takes from possessions is a delight, but this delight, as they say, is a noose round the soul's neck that keeps humankind tied to the part that makes it mortal"; CH 7.3: pleasure causes one not to hear or observe what one must.

peeks above the non-rational, then reasoning draws the non-rational to itself.[6] When reasoning takes hold of the non-rational, it fills it with understanding <to oppose> irrational impulses.[7]

[6] Compare SH 8.6: "Everything non-rational is moved by a certain rationality." For peeking above (ἀνακύπτω), compare the peeking below (παρακύπτω) of the primal Human in CH 1.14 (Jean-Pierre Mahé, "Mental Faculties and Cosmic Levels in the Eighth and the Ninth," in Søren Giversen, Tage Petersen, and Jørgen Podemann Sørensen, eds., *The Nag Hammadi Texts in the History of Religions: Proceedings of the International Conference at the Royal Academy of Sciences and Letters in Copenhagen, September 19–24, 1995* [Copenhagen: C. A. Reitzel, 2002], 73–83 at 77).

[7] Compare SH 17.3, 6: "Reasoning fills up the insufficiency of desire. The virtue of justice is born … when [drive and desire] are controlled by the soul's rationality … The discursive reason of reality, then, is knowledge of calculations that bestows a faded image of rationality in what is non-rational."

OH 5

The Process of Generation

1. A figure is an appearance and likeness of the generic form specific to bodies.[1] 2. A generic form is the pattern of the figure. Through the generic form and figure (Nature) acts as an artificer. She works in this way: when human sperm {. . .} collects in the brain and floats on top of it, (it becomes) a foam having in itself the power of generation.[2]

3. Whenever this (animal) has an impulse for sex, the above-mentioned sperm forcefully shoots into the womb.[3] 4. When the woman's reproductive matrix receives the sperm, it transforms it.[4] The matrix separates the fluid and corrupted element (from the sperm) and molds what remains with the cooperation of the breath-power contained in the sperm. It enlarges (the fetus), and once enlarged, it becomes an (embryonic) image.[5] 5. The matrix shapes and likens (the fetus) into the appearance of a likeness. When the likeness is generated, it is manifest in the body.

[1] Compare SH 15.4: "the generic form (τὸ εἶδος) is conveyed in the figure. The generic form is the means through which the (fetal) image is imaged."

[2] Compare SH 22.1: "When nourishing blood <foams up> and the genitals store away the seed, it somehow happens that a certain substance is breathed out from all parts of the body by divine operation." For sperm as foam, a theory attributed to Pythagoras, see Pseudo-Plutarch, *Opinions of the Philosophers* 5.3.2; Aristotle, *Generation of Animals* 2.2, 736a13–14: "productive foam causes semen to be white." For semen as strained and concocted blood, see Aristotle, *Generation of Animals* 1.19, 726b1–13.

[3] Compare *Excerpt of the Perfect Discourse* (NHC 6,8) 65.15–21 corresponding to *Ascl.* 21: "If you wish to see the reality of this mystery, then you should see the wonderful representation of the intercourse that takes place between the male and the female. For when the semen reaches the climax, it leaps forth."

[4] Compare SH 15.4: "This life-breath, injected into the womb, was not barren in the seed. As a productive force, life-breath begins the work of transformation."

[5] Compare SH 15.4: "When the seed is transformed, it becomes capable of growth and mass. The formed image is drawn in the mass which is shaped . . . The generic form is the means through which the (fetal) image is imaged."

6. The body takes on the likeness of the animal's shape in the womb. As it is molded in the uterus, (the fetus) breathes.[6]

7. Now the constitution (of the fetus) fitted together is the result of set measurements, and its features are, so to speak, loci of the generic forms specific to bodies.[7] 8. For whenever the feature receives the generic form, immediately the feature becomes like the generic form, and thus the feature becomes the design of the generic form according to the feature, and the feature is a bodily configuration. 9. The generic form precedes the configuration and the configured body is shaped, turned into a likeness, and made visible. 10. One birth differs from another, and the entity born differs from another.

11. Herein is the principle of the original creation, which is the birth of all things.[8] 12. As much as consciousness differs from consciousness's activity, so much does deity differ from divine activity, for what is godlike is made into god by God.[9]

[6] Other authors deny that the fetus breathes (Porphyry, *To Gaurus* 3.4; 10.3; *Ref.* 6.14.11). Compare SH 15.5: "life-breath does not possess vital motion in its womb, but only the motion that provides initial growth." See further I. M. Lonie, *The Hippocratic Treatises "On Generation", "On the Nature of the Child" and "Diseases IV"* (Berlin: de Gruyter, 1981), 146–56.

[7] SH 15.5: "Nature, serving as midwife, brings to birth what is in the womb into the outside air according to fixed measurements (of time)"; SH 16.3: "nor can it [the body] attain bodily structure apart from harmony."

[8] The creation of the human is related to the creation of the cosmos. They both instantiate the same principle.

[9] Compare CH 9.1: "consciousness differs from the activity of consciousness as much as God differs from divinity (νοήσεως ὁ νοῦς διαφέρει τοσοῦτον ὅσον ὁ θεὸς θειότητος)." The meaning of νόημα here in OH 5.12 and in SH 18.1 seems equivalent to νόησις ("thinking," "the activity of consciousness"). On God as the basis of deification, compare *Ref.* 10.34.5: "after you become a good imitator of the Good, you will be honored by him as one like him. God is not poor; for his glory, he makes you also a god!"

Vienna Hermetica (VH 1–2)

Introduction

The Vienna Hermetica consist of four fragments on the backside of two papyri housed in Vienna (*P. Graec. Vindob.* 29456 recto and 29828 recto). They belong to a single roll papyrologically dated to the end of the second or the beginning of the third century CE. The fragments attest a Hermetic collection of at least ten tractates, the ninth called "On Energies." They were initially published by H. Oellacher in 1951.[1] In 1984, Jean-Pierre Mahé published an improved text with commentary.[2]

On the front side of the papyri are fragments of the Jewish romance called *Jannes and Jambres*. These two characters are magicians said to have opposed Moses in Egypt.[3] The Jewish text on the front of the papyrus and the Hermetic text on the back may represent two different stages in the use of the papyrus. Usually, the back of the papyrus was inscribed first. If the writing on the back became effaced or the owner of the roll wanted to copy out another text, the front of the papyrus was sometimes used. If so, the Hermetic text on the back was the first text inscribed on the papyrus. Not long afterward, it seems, the other side was used to copy out the Jewish romance.

Possibly the owner of the papyrus desired both these texts for his or her library. The owner was not necessarily Jewish, but apparently someone interested in both (para-)biblical texts and Egyptian wisdom. The use of an

[1] H. Oellacher, "Papyrus- und Pergamentfragmente aus Wiener und Münchner Beständen," in *Miscellanea Giovanni Galbiati*, 3 vols., Fontes Ambrosiani 26 (Milan: Hoepli, 1951), 2.182–88.

[2] Jean-Pierre Mahé, "Fragments hermétiques dans les papyri Vindobonenses graecae 29456r° et 29828r°," in E. Lucchesi and H. D. Saffrey, eds., *Mémorial André-Jean Festugière: Antiquité païenne et chrétienne*, Cahiers d'orientalisme (Geneva: Cramer, 1984), 51–64 at 60. Mahé's text is used as the basis for the following translation.

[3] Jannes was known to Pliny the Elder in the first century CE (*Natural History* 30.1.11) and by Apuleius and Numenius in the second century CE (Apuleius, *Apology* 90; Numenius frag. 9, 10A [des Places]). The reference to Jannes and Jambres in 2 Timothy 3:8 can be dated to the early second century.

abbreviation (a *nomen sacrum*) for the name of God on the recto of the papyrus may suggest that its owner, or at least its scribe, was Christian. As Mahé notes, a third-century papyrus from Berlin (*Papyrus Berol.* 9794) juxtaposes a Hermetic prayer (CH 1.31–32) with Christian prayers, and the scribe of Nag Hammadi codex VI combined both Christian and Hermetic texts.[4] As can be surmised from the FH material, Christians were the most avid readers of Hermetica beginning in the third century CE.

If the two texts on the front and back of the papyrus are connected by the common interests of their reader(s), then Hermes Thrice Great might have been categorized as an Egyptian magician or wonderworker like Jannes and Jambres.[5] What Hermes says, however, has nothing to do with the practice of magic. Instead, Hermes discourses like a philosopher. Most of what he says has unfortunately been lost. The scant fragments that remain touch on two key themes in the Hermetica. First, humans alone have reason, and second, God is too great to be named.

[4] Mahé, "Fragments hermétiques dans les papyri Vindobonenses," 61.
[5] Mahé, "Fragments hermétiques dans les papyri Vindobonenses," 60.

VH 1

Humans Alone Have Reason

Hermes: <All> animals ... were <or>dained to be unreasoning, but those which are part of ... appear as energies ... <according t>o the manifestations of God.[1]

Tat: You speak truth, father, and have de<monstr>ated this point as well.[2]

Hermes: And you will discover God, O Tat, supplying a host of benefits among each one of us, whomever he wills (to benefit).

Tat: For this reason also, only <the> human race is <endowed with consciousness, O fa>ther.[3] The human race alone both knows God <and is kno>wn.[4] All the other animals are too <bent downwa>rd to under-s<tand> God, but those which are known all has[ten] ... toward the one who is eternally <born> ... to God.[5] This (teaching) is above le<arning[6] ... it is not a single thing in this world below ... <among every>thing born, <hu>manity has the ability to un<ite essentially> with God.[7]

1 For animal intelligence, compare SH 4.1–5 above with notes.

2 Here accepting Mahé's correction of τουτων to τουτον ("this point").

3 Compare CH 12.12: "God gave two gifts to humanity above all mortal animals: consciousness and reason (τόν τε νοῦν καὶ τὸν λόγον)"; *Ascl.* 6: "Of all living things, consciousness equips only the human, exalts it, raises it up to understand the divine plan"; *Excerpt from the Perfect Discourse* (NHC VI,7) 66.31–33 (corresponding to *Ascl.* 22): "to humans alone he accorded gnosis and knowledge"; *Prayer of Thanksgiving* (NHC VI,7) 64.8–10 (corresponding to *Ascl.* 41): "he bestowed on us consciousness, reason, and gnosis."

4 Compare CH 1.31: "Holy is God, who desires to be known and is known by his own people" (ὅς γνωσθῆναι βούλεται καὶ γινώσκεται τοῖς ἰδίοις); CH 10.15 (God is not ignorant of humanity but knows humanity fully and wants to be known). See further Festugière, *RHT*, 4.56–59; Mahé, "Fragments hermétiques," 56–57.

5 On hastening, compare CH 4.5: "those who participate in the gift that comes from God ... hasten toward the one and only"; SH 2B.7: consciousness "rushes toward the good."

6 For the Hermetic initiate, lessons are not taught, but remembered and experienced (CH 13.2). See further Wouter Hanegraaff, "Altered States of Knowledge: The Attainment of Gnōsis in the Hermetica," *The International Journal of the Platonic Tradition* 2 (2008): 128–63.

7 It is consciousness (νοῦς) that allows humanity to unite with God. Compare CH 12.19: "Humanity is both receptive of God and able to unite essentially with God" (ὁ ἄνθρωπος, ὁ καὶ τοῦ θεοῦ δεκτικὸς καὶ τῷ θεῷ συνουσιαστικός); *Ascl.* 5: "the one who has joined himself to the gods in divine reverence, using the mind (*mens*) that joins him to the gods, almost attains divinity."

VH 2

On Energies

... since he is good ... energy ... he being so great, these things ... On the topic of energies let what has been said suffice.[1]

(End of) Discourse 9

(Beginning of) Discourse 10

<In the> General (Discourses), O Tat, I have often spoken about ... in many discourses.[2] Now I consider it necessary (that this discourse) ... <my good> man, be for you.

On the subject of ... for ... in need of existing things, there is one thing or w<ondrous> signs ...

God without Name

The one God <requires no> name.[3] For the being <without a name> is <on>e ... God.[4] I persist with the <appellation> 'God,' since I desire to show what it signif<ies> ... the energy <and?> ... <the?> nature of his will ... in every place ... and it has come to be. For what is worthless ... no one ...

Note: Vienna fragments 3 and 4 are too lacunose to translate.

[1] On the topic of energies, see SH 3 and SH 4.6–9.

[2] On the General Discourses, see SH 3.1 with note 3 there.

[3] Cf. SH 1.2: "What cannot be expressed – this is God."

[4] Other possible translations: "The unique One who (truly) exists <does not have a name>" *or:* "Unique is the one who (truly) exists <and without name>." Compare FH 3a: "God is one. He who is one has need of no name, for he who truly exists is without name"; FH 3b (from Lactantius): "Hermes also affirms that God is without name because he needs no proper designation, since he is unique"; FH 11b (from Lactantius): "Hermes said that his name could not be expressed by a mortal mouth"; CH 5.10: "This is the God who is greater than any name"; *Ascl.* 20: "Given the greatness of this divinity, none of these titles (God, father, master of all) will name him precisely."

Hermetic Fragments from Various Authors (FH 1–45)

General Introduction

When approaching the Hermetic fragments, one must distinguish between a direct citation, a paraphrase, the employment of Hermetic ideas, and the mere naming of Hermes Thrice Great. In this section (FH), I strive to print only direct citations or paraphrases of Hermes Thrice Great. Moreover, I favor passages that do not appear elsewhere in Hermetic literature. Thus citations of CH and *Ascl.* by later authors are not included. Those interested in authors who employ Hermetic ideas or who refer in passing to Hermes should proceed to the Testimonies concerning Hermes Thrice Great (TH).

Fragments 1–37 as printed here adhere to the ordering in the edition of Nock and Festugière, *Corpus Hermeticum*, vol. 4, pages 101–50 (published in 1954). In 2009–11, Paolo Scarpi published an Italian edition of the fragments with a slightly different numbering system (*La Rivelazione segreta di Ermete Trismegisto*, vol. 2, pages 5–36). Scarpi's system tends to combine citations that are directly juxtaposed in the works of ancient authors. The logic of his ordering is acknowledged. For the sake of consistency and ease of citation, however, the internationally recognized numbering of Nock and Festugière is maintained.

The present translation supplements the edition of Nock and Festugière in several ways. At times, these editors did not include important citations from the authors they included. For instance, in the case of Tertullian, they cited and translated a single passage from his work *On the Soul*. Yet there are at least four relevant passages in Tertullian that relate to Hermes or Hermetic lore. These passages have been included below for the sake of completeness. The same practice is followed with other authors (such as Zosimus and John Lydus). In the case of Cyril, a long addendum has been added that traces the reception of specifically Cyrillian fragments in John Malalas, the *Tübingen Philosophy*, and several important Syriac texts. Nock and Festugière ended their edition with FH 37 (John Lydus). This translation includes fragments from additional authors such as Gregory of Nazianzus, Didymus of Alexandria, Gaius Iulius Romanus, Augustine, Quodvultdeus, Albert the Great, and Nicholas of Cusa.

There are no overarching themes that unite all the Hermetic fragments here translated. Their contents are dictated by the interests of those who quoted them. Frequently those interests also dictated the phrasing – or paraphrasing – of a particular quote. In some cases, modification of Hermetic ideas occurred either by contamination with other systems of thought or by forced interpretations. These kinds of modifications are prevalent among Christian authors who were, it seems, the most avid, if not the most careful, readers of the Hermetica in Late Antiquity. Of the forty-five fragments printed below, thirty-nine derive from Christian authors. The most frequent citers of Hermetica are Lactantius and Cyril, from whom twenty-six (thirteen each) of the fragments derive. The fragments are ordered by the date of the author who cites them, beginning with Tertullian in the early third century CE and ending with Nicholas of Cusa in the mid fifteenth.

Tertullian

Introduction

Quintus Septimius Florens Tertullianus – widely known as Tertullian – lived from approximately 160 to 225 CE. He converted to Christianity around 197 and became one of the first Christian theologians in the Latin west. His home was Carthage in North Africa where he received rhetorical and philosophical training. Later in life, Tertullian joined a rigorist renewal movement in Christianity known today as "Montanism." He is the first Latin writer to mention Hermes Thrice Great, and he provides the earliest reception of the Hermetic tradition in Latin.

Tertullian wrote thirty-one surviving treatises, but he mentions Hermes in only two. In his *Against the Valentinians* 15.1 (written 207–12 CE), he mentions Hermes Thrice Great in connection with speculation about the origin of matter. In his work *On the Soul* 2.3 (written about 210–13 CE), Tertullian mentions Hermes as one among several authorities who wrote holy scripture and were deemed to be divine. In this work, Tertullian goes beyond the common tradition that Plato visited Egypt by claiming that Plato closely approximated the teachings of Hermes. Tertullian also cites a certain Albinus to the effect that the Egyptian Hermes discovered the doctrine of reincarnation (*On the Soul* 28.1). Finally, Hermes is cited as a witness to the last judgment (*On the Soul* 33.2).

Even though Tertullian grants Hermes a measure of authority, overall his attitude toward the Egyptian sage was not only competitive but also hostile. According to Tertullian, philosophers only happen upon the truth by a kind of blind chance (*On the Soul* 2.1). Hermes's writings are not scripture. However great and authoritative Hermes seems to be, he came later than Moses, who was, unlike the Thrice Great, truly inspired.[1]

[1] On Tertullian see further, Claudio Moreschini and Enrico Norelli, *Early Christian Greek and Latin Literature: A Literary History*, trans. Matthew J. O'Connell, 2 vols. (Peabody, MA: Hendrickson, 2005), 1.332–33, 348–50; Geoffrey D. Dunn, *Tertullian* (London: Routledge, 2004), 3–11. Löw,

FH 1a

Tertullian, Against the Valentinians *15.1*[2]

Come now, let the Pythagoreans learn, and let the Stoics recognize along with Plato himself the source of matter which they want to be "unborn," and which they treat as the origin and substance for every mundane structure! This teaching that famous Hermes Thrice Great, teacher of all the natural philosophers, did not recognize.[3]

FH 1b

Tertullian, On the Soul *2.1, 3*[4]

Clearly I will not deny that sometimes the philosophers perceived matters resembling our doctrines ... It appears that (philosophy) drew these from putative sacred writings, since antiquity considered many authors to be gods, not to mention deified men like Hermes the Egyptian, to whom Plato especially adapted himself.

FH 1c

Tertullian, On the Soul *28.1*[5]

Now who is the source of that ancient teaching mentioned by Plato about the two-way traffic of souls? They depart from here, arrive there, then come back here and are born, so that we have people returning alive from the dead. Some attribute the doctrine to Pythagoras. Albinus considers it to be a divine pronouncement, perhaps, of the Egyptian Hermes.

Hermes, 48–59; Claudio Moreschini, *Hermes Christianus: The Intermingling of Hermetic Piety and Christian Thought*, trans. Patrick Baker (Turnhout: Brepols, 2011), 28–30.

[2] The text used for the following translation was edited by Jean-Claude Fredouille, *Tertullien. Contre les Valentiniens Tome 1*, SC 280 (Paris: Cerf, 1980), 114.

[3] For the Hermetic understanding of matter, see SH 2A.13; SH 9; SH 11.2 §34; FH 18 (from Iamblichus); FH 45c (from Nicholaus of Cusa).

[4] The text used for the following translation was edited by J. H. Waszink, *Quinti Septimi Florentis Tertulliani De Anima* (rpt. Leiden: Boston, 2010), 3.

[5] The text used for the following translation was edited by Waszink, *De Anima*, 39.

FH 1d

Tertullian, On the Soul *33.2*[6]

This the Egyptian Hermes also knew (namely, that souls must retain their consciousness of past deeds). He said that the soul, when it departs from the body, is not poured back into the soul of the All but remains distinct so as to give an account to the father concerning the things it did in the body.[7]

[6] The text used for the following translation was edited by Waszink, *De Anima*, 47.

[7] Compare SH 25.3–4: "For souls released from bodies do not pour forth in a jumbled heap into the air . . . dispersed amidst all the remaining boundless breath . . . The soul is its own proper entity." On rendering an account, note SH 7.3: humans "are subject to Justice due to their mistakes during this life;" CH 10.16: "When the soul rises up to itself . . . the mind . . . leaves the soul to judgment and the justice it deserves"; *Ascl.* 28: "When the soul withdraws from the body, it passes to the jurisdiction of the chief daimon who weighs and judges its merit"; 2 Cor 5:10: "all of us must appear before the judgment seat of Christ, so that each may receive recompense for what has been done in the body." For the soul of the All, compare CH 10.7: "In the General Discourses did you not hear that all the souls whirled about in all the cosmos . . . come from the one soul of the All?" See further Löw, *Hermes*, 59–64.

Pseudo(?)-Cyprian

Introduction

The work entitled *Idols are Not Gods* (*Quod idola dii non sint*, hereafter *Idols*) offers a sharp polemic against non-Christian religions and a brief exposition of the Christian faith. It has been traditionally ascribed to Cyprian, bishop of Carthage (who lived about 200–58 CE).[1] Both Jerome (*Epistle* 70.5) and Augustine (*On Baptism* 6.44.87) assigned the treatise to Cyprian, but it is not found in the manuscripts of his works. Pontius, Cyprian's biographer, does not ascribe the work to Cyprian either, and it is not listed in an early catalogue of Cyprian's oeuvre, a catalogue compiled about 359 CE.

Whoever the author of *Idols* was, he borrows from the Latin writers Minucius Felix and Tertullian (both active in the late second and early third centuries CE). Indeed, chapters 1–9 of *Idols* constitute an abridgement of Minucius Felix's dialogue called *Octavius*.[2] The sentence quoted as FH 2, however, does not appear in Minucius. Nevertheless Augustine quoted our very passage from *Idols* in his *On Baptism* (6.44.87), and so transmitted it to the Middle Ages.

Specifically, *Idols* begins as a vigorous polemic against deification as it was conceived and practiced in Greek and Roman civil religion. The author then turns to declare the unity and incomprehensibility of God, a doctrine for which Hermes is invoked as witness. If *Idols* is by a (probably young) Cyprian, it can be dated to the second quarter of the third century CE. If, as some scholars believe, the work uses passages from Lactantius, it must

[1] An English translation of the whole work can be found in *The Complete Works of Saint Cyprian of Carthage*, ed. Phillip Campbell (Merchantville, NJ: Evolution, 2013), 109–15.

[2] The passage that mentions Hermes agrees closely with Minucius Felix, *Octavius* 26.7–27.1. A comparison of these texts can be found in Joseph Bidez and Franz Cumont, *Mages hellénisés: Zoroastre, Ostanès et Hystaspe d'après la tradition grecque*, 2 vols. (Paris: Belles Lettres, 1938), 2.289–92.

be dated not long after 320 CE. In the latter case, the actual author and specific provenance of the work remain unknown.[3]

FH 2

Idols Are Not Gods *6*

Hermes Thrice Great as well affirms that there is one God and confesses that he is unable to be grasped and beyond human valuation.[4]

[3] See further Fowden, *Egyptian Hermes*, 211, n. 88; Löw, *Hermes*, 65, n. 239; Moreschini, *Hermes Christianus*, 30–31; Klaus Sallmann, *Die Literatur des Umbruchs von der römischen zur christlichen Literatur 117 bis 284 n. Chr.* (Munich: Beck'sche, 1997), 583–84.

[4] In context, Hermes Thrice Great is mentioned along with the Persian sage Ostanes and Plato as foreign witnesses to the incomprehensibility and unity of God (see further *Idols* 8–9). God's unity is selectively attested in Hermetic writings (for example, in *Ascl.* 3; CH 5.2; 11.5, 11; VH 2). For the unknowability of God, compare *Ascl.* 31, where God is both incomprehensible (*incomprehensibilis*) and beyond valuation (*inaestimabilis*). Compare also SH 1.1 (≈ FH 25); FH 3a–b (from Lactantius) below. God's unknowability might be rooted in Egyptian theology (Amun is the Hidden One), but the idea is conventional in Middle Platonism. See further Francesca Calabi, ed., *Arrhetos Theos: L'ineffabilità del primo principio nel medio platonismo* (Pisa: ETS, 2002). The originality of this fragment is in question. Yet Löw argues that nowhere is the declaration of God's unity and incomprehensibility conjoined as here (*Hermes*, 68).

Lactantius

Introduction

L. Caelius Firmianus Lactantius lived from approximately 250 to 325 CE. He was born and educated in the Roman province of Africa (roughly modern Tunisia). Around 297, he was appointed to the official chair of Latin rhetoric in Nicomedia (in what is now northern Turkey). There, at the seat of the emperor Diocletian, Lactantius witnessed first-hand the storm cloud of imperial persecution gather against Christians. During the initial waves of persecution, Lactantius lost or relinquished his post. Though impoverished, he was spurred to write his seven-volume *Divine Institutes* (between 305 and 313) to defend Christianity as the true philosophy.

In his *Divine Institutes*, Lactantius addressed magistrates and public intellectuals. He attacked Hellenic religion and philosophy while defending Christian theology and moral principles. Yet Lactantius did not aim to destroy Hellenic culture. He aimed to salvage its best fruits and blend them with his own Christian worldview. The Greeks had enough knowledge and prophecies to come to Christ on their own. Accordingly, Lactantius quoted the finest minds of the Hellenic tradition in order "to make clear that not only among us, but also among those who persecute us, the truth, which they refuse to acknowledge, is safely kept."[1]

Yet Hermetic religion gave Lactantius something more. Here was a true, divinely revealed philosophy whose ultimate goal was piety toward God. In terms of its basic structure, this was exactly how Lactantius wished to present Christian thought. It is no surprise, then, that Lactantius maintained a positive view of Hermes. Hermes was an authoritative Egyptian sage and theologian who preached Christian theology before Christ. In

[1] Lactantius, *Divine Institutes* 7.25.1. Lactantius composed an *Epitome of the Divine Institutes* around 317 CE. This work was not only an abridgement, but sometimes added details and sharpened arguments found in the larger work.

part to confirm this portrait of Hermes, the Latin orator transcribed quotations in which Hermes affirmed the unity of God, the unknowability (hence namelessness) of God, the creation of the world, humanity made in God's image, and the procession of the Word (or *Logos*). Speaking generally, Lactantius remarked that Hermes Thrice Great "said everything about God the father and much about the son which is contained in the divine secrets."[2]

Lactantius read Hermes with Christian eyes, feeding Hermetic thought through the grinder of a preconceived Christian theology. At the same, however, Lactantius opened himself to significant influence from Hermetic thought. He showed that Hermetic and Christian thought were fundamentally compatible, an idea that would have a long history. The African's testimony about Hermes indicates how highly this Egyptian sage was viewed among educated writers in the early fourth century CE. The respect for Hermes as a prophet of Christian truth continued far into the Middle Ages and in part explains why Byzantine scholars collected and preserved what we call the *Corpus Hermeticum*.[3]

Importantly, Lactantius quoted a number of texts later incorporated into the *Corpus Hermeticum*.[4] He is also the first writer to cite the *Logos Teleios* or *Perfect Discourse*. Lactantius knew this work in Greek and translated parts of it. The *Perfect Discourse* was later fully rendered into Latin by an unknown translator.[5] According to Claudio Moreschini, Lactantius also had access to another Hermetic treatise akin to the doctrine of Plato's *Timaeus*. The traces of this treatise, according to Moreschini,

[2] Lactantius, *Divine Institutes* 4.27.19. In context, Lactantius indicates that Hermes gained his knowledge through necromancy. See further Löw, *Hermes*, 121–24, 245–53.

[3] On Lactantius, see further Wlosok, *Laktanz*, 180–231; Fowden, *Egyptian Hermes*, 204–11; Moreschini and Norelli, *Early Christian Literature*, 398–405; van den Broek, "Hermes and Christ: 'Pagan' Witnesses to the Truth of Christianity," in van den Broek, ed., *From Poimandres*, 115–44 at 130–36; Elizabeth DePalma Digeser, *The Making of a Christian Empire: Lactantius & Rome* (Ithaca: Cornell University Press, 2000), 67–90; Moreschini, *Hermes Christianus*, 33–48; Jochen Walter, *Pagane Texte und Wertvorstellungen bei Lactanz*, Hypomnemata 165 (Göttingen: Vandenhoeck & Ruprecht, 2006), 152–71; Johannes van Oort, "Augustine and Hermes Trismegistus: An Inquiry into the Spirituality of Augustine's 'Hidden Years,'" *Journal of Early Christian History* 6 (2016): 55–76 at 66–68.

[4] Lactantius quoted CH 10.5 (*Divine Institutes* 1.11.61); CH 9.4 (*Divine Institutes* 2.15.6; 5.14.11), CH 12.23 (*Divine Institutes* 6.25.10); CH 16.15–16 (*Divine Institutes* 2.15.7).

[5] Lactantius quoted *Ascl.* 8 (*Divine Institutes* 4.6.4), *Ascl.* 11 (*Divine Institutes* 7.9.11), *Ascl.* 25 (*Divine Institutes* 2.15.8), *Ascl.* 26 (*Divine Institutes* 4.6.9; 7.18.3–4; *Epitome of the Divine Institutes* 66.6), *Ascl.* 28 (*Divine Institutes* 2.14.6); *Ascl.* 29 (*Divine Institutes* 2.15.6); *Ascl.* 41 (*Divine Institutes* 6.25.10–11). These references and those from the previous note derive from Holzhausen, *CH Deutsch* 2.570–71. A fuller list can be found in Wlosok, *Laktanz*, 261–62; Löw, *Hermes*, 258–60.

appear in FH 3a–4b, 7 as well as another work of Lactantius entitled *The Wrath of God* 11.11–12.[6]

FH 3a

Lactantius, Divine Institutes *1.6.1–4*

Now we pass on to divine testimonies. First of all, I cite one testimony that resembles divine (revelation) both because of its great antiquity and because the one I will name was transferred from the human realm to the gods.

In Cicero, Gaius Cotta the priest disputes against the Stoics about religious rites and the variety of opinions customarily held about the gods so as to make all things uncertain in the manner of Academic philosophers. He says that there were five persons called Hermes and, after enumerating four of them in order, he says that the fifth was the one who killed Argus.[7] For this reason, he fled to Egypt and delivered to the Egyptians both laws and literature. The Egyptians called this Hermes "Thoyth," and their first month, namely September, is named after him. This same man founded a city which even now is called "Hermopolis" in Greek, and the people of Faenia worship him with devotion.[8]

Although he was a human being, he (Hermes) was of the greatest antiquity and most learned in every kind of teaching to such an extent that, by virtue of his knowledge of many topics and sciences, he gained the title "Thrice Great."[9]

Hermetic Theology

This man wrote books – in fact, many books – pertaining to the investigation of divine matters. In them, he asserts the majesty of the highest and singular God and invokes him with the same names that we use, namely

[6] Moreschini, *Hermes Christianus* 39. See further his *Dall' "Asclepius" al "Crater Hermetis": Studi sull' Ermetismo latino tardo-antico e rinascimentale* (Pisa: Giardini, 1985), 29–31.

[7] Argus was the many-eyed monster posted by Hera to guard Zeus's bovine lover Io. See further Timothy Gantz, *Early Greek Myth: A Guide to Literary and Artistic Sources* (Baltimore: Johns Hopkins University Press, 1993), 199–202, 219, 232.

[8] Lactantius took his information here from Cicero, *Nature of the Gods* 3.56 (= TH 2). Faenia was in northeastern Arcadia (in central Greece). Pausanias calls it "Pheneüs," affirming that Hermes was the god most honored there (*Description of Greece* 8.14.6–10). See further Löw, *Hermes*, 102–10.

[9] Compare Isidore of Seville: "who on account of his knowledge of many arts (*multarumque artium scientiam*) was called 'Thrice Great'" (*Etymologies* 8.11.45 = TH 23b).

"lord" and "father."[10] Moreover, to prevent someone from inquiring after God's name, he said that God was without name, since he needs no particular name on account of his very unity. To quote his own words: "God is one. He who is one has need of no name, for he who truly exists is without name."[11]

FH 3b

Lactantius, Epitome of the Institutes *4.4–5*

Hermes, on account of his virtue and his knowledge of many arts, merited the name "Thrice Great," excelled the philosophers in doctrine, and preceded them in age. Among the Egyptians, he is worshiped as a god. While affirming the majesty of the singular God with limitless praises, Hermes calls him "lord" and "father." Hermes also affirms that God is without name, as he needs no proper designation, since he is unique.[12]

FH 4a

Lactantius, Divine Institutes *1.7.2*

God without Parents

Does not that famous Hermes Thrice Great,[13] whom I mentioned above, call God not only "motherless" as did Apollo, but "fatherless" as well, since his origin is not some other being?[14] For he who himself fathered all beings cannot be fathered by any other.

[10] The names "lord" (*dominus*) and "father" (*pater*) appear, for instance, in CH 5.2; 13.21; *Ascl.* 22–23, 26, 29. These titles appear frequently in ancient Mediterranean religions to refer to superior beings with whom one has a special relation.

[11] The final quote is cited in Greek. In the context of this passage, Lactantius has been arguing for the unity of God. For the Hermetic theology expressed here, compare CH 5.1: "the God who is greater than any name"; *Ascl.* 20: "given the greatness of this divinity, none of these titles [God, father, master of all] will name him precisely . . . he is nameless or rather he is all-named since he is one and all"; SH 1.2: "what cannot be expressed – this is God"; SH 6.19: "the name greater than God"; FH 11a–b: God's name cannot be expressed "by mortal mouth"; VH 2: "The one God [requires no] name"; Philo: "no name at all can properly be used of me [God]" (*Life of Moses* 1.75). See further Festugière, *RHT*, 4.69–70; Löw, *Hermes*, 129–38. For the hidden divine name in Egyptian thought, see Scott, "Egyptian Elements," 49–53.

[12] See further Löw, *Hermes*, 113–15, 138–40; Wlosok, *Laktanz*, 232–46; Sfameni Gasparro, "L'ermetismo nelle testimonianze dei Padri," 265–67.

[13] Here Lactantius used the Latin version of "Thrice Great," namely *Termaximus*.

[14] In an oracle ascribed to Apollo that Lactantius quoted immediately before this (*Divine Institutes* 1.7.1), God is called "motherless" (ἀμήτωρ) and "incapable of being named with a word." The

FH 4b

Lactantius, Divine Institutes *4.13.2*

That very one, God the father, source and beginning of reality, because he lacks parents, is most truly called "fatherless" and "motherless" by the Thrice Great, since he was not born from any other being.[15]

FH 4c

Lactantius, Epitome of the Divine Institutes *4.4*

(Hermes also affirms) that God does not have any parents because he himself exists from himself and through himself.[16]

FH 5a

Lactantius, Divine Institutes *1.11.61*

The Few who Know

The Thrice Great authorizes this truth[17] when he said that there were extremely few in whom was the perfect teaching. Among these few, he named his relations Ouranos, Saturn, and Mercury.[18]

same oracle in a fuller form was inscribed at Oenanda in Asia Minor. See further Robin Lane Fox, *Pagans and Christians* (New York: Alfred A. Knopf, 1987), 168–261; 711–27; Löw, *Hermes*, 142–44.

15 "Without father" and "without mother" are quoted in Greek. In context, Lactantius argued for both the divinity and humanity of Christ. Christ is born into the world so that he, like the father, can be in his spiritual birth without mother, and in his fleshly birth without father (compare Hebrews 7:3). For God as his own father and mother, compare FH 13. Bleeker quotes an Egyptian prayer to Thoth as the one "who hath created himself, he was not born" (*Hathor and Thoth*, 153). Atum the primal creator also lacks parents. See further Löw, *Hermes*, 206–8.

16 This quote follows immediately from frag. 3b above.

17 Namely, that Saturn was not born in heaven, but from a man named Ouranos (= "Heaven/Sky" in Greek).

18 On Saturn (= Kronos), see Plato, *Laws* 713c (Kronos, an ancient culture hero); CH 10.5 (Kronos, ancestor of Hermes). More obscure references to Kronos can be found in NF 1.122, n. 22. The distinction between Mercury and the Thrice Great may also be assumed in SH 23.29. Three different persons called Hermes are distinguished by Abū Maʿshar (TH 28; compare TH 31 from the Prefaces to the *Composition of Alchemy* and *Six Principles of Nature*). See further Löw, *Hermes*, 145–48.

FH 5b

Lactantius, Epitome of the Divine Institutes *14.3*

When the Thrice Great mentioned that extremely few are men outfitted with complete instruction, he enumerated his relations Ouranos, Saturn, and Mercury.

FH 6

Lactantius, Divine Institutes *2.8.48*

The world is the product of divine Providence. I will say nothing of the Thrice Great who preaches his teaching.[19]

FH 7

Lactantius, Divine Institutes *2.8.68*

The Inscrutability of God

The works of God are seen by the eyes; but how he made them, not even the mind can behold.[20] The reason is, as Hermes said, "the mortal cannot approach the immortal, nor the temporal the eternal, nor the corruptible what is incorruptible."[21] He means coming close and pursuing (the divine) with consciousness.

[19] Lactantius grouped Hermes with the Sibyl, the Hebrew prophets, the Pythagoreans, the Stoics, and the Peripatetics who teach divine providence. Compare SH 12.1: "Providence is the reason of the celestial God"; SH 14.1: "Providence firmly governs the whole world." See further Löw, *Hermes*, 149–51.

[20] In context, Lactantius argues against the Epicureans.

[21] Compare CH 5.2: "the one who alone is unbegotten is also unimagined and invisible, but in presenting images of all things he is seen through all of them and in all of them ... Only understanding ... sees the invisible, and if you have the strength, Tat, your mind's eye will see it ... Can you have a vision of the image of God? If what is in you is also invisible to you, how will God reveal his inner self to you through the eyes?"; SH 1.2: "Bodies are seen by eyes, and sights are spoken by the tongue. But what is bodiless, invisible, without shape, and not consisting of matter cannot be grasped by our senses." See further Löw, *Hermes*, 176–78.

FH 8a

Lactantius, Divine Institutes *2.10.14*

Made in God's Image

This (teaching) Hermes also hands on, who not only said that humanity was made by God in the image of God, but also tried to explain how, by complex reasoning, God formed each part of the human body – not a single part any less valuable for its necessary utility than for its beauty.[22]

FH 8b

Lactantius, Divine Institutes *7.4.3*

But Hermes was not ignorant that humanity was both crafted by God and in God's image.[23]

FH 9

Lactantius, Divine Institutes *2.14.6*

Hence the Thrice Great's word for the devil is "the ruler of daimones."[24]

[22] In context, Lactantius may imply that Hermes taught that humanity was molded from clay. The god Khnum in native Egyptian lore was said to have shaped the human body from clay. Compare CH 5.6: "consider how the human being is crafted in the womb, examine the skill of the craftwork carefully, and learn who it is that crafts this beautiful, godlike image of humankind." Humans are called God's image in the Egyptian text *Wisdom of Merikare* (references in Erik Iversen, *Egyptian and Hermetic Doctrine* [Copenhagen: Museum Tusculanum, 1984], 16). Yet Lactantius is selective: humankind, according to *Ascl.* 10, is in fact "the second image of God"; the first image is the cosmos. See further Sfameni Gasparro, "L'ermetismo nelle testimonianze dei Padri," 282; Löw, *Hermes*, 151–55.

[23] In context, Lactantius opposes the (Stoic) idea that human beings arose in various parts of the earth. See further Löw, *Hermes*, 155–57.

[24] In context, Lactantius discusses his theory about the origin of daimones, in dependence on the Watcher myth in 1 Enoch 1–36. For the point he makes, Lactantius likely draws from *Ascl.* 28, where the soul comes into the power of the chief daimon (*in summi daemonis potestatem*). *Summi daemonis* may be a rendering of δαιμονιάρχου, "the ruler of daimones." Compare "the great Daimon" (*noq ᵉndaimōn*) set up by God as overseer and judge of human souls in *Excerpt from the Perfect Discourse* (NHC VI,8) 76.22–23. See further Mahé, *HHE*, 2.257–59; Löw, *Hermes*, 163–65.

FH 10

Lactantius, Divine Institutes *2.15.6*

Defining Devotion

Furthermore, Hermes affirms that those who know God are not only safe from the attacks of daimones but are not even held in the grip of Fate.[25] "Devotion," he says, "is the one safeguard. No evil daimon or Fate rules over the devout human being, for God protects the devout from all evil. The one and only good for human beings is devotion."[26]

What devotion is he shows in another passage using these words: "Devotion is the knowledge of God."[27]

FH 11a

Lactantius, Divine Institutes *4.7.3*

The Inexpressible Name

Next, it (the name of God's son) cannot be expressed by a human mouth, as Hermes expressly teaches: "The cause of this {cause} is the will of {the unborn Good}, whose name cannot be spoken by a human mouth."[28]

[25] Compare Tatian, *Oration* 9.6: "But we [Christians] are above Fate . . . and not driven by Fate we reject its regulators." See further FH 20 (from Zosimus) and FH 39a–b (from Didymus of Alexandria).

[26] Lactantius quotes this Hermetic passage in Greek. Compare *Ascl.* 29: "the upright person's defense lies in devotion to God and supreme fidelity"; Cyril, *Against Julian* 4.23.11–13: "Hermes writes to Asclepius about sacrilegious daimones . . . 'There is one safeguard, necessary indeed, namely devotion.'" See further Löw, *Hermes*, 166–71.

[27] The Greek word for knowledge here is γνῶσις. Lactantius repeated this quotation in *Divine Institutes* 5.14.11 (see Löw, *Hermes*, 218–20). Compare CH 9.4: "Devotion [or reverence] is the gnosis of God"; Cicero, *Nature of the Gods* 2.153 (piety or devotion arises from knowledge of the gods). See further Löw, *Hermes*, 171–75.

[28] In pointed brackets is the unintelligible phrase †τοῦ αἰτίου ἡ τοῦ θεαγενετου αγαθο†. Translated here is τοῦ αἰτίου ἡ τοῦ θεοῦ ἀγενήτου ἀγαθοῦ βούλησις. In his edition, Pierre Monat prints <τοῦ αἰτίου ἡ τοῦ θεοῦ ἅτε τοῦ ἀγαθοῦ> βούλησις ("the cause of this cause is the will of God inasmuch as he is the Good" [Lactance, *Institutions divines livre IV*, SC 377 [Paris: Cerf, 1992], 68]). In the Hermetic quote, the unspeakable one is the unborn Good or high God, not the son of God. Lactantius apparently understood the "cause of this cause" as the high God, and God's son to be the will (or Will) of the high God. Compare Scott, *Hermetica*, 4.16, n.8. See further Löw, *Hermes*, 211–18. Moreschini observes: "the phrase: 'the creator Logos [who] is lord of all things' should . . . be understood as: 'the Logos that *belongs to the lord of all things*' i.e., the first god. The first god is indicated by the word 'him' (*ekeinon*) and, a little later, by all-perfect'" (*Hermes Christianus*, 86, n.182).

FH 11b

Lactantius, Epitome of the Divine Institutes *37.8*

Hermes said that his name could not be expressed by a mortal mouth.[29]

FH 12a

Lactantius, Divine Institutes *4.7.3*

God Prior to Thought

Shortly thereafter, he says to his son: "There is an inexpressible and holy discourse (*or:* Word) of wisdom concerning the sole lord of all and the God prior to thought.[30] To speak of this being is a superhuman task."[31]

FH 12b

Lactantius, Divine Institutes *4.9.3*

Word beyond Description

For the Thrice Great who investigated, I know not how, nearly all truth, often described the power and majesty of the discourse [*or:* Word].[32] So he declares in what was cited above,[33] where he confesses that there is an unspeakable holy discourse [*or:* Word] whose description exceeds human ability.

[29] In context, Lactantius was arguing that the name of God's son is inexpressible. Yet it is now impossible to determine whether "his" in the paraphrase of the Hermetic citation originally referred to the high God or a second god figure. See the previous note. Compare *PGM* 13.763–65: "Come to me, you from the four winds, ruler of all, who breathed spirit into people for life, whose is the hidden and unspeakable name – it cannot be uttered by a human mouth."

[30] For the God prior to thought (προεννοούμενος), compare FH 17, 30, 36 below. Lactantius may have understood the Greek to mean "the God already conceived," namely the father.

[31] "This being" in the Hermetic context is probably the high God, but Lactantius understood him to be the Word. Compare FH 11b above.

[32] In context, Lactantius argues that the son of God is initially born by the spirit and voice (*voce*) of God. He took *verbum*, representing the Greek λόγος, to refer to the second god or Word. See the comments of Löw, *Hermes*, 119–21, 215–17.

[33] Namely FH 12a.

FH 13

Lactantius, Divine Institutes *4.8.4–5*

God of Both Sexes

4. Unless perhaps we conceive of God as Orpheus thought, as both male and female since he could not otherwise generate unless he had the power of both sexes.[34] Orpheus assumes that God either coupled with himself or could procreate without coupling.[35] 5. But Hermes also was of the same opinion when he called God androgynous <...>; "his own father" and "his own mother."[36]

[34] In context, Lactantius discourses on the double birth of God's son: from eternity and in time (the incarnation). He opposes the idea that God required a partner (a kind of mother goddess) to generate his son. On the dual-gendered divine, see CH 1.9: "the Consciousness who is God is androgynous"; *Ascl.* 21: "'Do you say that God is of both sexes, Thrice Great?' 'Not only God, Asclepius, but all things'"; FH 37a below (androgynous Aphrodite). For the ancient Egyptian background, see Hornung, *Conceptions*, 171–72; Jan Zandee, "Der androgyne Gott in Ägypten: Ein Erscheinungsbild des Weltschöpfers," in Manfred Görg, ed., *Religion im Erbe Ägyptens: Beiträge zur spätantiken Religionsgeschichte* (Wiesbaden: Harrassowitz, 1988), 240–78 at 270–77. Compare the hymn to Zeus passed on by Pseudo-Aristotle: "Zeus is a male; Zeus is an undying maiden" (*On the Cosmos*, 401b1–2) with the comments of Festugière, *RHT*, 4.45–51. See further Marie Delcourt, *Hermaphrodite: Mythes et rites de la bisexualité dans l'antiquité classique* (Paris: University Presses of France, 1958), 105–12.

[35] In Orphic myth, the god Phanes is both male and female (Bernabé, *OF* 134) and is called αὐτοζῷον (self-existent) (Bernabé, *OF* 137).

[36] Here following the edition of Heck and Wlosok (*Divinarum Institutionum libri*, fasc. 2, 333) who print ἀρσενιόθηλυν ... † αὐτοπάτορα et αὐτομήτορα, citing CH 1.9, 16. The notion of a self-caused creator (such as Atum, Ptah, or Amun) is native to ancient Egypt, as documented by James P. Allen, *Genesis in Egypt: The Philosophy of Ancient Egyptian Creation Accounts* (New Haven: Yale Egyptological Seminar, 1988), 48–55; Iversen, *Egyptian and Hermetic Doctrine*, 23–24; Scott, "Egyptian Elements," 35–41; Moreschini, *Hermes Christianus*, 37–38; and Jean-Pierre Mahé, "La création dans les Hermetica," *Recherches Augustiniennes* 21 (1986): 3–53 at 10–15. Sometimes Thoth himself is called "self-caused" and "self-begotten" (Boylan, *Thoth*, 119). On self-generation, compare *Ascl.* 14 ("the things from which all come to be can easily come to be from those that have come to be from themselves"); SH 23.58 ("self-born Divinity"); FH 37a (androgynous Aphrodite). The idea of a self-generating divinity was also known in the Greek world. Aelius Aristides proclaimed that Zeus was "born of himself ... (he is) father to himself and one too great to be born from another ... he created himself from himself" (trans. Behr). Porphyry depicted the offspring of the Good as self-born (αὐτογέννητος), father of itself (αὐτοπάτωρ) proceeding from God in a self-born way (αὐτογόνως) (frag. 223, Smith). Similarly Iamblichus (*On the Mysteries* 8.2) spoke of a self-fathering, self-generating deity (αὐτοπάτωρ and αὐτογόνος) below the One. Clement of Alexandria spoke of the unutterable aspect of God as father and the part in sympathy with humans as mother (*Who is the Rich Man*, 37). The author of *Ref.* cited a Naassene hymn: "From you ... O Human whose name is great, comes father, and because of you there is mother" (5.6.5; compare Monoïmus in *Ref.* 8.12.5). Compare Firmicus Maternus: "Whoever you are, God ... you are your own father and son" (*Mathesis* 5, pref. 3). For further texts see Versnel, *Ter Unus*, 227–30; Zandee, "Androgyne Gott," 240–70; Löw, *Hermes*, 203–6.

FH 14

Lactantius, Divine Institutes *7.9.11*

Seeing God

This contemplation the Thrice Great most justly named "theoptical," a kind of vision that non-speaking animals do not have.[37]

FH 15

Lactantius, Divine Institutes *7.13.3*

Humanity at the Midpoint

Hermes, when he described human nature to teach how it was made by God, proposed the following: "Indeed [the same] from both natures, the immortal and mortal, he made the single nature of the human being, making it in one respect immortal, in another respect mortal.[38] Indeed, by setting humanity midway between the divine, immortal nature and the mortal, changeable nature he established his set purpose: that humanity might behold all things, and before all things be in wonder."[39]

[37] In context, Lactantius contrasted the prone, downward-looking gaze of many animals with the erect stature and uplifted sight of human beings. On the God-seeing soul, compare FH 16 below; SH 2A.6: "God grants the power of vision" (τὴν θεοπτικὴν δύναμιν); SH 7.3: "the power of seeing the divine" (θεοπτικὴ δύναμις). Iamblichus spoke of a "God-seeing soul" (*On the Mysteries* 8.6 = FH 16). See further Wlosok, *Laktanz*, 205–10; Löw, *Hermes*, 178–84; Sfameni Gasparro, "L'ermetismo nelle testimonianze dei Padri," 272–75.

[38] In context, Lactantius argues for the immortality of the soul against Lucretius the Epicurean. He quotes Hermes here in Greek. For Hermetic parallels, compare CH 1.15: "humankind is twofold – in the body mortal but immortal in the essential person"; *Ascl.* 8: "God covered him [humanity] with a bodily dwelling and commanded that all humans be like this, mingling and combining the two natures into one in their just proportions. Thus God shapes humankind from the nature of soul and of body, from the eternal and the mortal . . . so that the living being so shaped can prove adequate to both its beginnings, wondering at heavenly beings and worshiping them"; *Ascl.* 10: "Thus humankind is divine in one part, in another part mortal, residing in a body"; *Ascl.* 22: "God made humankind good and capable of immortality through its two natures, divine and mortal."

[39] Compare CH 4.2: "the human became a spectator of God's work (the cosmos)"; CH 14.4: "This is the proper way to understand and, having understood, to be astonished and, having been astonished, to count oneself blessed for having recognized the father." *Ascl.* 8: the highest God "wanted there to be another to admire the one (sensible god, or cosmos) he had made from himself, and straightaway he made humankind." See further Löw, *Hermes*, 160–62.

Iamblichus

Introduction

Iamblichus was born around 240 CE in the city of Chalcis by the Belus river (in modern northwestern Syria). Probably he studied with the Neoplatonist philosopher Porphyry in Rome before setting up his own Neoplatonist school in Apamea of Syria. He wrote a ten-volume *Compendium of Pythagorean Doctrine* as a kind of introductory course for his students. The first volume, *On the Pythagorean Way of Life*, survives in full. The second volume is an exhortation to philosophy modeled on a similar work of Aristotle. Fragments of Iamblichus's commentaries on some Platonic dialogues survive. In his *Anthology* book 1.49, Stobaeus also included large fragments of Iamblichus's work *On the Soul*.

Two of the three Hermetic fragments printed here derive from Iamblichus's work *On the Mysteries of Egypt*; and the third seems to depend on it. The title *On the Mysteries* was bestowed on the work by Marsilio Ficino in the fifteenth century. The work is in fact a lengthy reply to Porphyry's letter to an Egyptian priest called Anebo. In the letter, Porphyry strongly criticized the practice of theurgy. Theurgy is a term hard to define concisely, but it involves soul-cleansing rites that lead to encounters with gods and the soul's purification. Iamblichus defended theurgy as the universal path to salvation – a path Porphyry was unable to provide.

Iamblichus did not write his response to Porphyry in his own name. Rather, he took up the persona of a venerable Egyptian priest called Abammon, supposed teacher of Anebo.[1] It is this Egyptian persona that in part leads Iamblichus to relate a number of Egyptian theological

[1] See further H. D. Saffrey, "Réflexions sur la pseudonymie Abammôn-Jamblique," in John Clearly, ed., *Traditions of Platonism: Essays in Honour of John Dillon* (Aldershot: Ashgate, 1999), 307–18.

teachings. The source of these teachings was reputed to be Thrice Great Hermes.[2]

FH 16

Iamblichus, On the Mysteries *8.6*

Two Souls

You then claim that most Egyptians make what is in our power depend on the movement of the stars.[3] The true situation I must interpret for you at length from Hermetic conceptions. These writings declare that the human being has two souls, one from the first Intelligible, sharing in the power of the creator, the other set in us from the revolution of the heavens.[4] Into this latter (soul) slinks the God-seeing soul.[5] This being the case, the soul which descends to us from the (celestial) realms accommodates itself to the

[2] For Iamblichus, see further Fowden, *Egyptian Hermes*, 131–41; John M. Dillon, *Iamblichi Chalcidensis in platonis dialogos Commentariorum fragmenta*, Philosophia Antiqua 23 (Leiden: Brill, 1973), 3–66; Clarke, Dillon, and Hershbell, *Iamblichus: De mysteriis*, xviii–lii.

[3] Iamblichus treats the theme of astrology and Hermetic thought in *On the Mysteries* 8.4. The Egyptians, he says, recommend the practice of sacred theurgy which allows an ascent to the creator and the ability to become superior to Fate.

[4] Other Hermetic texts (for instance, CH 16.15; SH 2B.5–7) acknowledge the standard Platonic friction between the parts of the soul, but the division into two souls is never so explicit. Evil dispositions accrue from the planets in CH 1.25, but these dispositions do not constitute another soul. Two kinds of consciousness (νοῦς) are distinguished in DH 8.4 (Greek fragment in Mahé and Paramelle, "Nouveaux parallèles," 125; English translation in Salaman and others, *Way of Hermes*, 142). Perhaps we are to think of native Egyptian notions such as the *ka* and *ba* (for which see James P. Allen, "Ba," in Donald B. Redford, ed., *The Oxford Encyclopedia of Ancient Egypt*, 3 vols. [Oxford: Oxford University Press, 2001], 1.161–62; Andrey O. Bolshakov, "Ka," in *ibid.* 2.215–17). In the context of Greek philosophy, the theory of two souls might have been inspired by Plato's *Timaeus* 41–42, where the immortal soul given by the Craftsman is distinguished from the mortal soul made by the young gods. A doctrine of two souls (one rational, one irrational) is attributed to the Neopythagorean Numenius (frag. 44, des Places, a quotation of Porphyry taken from Stobaeus, *Anthology* 1.49.25a). See further Dillon, *Middle Platonists*, 376–78; Robert Petty, *Fragments of Numenius of Apamea: Translation and Commentary* (Westbury, Wiltshire: The Prometheus Trust, 2012), 204–5. Clement of Alexandria says that Isidore, son of Basilides, believed in two souls (*Stromateis* 2.20.113.3; compare Plotinus, *Enneads* 2.9.5.16–17). Origen discusses the scriptural support for two souls in *On First Principles* 3.4. Fowden notes an unpublished Byzantine text that claims that Plato followed the teachings of Hermes and Bitys in maintaining that a human has two distinct souls, a rational one from the Craftsman and an irrational one arising from the substance of heaven (*Egyptian Hermes*, 152, n.40). This text, however, may in fact be dependent on our very passage from Iamblichus (FH 16).

[5] The God-seeing (divine) soul is apparently nested in the (mortal) soul. On the God-seeing soul, compare SH 2A.6: "God grants the power of vision" (τὴν θεοπτικὴν δύναμιν); SH 7.3: "the power of seeing the divine" (θεοπτικὴ δύναμις); Josephus, *Against Apion* 1.232 (Pharaoh Amenophis wants to become a contemplator [θεατήν] of the gods); Philo, *Change of Names*, 7 (Moses becomes a "contemplator of the divine nature and a viewer of God [θεόπτης]").

circuits of those realms, but that which is present to us in an intelligible mode from the intelligible realm transcends the cycle of generation, and it is in virtue of it that deliverance from Fate comes as well as the ascent to the intelligible gods.[6]

FH 17

Iamblichus, On the Mysteries *10.7*

Union with God

As for the Good in itself, the Egyptians consider the divine good to be the God prior to thought, and the human good to be union with this God.[7] Bitys translated this teaching from the Hermetic writings.[8]

FH 18

Iamblichus in Proclus, Commentary on Plato's Timaeus *117d*[9]

The Principle of Matter

To be sure, Egyptian tradition says the same thing about matter. The divine Iamblichus related, at any rate, the opinion of Hermes that the principle of matter derived from the principle of being.[10] In fact, it is likely that Plato held his characteristic opinion about matter on Hermes's authority as well.[11]

[6] The basic point here is that divine νοῦς or consciousness is superior to Fate and allows one to ascend to God as in CH 1.24–26. Affective maladies are shed as the soul rises through the successive planetary spheres. A later Hermetic interpreter might have conceived of these maladies as part of a mortal soul.

[7] On the God prior to thought, compare FH 12a, 30, 36. For the Good identified with God, see CH 2.14–16. In CH 1.26, redeemed humans are said to "enter into God."

[8] For Bitys (or Bitos) see FH 21 (from Zosimus) with notes.

[9] Dillon prints this passage as fragment 38 of Iamblichus's *Commentary on the Timaeus* (*In Platonis Dialogos*, 141). Possibly Proclus was dependent on Iamblichus, *On the Mysteries* 8.3 (quoted in the next note).

[10] Compare Iamblichus: "As for matter, God derived it from the principle of being [*or:* substantiality], when he had abstracted the principle of matter [*or:* materiality] from it; this matter, which is endowed with life, the Craftsman took in hand and from it fashioned the simple and impassible (heavenly) spheres, while its lowest residue he crafted into bodies which are subject to generation and corruption" (*On the Mysteries* 8.3). For commentary on FH 18, see Dillon, *In Platonis Dialogos*, 312–13; Bull, "Tradition of Hermes," 132–33. For God making the matter of human souls out of his own essence, see SH 23.14–15.

[11] See further Festugière, *RHT*, 4.35–53.

Zosimus

Introduction

Zosimus of Panopolis, or present-day Akhmim in Middle Egypt, was a pioneering Greek alchemist who lived during the late third and early fourth centuries CE. At some point, Zosimus probably resided or at least sojourned in Alexandria, Egypt. He is known for combining technical knowledge of alchemy (the science of transforming metals) with a gnostic spirituality based on self-knowledge and the triumph over Fate. He believed that alchemical knowledge should be public and that the practice of alchemy required ritual acts of self-purification.

Zosimus's familiarity with the Hermetica is shown by his allusion to CH 1 and 4 in his treatise *The Final Count*. According to the *Suda*, he wrote twenty-eight treatises each entitled by a letter of the alphabet.[1] Zosimus himself referred to his treatises called by the letters kappa and omega. In the manuscripts that survive, Zosimus's treatise *On the Letter Omega* is found as the opening treatise or introduction to a book called *Authentic Commentaries* (or *Authentic Memorials*) *concerning Instruments and Furnaces*. It is addressed to his fellow alchemist and (spiritual) sister Theosebeia. In *On the Letter Omega*, Zosimus assumed that Mani, founder of Manicheanism, is still alive. This information indicates that the text was composed before or not long after 278 CE.

Sections 4–7 of the treatise can be briefly described here. After a short discussion of the symbolic meaning of the letter omega (which is related to both Ocean and the planet Saturn = Kronos), Zosimus immediately turned to attack his opponents. His alchemist rivals, affirmed Zosimus, are dominated by Fate like people deprived of divine consciousness. These rivals are not true philosophers, for philosophers (among whom he counted Zoroaster

[1] If the report is true, Zosimus may have supplemented the twenty-four letters of the Greek alphabet with other Coptic letters or with Greek letters out of use (such as the digamma).

and Hermes) transcend Fate. According to Zosimus, the Persian Zoroaster boasted that he had mastered Fate by the use of magical spells. Hermes, by contrast, recommended subduing Fate by self-knowledge and contemplation of the ever-transforming Logos – here called God's son. Hermes's admonitions are especially authoritative because, as the Egyptian Thoth, Hermes was also the first human being and the namer of all reality.[2]

FH 19

Zosimus, On the Letter Omega *4*

Those Driven by Fate

In his book *On Natures*, Hermes called such people[3] "devoid of consciousness," solely puppets led in the procession of Fate, unable to conceive of anything without a body – not even Fate herself, the slave driver they so richly deserve.[4] Rather, they revile her bodily training grounds, imagining it (the body) as something foreign, outside of her blessings.[5]

[2] On Zosimus, see further Jack Lindsay, *The Origins of Alchemy in Graeco-Roman Egypt* (New York: Barnes & Noble, 1970), 323–57; Howard M. Jackson, ed., *Zosimos of Panopolis on the Letter Omega* (Missoula, MT: Scholars Press, 1978), 1–14; Fowden, *Egyptian Hermes*, 120–26; Michèle Mertens, "Alchemy, Hermetism and Gnosticism at Panopolis c. 300 A.D.: The Evidence of Zosimus," in Arno Egberts, ed., *Perspectives on Panopolis: An Egyptian Town from Alexander the Great to the Arab Conquest: Acts from an International Symposium held in Leiden on 16, 17 and 18 December 1998* (Leiden: Brill, 2002), 165–76; Jean Letrouit, "Hermétisme et alchimie: contribution à l'étude du Marcianus graecus 299 (= M)," in Carlos Gilly and Cis van Heertum, eds., *Magia, alchimia, scienza dal '400 al '700: L'influsso di Ermete Trismegisto*, 2 vols. (Venice: Centro, 2002), 1.85–112. The numbering of *On the Letter Omega* follows Jackson, *Zosimos of Panopolis*, 20–21. The text for the translation is based on the most recent critical edition by Michèle Mertens, *Zosime de Panopolis: Mémoires authentiques. Les alchimistes grecs* IV/1 (Paris: Belles Lettres, 1995), 1–4 with notes on 53–86. Bidez and Cumont printed a partial excerpt of *On the Letter Omega* with notes in *Mages Hellénisés* 2.243–45. Festugière provided a French translation and notes for the whole treatise in *RHT* 1.263–74.

[3] Zosimus refers to his alchemist opponents who criticized his treatise *On Furnaces and Instruments*.

[4] For people without consciousness, compare CH 4.4: "those who missed the point of the proclamation are people of reason because they did not receive consciousness (νοῦς)." For those led in procession, compare CH 4.7: "just as processions passing by in public cannot achieve anything of themselves, though they can be a hindrance to others, in the same way, these people are only parading through the cosmos, led astray by pleasures of the body"; *Ascl.* 7: "Not all have gained true understanding (*intelligentiam veram*), Asclepius. They are deceived, pursuing, on rash impulse and without due consideration of reason, an image that begets malice in their minds." Compare also Parmenides: "For helplessness in their breasts is what steers their wandering minds. They are carried along in a daze, deaf and blind, uncritical tribes" (frag. 6.5–7, Gallop). See further Nock, "Diatribe," in his *Essays* 1.28–30.

[5] The bodily "training grounds" or "schools" (παιδευτήρια) may be bodies themselves, or the afflictions of the body like poverty and pain. I reject the μηδέν added by Reitzenstein and take ἄλλο to refer back to the bodily training grounds or simply the body (τὸ σῶμα) itself. For souls lamenting their embodiment, compare SH 23.31–37.

FH 20

Zosimus, On the Letter Omega *5*

Philosophers above Fate

Hermes and Zoroaster taught that the philosophers as a class are above Fate, for they neither rejoice in her beneficence – for they prevail over pleasures – nor are they thrown by the troubles that Fate sends.[6] At all times they live their lives in the inner courtyard,[7] not accepting the fair gifts of Fate because they look toward the end of evils.[8]

FH 21a

Zosimus, On the Letter Omega *7*

Living by Spirit, Following God's Son

Zoroaster, boasting in his knowledge of all higher realities and the magic of his embodied speech,[9] claims that he repels all the evils of Fate, both those particular and those universal.[10]

[6] Hermes Thrice Great and "Zoroastris" are also mentioned together in *Ref.* 5.14.7 (= TH 9). See further Bidez and Cumont, *Mages hellénisés,* 1.1–163; 2.7–263. For the dichotomy of many subject to Fate and the few who flee it, see Iamblichus, *On the Mysteries* 5.18. Hans Lewy quotes two *Chaldean Oracles* fragments which declare that theurgists are above Fate. The most relevant quotation is: "The theurgists are not reckoned among the herd of people subject to Fate" (*Chaldean Oracles and Theurgy: Mysticism, Magic and Platonism in the Later Roman Empire* [Cairo: French Institute of Oriental Archaeology, 1956], 212).

[7] NF print ἐν ἀϋλίᾳ, or "in immateriality." Here we read ἐναυλίαν ἄγοντας with Jackson (*Zosimos,* 22) and Mertens (*Alchimistes,* 3), following codex Venetus Marcianus 299 (tenth to eleventh centuries). Jackson comments: "the force of the expression being that philosophers, by their realization of kinship with God through mind, the divine element awakened within them, pass the whole of their lives in the court of their Father, the divine King who is Mind" (*Zosimos,* 43, n.20). As a parallel, Mertens (*Alchimistes,* 69–70) quotes Arnobius who referred to (possibly Hermetic) "upstarts" (*viri novi*) wanting to dwell in the divine court (*Against the Nations* 2.33, *in aulam dominicam*; 2.37, *aulam regiam*).

[8] Compare the polemic of Arnobius: "Let not what is said by some dilettantes who arrogate many matters to themselves, deceive or flatter you with windy hope that they are born of God and not liable to the laws of Fate (*nec fati obnoxios legibus*), that if they lead a life of restraint, his courtyard (*aulam*) lies open to them and that after the death of the body they are brought back without any hindrance at all to their ancestral seat" (*Against the Nations* 2.62). See further Festugière, "La doctrine des 'viri novi' sur l'origine et le sort des âmes d'après Arnobe II, 11–64," in *Mystique,* 261–312 at 299–302; Festugière, *RHT,* 1.263, n.1; 1.266–68.

[9] Embodied speech may simply refer to human languages as opposed to superior forms of (soundless) communication. Compare Plato, *Charmides,* 157a, where healing charms consisting of beautiful words produce a spiritual benefit (namely, temperance).

[10] Particular evils affect the individual (for instance, disease); universal evils affect the human race (for instance, wars).

Hermes, however, in his *On the Inner Courtyard*,[11] criticizes magic as well by claiming that the spiritual person gifted with self-knowledge must not rectify anything through magic even if it is considered noble.[12] Nor must the spiritual human compel Necessity, but rather let it proceed according to its own nature and judgment.[13] The spiritual person must advance solely by inquiring into the self.[14] Upon recognizing God, he or she must lay hold of the unnamable trinity, letting Fate do what it wants to the glob of clay in its possession, namely the body.[15]

By so exercising your consciousness and conduct, he says, you will see the son of God becoming all things for the sake of holy souls.[16] He undergoes these transformations to draw the soul away from the region of Fate into the bodiless realm.[17] Behold him becoming all things – god, angel, and a human subject to affections.[18] Since he is able to do all things, he becomes everything he wants.[19] He obeys the Father as he passes

[11] Here reading Περὶ ἐναυλίας with Jackson (*Zosimos*, 24), Fowden (*Egyptian Hermes*, 124, n.34), and Mertens (*Alchimistes*, 3). Manuscripts K and M read Περὶ ἀναυλίας. W. Kroll, Scott, NF, and Holzhausen emend to Περὶ ἀϋλίας (*On Immateriality*).

[12] On the spiritual human (τὸν πνευματικὸν ἄνθρωπον), compare 1 Corinthians 2:14–16; 15:45–52.

[13] For the judgment of Necessity, compare SH 13.

[14] Compare CH 1.19–21: "The one who recognized himself attained the chosen good, but the one who loved the body that came from the error of desire goes on in darkness ... He who was understood himself advances toward God ... because ... the Father of all things was constituted of light and life, and from him humanity came to be ... So if you learn that you are from light and life and that you happen to come from them, you shall advance to life once again."

[15] Instead of πηλῷ ("glob of clay"), Marcianus 299 reads σπηλῷ ("cave"), perhaps under the influence of Plato's famous allegory of the cave at the beginning of the *Republic* book 7. Scott believed that "the unnamable trinity" was a Christian gloss (*Hermetica*, 4.119). Bull maintains that this whole passage has been influenced by probably gnostic Christian ideas ("Tradition of Hermes," 406–7; note the Peratic trinity in *Ref.* 5.12.2). Bull agrees with Jackson that Trinitarian speculation was not exclusively Christian (*Chaldean Oracles* frags. 2, 23, 26–29, 31 [Majercik]; see further Morenz, *Egyptian Religion*, 142–46; Mahé, *HHE*, 1.48–52; 2.344–47). Yet Jackson's proposed trinity of father, Logos-son, and cosmos (or human endowed with consciousness) (*Zosimos*, 44, n.26) is not "unnamable." A better analogy is God, Father, and the Good (CH 10.14; compare "God, Father, Master of All" in *Ascl.* 20 and the "Unbegotten," "Begotten" and "Self-begotten" God in *Disc. 8–9* [NHC VI,6] 57.13–16; 63.21–23). Allen quotes a possible Egyptian parallel in the 300th Chapter of the Leiden papyrus: "All the gods are three: Amun, the Sun, and Ptah, without their seconds. His identity is hidden in Amun, his is the Sun as face, his body is Ptah" (*Genesis in Egypt*, 54, 62).

[16] Typically in Hermetic theology, the son of God is the cosmos (CH 9.8 and 10.14). It can also designate the Hermetic initiate, as in CH 13.2, 14. In CH 1.6, the son of God is the Logos, but his role is not salvific, as in our passage from Zosimus. Here the son of God is Christ, and what follows seems to come primarily from a Christian gnostic source authored or attributed to Nicotheus.

[17] One can also translate the last clause: "to the Incorporeal (God)."

[18] Mahé attributed this latter phrase to Christian redaction, *HHE*, 2.395, 9.6, n.2. Compare Philippians 2:6–7: "though he existed in the form of God, he did not consider equality with God something to be plundered; rather he emptied himself, taking the form of a slave, arriving in the likeness of human beings." Compare DH 9.6: "Because of man, God changes and turns into the form of man."

[19] One can also translate the last clause: "what he wills comes to pass."

through every body.[20] He enlightens the consciousness of each soul,[21] spurring it upward to the blessed region where indeed (the consciousness) was before the bodily (realm) came to be. (Consciousness) follows God's son, yearning for him and led into that light.

Behold the tablet that Bitos wrote,[22] and (the writings of) thrice-great Plato, and the infinitesimally great Hermes, and you will see that "Thouth" in the primal priestly language is translated "the first human being." He is the interpreter of all things that exist, the one who gave names to all bodily reality.[23] The Chaldeans, Parthians, Medes, and Hebrews call him "Adam," which means "virgin earth," "bloody earth," "fiery red earth" and "fleshly earth."[24] These writings were discovered in the libraries of the Ptolemies, stored away in each sanctuary, especially in the Serapeum.[25] At this time (Ptolemy) enjoined Asenas the high<priest> of Jerusalem to send Hermes who translated everything in Hebrew into Greek and Egyptian.[26] …

[20] Festugière originally understood, "He obeys the Father" as a Christian gloss (*RHT*, 1.267, n.1). The son's ability to pass through every body assimilates him to the Stoic πνεῦμα as well as the Philosophers' Stone (TH 30a: "it conquers every subtle reality and passes through every solid object"). Compare *SVF* 2.1027: "a spirit pervading the whole world" (πνεῦμα διῆκον δι' ὅλου τοῦ κόσμου); *SVF* 2.473 (πνεύματός τινος διὰ πάσης αὐτῆς [i.e., οὐσίας] διήκοντος). The doctrine was later claimed for Egypt: "among them (the Egyptians) that which pervades the whole cosmos is Spirit" (Horapollo, *Hieroglyphics*, 1.64).

[21] Here reading τὸν ἑκάστης νοῦν with the MSS.

[22] For Bitos (or Bitys), see FH 17 and TH 12 (from Iamblichus). Jackson comments: "Bitos, or Bitus, if he existed, would have been, like Manetho or Chaeremon, a Hellenized Egyptian priest and interpreter of native Egyptian traditions to the Greeks" (*Zosimos*, 46, n.37). Bitys is twice mentioned by Iamblichus. In one passage, Bitys finds the teaching of Hermes inscribed in hieroglyphs in shrines around Saïs in Lower Egypt. He translated the hieroglyphs for king Ammon and handed on the name of God (*On the Mysteries* 8.5). In another context, Bitys is said to translate Hermetic books that speak of union with God (10.7 = FH 17 above). See further Fowden, *Egyptian Hermes*, 150–53; Michel Tardieu, "Bitys," in *DPA* 2.113–15.

[23] Cf. Gen 2:20 (Adam names the animals). For primal Human speculation, see *Ref.* 5.7.3–6 (the Naassenes); Irenaeus, *Against Heresies* 1.30.1 (the Ophites). See further Stroumsa, *Another Seed*, 141–43.

[24] Based on a play on words, Adam (אדם) was taken from אדמה ("soil"; "ground") and related to אֹדם, or "red," and דם, or "blood." Hesychius, *Lexicon*, under the headword ἀδάμα records παρθενικὴ γῆ ("virgin earth"). "Virgin" may derive from the Greek ἀδμής ("unbroken," "unwedded"). Compare *Orig. World* (NHC II,5) 108.20–26: "Since then this messenger has been called Adam of light, which means 'the enlightened person of blood.' The earth upon <which the light of Forethought> spread was called holy Adamas, which means 'the holy adamantine earth.' From that time on all the authorities have honored the blood of the virgin" (trans. Marvin Meyer).

[25] "Each sanctuary" may refer to the two famous libraries of Alexandria, the palace library and the library in the temple of Sarapis.

[26] Asenas may be named after Asenath, the Egyptian wife of Joseph (*Joseph and Asenath* in *OTP* 2.177–248). For Hermes's work as a translator, compare the myth of the Septuagint found in the *Letter of Aristeas* (*OTP* 2.7–34). It is not directly said that Hermes translated the Septuagint (along with other Hebrew texts), although it may be implied.

Only the Hebrews and the holy books of Hermes speak these things about the luminous Human and his guide, the son of God, along with the earthly Adam and his guide, the counterfeit who blasphemously and deceitfully says that he is the son of God.[27]

FH 21b

Zosimus Quoted by George Syncellus, Chronological Excerpts *24*[28]

It is worthwhile citing a passage from Zosimus, the philosopher of Panopolis, about these matters. The passage derives from his writings to Theosebeia, namely the ninth book of his *Imouth.*[29] It reads as follows:

"The holy scriptures or books, my lady, affirm that there is a race of daimones who have intercourse with women. Hermes also mentioned this in his *Discourses on Nature,* as well as nearly every treatise, both public and hidden. The ancient and divine scriptures said this, namely that certain angels lusted after women.[30] After they came down, they taught them all the works of nature. Having fallen because of these women, he says, they remained outside of heaven because they taught humankind everything evil and nothing benefiting the soul. The same scriptures say that from them the giants were born.[31] From them was the teaching about these arts, first handed down by Chemeu. He called this the *Book of Chemeu,* whence also the art is called *chēmeia.*"[32]

[27] Compare 2 Thessalonians 2:7–12. See further C. G. Jung, *Psychology and Alchemy,* trans. R. F. C. Hull (London: Routledge & Kegan Paul, 1953), 346–57.

[28] The text for the following translation is taken from Alden A. Mosshammer, ed., *Ecloga Chronographica,* BSGRT (Leipzig: Teubner, 1984), 14. There are parallels in a Syriac text described by Mertens, *Alchimistes,* lxxv.

[29] Imouth or Imouthes = Asclepius.

[30] Compare Genesis 6:1–4.

[31] Zosimus summarizes the plot of 1 Enoch 6–8, considered scripture by some early Christian groups (1 Enoch is quoted in Jude 14–15). All of 1 Enoch was later canonized by the Ethiopian church. The first Hermes was later identified with Enoch (TH 26 from Abū Ma'shar).

[32] The fallen angels are said to teach the arts of sorcery, metallurgy, and root-cutting (1 Enoch 7–8), but *chēmeia* (apparently = alchemical arts) is an interesting addition. See further Festugière, *RHT,* 1.255–60; Stroumsa, *Another Seed,* 139–41; Mertens, "Sur la trace des anges rebelles dans les traditions ésotériques du début de notre ère jusqu'au xviie siècle," in *Anges et demons. Actes du colloque de Liège et de Louvain-la-Neuve (25–26 novembre 1987),* ed. J. Ries and H. Limet (Louvain-la-Neuve: Centre d'histoire des Religions, 1989), 383–98; Mertens, *Alchimistes,* xciii–xcvi; Kyle A. Fraser, "Zosimos of Panopolis and the Book of Enoch: Alchemy as Forbidden Knowledge," *Aries* 4 (2004): 125–47.

Ephrem the Syrian

Introduction

Ephrem the Syrian (306–73 CE) was born in Nisibis in what is now eastern Turkey. He was raised Christian and earned fame as a writer of hymns, homilies, and commentaries in Syriac. After his forced migration to Edessa in 363, he encountered a variety of Christians (Arians, Marcionites, Gnostics, and Manichaeans) against whom he wrote – and taught his choirs to sing – his *Hymns against Heresies*.

Ephrem wrote his prose refutation against Mani (founder of the Manicheans) around 365. In it, he opposed the view that Mani's doctrine agreed with the teachings of Hermes, Plato, and Jesus. It was a Manichean claim that the Egyptian Hermes, the Greek Plato, and the Judean Jesus were "heralds of that Good (Realm) to the world" (the realm of Light).[1] As evidence, Ephrem cited different Manichean teachings to show that they are not documented in Hermetic, Platonic, and Christian lore.[2]

FH 22

Ephrem the Syrian, Prose Refutations *2.208–10*

And if they should assert out of (misplaced) reverence that there were ancient teachers of (Manichaean) truth – for they say of the Egyptian

[1] Translation by J. C. Reeves, *Heralds of That Good Realm: Syro-Mesopotamian Gnosis and Jewish Traditions* (Leiden: Brill, 1996), 12.

[2] On Ephrem, see further Ephrem the Syrian, *Hymns*, trans. Kathleen E. McVey (New York: Paulist Press, 1989), 3–28; Edmund Beck, *Ephräms Polemik gegen Mani und die Manichäer im Rahmen der zeitgenössischen griechischen Polemik und der des Augustinus* (Louven: Secretariat of the CSCO, 1978); Sebastian Brock, *The Luminous Eye: The Spiritual World Vision of Saint Ephrem* (Kalamazoo: Cistercian Publications, 1992), 13–21; Sidney H. Griffith, "Setting Right the Church of Syria: Saint Ephraem's *Hymns Against Heresies*," in William E. Klingshirn and Mark Vessey, eds., *The Limits of Ancient Christianity: Essays on Late Antique Thought and Culture in Honor of R. A. Markus* (Ann Arbor: University of Michigan Press, 1999), 97–114.

Hermes and of the Greek Plato and of Jesus who appeared in Judea that 'they were heralds of that Good (Realm) to the world . . ."[3] For if it is so that they taught these (doctrines) of the Manichaeans, as they allege – if Hermes had knowledge of the Primal Man, father of the *ziwane*,[4] and if he had knowledge of the Pillar of Glory and of (the Realm) of Brightness and the Porter and the rest of the others regarding whom Mani taught about and also revered and addressed in prayer . . . and (if) then we discover that their doctrines or those of their adherents agree with one another, or (even) if one of theirs (agrees) with those of Mani, it (their allegation) is defensible. But if there is no agreement, refutation (of their allegation) is obvious.[5]

The Bowl of Forgetfulness

For Hermes taught that there was a bowl filled with whatever it was filled with and that there are souls excited by desire and they come down beside it, and, when they have come close to it, in it and by reason of it they forget their own place.[6]

Now Mani teaches that the Darkness made an assault upon the Light and desired it, while Hermes teaches that the souls desired the Bowl; and this is a little (more) probable, even though both are lying. But it is (more) probable, because it, the Soul, desires to remain in the body and delay in

[3] Reeves comments that the "authoritative predecessors" of Mani receive the technical designation "heralds of that Good (Realm)." In other words, they are the "messengers of the Realm of Light who announce among humanity the 'good news' of the Manichean gospel" (*Heralds*, 12).

[4] That is, "splendors" (referring to the five sons of the primal Human).

[5] This translation is taken with slight adaptation from Reeves, *Heralds*, 12, with the Syriac text from C. W. Mitchell (*St. Ephraim's Prose Refutations of Mani, Marcion, and Bardaisan*, 2 vols. [London: Williams & Norgate, 1921], 2.208–9).

[6] The bowl is reminiscent of the mixing bowl (κρατήρ) filled with consciousness (νοῦς) in CH 4.4. But the bowl in FH 22 is rather filled with forgetfulness (λήθη). Evidently, it refers to a bowl that souls drink before entering bodies. CH 1.14 speaks of immersion into the waters of Nature as the cause of spiritual self-estrangement. Compare Vergil: "They are the spirits owed a second body by the Fates. They drink deep of the river Lethe's currents there, long drafts that will set them free of cares, oblivious forever" (*Aeneid* 6.713–15, trans. Fagles); Arnobius, *Against the Nations* 2.25: "Is this that learned soul you speak about . . . flowing from living mixing bowls (*ex crateribus vivis*)?" Macrobius says that unembodied souls enter this world through the Bowl of Dionysus and hence become drunk and forgetful (*Commentary on the Dream of Scipio* 1.12.8). The mixing bowl (κρατήρ) is symbol of a flowing spring, which is indicative of birth (Porphyry, *Cave of Nymphs*, 69.1–2 Nauck). *Pistis Sophia* 3.131 speaks of archons who give "a cup of forgetfulness from the seed of evil" to a soul about to be reincarnated (Schmidt, *Pistis Sophia*, trans. MacDermot, 333).

its habitation and dwell in its house and be fondled in its bosom[7] . . . Neither Hermes nor Plato believe in the resurrection of the body.[8]

[7] Contrast SH 15.6: "the soul has no natural urge to be with a body"; SH 23.33–34 (the souls' complaint against embodiment); SH 25.4 (the soul's connection to the body is divinely compelled).

[8] The text for the "Bowl of Forgetfulness" fragment is taken with minor modifications from Scott, *Hermetica*, 1.164–65, which is dependent on the text of Mitchell, *St. Ephraim's Prose Refutations*, 2.210. The translation is that of F. C. Burkitt.

Cyril of Alexandria

Introduction

Cyril, bishop of Alexandria, Egypt, lived from approximately 378 to 444 CE. Likely in the years between 416 and 428, he composed a refutation of the emperor Julian's *Against the Galileans* (= Christians). Julian composed his work in the winter of 362–63 CE, about seventy years prior to Cyril's counterattack. Only the first ten books of Cyril's *Against Julian* survive complete. Most of the Hermetic fragments derive from books 1 and 2.

In *Against Julian*, Cyril argued that the Christian religion was superior to any Egyptian or Greek wisdom. In doing so, he preserved some of the Greco-Egyptian wisdom of the Hermetica. Like Lactantius, Cyril viewed Hermes as in part a prophet of Christian doctrines. Yet Cyril understood Hermes more negatively as a pagan "initiator, ever loitering in the temple precincts near the idols."[1] Hermes did, according to the Alexandrian bishop, have the good sense to adapt the books of Moses. This fact explains, for Cyril, why Hermes sometimes spoke in the language of Christian theology. Hermes's Christian insights, however, have much to do with Cyril's imagination.

It seems that Cyril became familiar with the Hermetica by reading Christian works like the *Exhortation to the Greeks on True Religion* (probably by Marcellus of Ancyra) and *On the Trinity* (by an unknown Egyptian writer). Stationed in Alexandria, Cyril was in a position to track down some Hermetic writings. He noted, for instance, the existence of fifteen books called *Hermaica* composed at Athens.[2] He also provided seventeen quotations from Hermetic writings, four of them known from elsewhere (CH 11.22; 14.6–10; *Ascl.* 29; SH 1.1), and thirteen distinctive fragments translated below. Among these latter fragments, he refers specifically to a third discourse to Asclepius, a first *Detailed Discourse* to

[1] Cyril, *Against Julian* 1.41. [2] Cyril, *Against Julian* 1.41.

Tat, as well as another unnumbered discourse to Asclepius. In some of these excerpts, Agathos Daimon and Osiris are the speakers. Although these figures are mentioned in surviving Hermetic tractates, they never elsewhere appear as partners in dialogue.[3]

FH 23

Cyril, Against Julian *1.48.14–1.49.7*

The Eternal Light-Consciousness

Hermes also says in his third discourse to Asclepius: "We cannot furnish such mysteries to the uninitiated.[4] Now listen with your consciousness: there was one single intelligible light before intelligible light; it exists always, a Consciousness shining from Consciousness, and there was nothing else except the unity of this Being, ever in itself and ever containing all things by its own Consciousness and Light and Spirit."[5]

Further on, he says: "Outside of this Consciousness there is no God, no angel, no daimon, (and) no other reality, for he is Lord of all and Father and God and Fount and Life and Power and Light and Consciousness and Spirit; and all things are in him and under him."

Now by speaking of "Consciousness from Consciousness," in my opinion, he speaks of the Son also as Light from Light.[6] He makes mention also of the Spirit as the one containing all things.[7] There is no angel or daimon or indeed any other nature or reality, he says, outside this divine

[3] The text used for the following translations is edited by Christoph Riedweg, Wolfram Kinzig, and Thomas Brüggemann, eds., *Kyrill von Alexandrien Werke. "Gegen Julian,"* 2 vols. (Berlin: de Gruyter, 2016–17). On Cyril, see further Fowden, *Egyptian Hermes*, 180; Norman Russell, *Cyril of Alexandria* (London: Routledge, 2000), 190–203; van den Broek, "Hermes and Christ," in *From Poimandres*, 115–44 at 136–42; Robert L. Wilken, "Cyril of Alexandria's *Contra Iulianum*," in *Limits of Ancient Christianity*, 42–62.

[4] Cyril may have derived this fragment from the author of *On the Trinity* (*PG* 39, cols. 757b–760a). Compare CH 5.1 (Hermetic teachings are mysteries); SH 11.4 (the teachings must not be delivered to the crowd). See further Sfameni Gasparro, "La gnosi ermetica come iniziazione e mistero," in her *Gnostica et Hermetica*, 309–30.

[5] In CH 1.5, a holy Word or Logos proceeds from divine Consciousness called Father, Life, and Light. Spirit and God are often names for the same being, or spirit is an extension of God, as in *PGM* 3.550–55. See further Sfameni Gasparro, "L'ermetismo nelle testimonianze dei Padri," 277–79.

[6] "Light from Light" (φῶς ἐκ φωτός) appears in the Nicene Creed (Jaroslav Pelikan and Valerie Hotchkiss, *Creeds & Confessions of Faith in the Christian Tradition*, 3 vols. [New Haven: Yale University Press, 2003], 1.162–63). This creedal explanation already occurs with the author of *On the Trinity* (*PG* 760a). See Scott and Ferguson, *Hermetica*, 4.174, n.3.

[7] In the Hermetic quote, however, Consciousness and Spirit are identified; they are not separate hypostases, as in Nicene belief.

supremacy or authority. Rather, he defines all things as in submission to authority and existing because of it.[8]

FH 24

Cyril, Against Julian *1.49.8–17*

The Divine Spirit

Again the same Hermes in the same third discourse to Asclepius when someone asks about the divine Spirit, speaks as follows.[9]

"Unless the lord of all foresaw and arranged that I reveal this teaching, you would not now be mastered by such a burning desire to investigate this question. Now listen to the rest of the teaching.

All things need this Spirit, whom I often mentioned before. For this is the Spirit that bears all things, giving them life and nourishment according to their worth; this Spirit depends upon the holy fountain; it is a help to spirits and ever productive of life for all beings, since it is one."[10]

FH 25

Cyril, Against Julian *1.43.14–29*

God Beyond Comprehension

Hermes the Thrice Great speaks somewhere as follows:

1. "It is difficult to understand God. Even for the person who can understand, to speak of God is impossible. After all, it is impossible to signify with a body what has no body. Likewise, the perfect cannot be comprehended by the imperfect. Moreover, it is grievous for the eternal to have fellowship with the ephemeral. The former lasts forever, while the latter passes away. The one is true, while the other is shrouded by appearances. The weaker stands apart from the stronger and the lesser

[8] Compare CH 9.9: "God holds within him the things that are; none are outside of him; and he is outside of none"; 12.23: "God is All. And the All permeates everything and surrounds everything"; CH 1.31: "Holy are you [God] who surpass every eminence (ὁ πάσης ὑπεροχῆς μείζων)."

[9] This fragment picks up immediately from the preceding. Cyril may have derived it from the author of *On the Trinity* (*PG* 39, columns 756b–757a), who quotes FH 23–24 in the reverse order. See further Claudio Moreschini, "La sapienza pagana al servizio della dottrina trinitaria secondo lo pseudo Didimo di Alessandria," *Augustinianum* 54 (2014): 199–216.

[10] Compare John 6:63: "it is the Spirit that gives life"; 2 Corinthians 3:6: "the Spirit gives life." See further Claudio Moreschini, "Dal *pneuma* ermetico allo Spirito cristiano," *Studi Classici e Orientali* 61 (2015): 451–60.

from the greater as much as the mortal is distant from the divine and immortal.[11]

2. If there is an incorporeal eye,[12] let it go out from the body to the vision of the Beautiful, fly up and soar on high,[13] seeking to behold not a shape nor a body, nor forms, but rather that which made these things, what is at rest, calm, stable, unchanging, the Everything and Alone, the One, the Being from itself, the Being in itself, the Being like itself which is like no other nor unlike itself."[14]

FH 26

Cyril, Against Julian *1.44.1–11*

The Infinite God

Again, the same Hermes affirms:[15] "When conscious of that one and single Good, you can never say anything impossible, for he himself is utter potentiality.[16] Nor can you conceive of him as within or outside of anything, for, as a being without limit, he is the limit of all things; contained by nothing, he contains all things.

What then is the difference between bodies and what has no body, between things born and what is not born, between things subject to Necessity and the being who has supreme power in himself? What is the difference between earthly and heavenly things, things corruptible and things eternal? Is it not true that one type of being has supreme power in itself and the other is subject to Necessity? <Is it not true that some beings are above, perfect, and eternal while> things below are incomplete and corruptible?"[17]

[11] Thus far Cyril conforms to SH 1.1, minus the final "and immortal."
[12] Compare the "mind's eye" in CH 5.2; the "eyes of the heart" in Ephesians 1:18.
[13] Here reading αἰωρηθήτω with Riedweg (*Gegen Julian* 1.73, line 24), not θεωρείτω ("behold") printed in NF 4.130.
[14] Compare CH 4.9: "For the Good has neither shape nor outline. This is why it is like itself but unlike all others, for the bodiless cannot be visible to body." See further SH 1 with notes.
[15] This passage picks up immediately after FH 25. [16] On God as the Good see CH 2.15–16.
[17] In angled brackets I translate Scott's supplement: <τὰ μὲν γὰρ ἄνω, τέλεια ὄντα, ἀΐδιά ἐστι>. On divine ineffability, see Sfameni Gasparro, "L'ermetismo nelle testimonianze dei Padri," 267–69.

FH 27

Cyril, Against Julian *1.46.9–12*

The Fertile Word

Thrice Great Hermes utters the following about God: "For when his Word came forth, he was supremely perfect, fertile, and creative in the realm of nature which was itself fertile.[18] When the Word alighted upon fertile water, he made the water pregnant."[19]

FH 28

Cyril, Against Julian *1.46.13–18*

Word over Nature

The same Hermes once again[20] said: "The pyramid lies at the foundation of Nature and the intelligible world.[21] The pyramid has as its leader and superior the creative Word of the Master of all things. This Word is, after his Master, the first power, unborn, and unlimited. From his Master, the

[18] FH 27–35 are united by the theme of the creative Word. This idea is rooted more in Egyptian than Jewish or Christian mythology. See Mahé, "La création," 9–10.

[19] Compare Genesis 1:2: "a spirit of God was borne over the waters"; CH 1.5: "a holy Word mounted upon the <watery> nature, and untempered fire leapt up from the watery nature to the height above," CH 1.14: "When the Human saw in the water the form like himself as it was in nature, he loved it and wished to inhabit it; wish and action came in the same moment, and he inhabited the unreasoning form;" SH 15.2: "Fire, when it opposed water, dried a part of it so that <earth> arose, borne upon the water"; DH 2.4: "Water is a fecund essence." See also Holzhausen, *CH Deutsch* 1.198 on CH 15.

[20] This passage picks up immediately from FH 27.

[21] Festugière cited evidence from [Iamblichus], *Theology of Arithmetic* (one must add Sextus, *Against the Mathematicians* 7.100) that the pyramid is the first of the geometric solids which constituted the world's body (*Mystique,* 131–37). Festugière considered the pyramid to be equivalent to the Pythagorean Tetraktys, avowed to be the "source possessing the roots [i.e., elements] of ever-flowing nature" (Sextus, *Against the Mathematicians* 4.2; *Ref.* 1.2.9; 4.51.7; 6.23.4; 6.34.1). Specifically, the pyramid was viewed as the basic structural element of fire, indicating that the creative Word is lord of fire. By contrast, Mahé related the pyramid to the primal mound (the *Benben* stone) which rises out of the primal waters (Nun) in Egyptian mythology. "The pyramid texts represent the Demiurge Atum-Khepri 'rising on the mound' and producing the world by spitting … The magic ritual of the papyrus Bremner Rhind (fourth century BCE) shows an analogous Demiurge creating by his word the 'modes of existence,' i.e., the latent forms of things, provisionally kept in the Nun before the appearance of the world. A Greek speaker would probably call this an 'intelligible world' created by the 'Word-Demiurge.' Finally, in a praise of primordial Thebes inscribed at Karnak under Ptolemy VIII (145–116 BCE) one sees Amun 'take his stand on … the massive emergence' and supporting the four columns of heaven to 'found what is pronounced by his voice'" (Mahé, "La création," 30). See further Bull, "Tradition of Hermes," 135–36.

Word emerged.[22] He holds power over and rules the beings crafted through him.[23] He is the firstborn of the Totally Perfect Being, himself perfect and productive as his true son."

FH 29

Cyril, Against Julian *1.46.19–28*

The Word as True Son

And again[24] the same Hermes when one of the ministers of the sanctuaries[25] in Egypt asked: "Why then, greatest Agathos Daimon,[26] is the Word invoked with this name ('true son') by the lord of all?" he (Agathos Daimon) replied: "I mentioned this in the preceding discourses and you have not understood. The nature of his intelligible Word is a generative and creative nature. This is, as it were, his power to engender or his nature or his character – call it whatever you want to call it. Just keep this alone in mind, that he is perfect in a perfect being and issued from a perfect being he produces, creates and brings to life perfect blessings. Since, then, he is of such a nature, he is rightly called by this title."[27]

[22] More literally, "peeked out"; compare CH 1.14: "the Human broke through the vault and stooped to look (παρέκυψεν) through the cosmic framework."

[23] "Through him" (δι' αὐτοῦ) is ambiguous. Perhaps we should read δι' αὑτοῦ ("crafted through *himself*"). The creative Word who emerges from the Father is parallel to CH 1.6–11. See further Sfameni Gasparro, "L'ermetismo nelle testimonianze dei Padri," 279.

[24] This passage picks up immediately after FH 28.

[25] We might also translate: "one of the gods of the sanctuaries" (perhaps Osiris).

[26] Agathos Daimon (the Good Daimon) protected households in the form of a snake. At Alexandria, Agathos Daimon was a state deity sometimes identified with Sarapis. He is the father of the second Hermes according to a (pseudonymous) letter of Manetho cited by George Syncellus (= TH 10b). Manetho places Agathos Daimon in his list of divine kings after Hephaestus (Ptah) and Helios (Re) (Waddell, *Manetho*, 209). See further P. M. Fraser, *Ptolemaic Alexandria*, 2 vols. (Oxford: Clarendon Press, 1972), 1.209–11; 2.355–59; Copenhaver, 164–65. Agathos Daimon appears in CH 10.23 as divine Consciousness instructing Hermes. His words are reported in CH 12.1, 8, 13. Agathos Daimon is also frequently invoked in magical papyri, for instance *PGM* 7.1023: "Grant [victory] because I know the names of Agathos Daimon"; *PGM* 8.49–51: "I know you Hermes . . . turn to me with . . . Agathos Daimon"; *PGM* 12.243–44: "Heaven is your head; ether, body; earth, feet; and the water around you, ocean, [O] Agathos Daimon" (trans. Morton Smith).

[27] The Word as creator is like his divine Father and thus his true son. Hermes as Logos had a demiurgic role, and in the Greek world he was son of the high God Zeus.

FH 30

Cyril, Against Julian *1.46.29–34*

The Word and the Father

The same Hermes in the first of his *Detailed Discourses*[28] to Tat speaks about God as follows: "The Word of the Craftsman, my child, is eternal, self-moved, without growth, without diminishment, without change, without corruption, unique, always like himself, equal and uniform, stable, well-ordered, existing as one after the God who is known before all things."[29]

By this designation (the God known before all things) he signifies, in my view, the father.

FH 31

Cyril, Against Julian *2.29.19–2.30.8*

Indeed Plato declares with gusto, "Gods of gods, works of whom I am the creator and father."[30] We already cited the Greek oracles on these subjects, so I will refrain from repetition and proceed to mention the discourses of Hermes Thrice Great. He spoke as follows in his discourse to Asclepius.[31]

The Origin of Earth

Osiris, he says, spoke: "Then, O greatest Agathos Daimon, how did the earth in its entirety appear?" Then the great Agathos Daimon said: "By an orderly process of evaporation, as I said. From that time, when the abundant waters were ordered[32] to retreat into themselves, the earth in its entirety appeared muddy and quivering.[33] When finally the sun shone

[28] *Disc. 8–9* (NHC VI,1) 63.2–3 distinguishes between general and detailed discourses.

[29] As equal and uniform, the Word resembles the cosmos made by the Craftsman in Plato, *Timaeus* 34b: "smooth and even all over, and equal from the center" (λεῖον καὶ ὁμαλὸν πανταχῇ τε εκ μέσος ἴσον). Here God is προεγνωσμένον ("known before all things"); in FH 12a, 17, 36, God is "prior to thought" (προεννοούμενος).

[30] Plato, *Timaeus* 41a.

[31] Oddly, the following discourse presents Agathos Daimon, not Hermes, as speaking to Osiris, not Asclepius.

[32] Other manuscripts read, instead of ἀπὸ τοῦ ("from that time"), ἀπὸ τοῦ κυρίου ("ordered by the lord") or ἀπὸ θεοῦ ("by God").

[33] Compare SH 23.51: "the earth was still quivering as it was congealed by the shining sun"; *PGM* 13.167–69: "Then he [an unidentified God] laughed a second time. All was water. Earth, hearing

and began the heating and drying process, the earth was hardened in the midst of the waters, completely surrounded by water."[34]

FH 32a

Cyril, Against Julian *2.30.9–11*

Creation by Voice

Moreover, in another passage (he says):[35] "The creator and Lord of all pronounced with his voice: 'Let earth come to be and the firmament appear!' And immediately the beginning of his creation, earth, came into existence."[36]

FH 32b

Cyril, Against Julian *2.30.12–18*

The Origin of the Sun

So much he says concerning earth. Concerning the sun he speaks in turn.

Osiris said: "O thrice great Agathos Daimon, from what source did this great sun blaze forth?"[37] Then the great Agathos Daimon said: "Osiris, do you want us to recount how the sun was born and the origin of its shining? It shone forth by the providence of the master of all. This is the origin of the sun from the master of all, made through his holy and crafting Word.'"[38]

the sound, cried out and heaved, and the water came to be divided into three parts" (trans. Morton Smith).

[34] The process described here recalls the primeval mound that rises out of the waters in some Egyptian creation myths.

[35] This passage picks up immediately from FH 31. The speaker is not clear, but judging from FH 31 Cyril believed that he was quoting Hermes. We might also supply "Agathos Daimon."

[36] Compare Genesis 1:6–9: "And God said, 'Let there be a firmament in the midst of the waters, and let it separate the waters from the waters' . . . And God said, 'Let the waters under the sky be gathered together into one place, and let the dry land appear'" (NRSV, modified). Creation by the spoken word is, however, a native Egyptian notion that appears in SH 23.10 (God creates Nature by voice). For relevant Egyptian texts, see Allen, *Genesis in Egypt*, 36–47.

[37] With the epithet "thrice great," it is tempting to view Agathos Daimon as a manifestation of Hermes.

[38] It is not clear whether the last sentence continues the quote from Hermes or is Cyril's own summarizing comment. Compare CH 4.1: "the Craftsman made the whole world by reasoned speech [*or:* Word] (λόγῳ)."

FH 33a

Cyril, Against Julian *2.29.19–25*

The Formation of the Sun

Likewise the same Hermes says in his first *Detailed Discourse*[39] with Tat: "The lord of all immediately uttered by his own holy, intelligible, and creative Word, 'Let the sun exist!' And just when he spoke, Nature with a burst of wind drew up the fire naturally borne upward – I mean the unmixed, brightest, most intense and productive fire.[40] Nature performed this work by her own breath and raised the fire to the heights, away from the water."[41]

FH 34

Cyril, Against Julian *2.31.10–16*

The Bestowal of Necessity

Their Thrice Great Hermes again makes mention of this,[42] for he introduces God as saying to his creatures: "I will bestow upon you my subjects the command given to you through my decree,[43] as Necessity; for this is the law that you possess."[44]

FH 35

Cyril, Against Julian *8.31.17–24*

The Order of Creation

Somewhere their Thrice Great Hermes spoke about the master craftsman God of all: "In addition, he established order in disorder[45] as a perfect and wise being in order to make the intelligible entities preeminent and first in

[39] Compare FH 30.

[40] The act of speaking the sun into existence resembles Genesis 1:14–16. But interest in the mechanics of the sun's formation indicates a wider (Egyptian) mythological background.

[41] In CH 1.5 fire is drawn up to the height, but Nature is not the actor.

[42] Namely that God organizes his creation as he intends (Cyril, *Against Julian*, 2.31.6–9).

[43] Or "Word" (διὰ τοῦ λόγου).

[44] Compare God's speech to the souls in Plato, *Timaeus* 41e–42d; SH 23.17, 38–42.

[45] Accepting Scott's emendation of [καὶ] ἀταξίᾳ ("in disorder") for the manuscript reading καὶ ἀταξίαν ("and disorder") (Scott, *Hermetica*, 4.223, n.16). Holzhausen proposes τάξιν κατ᾽ ἀξίαν, which he translates *nach Rang und Wert* (*CH Deutsch*, 2.599, n.71). Compare Plato, *Timaeus* 30a: the Craftsman "brought it out of disorder into order" (εἰς τάξιν . . . ἐκ τῆς ἀταξίας); Philo wrote that Hermes's garb is a manifestation of "order in disorder" (τάξιν ἐν ἀταξίᾳ) (*Embassy to Gaius* 94).

rank as eldest and superior, while he subordinated things sensible as second to these. Thus what is heavy and borne beneath the intelligible contains within itself a wise creative Word. His Word has a share in creative nature as a productive and life-giving being."[46]

Compare CH 5.4: "if the unordered is deficient . . . it is still subject to a master who has not yet imposed order on it."

[46] Compare CH 1.14, 16: "Nature took hold of her beloved [the Human], hugged him all about and embraced him . . . When Nature made love with the Human, she bore a wonder most wondrous . . . seven humans, androgynous and exalted."

Addendum: The Reception of Hermetic Fragments from Cyril

The following six sources all appear to be dependent upon an excerpted collection of Hermetic fragments made (at least in part) from Cyril's work *Against Julian*. It is logical, therefore, to present them here.

In terms of sheer data, these authors contribute little that is absolutely new to our knowledge of Hermetic lore. They are vital, however, for understanding the reception of the Hermetica among Christian authors in Late Antiquity and beyond. In these fragments, one can observe the progressive Christianization of Hermes, lauded as no less than the prophet of the Trinity.

John Malalas (491–578 CE), *Chronography* 2.4[1]

In the times of the reign of the aforementioned (Pharaoh) Sostris lived Hermes Thrice Great the Egyptian. He was a man fearsome in wisdom, who said that the name of the unspeakable creator consisted of three persons but one divinity. Thus the Egyptians called him "Hermes Thrice Great."[2]

Hermes has been cited in his many treatises to Asclepius as having said the following about God's nature: "Unless the Lord of all foresaw that I reveal this teaching, you would not now be mastered by such a burning desire to investigate this question.[3]

We cannot furnish such mysteries to the uninitiated. Now listen with your consciousness: there was one single intelligible light before intelligible light; it exists always, a Consciousness shining from Consciousness, and there was nothing else except the unity of this Being, ever in itself and ever

[1] The text that serves as the basis for the following translation is edited by Ioannes Thurn, ed., *Ioannis Malalae Chronographia*, Corpus Fontium Historiae Byzantinae 35 (Berlin: de Gruyter, 2000), 19–20, 265.

[2] Mahé quotes a parallel Armenian text (*Testimony of the External Philosophers concerning Divinity*) to the effect that "Hermes the illustrious philosopher said (that there existed) three celestial powers, very great, ineffable, creators of all (beings), and that therein consists the sole divinity" (*HHE*, 2.346).

[3] This is the first line of FH 24 from Cyril, *Against Julian* 1.49.10–12.

containing all things by the same Consciousness and Light and Spirit. Outside of this Consciousness there is no God, no angel, no daimon, (and) no other reality, for he is lord of all and father and God; and all things are in him and under him.[4]

For when his Word came forth, he was supremely perfect, fertile, and creative in the realm of nature which was itself fertile. When the Word fell into fertile water, he made the water pregnant."[5]

Having declared this, he prayed: "I swear by you, Heaven, wise work of a great God, be propitious! I swear by you, Voice of the Father which he uttered at first when he fixed all the universe by his will."[6]

This voice of the Father, which he uttered at first, is his only-born Word.[7]

These passages, also collected by the most holy Cyril in his *Against Julian the Emperor*, are adduced to show as more precise proof that even Thrice Great Hermes, though ignorant of the future, confessed the single substance of the Trinity.[8]

John Malalas, *Chronography* 13.36

During his (Gratian's) reign, Theon the most wise philosopher taught and interpreted the astronomical matters along with the treatises of Hermes Thrice Great and Orpheus.[9]

[4] This paragraph is a slightly shorter version of FH 23 from Cyril, *Against Julian* 1.48.15–23.

[5] This paragraph is identical to FH 27 from Cyril, *Against Julian* 1.46.9–12.

[6] In the text of Cyril, a form of this quote is attributed to Orpheus, not Hermes (*Against Julian* 1.46.2–4). It reads: "I swear by you, sage work of a great God! / I swear by you, speech of the Father which he uttered at first / when he fixed all the universe by his own counsels."

[7] This is a Christianizing comment of Cyril. In the text of Malalas, however, one could mistakenly read it as part of the quote of "Hermes." In later tradition, this is how it was taken (see below).

[8] The testimony of Malalas was adapted and abbreviated by John of Antioch in the early seventh century CE (frag. 9, *Fragmenta ex Historia chronica*, ed. Umberto Roberto [Berlin: de Gruyter, 2005], 24–27). The author of the seventh-century CE *Paschal Chronicle* 85.8–86.12 (Dindorf) follows Malalas more closely. This passage from Malalas was also slightly adapted in the 1050s by the Byzantine writer George Cedrenus, *A Concise History of the World* 24.3 printed in Luigi Tartaglia, ed., *Georgii Cedreni historiarum compendium* (Rome: Bardi, 2016), 102.

[9] The emperor Gratian reigned from 367 to 383 CE. Theon of Alexandria (approximately 335–405 CE) was a famous astronomer and mathematician. In the *Palatine Anthology* (9.491), a line in SH 29 was attributed to him: "Moon, Jupiter, Mars, the Paphian, Saturn, Sun, and Mercury." Theon's daughter Hypatia, dismembered by a Christian mob in 415 CE, earned fame as a mathematician and philosopher.

Tübingen Theosophy *(around 500 CE)*[1]

2.32 A Fragment of Hermes to Asclepius about God

We cannot furnish such mysteries to the uninitiated. Now listen with your consciousness: there was one single intelligible light before intelligible light; it exists always, a Consciousness shining from Consciousness, and there was nothing else except the unity of this Being, ever in itself and ever containing all things by its own Consciousness and Light and Spirit.[2]

2.33 The Same Writer from the Same Discourse

Outside of this (Consciousness) there is no God, no angel, no daimon, (and) no other reality, for he is lord of all and father and God and Fount and Life and Power and Light and Consciousness and Spirit; and all things are in him and under him.[3]

2.34 The Same Writer to Tat from the First Book of the *Detailed Discourses* about God

The Word of the Craftsman, my child, is eternal, self-moved, without growth, without diminishment, without change, without corruption, unique, always like himself, <equal and uniform, stable, well-ordered>, existing as one after the God who is known before all things.[4]

2.35 <From the Same Author about God>

For when his Word came forth, he was supremely perfect, fertile, and creative in the realm of nature which was itself fertile. When the Word alighted upon fertile water, he made the water pregnant.[5]

[1] The anonymous *Theosophy* originally comprised eleven books. The first seven concerned the "orthodox faith." Books 8–10, from which the fragments derive, attempted to show how "the oracles of the Greek gods and the so-called theologies of the Greek and Egyptian sages as well as the Sibylline oracles agree with the objective of the divine scriptures" (§1). Book 11, finally, presented a brief chronicle from Adam to the reign of the Emperor Zeno (died in 491 CE). The following translations are based on the text edited by Pier Franco Beatrice, *Anonymi monophysitae Theosophia: An Attempt at Reconstruction* (Leiden: Brill, 2001), 37–38. See further Beatrice, "Pagan Wisdom and Christian Theology according to the *Tübingen Theosophy*," *Journal of Early Christian Studies* 3 (1995): 403–18.

[2] The fragment is identical with FH 23 from Cyril, *Against Julian* 1.48.15–19.

[3] The fragment is identical with FH 23 from Cyril, *Against Julian* 1.48.20–23.

[4] The fragment is nearly identical with FH 30 (from Cyril, *Against Julian* 1.46.30–33), from which the phrase in angled brackets is added.

[5] The fragment is identical to FH 27 from Cyril, *Against Julian* 1.46.9–12.

2.37 Hermes the Greatest on the Almighty[6]

Be wakeful with your eye of sleepless fire, you who enliven the course of the aether, control the heat of the sun, send the clouds in the whirlwind, whose name the world cannot contain.[7] I have known thee, you uncorrupted, ever-flowing, all-seeing, fearsome eye,[8] father of worlds, the only God, taking your commencement from no being!

After you, I celebrate the one single son derived from you, whom you fathered by indescribable strength and piercing voice[9] all at once without jealousy and without suffering, to be your own unborn[10] Word, a god in essence and from (divine) essence[11] who manifests the incorruptible and entirely equal[12] image of you his Father, so that he is in you and you in him, the mirror of (your) beauty, the face bestowing mutual joy![13]

2.42 Hermes from the Third Discourse to Asclepius

Unless the Lord of all foresaw and arranged that I reveal this teaching, you would not now be mastered by such a burning desire to investigate this question. Now listen to the rest of the teaching.

[6] In his edition of the Hermetic fragments from diverse authors, A. D. Nock added a postscript in which he printed the Greek text of a "Hymn to the Almighty" ascribed to Hermes. Nock derived his Greek text from Hartmut Erbse, who defended the authenticity of the fragment (*Fragmente griechischer Theosophien* [Hamburg: Hanischer Gilden, 1941], 203). Nock, who saw Christian influence in the fragment, was inclined to reject it. If the fragment is genuine, it has undergone heavy Christian editing.

[7] Compare FH 3a with notes. Scarpi, 2.39, notes that *PGM* 12.237–40 is "a sort of evocation of this passage" insofar as the almighty Forefather (ὁ παντοκράτωρ θεός) of the gods has a hidden and secret name (κρυπτὸν ὄνομα ἄρρητον).

[8] Compare the "incorporeal eye" of FH 25, and the "eye of the tormenting angels who control Tartaros – an eye that ever maintains its threatening stare" in *Ref.* 10.34.2.

[9] Here Beatrice prints ὃν ῥώμῃ ἀπορρήτῳ καὶ ὀξυτέρᾳ νοῦ καὶ φωνῆς ("whom you fathered by the unspeakable and piercing strength of your mind and voice").

[10] "Unborn" (ἀγένητον) is a correction of Erbse. MSS read either ἀγενοῦς ("[Word] of the Unborn") or ἀγεννήτως ("in an unborn way").

[11] The language may depend on John 1:1: "the Word was (a) god." Compare the Nicene Creed "Light from Light"; FH 23: "there was one single intelligible light before intelligible light; it exists always, a Consciousness shining from Consciousness."

[12] Translating πανομοίαν ("entirely equal") with Pitra and Nock. Erbse printed πᾶν ὁμοίαν.

[13] Compare John 14:10: "Do you not believe that I am in the Father and the Father is in me?"; John 17:21: "As you, Father, are in me and I am in you." Wisdom 7:26: "she [Wisdom] is a spotless mirror of the working of God and an image of his goodness." CH 1.9: "The mind who is God . . . by speaking gave birth to a second mind, a craftsman . . . a god of fire and spirit"; CH 1.12: "Consciousness the father of all . . . gave birth to a Human like himself whom he loved as his own child. The Human was most fair: he had the father's image."

All things need this Spirit, whom I often mentioned before. This is the Spirit that bears all things, giving them life and nourishment according to their worth; this Spirit depends on the holy fountain; it is a helpful spirit and ever productive of life for all beings, since it is one.[14]

1.40[15]

To the person who asked if by a circumspect life one can draw near to God, Apollo replied:

> You seek to find a prize equal to a god; you cannot.
> Only praiseworthy Hermes of Egypt took this prize,
> Moses of the Hebrews, and the wise man of Mazaca,[16]
> Whom once the land of renowned Tyana nourished.
> Yes, hard it is for mortal eyes to look upon deathless reality
> Unless one has a covenant with the gods.

Prophecies of the Pagan Philosophers in Abbreviated Form *(Sixth or Seventh Century CE)*[1]

4. Hermes Thrice Great Also Speaks about the Trinity

This man was from Egypt, outstanding in wisdom; he interpreted and said that the name of the ineffable one and the maker consists of three-fold powers of majesty, but the godhead, he said, is one.[2] For this reason, he was called by the Egyptians "Thrice Great," that is, of three-fold greatness,

[14] The fragment is virtually identical to FH 24 (from Cyril, *Against Julian* 1.49.14–17), the only significant difference being that Nock prints ἐπίκουρον πνεύμασι ("a help to spirits") and Beatrice prints ἐπίκουρον πνεῦμα ("helpful spirit").

[15] For the sake of completeness, I translate the following oracle (probably third century CE), which mentions the Egyptian Hermes among other sages (Moses and Apollonius of Tyana). The text is taken from Beatrice, *Theosophia*, 21. Cf. the oracles cited by Porphyry, fragments 323–24 (Smith). See further Aude Busine, "Hermès Trismégiste, Moïse et Apollonius de Tyane dans un Oracle d'Apollon," *Apocrypha* 13 (2002): 227–44.

[16] The reference is to Apollonius of Tyana. Mazaca or Caesarea in Cappadocia (modern Kayseri) was the capital of the Roman province of Cappadocia in what is now central Turkey.

[1] These "prophecies" come from a Syriac collection addressed to the pagan residents of Harran (on the southeastern border of modern Turkey). The translations are taken in slightly adapted form from Sebastian Brock, "A Syriac Collection of Prophecies of the Pagan Philosophers," *Orientalia Lovaniensia Periodica* 14 (1983): 203–46 (215–16, 218–19 [text], 228–31 [translation]).

[2] Compare the "Unbegotten," "Begotten," and "Self-begotten" God in *Disc. 8–9* (NHC VI,6) 57.13–16; 63.21–23.

for it is shown in his various treatises addressed to his friend Asclepius, where he speaks of the divine nature as follows:

> Unless there was some concern on the part of the lord of all, with the result that the Word revealed (it) to me, then no desire such as this would have seized hold of you that you should enquire about it.[3]
>
> For it is not capable of being found by those who are not worthy of such mysteries as these. But listen with the mind, how the intelligible light was all alone on its own before the sensible light; and it is at all times the mind which illumines the intelligence.[4]

After a little, he said: "The Word which was born from him is perfected in everything and is creator as well."[5]

Having said this, he prayed, "I adjure you, O heaven, work of wisdom of the great God, be forgiving. I adjure you, first voice of the Father, which spoke when he made firm the entire universe by (his) will, the first voice of the Father which he spoke to the only-begotten, his Word."[6]

14. Hermes on the Son

> The Word of the same was born, being perfect in everything, as one born and the creator, having descended into a mother who gave (him) birth, and dwelled in nature; and he caused the waters to conceive.[7]

19. Hermes on the father and on the son

> Therefore he resembles the power of the father who is with him. The son is therefore in the father and the father in the son, for he is the cause for everything to come into being; child of the father, who is light of light, who is from fire and with fire; so too the mind which is with the father is also the Word in light.[8]

[3] FH 24 from Cyril, *Against Julian* 1.49.10–12.

[4] A transmuted form of the first part of FH 23 from Cyril, *Against Julian* 1.48.15–18.

[5] Compare the beginning of FH 27 from Cyril, *Against Julian* 1.46.9–11.

[6] In the text of Cyril, a form of this quote is attributed to Orpheus, not Hermes (*Against Julian* 1.46.2–4). This misattribution is also attested in John Malalas (above).

[7] A statement about creation is refashioned into a prophecy of the virgin birth. Compare the latter part of FH 27 from Cyril, *Against Julian* 1.46.11–12.

[8] Some phrases here resemble Cyril's Christian commentary on FH 23 from Cyril, *Against Julian* 1.49.1–7. Compare also the *Hymn to the Almighty* cited as part of the *Tübingen Philosophy* above. Section 21 of the same Syriac work offers an abbreviated translation of CH 13.1–2. See further Van Bladel, *Arabic Hermes*, 83–85.

Jacob of Edessa, Hexaemeron *(Shortly after 700 CE)*[1]

Behold, there was a man, Egyptian by race, most celebrated and honored among the Greeks whom they called "Hermes Thrice Great." He spoke discourses to those who questioned him, discourses which pointed toward truth and which are not foreign to the discourses of the Spirit.

When a certain Osiris, they say, asked him about the generation of the sun, it is written that he responded to him: "Osiris, do you want me to speak about the generation of the sun when it appeared? It appeared by the Providence of the universal lord."[2] There is the generation of the sun from the universal lord, for it was made by his sacred Word.

When he again asked how it was made, he responded after other matters in this way: "The lord of all immediately cried out to his Word who was holy, understanding, and effective: 'Let the sun exist!' As soon as he said this, there appeared that fire which naturally extends on high, that fire, I mean, which is most preeminent and luminous, most powerful and longest enduring. Nature drew the fire out by its own breath and drew it up into the height above the waters."[3]

I think that no one would say that these words are far distant from the truth of the words of the Spirit of truth. In fact, I would declare them to be extremely close. In effect, I affirm the providence of God, the universal lord. Further, I affirm that the sun was made by the universal lord through his holy Word.

Moreover, when the universal lord cried out to his holy Word, "Let the sun exist!" Nature the creatrix by her own breath drew out over the waters a sphere of shining, productive fire. In this way, he says that the sun appeared.[4]

Now who would say that this was not the Spirit spoken of by Moses who dictated: "God said, let there be luminaries," and who sung through David: "By the Word of the lord the heavens were made and by the spirit of his mouth all their powers"?[5] It is this Spirit who also put these words

[1] The text used as the basis for the following translation is the Latin translation of the Syriac made by A. Vaschalde, *Iacobi Edesseni Hexaemeron seu In opus creationis libri septem*, Corpus Scriptorum Christianorum Orientalium 97, Scriptores Syri 48 (Leuven: L. Durbecq, 1953), 125–26. The Syriac text can be found in I.-B. Chabot, ed., *Iacobi Edesseni Hexaemeron seu In opus creationis libri septem*, Corpus Scriptorum Christianorum Orientalium, Scriptores Syri 56 (Paris: Republic, 1928), 149–50 (149b11–150a17).

[2] The text is close to FH 32b from Cyril.

[3] A version of FH 33a from Cyril.

[4] How Jacob would explain "Nature the creatrix" is unclear.

[5] Genesis 1:14; Psalm 32:6.

into the mouth of Hermes the Egyptian so that through them he could reveal all truth and declare it.

Suda (a Byzantine Dictionary of the Tenth Century CE) under the Headword "Hermes the Thrice Great"[1]

Hermes Thrice Great was an Egyptian sage. He flourished before the Pharaoh.[2] He was called "Thrice Great" because he proclaimed concerning the Trinity that a single deity existed as triune, as follows: "There was an intelligible light prior to intelligible light; and there always was a brilliant consciousness from consciousness, and there was nothing else apart from the unity of this consciousness. Moreover, there was a spirit embracing all things. Outside of this, there was no god, nor angel, nor any other substance, for he is lord and father and God of all, and all things are beneath him and in him."[3]

"His Word is completely perfect and fertile and creative; as a child[4] in a fertile nature and in fertile water, he made the water pregnant."[5]

After declaring this, he prayed: "I swear by you, heaven, the wise work of a great God; I swear by you, voice of the father which he uttered at first when he established the world in its entirety; I swear by you according to his only-born Word and according to the father, who embraces all things, be gracious, be gracious!"[6]

Bar Hebraeus (1226–86 CE), Candelabra of the Sanctuary, Base III[1]

One alone is the intellectual light, (consisting) of intelligible fire: and the intellect which is at all times illumined in an illumined mind. There is

[1] The translation of the following fragment is based on the text edited by Ada Adler, ed., *Suidae Lexicon*, 5 vols. (Stuttgart: Teubner, 1967), 2.413–14, §3038.

[2] Perhaps the Pharaoh in the time of Moses is meant (the only well-known Pharaoh in biblical tradition). If so, Hermes Thrice Great precedes the Hebrew sage. This line (ἤκμαζε δὲ πρὸ τοῦ Φαραώ) reappears in Zonaras, *Lexicon* under epsilon, page 860, line 13 (Tittman).

[3] An adaptation of FH 23 from Cyril, *Against Julian* 1.48.16–23.

[4] The Suda reads παῖς ὢν – a Christianizing variant – but Cyril and Malalas have the original reading πεσών ("having fallen upon").

[5] An adaptation of FH 27 from Cyril, *Against Julian* 1.46.9–12.

[6] In the text of Cyril, a form of this quote is attributed to Orpheus, not Hermes (*Against Julian* 1.46.2–4). In 1574, Flussas (François Foix de Candalle) combined SH 2A, SH 1, Stobaeus's Greek quote of *Ascl.* 27 (*Anthology* 4.52, second part of §47), and this passage from the *Suda* to form CH 15. The *Suda* passage evidently draws upon John Malalas, cited above.

[1] Employed below with minor changes is the translation of Sebastian Brock, "Some Syriac Excerpts from Greek Collections of Pagan Prophecies," *VC* 38 (1984): 77–90 at 83–84. For the MSS used to

nothing else in its mixture, and in spirit it encircles everything. And outside this one there is no god, no angel, no demon, no essence whatsoever; but he is lord of all and God and father, and everything is in him and under his authority whose Word, having in perfect fashion proceeded from him and been born, is maker of all; and having at his generation overshadowed the nature of the waters, he caused the waters to bring forth.[2]

establish the text, see *ibid.*, 80. We know that Cyril's *Against Julian* was known in a Syriac translation, part of which survives (Van Bladel, *Arabic Hermes*, 199, n. 135).

[2] This fragment, which Bar Hebraeus took from a Syriac collection of oracles, represents a fused and transmuted form of FH 23 and 27 (from Cyril, *Against Julian* 1.48.16–12; 1.46.9–12), perhaps mediated by the Hermetic quotes in the anonymous Syriac writer quoted above. Another fragment of Bar Hebraeus (translated by Brock, "Some Syriac Excerpts," 86) is a partial rendition of the Hymn to the Almighty from the *Tübingen Theosophy* 2.37 or a collection dependent upon it. See further Van Bladel, *Arabic Hermes*, 127–28.

Marcellus of Ancyra

Introduction

Marcellus, bishop of Ancyra, lived from about 285 to 374 CE. He was a strong supporter of the Nicene theology in which divine father and son are seen as a single substance. Nevertheless, he lived during a time when forms of Arian Christology (in which Christ is ontologically subordinate to the father) predominated. In 336, Marcellus was deposed from his position for criticizing his Arian opponent Asterius. Although restored in 337, he was expelled again two years later. Probably in exile sometime between 340 and 350, Marcellus wrote a letter called *On the Holy Church* attacking the putative divisiveness of other Christian groups.[1]

Even to fellow supporters of Nicea, Marcellus became something of an embarrassment. The bishop of Ancyra strongly emphasized the unity of God, arguing that the divine son and holy spirit only emerged as independent entities for the purposes of creation and salvation. After salvation is complete, Marcellus argued, both son and spirit will be subsumed again into the divine unity of the father.[2]

Although deemed a heretic by many in his time, Marcellus fought fiercely against those whom he perceived to be heretics. In this passage from *On the Holy Church*, he attributes the heresy of his opponents primarily to three figures: Plato, Aristotle, and Hermes Thrice Great.

[1] Formerly *On the Holy Church* was attributed, or partially attributed, to Anthimus, bishop of Nicomedia, who was martyred during the Diocletian persecution (either in 303 or 311 CE). Despite some opposition (R. P. C. Hanson, "The Date and Authorship of Pseudo-Anthimus 'De Sancta Ecclesia,'" *Proceedings of the Royal Irish Academy* 83c [1983]: 251–54), the ascription to Marcellus has proved cogent. See the history of research in Alistair H. B. Logan, "Marcellus of Ancyra (Pseudo-Anthimus), "'On the Holy Church': Text, Translation, and Commentary," *Journal of Theological Studies* 51 (2000): 81–112 (81–89). For the historical context of the work, see Sara Parvis, *Marcellus of Ancyra and the Lost Years of the Arian Controversy 325–345* (Oxford: Oxford University Press, 2006), 186–92. The translation below is based on Logan, "Marcellus," 91–92.

[2] For a more detailed discussion of Marcellus's theology, see Maurice James Dowling, "Marcellus of Ancyra: Problems of Christology and the Doctrine of the Trinity" (Ph.D. diss., Queen's University, Belfast, 1987), 58–268.

Unlike Lactantius, Marcellus is not at all friendly toward Hermes. Alistair H. B. Logan suggests that Marcellus vilified Hermes precisely to counter the tendencies of Lactantius and Eusebius, both of whom appealed to pre-Christian Hellenic authors to validate Christian doctrines.[3]

FH 36

Marcellus of Ancyra, On the Holy Church *7–16*

Hermes Source of Heresies

All these[4] derived the starting points of their impiety from the philosophers Hermes, Plato, and Aristotle.[5]

Now about the heresy of the Ariomaniacs[6] – a plague on God's church – it is necessary to clarify its status as well, so that you can know that they filched the dogmas of the ancients by deceitful sophistry.

These are the people, then, who teach three hypostases, just as Valentinus the chief heretic first concocted them in his book entitled *On the Three Natures*. He indeed was the first to concoct three hypostases and three persons of Father, Son, and Holy Spirit, and he is caught red-handed having filched this teaching from Hermes and Plato.

The Second God

Accordingly, this is why they in turn fabricate a second god created by the father before the ages, as their leader Asterius said. He was taught by Hermes surnamed Thrice Great.[7] For Hermes mouths this doctrine to Asclepius the doctor: "Therefore listen, Asclepius. The lord and creator of

[3] Logan, "Marcellus," 89. See further Markus Vinzent, ed., *Markell von Ankyra: Die Fragmente. Der Brief an Julius von Rom.* Supplements to VC 39 (Leiden: Brill, 1997), xiii–xci; Joseph T. Lienhard, *Contra Marcellum: Marcellus of Ancyra and Fourth-century Theology* (Washington, DC: Catholic University of America Press, 1999), 1–20.

[4] Marcellus refers to a motley group of early Christians he calls "gnostics" and "the rest of the mob of heretics," for instance Simon, Saturninus, Basilides, Marcus the Valentinian, Carpocrates, Prodicus, Epiphanes, Marcion, Lucian, and Cerdo.

[5] For the argument that Christian heretics derived their doctrines from philosophers, see Irenaeus, *Against Heresies* 2.14; Tertullian, *Prescription against Heretics* 7.3–8; and especially *Ref.* 1, *pref.* §§8–9 with M. David Litwa, ed., *Refutation of All Heresies: Translated with an Introduction and Notes* (Atlanta, GA: SBL Press, 2016), xlv–l. Logan speculates that Marcellus may have received his knowledge of the Hermetica from the writings of Lactantius or perhaps an independent collection from Egypt ("Marcellus," 103–4).

[6] A derogatory term for the various followers of Arius.

[7] Lactantius tentatively derives Plato's views on a first and second God from Hermes (*Epitome of the Divine Institutes* 37.4–6). Eusebius of Caesarea referred to Christ as a "second god" (*Preparation for the Gospel* 7.13.2; *Ecclesiastical History* 1.2.5). He was anticipated by Origen (*Against Celsus* 6.61) and Justin Martyr (*Dialogue with Trypho* 55.1).

all things, whom we traditionally call God, made a yet second god that is visible and perceptible."[8] This is the passage whence flows Asterius's reading "only begotten god" against (the testimony of) the divine John who said "only begotten son."[9]

Then again the Thrice-Great says: "When therefore he made this first and sole and one (god), it appeared beautiful to him and bursting with all goods, he was delighted and loved it exceedingly as his own offspring."[10]

This, then, was the source from which their notion of a first and second god originated. It was on account of this, too, that Eusebius of Caesarea wrote "unbegotten."[11]

Furthermore, what was the source for their declaration that the Word of God is subordinate to the will of God? Did they not learn this too from the Thrice Great? For he speaks about the second god after the primal God as follows: "We will know the God prior to thought who has all things in common with the one who willed him except in two respects: by the fact that he is embodied and by the fact that he exists in visible form."[12]

By hankering after these (doctrines), they horribly fell short of the true knowledge, boasting of being disciples of Hermes and Plato and Aristotle rather than of Christ and his apostles!

[8] This quote represents a Greek version of *Ascl.* 8: "When the master and shaper of all things, whom rightly we call God, made a god next after himself who can be seen and sensed [namely the cosmos] . . . then, having made this god as his first production and second after himself, it seemed beautiful to him since it was entirely full of the goodness of everything, and he loved it as the progeny of his own divinity." Lactantius also quotes the Greek version of *Ascl.* 8 in his *Divine Institutes* 4.6.4: "In the book called *Perfect Discourse*, Hermes used these words: 'The Lord and Maker of all things, whom we usually call God, created the second God visible and sensible . . . When he had created him as his first and unique creation . . . he loved and cherished him as his only son." The first part of this quote (without the mention of God's "son") also appears in Lactantius, *Epitome of the Divine Institutes* 37.5. On the divinity of the world, see Jean Pépin, "Cosmic Piety," in A. H. Armstrong, ed., *Classical Mediterranean Spirituality: Egyptian, Greek, Roman* (London: SCM Press, 1989), 408–36. On the Christian understanding of *Ascl.* 8, see Löw, *Hermes*, 197–203; Stephen Gersh, *Middle Platonism and Neoplatonism: the Latin Tradition*, 2 vols. (Notre Dame, IN: University of Notre Dame, 1986), 1.370–73; Paolo Siniscalco, "Ermete Trismegisto, profeta pagano della rivelazione cristiana," *Atti dell'Accademia delle Scienze di Torino* 101 (1966–67): 83–117 at 89–102.

[9] The manuscripts of John 1:18 disagree on whether to read "only begotten son" (ὁ μονογενὴς υἱός) or "only begotten God" (μονογενὴς θεός).

[10] A continuation of the *Ascl.* 8 quote. Marcellus cites more of the text than is contained in Lactantius, *Divine Institutes* 4.6.4, which indicates that Marcellus was not entirely dependent upon him.

[11] Note that Hermes never claims that the cosmos was unbegotten. According to Marcellus frag. 118 (Vinzent = Eusebius, *Against Marcellus* 1.4.26), Eusebius spoke doctrines like those of Hermes (Εὐσεβίου . . . Ἑρμῇ ὁμοίως εἰρηκότος). It is true that Eusebius made use of Hermetic texts (for instance, CH 7.1 in *Against Hierocles* 42) without acknowledgement. The ellipsis indicates the omission of a section wherein Marcellus quotes Plato, *Timaeus* 68a and 52a, wrongly citing the *Gorgias*.

[12] The God prior to thought here refers to the second god or cosmos. Compare CH 8.2; FH 12a, 17, 30. The Hermetic cosmos, or second god, is embodied and visible. Marcellus took the embodiment to refer to Christ's incarnation.

John Lydus

Introduction

John Lydus was born in 490 CE in the city of Philadelphia in Lydia (southwestern Turkey). He filled lucrative political offices in Constantinople mainly during the reign of the emperor Justinian (527–65 CE). After retiring around 552, he retained his teaching post at the imperial court. During this time, he occupied himself with compiling works on Roman antiquities. One of these is his *On Months*, a motley work treating ancient legends, festivals, and the marking of time (days, months, and so on). In this work, Lydus quotes portions of the *Asclepius* (not printed here) as well as otherwise unattested Hermetic fragments translated below.[1]

FH 37a

John Lydus, On Months *4.64*

Androgynous Aphrodite

Hence Hermes in his *Creation of the Cosmos* relates that the parts above Aphrodite's waist are masculine and the parts below it feminine.[2] Whence

[1] Lydus quotes *Ascl.* 19, 39 in *On Months* 4.7; he quotes *Ascl.* 28 in *On Months* 32, 149. For the life and works of Lydus, see further Anastasius C. Bandy, ed. and trans., *On the Months (De Mensibus)* (Lewiston: Edwin Mellen, 2013), 1–46. The text on which the following translations are based is edited by Richard Wuensch, *Ioannis Lydi liber de mensibus* (Stuttgart: Teubner, 1967), 71, 90–91, 117, 167.

[2] The precise identity of this Aphrodite is unclear. There was a Hermetic treatise called *Aphrodite* (SH 22). An androgynous divine Consciousness (Νοῦς) appears in CH 1.9; compare *Ascl.* 20: "God ... completely full of the fertility of both sexes and ever pregnant with his own will, always begets whatever he wishes to procreate." See also FH 13 (= Lactantius, *Divine Institutes* 4.8.4–5) above with notes. Griffiths quotes the *Coffin Texts* where the Egyptian creator Atum says: "I am he who engendered Shu (Air); I am he-she" (*Iside*, 464). The dual sexuality is also reminiscent of Hermaphroditus, reputed son of Hermes and Aphrodite in Greek mythology (Diodorus, *Library of History* 4.6.5; Ovid, *Metamorphoses* 4.274–388; Lucian, *Dialogues of the Dead* 15.2). Indeed, Lydus mentions Hermaphroditus later in *On Months* 4.64. Other gods of Late Antiquity were dual

the Pamphylians once worshiped a bearded Aphrodite.[3] They concur that she was born from the genitals of Kronos – that is, from eternity – and that the nature of events is eternal and incorruptible.

FH 37b

John Lydus, On Months *4.7*

Chance, Fate, Necessity

The name of Chance and Fate is put forth in reference to birth. Hermes testifies to this in the so-called *Perfect Discourse*: "The so-called seven spheres have a principle called Chance or Fate which changes all things and does not permit them to remain in the same state. Fate is the fated energy or God himself or the order arrayed after it, joined with Necessity and spread throughout all things in heaven and on earth. Fate gives birth to the very principles of things, and Necessity compels their end results. Order and law follow in turn, such that there exists nothing unordered."[4]

Porphyry appears to agree more with Hermetic teachings concerning Chance when he says, "The ancients connected Chance to the number seven, since seven controls the spinning of the seven (planetary spheres). Seven is the queen of whatever is spun for the living creature as well as the energy outside of it which derives from her."[5]

FH 37c

John Lydus, On Months *4.32, 149*

Three Kinds of Angel

The Egyptian Hermes says in his treatise called *Perfect Discourse* that there are punishing angels in matter itself who punish the human race according to its deserts. There are also purifying daimones fixed in the air that purify

gendered. Valerius Soranus (around 100 BCE) referred to Jupiter as mother of the gods (Augustine, *City of God* 7.9); Phanes among the Orphics was also of both sexes (Bernabé *OF* 134). An androgynous god Aphrodite-Aphroditus was worshiped on Cyprus. Hesychius, *Lexicon*, under the headword Ἀφρόδιτος (Latte) observed: "Paion who wrote about Amathus (on Cyprus) says that the goddess (Aphrodite) was depicted as a man on Cyprus." See further Delcourt, *Hermaphrodite*, 79–82, 115–29; Copenhaver, *Magic*, 180–82.

[3] For the bearded Aphrodite with male genitals see also Macrobius, *Saturnalia* 3.8.2.

[4] A Greek version of *Ascl.* 39.

[5] This quote also appears as Porphyry fragment 467 (Smith). The idea of "chance" here seems roughly equivalent to Fate (εἱμαρμένη) elsewhere in Hermetic literature.

souls after death as they try to course up through the zones of hail and fire in the air. These zones the poets and Plato himself in his *Phaedo* call "Tartarus" and "Pyriphlegethon."[6] Finally, the savior daimones, arrayed near the lunar region, save souls.[7] . . .

The <Egy>ptian Hermes in his treatise entitled *Perfect Discourse* says that the souls transgressing the rule of devotion, when freed from the body, are handed over to the daimones and carried through the air <as if shot out by a sling> through the zones of fire and hail which the poets call "Pyriphlegethon" and "Tartarus."[8] Hermes, for his part, is concerned solely with the purification of souls.

FH 37d

John Lydus, On Months *4.53*

There is much past and present disagreement about the god worshiped by the Hebrews. The Egyptians and Hermes first of all, spoke theologically about (the Hebrew god) as Osiris, the one who (truly) exists.[9]

[6] Compare Plato, *Phaedo* 107d, 112a–14b; *Gorgias* 524a–d; *Republic* 614c.

[7] For the idea of a punishing daimon, see CH 1.23; *Ascl.* 28, 33b and FH 9 (= Lactantius, *Divine Institutes* 2.14.6) above.

[8] Nock adopts the emendation of Scott σφενδονούμεναι ("as if shot out by a sling"). The demonology developed here is briefly commented on by Mahé, *HHE*, 2.256–59; Quispel, "Reincarnation and Magic in the *Asclepius*," in van den Broek, ed., *From Poimandres*, 167–231 at 183–85.

[9] Compare Philo, *Change of Names* 11; *The Worse Attacks the Better* 160 (God alone belongs to the realm of true Being). Occasionally Greco-Roman writers identified the Hebrew God with Dionysus (for instance, Tacitus, *Histories* 5.5, Plutarch, *Table Talk* 4.6; compare Cornelius Labeo in Macrobius, *Saturnalia* 1.18–21), who was in turn identified with Osiris.

Gregory of Nazianzus

Introduction

Gregory of Nazianzus (who lived from approximately 330 to 390 CE) was a well-educated Christian theologian who had a brief reign as bishop of Constantinople (381 CE). A sophisticated poet and homilist, Gregory is perhaps best known for helping to define orthodox discourse about the Christian trinity. He defended the Nicene position that father and son were of the same (unknowable) substance, and that the holy spirit shared that substance.

Five orations on the mystery of the trinity were delivered in or near Constantinople around 380 CE. In the second of these, Gregory quoted Hermes Thrice Great as a "Greek theologian" who affirmed God's ineffability. He quoted Hermes without attribution, perhaps because he did not know it (Hermes was usually called "Egyptian," not Greek). Nevertheless, Gregory's desire to play a game of one-upmanship may have led him to suppress the name of his perceived theological competitor.[1]

[1] For Gregory, see further Frederick W. Norris, *Faith Gives Fullness to Reasoning: The Five Theological Orations of Gregory Nazianzen: Introduction and Commentary* (Leiden: Brill, 1991), 1–82; John A. McGuckin, *St. Gregory of Nazianzus: An Intellectual Biography* (Crestwood, NY: St. Vladimir's Seminary Press, 2001), 283–89; Lionel Wickham, *St. Gregory of Nazianzus on God and Christ: The Five Theological Orations and Two Letters of Cledonius* (Crestwood: St. Vladimir's Seminary Press, 2002), 9–23; Brian E. Daley, *Gregory of Nazianzus* (London: Routledge, 2006), 3–49. The following translation is based on the text edited by Paul Gallay, *Grégoire de Nazianze Discours 27–31 (Discours théologiques)*, SC 250 (Paris: Cerf, 1978), 106–8.

FH 38

Gregory of Nazianzus, Oration *28.4*

It suffices to quote again: "To understand God is difficult, to express him is impossible."[2] So one of the Greek theologians philosophized – and not without sleight of hand, in my view – so as to seem to have grasped that God is difficult to speak of while dodging the charge that he is inexpressible.[3] But according to my doctrine, if it is impossible to express him, it is more impossible to understand him. For a concept may perhaps be expressed in words – even if hazily and not adequately – to someone not completely deaf and intellectually sluggish. But to comprehend so great a matter by the mind is utterly impossible and impracticable – and I do not just mean to slothful and sinking souls, but also to those perfectly sublime and beloved by God. The same applies to every nature born in this world, blocked from understanding the truth by this gloomy darkness and the gross portion of flesh.[4]

[2] The sentence appears in fuller form in SH 1.1; FH 25 (from Cyril); TH 24 (the *Passion of Artemius*).

[3] The "Greek theologian" quoted here is Hermes Thrice Great, not Plato, as established by Jean Pépin, "Grégoire de Nazianze, lecteur de la littérature hermétiques," *VC* 36 (1982): 251–60. Gregory's selective quotation and corrective comment may express defensiveness or simply one-upmanship. There is a possibility that the Emperor Julian (*Orations* 4.131d–132a) also knew the same Hermetic quotation. It is more likely, however, that Julian adapts Plato, *Timaeus* 28c. See further Scott, *Hermetica*, 3.301.

[4] Gregory would apparently agree with the Hermetic author that "there is no truth upon earth ... Truth is the most perfect excellence, the undiluted good itself; it is what is not muddied by matter nor shrouded by a body" (SH 2A.8–9).

Didymus of Alexandria

Introduction

Didymus of Alexandria (313–398 CE) was a famous early Christian teacher dwelling in Egypt. Although he lost his sight at the age of four, Didymus was universally lauded for his vast memory and versatile learning. He is reputed to have commented on nearly every biblical book and to have written treatises (of which *On the Holy Spirit* survives). The church historian Rufinus (340–410 CE) placed Didymus at the head of an Alexandrian Catechetical School, although both the accuracy and the meaning of his testimony is disputed.

If Didymus is the author of *On the Trinity*, he quoted from a collection of at least three treatises by Hermes to Asclepius.[1] Cyril of Alexandria later incorporated these quotations in his *Against Julian* (see FH 23–24). Didymus also knew what is now called CH 6 (*The Good is God Alone*) and possibly a treatise similar to CH 13 (*On Rebirth*).

Because of their association with Origen of Alexandria, the works of Didymus were not widely copied after 553 CE (the fifth Ecumenical Council). Thus most of Didymus's works are lost. Yet in 1941, an accidental find at a munitions dump near Tura, Egypt (south of Cairo) brought to light several codices of his oeuvre. Among these were certain commentaries – or more precisely, lecture notes – on Ecclesiastes and Psalms 20–44. Both contain important Hermetic fragments parallel to each other, which are translated below.

[1] For the works of Didymus, see Grant. D. Bayliss, *The Vision of Didymus the Blind: A Fourth-century Virtue-Origenism* (Oxford: Oxford University Press, 2015), 46–55.

FH 39a

Didymus of Alexandria, Commentary on Ecclesiastes *5–6, 167.15–23*[2]

That Egyptian whom they call "Thrice Great" said: "The sage breaks the bond of Fate. He is not subject to the power of Necessity and is not subject to the power of the cosmos, but exists above heaven. The sage's thinking has transcended mere appearances."[3]

They say that the human herd is subject to Fate. Yet the one who has transcended human life is able to say: "I look not at what appears, but at what is not seen."[4] Since what appears is temporary and what does not appear is eternal, the sage does not waste away among these things. Riches do not inflate him, nor does poverty bring him down. The sage does not suppose that disrepute is a great evil, or that honor and fame from the masses is something worthwhile.

FH 39b

Didymus the Blind, Psalm Commentary *22–26.10, 88.8–18*

"Deliver me from my constraints!"[5] The Psalmist calls his afflictions "constraints." He does this also in other passages as well: "Then they cried to the Lord and he delivered them from their constraints."[6] Thus one need not listen to those who introduce birth horoscopes, for they say that Fate

[2] The text for the following translation is taken from L. Koenen and J. Kramer, ed., *Didymus der Blinde, Kommentar zum Ecclesiastes (Tura Papyrus), Teil III, Kommentar zu Ecclesiastes Kap. 5 und 6.* In Zusammenarbeit mit dem Ägyptischen Museum zu Kairo (Bonn: Rudolf Habelt, 1970); M. Gronewald, ed., *Psalmenkommentar (Tura Papyrus), Teil II, Kommentar zu Psalm 22–26, 10* (Bonn: Rudolf Habelt, 1968). The papyrus page and line numbers are taken from these editions.

[3] This fragment best resembles content from the fragments of Zosimus (FH 19–21). In FH 19, those without divine consciousness are said to be controlled by Fate. Philosophers are above Fate according to FH 20. In FH 21, it is clarified that Fate has control of the body and that philosophers should not use magical means to overcome Necessity. According to Hermetic teaching, the body is subject to Fate, but consciousness (or νοῦς) is not (CH 1.15; SH 20.7). Thus humans fall under Fate because of their nativity or birth (SH 7.3). Compare also TH 12 (from Iamblichus, *On the Mysteries* 8.4) where Hermes is the philosopher's guide for theurgic ascent to attain the realm above Fate.

[4] Compare CH 13.11: "I no longer picture things with the sight of my eyes but with the mental energy that comes through the powers"; 2 Corinthians 4:18: "we look not at what can be seen but at what cannot be seen, for what can be seen is temporary, but what cannot be seen is eternal."

[5] Psalm 24:17 70. The word "constraints" (ἀναγκῶν) is the genitive plural of ἀνάγκη, the term for Necessity. We might thus translate it "the constraints of Necessity."

[6] Psalm 106:6, 70.

parcels out certain matters to human beings.[7] Yet when one becomes godly and wise according to God, one exits the chain of causation.

Furthermore, the learned Egyptians – among them Hermes Thrice Great – declare: "the sage is not subject to Fate and stands outside the cosmos." As the Savior said, it is possible to be in the cosmos and no longer of it[8] if one extends one's consciousness above and possesses heavenly citizenship.[9]

Thus these people lisp our doctrines when they say that the sage breaks the bond of Fate. Thus many of those who deal in birth horoscopes understand these words: "I am subject to <condemnations>.[10] From these deliver me, and break the bond of Fate!"

[7] The Christian polemic against horoscopic and other forms of astrology had a long history. See, for instance, the author of *Ref.* 4.1.1–4.7.3; 5.12.1–5.18.1. See further Tim Hegedus, *Early Christianity and Ancient Astrology*, Patristic Studies 6 (New York: Peter Lang, 2007); Denzey Lewis, *Cosmology and Fate*. Recent scholarship dispels the idea that early Christians did not use astrology. See Kocku von Stuckrad, "Jewish and Christian Astrology in Late Antiquity – a New Approach," *Numen* 47 (2000): 1–40; Ute Possekel, "Bardaisan and Origen on Fate and the Power of the Stars," *Journal of Early Christian Studies* 20 (2012): 515–41.

[8] Compare John 15:19; 17:14, 16.

[9] Philippians 3:20.

[10] Here the MS reading κρισσαί is emended to κρίσεις ("condemnations").

Gaius Iulius Romanus

Introduction

In 1988, I. G. Taifacos drew attention to a previously unnoticed Hermetic fragment.[1] It is quoted by Gaius Iulius Romanus, a grammarian, probably from Italy, who lived during the late third and early fourth centuries CE. Substantial portions of his work called *Starting Points* (*Aphormōn*) are preserved by the grammarian Charisius in the fourth century.[2]

FH 40

Gaius Iulius Romanus Quoted by Charisius, The Art of Grammar *2.16*

For, as Hermes in *The Secret Discourse* writes, "Rotten seed is embedded in the name for pig (*huos*), <for the *hu* designates rottenness, and *on* the material substrate.>[3] In the same way, the human race arose from fire and the robe of death."[4]

[1] I. G. Taifacos, "C. Iulius Romanus and his Method of Compilation in the *Aphormai* " (Ph.D. diss., London, 1988): 31–35.

[2] The following translation is based on the text edited by Charles Barwick and F. Kühnert, eds., *Flavii Sosipatri Charisii. Artis grammaticae libri v* (Stuttgart: Teubner, 1997), 312. See further Sallmann, *Literatur*, 236–37.

[3] The received text says: τὸ γὰρ ὕσπορός ἐστιν, τὸ δέ ὕον οὐσία. Accepted here is the emendation of Fabricius: τὸ γὰρ ὔ σαπρόν ἐστιν, τὸ δέ ὄν οὐσία. The point seems to be that a Greek would respond to a rotten smell with "*hu*!" like the English "pee-yew!"

[4] In CH 7.2, the human body is called "the garment of ignorance . . . the living death." For humanity arising from fire, see SH 23.14: God "took a sufficient amount of breath from himself and, by an act of intellect, mixed it with fire." Humanity's nature is twofold: "in the body mortal but immortal in the essential person" (CH 1.15).

Augustine

Introduction

Aurelius Augustine (354–430 CE) was a Latin-speaking rhetor who became bishop of Hippo in North Africa (395 CE). A few formulations in Augustine's *Confessions* may have been inspired by texts now known as CH 5 and 7.[1] Nevertheless, his primary engagement with Hermes and Hermetic texts appears in his *City of God* (written after 410 CE). The bishop of Hippo quoted select portions of the Latin translation of the *Perfect Discourse* called the *Asclepius*. The version of the *Asclepius* he used resembles the later medieval versions that scholars use to establish the modern text. One might argue, therefore, that citations from Augustine add nothing new to our knowledge of Hermetic lore.

Augustine offers, however, his influential – though almost entirely hostile – interpretation of the *Asclepius*. Augustine launched his attack upon Hermes immediately after seeking to undermine the daimonology of the philosopher Apuleius. This North African Platonist had presented the daimones as mediators between gods and human beings. In the *Asclepius*, "Hermes" displayed a different view. He presented daimones (or spirits) as gods who are able to inhabit statues.[2]

[1] Augustine's phrase "the living death" (*mortem vitalem, Confessions* 1.7; 5.14) corresponds to "the living death" (τὸν ζῶντα θάνατον) in CH 7.2. The title of his first book, *De pulchro et apto* (*On the Beautiful and the Harmonious*) is said to correspond with the Hermetic phrase "all things very beautiful and all things measured out" (πάντα περικαλλῆ καὶ πάντα μεμετρημένα, CH 5.7, Van Oort, "Augustine and Hermes," 69–71).

[2] This religious practice would seem to have some analogy in the Egyptian Opening of the Mouth ritual, for which see Jan Assmann, *Death and Salvation in Ancient Egypt*, trans. David Lorton (Ithaca: Cornell University Press, 2001), 310–29; Mark Smith, *The Liturgy of the Opening of the Mouth for Breathing* (Oxford: Ashmolean Museum, 1993); Eugene Cruz-Uribe, "Opening of the Mouth as Temple Ritual," in E. Teeter and J. A. Larson, eds., *Gold of Praise. Festschrift E. F. Wente* (Chicago: Oriental Institute, 1999), 69–73. More relevant here, however, are divine statues in Egypt which were known to give oracles, send dreams, and heal diseases (examples cited in Derchain, "Authenticité," 187; with a general discussion in Morenz, *Egyptian Religion*, 150–56; Hornung, *Conceptions*, 135–36). Compare *PGM* 5.370–446 (animating a statue of Hermes for a dream oracle);

In his attack upon Hermes, Augustine demonstrated considerable rhetorical skill and bravado. By no means did he sympathetically attempt to discern the meaning of Hermetic discourse. On the contrary, he carefully selected what to extract and exclude from the *Asclepius*. He hammered relentlessly on what he considered to be the weak point of Hermetic religion: "man-made gods." Yet the bishop of Hippo evinced no interest in understanding the conceptual background of ritually animated statues, or the reasons why the Hermetic author would have considered such animation misguided.

Furthermore, Augustine treated the morally ambiguous daimones as purely evil in accordance with his Christian worldview. (For Augustine, the daimones were demons.) Any benefits that the daimones actually bestowed he discounted as deceptive. On the topic of deified men, Augustine neglected to mention the Christian worship of Jesus – manifestly a human being – and did everything he could to distinguish the cult of martyrs from the worship of deified heroes. The idea that the true (divine) self of the elder Asclepius went to heaven (as did many Christian martyrs), Augustine simply dismissed.

In sum, although Augustine's arguments have been praised for their acuteness, one needs always to be aware of how deeply polemical and one-sided they are. Augustine lived at a time when the practice of native Egyptian religion was technically illegal, and when Hermetic communities – if they existed – had probably passed into history. Yet even in the 420s CE, Augustine's ideological battle against traditional African and Greek religions was hardly won. In his final decade, Augustine fought in the trenches to win a war of words against Egypt's most exalted sage.[3]

Julian of Laodicea (about 500 CE), *On the Setting up of Statues* in *CCAG* 8.4.252–53. See further Mahé, *HHE*, 2.98–102, 224, 315, 385. For animated statues in a Greek context, see Sarah Iles Johnston, "Animating Statues: A Case Study in Ritual," *Arethusa* 41 (2008): 445–77.

[3] See further Mahé, *HHE*, 2.56–58; Fowden, *Egyptian Hermes*, 209–11; Pier Franco Beatrice, "Hermetic Tradition," in Allan D. Fitzgerald, ed., *Augustine Through the Ages: An Encyclopedia* (Grand Rapids, MI: Eerdmans, 1999), 429–31; van den Broek, "Hermes and Christ: 'Pagan' Witnesses to the Truth of Christianity," in van den Broek, ed., *From Poimandres*, 115–44 at 139–41; Moreschini, *Hermes Christianus*, 74–79; Wouter J. Hanegraaff, "Hermetism," in Karla Pollmann and Willemien Otten, eds., *The Oxford Guide to the Historical Reception of Augustine*, 3 vols. (Oxford: Oxford University Press, 2013), 2.1135–39; Van Oort, "Augustine and Hermes," 71–73. The text used for the following translation is that of Bernard Dombart and Alphonse Kalb, eds., *Sancti Aurelii Augustini De Civitate Dei libri i–x*, CCSL 47 (Turnhout: Brepols, 1955), 239–48.

FH 41

Augustine of Hippo, City of God *8.23–26*

23. The Egyptian Hermes, whom they call Thrice Great, both thought and wrote differently about them (daimones). Apuleius denies that they are gods. Yet when he says that they hold the middle place between gods and humans so as to seem necessary (for communication) with the gods, he does not distinguish their cult from the worship of the higher gods.

That famous Egyptian (Hermes), however, says that some gods are made by the supreme God, and others by human beings. Anyone who hears this as I have stated it, supposes that he refers to images, because they are the works of human hands. Yet he asserts that visible and tangible images are, as it were, only bodies of the gods, and that there dwell in them certain spirits who are invoked. These spirits have power either to inflict harm or to fulfill the desires of those who render them divine honors and cultic service.[4]

By "making gods," he means uniting these invisible spirits by a certain ritual to the visible objects of bodily nature so as to make, as it were, animated bodies, images dedicated and subject to these spirits. He adds that human beings received this great and wondrous ability to make gods. I will quote the words of this Egyptian as they have been translated into our tongue:

> Now since we have introduced the topic of the kinship and participation between human beings and gods, realize, Asclepius, the power and efficacy of humankind. Just as the lord and father – or to use his highest name, God – is the producer of heavenly gods, so humanity is the maker of gods who are content to dwell near humans in temples.

And a little later[5] he says:

> Thus humanity, ever mindful of its nature and origin, perseveres in that imitation of divinity. Just as the father and lord made eternal gods to be similar to himself, so humanity molds its gods according to the likeness of its facial features.[6]

Asclepius, to whom he was speaking for the most part, answered him and said, "Do you mean statues, Thrice Great?" He replied: "Yes, statues,

[4] Augustine omits Hermes's statement that the spirits have power to do good as well (*Ascl.* 24).

[5] Augustine omits a passage in which Hermes says that humans form "the *figures* of gods" (*species vero deorum*), not the gods themselves (*Ascl.* 23).

[6] *Ascl.* 23. Statue-making is a form of imitating God.

Asclepius. Do you see how much even you lack faith? I speak of statues animated by consciousness and full of spirit, statues that perform so many great deeds, statues that know the future and foretell it by lots, by prophets, by dreams, and by many other means; statues that cause human illnesses and cure them, who provide woe or blessing according to what is deserved.

Do you not know, Asclepius, that Egypt is the image of heaven? Rather, it is truer to call Egypt the instantiated and transposed image of all that is governed and transacted in heaven. If we must speak what is more true, our land is the temple of the whole world! And since it befits the prudent to know all things beforehand, it is not permitted to be ignorant of this: a time will come when it will appear that the Egyptians have worshiped divinity with pious mind and regular ritual to no end."[7]

Hermes, pursuing this subject at length, seems to predict the present time. During this time, the Christian religion, the more true and holy it is, the more vehemently and freely it overthrows all lying fabrications . . .

But when Hermes predicts these things, he speaks as one who is a friend to these same mockeries of demons, and does not clearly express the Christian name. On the contrary, he bewails these rites by whose implementation Egypt is preserved as the heavenly image – as if they had already been removed and abolished. Thus he testifies to these future events by a kind of tearful prediction.

Now it was about such things that the apostle said, "Although they knew God, they did not glorify him as God nor give thanks, but became futile in their thinking, and their foolish heart was darkened."[8] For Hermes makes many truthful statements about the one true God, creator of the world. Thus I know not how he fell so low by the darkening of his heart so as to want humans always to be subject to – as he admits – man-made gods. And I know not how he bewails the future removal of these rites as if it involved anything unhappy for humanity. . . [9]

These vain, deceitful, dangerous, sacrilegious rites the Egyptian Hermes lamented, for he knew that a time would come when they would be removed. Yet he mourned with impudence just as he impudently foreknew. For it was not the holy spirit who revealed these things to him, as he had to the holy prophets . . . No, those spirits showed to the Egyptian the

[7] *Ascl.* 24. Here it is worth noting that Hermes says "it will *appear*" (*appareat*) – not that the Egyptians did in fact worship in vain. For a different – in some ways more accurate – translation of the same passage, see *Excerpts from the Perfect Discourse* (NHC VI,8) 69–70.

[8] Romans 1:21. Compare Augustine, *Confessions*, 7.9.14.

[9] What Hermes actually bewails is the *appearance* that Egyptians worshiped in vain.

time of their own destruction – the very spirits who, when the Lord was present in flesh, said with trembling, "Do you come here to destroy us before the time?"[10] ...

This (Hermes), blown here and there by every wind of doctrine,[11] and mixing true things with false, bewails a religious system as if destined to perish – a system which he later admits to be wrong.

24. After many topics, Hermes again comes back to the subject of man-made gods, remarking:

> "... Let us return to the human being and to reason, the divine gift by virtue of which the human being is a rational animal. For the things said about humanity, though wonderful, are not as wonderful (as reason). The fact that humanity has the ability to discover and to produce the divine nature surpasses all other wonders.

Thus, because[12] our ancestors greatly erred about the account of the gods as unbelieving and unconcerned about divine service and worship, they invented the technique of producing gods. To their invention they added and mixed in a power conforming to the natural world. Since they could not make gods, they invoked the souls of daimones or angels to enter the holy images and divine mysteries so that the likenesses would have the power to do good or evil."[13]

... Does Hermes say that they *moderately* erred in discovering the god-making technique, or was he content simply to say that "they erred"? No; he must add they "greatly erred." This great error and incredulity that did not attend to divine worship and service discovered the god-making technique. And yet ... this man of wisdom grieves as though divine religion were to be ruined at some future time!

Is he not compelled by divine power on the one hand to betray the past error of his ancestors[14] and on the other hand by diabolical power to lament the future punishment of demons? For if their ancestors, by erring greatly with respect to their knowledge of the gods, and erring through

[10] Hermes was not divinely inspired. Contrast Jacob of Edessa in the above *Addendum: The Reception of Hermetic Fragments from Cyril.*

[11] An allusion to Ephesians 4:14.

[12] According to Scott (*Hermetica*, 3.220), Augustine fundamentally misunderstood this passage because he read *quoniam* ("*because* our ancestors greatly erred") which is a mistranslation of ἐπεί ("*after* our ancestors great erred, they invented the art of producing gods"). Yet *quoniam* can also mean "after" (*OLD* 1567, definition 1 under the headword *quoniam*). Augustine's misreading is his own interpretive choice.

[13] *Ascl.* 37.

[14] Notice how Augustine affirmed that Hermes was under divine influence although earlier he denied that Hermes was inspired by the Holy Spirit.

incredulity and mental aversion from divine worship and service, invented the god-making technique, what wonder is it that this detestable technique – that makes whatever is opposed to divine religion – be removed by divine religion? . . .

For if he had only said, without mentioning the causes, that his ancestors had discovered the god-making technique, it would have been our duty, if we paid any regard to what is right and pious, to take note and observe that they would never attain to this god-making technique if they had not wandered from the truth . . . If, moreover, we say that the causes of this technique are peoples' great error and unbelief, along with their erroneous and faithless mental aversion to divine religion, the shamelessness of those who resist the truth could in some way be tolerated.

Yet when this same man admires above all else the power of this god-making technique among humans and laments the coming time when all these idols instituted by men will even be illegal,[15] what ought we to say – or rather do – but give as much thanks as we can to our lord God who removed these things by causes opposed to those by which they were instituted?

(Hermes) even admits and reveals the causes for this situation, saying that his ancestors by great error, unbelief, and by ignoring the divine worship and service discovered the god-making technique. . . .[16]

Even Hermes himself was amazingly compelled to confess that the things whose removal he resisted and lamented were instituted not by prudent, faithful, and religious men, but by erring and unbelieving ones who were averse to the worship and service of the gods.

Although he *calls* them gods, still when he says that they were made by such people as we certainly ought not to be, he shows – willingly or not – that they are not to be worshiped by those unlike these god-makers – that is by prudent, faithful, and religious people. At the same time, he shows

[15] Augustine probably had in mind the emperor Theodosius proscribing the public practice of non-Christian religions in 393 CE.

[16] Notice the subtle distortion here. In the Latin *Asclepius*, the text does not say that the Egyptians erred in making the statues. "In fact, according to the author of the Hermetic text, the making of idols was not due to an error but, on the contrary, was a remedy introduced specifically to correct the earlier, seriously mistaken idea of the ancients on the gods, an idea resulting from their unbelief and their indifference to worship and divine religion" (Beatrice, "Hermetic Tradition," 430). Hermes does not lament the statue-making practice; rather, he celebrates it (*Ascl.* 23). What Hermes laments is the later downfall of Egyptian religion, which he puts in apocalyptic terms. Augustine read the statue-making practice (*Ascl.* 37) in light of the Hermetic apocalypse (*Ascl.* 24) – as if the apocalypse was or had already occurred.

that the very people who made them wanted beings who were not gods to be considered gods ...

Such are their gods, the gods of such people and made by such people – they are demons come into idols by an unknown technique and fastened in bonds by their own lust. When Hermes calls these gods "man-made," he does not grant them what the Platonist Apuleius did ... namely that they be made by God to be messengers and mediators among the gods ... What kind of god is it that is made by a person in error and unbelief and turned away from the true God?[17]

Moreover, if the demons which are worshiped in the temples, introduced by some unknown technique into images ... if those demons are neither mediators nor interpreters between humans and the gods ... then it remains to be affirmed that what power they possess they possess as demons, doing harm by bestowing pretended benefits – which harm all the more by deceit – or else they do harm openly ...

26. It is certainly a remarkable thing how this Egyptian, when lamenting the future time when these things will be removed from Egypt ... says, among other things: "Then shall that land, the most holy place of shrines and temples, be full of tombs and corpses"[18] – as if honestly, were these things not removed, people would cease to die! ...

Yet he appears to lament that the memorials of our martyrs will succeed their temples and shrines – or so it seems to those with perverted minds averse to us. They suppose that the gods worshiped by pagans in temples are equivalent to the dead venerated by us in tombs.

Hermes himself in that same book in which he, as if foretelling future things, ... testifies that the gods of Egypt were dead men ... He says: "Take your grandfather, Asclepius, the first inventor of medicine to whom a temple was consecrated on a mountain of Libya near the shore of the crocodiles. In this temple lies his earthly self, meaning his body. His real remains – or rather his whole self, if the whole human consists in living

[17] Hermes never said that the statues were made by such people. Compare Iamblichus: "For one absurdity appears from the outset, if daimones are deemed to be created and perishable; another even more appalling absurdity is if they are created ... for certainly the daimones exist prior to both soul and bodily powers" (*On the Mysteries* 3.22). "But not even is a human able to shape forms of daimones by any artificial means, but on the contrary, he himself is shaped and created by the daimones in so far as he shares in a perceptible body" (3.30, trans. Clarke, Dillon, and Hershbell, modified).

[18] Augustine leaps back to *Ascl.* 24. When it comes to the downfall of Egyptian religion, Augustine counts Hermes among the prophets.

consciousness – returned in a better state to heaven.[19] By his divine power, he affords all the aid to ailing humans he once did when he bestowed the art of medicine."[20]

Behold, he said that a dead man was venerated as a god in the place where he had his tomb![21] Hermes was deluded and deceived in saying that Asclepius journeyed back to heaven.

Then he adds: "Does not Hermes my grandfather whose name I bear, while dwelling in the country named after him, help and preserve all mortals who come to him from everywhere?"[22]

This elder Hermes, or Mercury,[23] is given out as Hermes's grandfather in Hermopolis, the city named after him. Behold! Here are two gods whom he affirms to have been men: Asclepius and Mercury. Now concerning Asclepius, both the Greeks and Latins think the same thing; but as to Mercury, there are many who do not think that he was mortal, though Hermes testifies that he was his grandfather . . .

Hermes goes on to add: "Indeed we know how many good things Isis wife of Osiris bestows when she is kindly and what great opposition she offers when enraged."[24]

Then, to show that there were gods of this type made by men through this technique . . . he goes on to say:

> For it is easy for earthly and material gods to be angry, being made and composed by men from both natures.[25]

By "from both natures," he means from soul and body, the soul being the demon and the body the statue. He continues:

> Thus it arose that animals were called sacred among the Egyptians and their souls worshiped throughout each city. Some of them were consecrated

[19] The view expressed here is different than the veneration of the martyrs' relics (often consisting of body parts). In general, Hermetic texts do not view the corpse as something holy or capable of consecration. The body is left behind, as in CH 1.24 and the end of *Ascl.* 27. Mahé quotes a comparable Greek inscription in the fourth-century BCE tomb of Petosiris: "I invoke Petosiris whose corpse lies under earth but whose soul resides in the residence of the gods" (*HHE*, 2.306, n.148). The residence of the gods was in general the sky, in which the deified dead could shine as stars (Plutarch, *Isis and Osiris* 21 [*Moralia* 359c–d]; Porphyry, *Abstinence* 4.10).

[20] *Ascl.* 37. Compare SH 23.6 (Asclepius an ancient follower of Hermes); SH 26.9 (Asclepius founds medicine and creative literature); Oxyrhynchus Papyrus XI.1381 (the report of a healing by Asclepius edited by Edelstein and Edelstein, *Asclepius*, 1.169–75). Augustine tells stories of miracles and healing worked at the tombs or sanctuaries of martyrs in *City of God* 22.8.

[21] Hermes never said that Asclepius was *venerated* at his tomb, or that his powers to heal were disseminated only at the tomb. Augustine apparently imported ideas from the cult of martyrs.

[22] *Ascl.* 37. Notice "from everywhere" (not just at his tomb).

[23] It is unclear why Augustine calls the *Elder* Hermes "Mercury."

[24] *Ascl.* 37.

[25] *Ascl.* 37.

> while still alive so that they are worshiped according to the laws (of each city), and so that the cities might be called by their names.[26]

Where then is that mournful complaint that the land of Egypt, the most holy dwelling of shrines and temples, will be utterly filled with tombs and corpses? Truly the deceitful spirit, at whose prompting Hermes spoke, was compelled to confess through him that already Egypt was a land utterly filled with tombs and corpses which they worship as gods![27]

[26] *Ascl.* 37. Animals consecrated while alive would include the Apis bull (the "living image of Osiris," Plutarch, *Isis and Osiris* 43 [*Moralia* 386c]) and any animal (such as the ibis) chosen for special sacralization and mummification (Diodorus, *Library of History* 1.84–90). On animal veneration and the Greek response to it, see further Philo, *Decalogue* 76–80; Plutarch, *Isis and Osiris* 71–76 (*Moralia* 379d–382a); Origen, *Against Celsus* 3.17.

[27] Hermes mourns the downfall of Egyptian religion because of foreign invasion and the prohibition of worship (*Ascl.* 24). He never says that Egyptians worship the dead or pay them honor at their tombs.

Quodvultdeus

Introduction

Quodvultdeus is the received name of a bishop who preached in Carthage until he was exiled to Italy in 439 CE. He is the author of twelve homilies (delivered approximately from 434–39 CE). In one of these, he clashes swords with Hermes Thrice Great. Although his pugnacious tone is reminiscent of Augustine, broadly speaking, Quodvultdeus engages Hermetic literature in the tradition of Lactantius. According to this approach, Hermes is a witness to Christian truth, and his testimony renders the unconverted Hellene without excuse.

At times, however, Quodvultdeus's Christian interpretation of Hermetic texts is even more forced than that of Lactantius. The Carthaginian bishop tended to break Hermetic quotations into fragmented soundbites that he occasionally cornered and countered with overbearing criticism. He had no reservation about blending these Hermetic soundbites with what he considered to be the clearer speech of Christian scripture. If Hermes was right in the main, Quodvultdeus nonetheless delighted in occasionally exposing the contradictions in the Egyptian's teaching and hounding Hermes for perceived error (in particular about God's "wife").

Cited here is Quodvultdeus's homily called *Against Five Heresies*. The five "heresies" attacked here are paganism, Judaism, Manichaeism, Sabellianism, and Arianism. Important for the history of interpretation is the fact that this work came to be attributed to Augustine. The tradition of interpretation represented by Quodvultdeus could thus serve as a proper counterweight to the even more hostile and critical portrayal of Hermes in the *City of God*. In short, Hermes could remain a prophet and a sage whose theology, if not perfect, manifested truth long before the time of Christ.[1]

FH 42

Quodvultdeus, Against Five Heresies *3.4–21*

4. Hermes, who is called "Mercury" in Latin, wrote a book called *Logos Teleios*, meaning *Perfect Word.* This book has a great reputation because great is the one about whom it is written. For what is more perfect than the Word who alone is free among those who have died?

5. Let us hear what Hermes says about the perfect Word: "The lord and maker of all gods made a second god <from> himself."[2] Shortly thereafter, to illustrate what he said, he reiterated: "Because he made him first, single and unique, he appeared good to him and most full of all goods."[3]

6. How much more fully does John the evangelist speak: "Of his fullness we received, grace for grace"?[4]

"He appeared good to him and most full of all goods." And then: "God rejoiced." With whom or what did he rejoice? Let the wisdom of God herself, the son of God, speak: "I was with him who was rejoicing."[5]

7. Thus "he rejoiced and greatly loved him as his own offspring."[6] Initially, Hermes spoke of him (the son of God) as made, but later called him "offspring."[7]

Likewise, in another passage he said, "the son of the blessed God and of Goodwill, whose name cannot be expressed by a human mouth."[8]

[1] For Quodvultdeus, see further A. D. Nock, "Two Notes," *VC* 3 (1949): 48–56; P. Desiderius Franses, *Die Werke des hl. Quodvultdeus Bischofs von Karthago gestorben um 453* (Munich: J. J. Lentnerschen, 1920), 72–73; Moreschini, *Hermes Christianus*, 79–82; Thomas Macy Finn, *Quodvultdeus of Carthage: The Creedal Homilies: Conversion in Fifth-century North Africa*, Ancient Christian Writers 60 (New York/Mahwah: Newman Press, 2004), 1–21. The text used for the following translation is taken from R. Braun, *Opera Quodvultdeo Carthaginiensi episcopo tributa*, CCSL 60 (Turnhout: Brepols, 1976), 265–68.

[2] *Ascl.* 8, also quoted in Lactantius, *Divine Institutes* 4.6.4. See further Siniscalco, "Ermete Trismegisto," 102–9.

[3] A continuation of the quote from *Ascl.* 8. [4] John 1:16. [5] Proverbs 8:30.

[6] A continuation of the quote from *Ascl.* 8.

[7] In Hermetic thought, the son of God is the cosmos, as in CH 9.8; 10.14.

[8] Compare FH 11a–b from Lactantius, *Divine Institutes* 4.7.3 and *Epitome of the Divine Institutes* 37.8. By referring to God's son as the one who is inexpressible, Quodvultdeus may assume the context of the passage in Lactantius. In the twelfth-century *Book of Alcidus*, the author "follows" Hermes in designating divine consciousness (νοῦς) as "son" (4.11, Lucentini).

8. You were looking, O pagan, for the wife of God ... **9.** You seek the wife of God. Let impure perversity, I implore you, be cast from your heart!

The wife of God is Goodwill[9] ... **10.** And yet Hermes confesses that the son of God is God ... **11.** Hermes says that the father is God as well as the son ...

13. In another passage he calls the son of God *symboulon*, that is "counsel" or "counselor."[10] And the prophet says: "His name will be called 'wonderful counselor,' 'mighty and powerful God.'"[11] ...

15. What are you doing, pagan? Open your ears ... I will not offer you my own authors – you have Hermes upon whom you bestow such honor and worship among the gods as to call the day of the Lord by his name.

16. Hear him, let him convince you, let him defeat you, so that when he conquers you, you will back down and believe me. Hermes said: "God loved his own offspring."[12] He said: "son of the blessed God and of Goodwill." And lest he put up with tedious questioning about his name, he immediately added: "Whose name is not able to be expressed by a human mouth."[13]

17. Why do you, Hermes, say that the name of God's son cannot be expressed? He is expressed by you, whom people consider to be not a human being but a god. He utters, moreover, to his son these words: "There is, my son, an inexpressible holy Word of holy wisdom."[14] Is this not "In the beginning was the Word"?[15]

18. Tell us, Hermes, does this Word of wisdom have a mother? He continues: "he is from the lord alone and from God the lord of all mortal things." And because he cannot be investigated by human beings, he adds: "he is above human beings."[16]

19. Thus because he is above human beings, I cannot express the name of God's son because I am not a god. Let human beings as merely human say what I am not; I do not know what I am.[17]

There is a Word of wisdom from the sole lord.[18]

[9] This is not a quote but a paraphrase of the material in FH 11a–b. Compare CH 13.1–2 (the Will of God sows the seed into the womb of wisdom). Philo, *Drunkenness* 30: God united with his knowledge to produce created reality.

[10] Compare Lactantius, *Divine Institutes* 4.6.9 (the Sibyl calls the second god σύμβουλον); SH 17.5: "This intelligent reality rules and governs as a ruler while its reason serves as counselor (σύμβουλος)."

[11] Isaiah 9:6. [12] Quodvultdeus returns to *Ascl.* 8. [13] Compare FH 11a–b from Lactantius.

[14] Compare FH 12a from Lactantius. The "son" referred to in this passage is the son of Hermes, probably Tat.

[15] John 1:1. [16] Compare FH 12a–b from Lactantius.

[17] Quodvultdeus impersonates what Hermes (ought to have) said.

[18] This is Quodvultdeus's telescoping paraphrase of FH 12a from Lactantius.

20. So do not suppose here, O pagan, that he is human or imagine that there was a marriage: he is from the sole lord and above human beings . . .

Recognize your God! It is he and no other, not Mars, not Jove, not Hermes, but the one Hermes confesses.

21. O Christian, why are you surprised that these people can say such things about the father and the son? "Even demons believe and tremble."[19] Indeed, in the gospels, when the Lord passes by, they say, "We know who you are: the son of God!"[20]

[19] James 2:19. [20] Mark 1:24; Matt 8:29.

Michael Psellus

Introduction

Michael Psellus (who lived approximately 1018–85 CE) demonstrated his rhetorical and intellectual talents early on during his education in Constantinople (modern Istanbul). After achieving prominence in the Byzantine imperial court, he was appointed to oversee the teaching of ancient philosophy. Psellus boasted that, "I found philosophy only after it had breathed its last, at least as far as its own exponents were concerned, and I alone revived it with my own powers."[1] As the advisor and tutor of emperors, he enjoyed great political prestige as the Byzantine Empire suffered decline.

Psellus left behind about 1,100 diverse works, many of them short essays and speeches. In some of these, he mentions Hermes Thrice Great – sometimes admiringly, more often critically. His citations and testimonies indicate that there was a much fuller body of Hermetic writings that existed in the golden era of Byzantine culture. Along with the following fragment, see also the testimonies of Psellus printed below in TH 29.

FH 43

Michael Psellus, Opusculum *19.148–50*[2]

Hermes Thrice Great dialogues with Asclepius as follows: "Let a man not cohabit with a man if he is infertile. For he will lie down as a corpse in mud."

[1] Psellus, *Chronographia* 6.37, quoted by Anthony Kaldellis, *Hellenism in Byzantium: The Transformations of Greek Identity and the Reception of the Classical Tradition* (Cambridge: Cambridge University Press, 2007), 189–224 at 193. See further Anthony Kaldellis, *Mothers and Sons, Fathers and Daughters: The Byzantine Family of Michael Psellos* (Notre Dame, IN: University of Notre Dame Press, 2006), 3–10.

[2] The text used for the following translation is edited by L. G. Westerink and J. M. Duffy, *Michael Psellus Theologica II* (Munich: K. G. Saur, 2002), 106.

Albert the Great

Introduction

Albert the Great was born around 1200 in southern Germany. He was famous already in his lifetime as a theologian and natural scientist. His many appointments as diplomat and administrator did not stop him from becoming one of the most prolific authors of the Middle Ages.

As a young man, Albert studied at the University of Padua, in Italy. There, it seems, he was persuaded by the preacher Jordan of Saxony to join the Dominican order in 1223 CE. He went to Paris around 1240, where he received his license as Master in Theology. Beginning around 1245, he held one of the prestigious chairs in theology at the University of Paris. In 1248, he was sent to Cologne to establish a school for higher learning.

Six years later, Albert became Prior Provincial of German Dominicans, a busy administrative post he held until 1257. After a short period of teaching at Cologne, he was appointed bishop of Regensburg (1260), an appointment he was able to resign two years later. From 1263 to 1264, Albert served as Preacher of the Crusade in all German-speaking lands. About 1270, Albert was stationed back at Cologne as a retired professor in residence. He died and was buried in that city about ten years later.

In his massive oeuvre, Albert makes about 125 references to Hermes or Hermes Thrice Great. Although most of his citations go back to passages in the *Asclepius*, Albert also cites the titles of other works attributed to Hermes. These include *On Alchemy, On Talismans, On Spells, On the Power of Stones, The Secrets of Aristotle, The Secret of Ultimate Secrets*, and *On Universal Virtue*. There does not seem to be firm evidence that Albert distinguished Hermes the philosopher from Hermes the scientist and technician. Albert does not always accept the views of Hermes, but in most cases he is cited with respect. The fragments that follow constitute only a small sample of Albert's engagement with Hermetic literature. Further testimonies are offered in TH 36.[1]

FH 44a

Albert the Great, Book of Minerals *3.1.6 (around 1254 CE)*[2]

Father Hermes Thrice Great . . . says, "Earth is the mother of metals and heaven their father," and "Earth is impregnated to produce them in mountains, fields, plains, streams, and all other places."[3]

FH 44b

Albert the Great, Book of Minerals *4.7*[4]

According to Hermes, gold is the only metal in which no disease appears, for neither of its material constituents is imperfect or inharmoniously

[1] For Albert the Great, see further James A. Weisheipl, "The Life and Works of St. Albert the Great," in Weisheipl, ed., *Albertus Magnus and the Sciences: Commemorative Essays 1980* (Toronto: Pontifical Institute of Mediaeval Studies, 1980), 13–51; Simon Tugwell and Leonard E. Boyle, *Albert & Thomas: Selected Writings* (New York: Paulist Press, 1988), 3–38; Kenneth F. Kitchell Jr. and Irven Michael Resnick, trans., *Albertus Magnus on Animals: A Medieval "Summa Zoologica"* (Baltimore: Johns Hopkins University Press, 1999), 1–42; Paolo Lucentini, "L'Ermetismo magico nel secolo XIII," in Menso Folkerts and Richard Lorch, eds., *Sic itur ad astra: Studien zur Geschichte der Mathematik und Naturwissenschaften: Festschrift für den Arabisten Paul Kunitzsch zum 70. Geburtstag* (Wiesbaden: Harrassowitz, 2000), 409–50 at 429–38, 439–40; David Porreca, "The Influence of Hermetic Texts on Western European Philosophers and Theologians (1160–1300)" (Ph.D. diss., University of London, 2001), 76–123; Claire Fanger, "Albertus Magnus," *DGWE* 9–12.

[2] The text used for the following translation is edited by Augustus Borgnet, *B. Alberti Magni. Opera omnia vol. 5. Mineralium libri quinque* (Paris: Vivès, 1890), 66.

[3] In context, Albert seems to be dependent on a version of the *Emerald Tablet* (TH 30). He probably quotes from a larger work containing it, possibly *The Secret of Ultimate Secrets* (= the *Secret of Secrets* ascribed to Aristotle). The latter work existed in Arabic by 950 CE and was translated into Latin shortly after 1230 CE. See further Steven J. Williams, *The Secret of Secrets: The Scholarly Career of a Pseudo-Aristotelian Text in the Latin Middle Ages* (Ann Arbor: University of Michigan Press, 2003), 7–30.

[4] The text used for the following translation is edited by Augustus Borgnet, *B. Alberti Magni. Opera omnia vol. 5. Mineralium libri quinque* (Paris: Vivès, 1890), 93.

mixed. Although like other metals, it is composed of sulphur and quicksilver, its sulphur is extremely bright and clean . . .

Hermes says in his *Alchemy*: "Sulphur itself, because of a certain affinity by which all metals are closely related to it, burns and reduces them all to ash, except only gold; for the pores (of gold) are tightly closed and cannot be opened" . . . Hermes, the root sustaining all philosophers,[5] says: "The medicine of the sun is red, that of the moon is white."[6]

FH 44c

On Intellect and the Intelligible *2.1.6 (1254–57 CE)*[7]

Hermes upbraided the ignorant commoners of old: "No human being gives attention to such matters in life.[8] Rather, they consume their lives in the manner of pigs."[9]

FH 44d

On Intellect and the Intelligible *2.1.9*

Hermes said: "The God of gods cannot be perceived on his own terms with his own name. Rather, those who by lengthy study separate themselves from the body barely graze him with their minds."

A person is thus united to the outer reaches of his light. When mixed with that light, one participates to some degree in divinity.

[5] In *On Minerals* 3.2.6, Hermes is similarly called the "prophet of philosophers."

[6] Here sun and moon refer to gold and silver, and the "medicine" refers to different red and white "elixirs" used to make metals take on a gold or silver tinge.

[7] The text used for translating FH 44c–d was edited by Augustus Borgnet, *B. Alberti Magni. Opera Omnia, vol. 9. De intellectu et intelligibili* (Paris: Vivès, 1890), 513, 517.

[8] What "Hermes" meant by "such matters" (*tales*) is unknown; in context, Albert speaks of seeing reality with the intellect.

[9] Compare CH 12.4: "When mind . . . gives way to longings, the rush of appetite drives such souls to the longings that lead to unreason and, like animals without reason, they never cease their irrational anger and irrational longing."

FH 44e

Albert the Great, Commentary on John *5:37–38* *(1256 CE, Revised 1270–75)*[10]

"A person will not see me and live" (Exod 32:20). He means that in human life, no one will see me even by intellect. Accordingly, Hermes Thrice Great says: "When the keenness of the mind is completely turned away from flesh, the mind barely grazes God."

[10] The text used for the following translation was edited by Borgnet, *B. Alberti Magni. Opera Omnia, vol. 24. Ennarrationes in Joannem* (Paris: Vivès, 1899), 227.

Nicholas of Cusa

Introduction

Nicholas of Cusa (1401–64 CE) is named after the town of his birth, Kues in southwestern Germany (today Bernkastle-Kues). As a young man, Nicholas first matriculated at the University of Heidelberg (1416). The following year, he moved on to the university of Padua, where he graduated in 1423 as Doctor in Canon Law. He also studied theology for a short time at Cologne (1425).

After his studies, Nicholas launched his career as an ecclesiastical statesman. Although he initially supported the subordination of popes to general councils, Nicholas became a firm proponent of papal authority. He was later appointed to several high positions in the ecclesiastical hierarchy. As a papal legate, he traveled to Constantinople to persuade Greek Orthodox Church leaders to negotiate a politically opportune, but ultimately abortive, reunion with the Roman church (1437–39). Later, he was appointed cardinal (1449), then bishop (1450), and ended his career as the pope's Vicar General (the effective governor of Rome).

The last quarter-century of his life, Nicholas published several dozen tractates mostly dealing with speculative theology. In some of these works, he quoted Hermes Thrice Great among other ancient authorities. The Hermes that Nicholas knew was the philosopher as opposed to the astrologer, alchemist, and magician. Nicholas does not appear to have had any independent sources for Hermetic lore beyond the *Asclepius*, a book which he personally annotated and assimilated into his own theology.

Nicholas of Cusa was still alive when Marsilio Ficino finished his Latin translation of the Greek *Corpus Hermeticum* in 1463. Yet when the translation was published in 1471, the cardinal had already passed away. Nicholas thus rightly serves as the final witness to the medieval reception of the Hermetica. After him, the *Corpus Hermeticum* would come to dominate the scholarly study of Hermetism, though the multifarious traditions of Hermes known in the medieval period were never entirely forgotten.[1]

FH 45a

Nicholas of Cusa, On Learned Ignorance *1.24 (1440)*[2]

Hence Hermes Thrice Great rightly remarks: "Because God is the totality of things, he has no proper name, for it would be necessary either to give him every name or to call everything by his name," since in his simplicity he enfolds the totality of all things.[3]

Hence as regards his proper name, it is the tetragrammaton or four-letter name which we call "ineffable." It is God's proper name for this reason: it does not suit God as regards any relation to creatures. Rather, it suits God according to his own essence. Thus one ought to interpret it, "One and All," or better: "All in One."

FH 45b

Nicholas of Cusa, On Learned Ignorance *1.25*[4]

Hermes said that all things, whether animals or non-animals, are of two sexes. For this reason, he said that the cause of all things, namely God,

[1] For Nicholas of Cusa, see further Donald F. Duclow, "Life and Works," in Christopher M. Bellitto, Thomas M. Izbicki, and Gerald Christianson, eds., *Introducing Nicholas of Cusa: A Guide to a Renaissance Man* (New York and Mahwah, NJ: Paulist Press, 2004), 25–58; J. M. Counet, "Cusa, Nicholas of (Niklaus Krebs)," *DGWE*, 293–96; Pasquale Arfé, "Ermete Trismegisto e Nicola Cusano," in Lucentini and others, eds., *Hermetism from Late Antiquity*, 223–44; Erich Meuthen, *Nicholas of Cusa: A Sketch for a Biography*, trans. David Crowner and Gerald Christianson (Washington, DC: Catholic University Press, 2010).

[2] The text used for the following translation is edited by Ernest Hoffmann and Raymund Klibansky, *Nicolai de Cusa. De Docta Ignorantia* (Leipzig: Meiner, 1932), 31. For Nicholas's additional Hermetic testimonies (mostly taken from *Ascl.*), see TH 38 below; Moreschini, *Hermes Christianus*, 121–24; Ebeling, *Secret History*, 55–57.

[3] Compare *Ascl.* 20: "God, father, master of all . . . none of these titles will name him precisely . . . I cannot hope to name the maker of all majesty, the father and master of everything, with a single name, even a name composed of many names; he is nameless or rather he is all-named since he is one and all, so that one must call all things by his name or call him by the names of everything"; CH 5.10: "This is the God who is greater than any name . . . There is nothing that he is not, for he also is all that is, and this is why he has all names, because they are of one father, and this is why he has no name, because he is father of them all."

[4] The text used for the following translation is edited by Hoffmann and Klibansky, *Docta Ignorantia*, 33.

enfolds within Godself the masculine and feminine sexes. Hermes believed that Cupid and Venus constituted the unfolding of God.[5]

FH 45c

Nicholas of Cusa, On Learned Ignorance 2.8[6]

Hermes said that matter (*hylē*) was the nurse of bodies and formlessness the nurse of souls.[7]

[5] Compare *Ascl.* 21: "'Do you say that God is of both sexes, Thrice Great?' 'Not only God, Asclepius, but all things ensouled and soulless, for it is impossible for any of the things that are to be infertile . . . For each sex is full of fecundity, and the linking of the two, or, more accurately, their union is incomprehensible. If you call it Cupid or Venus or both, you will be correct.'"

[6] The text used for the following translation is edited by Hoffmann and Klibansky, *Docta Ignorantia*, 55.

[7] Compare *Ascl.* 14–15: "There was God and *hylē* (which we take as the Greek for 'matter'), and attending matter was spirit, or rather spirit was in matter . . . Because these things had not come to be, they were not as yet, but by then they already were in that from which they had their coming to be . . . matter . . . has in itself the natures of all things inasmuch as it furnishes them most fertile wombs for conceiving." Hermann of Carinthia quoted "Hermes the Persian": "Form is the adornment of matter, whereas matter is the necessity of form" (*On Essences* 58vF, Burnett). For Hermetic reflections on matter, see also SH 9, FH 18.

Testimonies concerning Hermes Thrice Great (TH 1–38)

General Introduction

The Hermetic testimonies printed here range from the late third century BCE until the fifteenth century CE. The authors quoted are Jewish, Phoenician, Hellenic, Christian, and Muslim. They all present different portraits of Hermes that cannot easily be reconciled. For example, the Jewish writer Artapanus identified Hermes with Moses the great culture hero. The Christian Athenagoras indicated that Hermes was a deified king like Alexander the Great. Iamblichus the Neoplatonic philosopher presented Hermes as a god. Augustine, bishop of Hippo, depicted him as an idolater and demonically inspired prophet. The Alexandrian philosopher Hermias presented Hermes as triply incarnated. The Muslim writer Abū Maʿshar said that there were three different Hermeses. The first of these built the pyramids in Egypt; the second was a Babylonian scholar; and the third was an expert on poisons. According to the magical handbook the *Picatrix*, Hermes was the builder of a mystical, multi-colored city featuring a wondrous temple to the Sun and an array of animated statues.

Whatever their diversity of content, these testimonies show that Hermes the philosopher and culture hero was never far removed from Hermes the magus and master of esoteric lore. Hermes was the inventor of writing according to Philo of Byblos. Yet according to the same author, he used his magic spells to help Kronos defeat his enemies. Arnobius put Hermes in the company of Pythagoras and Plato. Yet the Peratic author linked Hermes with Ostanes and Zoroaster (called Zoroastris), the chief Persian magi.[1] For the philosopher Iamblichus, Hermes was the great guide to theurgists. In turn, most Arabic writers viewed Hermes as an expert on astrology and alchemy. Such testimonies indicate that the constructed boundary between "philosophical" and "technical" Hermetic writings remains questionable.

[1] Hermes's association with Zoroaster appears again in Michael Psellus (TH 29c) and is familiar from the fragments of Zosimus (FH 20–21).

Although the following testimonies are wide-ranging, they are hardly exhaustive. We do not trace the reception history of the *Asclepius* by Latin writers after Augustine, since this work has already been done.[2] Moreover, some works attributed to Hermes – such as the Arabic *Rebuke of the Soul* – are too long to be included here and are available elsewhere.[3] There are dozens more Arabic and medieval Latin sources that make mention of Hermes, often in passing.[4] A great number of these are alchemical, astrological, and magical texts that somehow feature Hermes or are attributed to him. Even today, this material remains largely uncharted by scholars. A full and exhaustive record of Hermetic testimonies can only await new critical editions and studies of these materials.[5]

[2] Paolo Lucentini, "L'Asclepio ermetico nel secolo XII," in *From Athens to Chartres. Neoplatonism and Medieval Thought. Studies in Honour of Edouard Jeaneau* (Leiden: Brill, 1992), 397–420; Porreca, "Influence of Hermetic Texts (1160–1300)," 15–279; Carlos Gilly, "Die Überlieferung des *Asclepius* im Mittelalter," in van den Broek, ed., *From Poimandres*, 335–67; Paolo Lucentini, "Hermetic Literature II: Latin Middle Ages," in *DGWE*, 499–529 at 499–510; Ebeling, *Secret History*, 54–55; Moreschini, *Dall' Asclepius*, 13–120; Moreschini, *Hermes Christianus*, 27–132; Heiduk, "Offene," 87–176.

[3] The date of this work is approximately 1200 CE. See Scott's translation of the Latin (not the original Arabic) in *Hermetica*, 4.277–352. Some of the Arabic sources edited by Scott are not included here because they do not actually concern Hermes Thrice Great or because they add no new information.

[4] Van Bladel notes: "Hermes is cited or discussed in at least seventy individual Arabic works by different authors from Andalusia to India, dating from the eighth to the eighteenth centuries; this is based only on preliminary gleanings of the bibliographical sources" (*Arabic Hermes*, 17). For a short survey of Arabic Hermetica, see Ebeling, *Secret History*, 44–51; Pierre Lory, "Hermetic Literature III: Arab," *DGWE* 529–33.

[5] Van Bladel promises a future study of the Arabic Hermetica that will include "an inventory of the actual texts attributed to Hermes in Arabic, most of which are still in manuscript, an outline of their chronology, and descriptions of the contents of the majority of them" (*Arabic Hermes*, vi). Important critical texts of medieval Latin Hermetica have started to appear in the series Corpus Christianorum Continuatio Mediaevalis published by Brepols (www.corpuschristianorum.org/series/pdf/CCCM_HERMES%20LATINVS_092016.pdf). Festugière gathered some of the undatable alchemical fragments attributed to Hermes in *RHT*, 1.242–60. H. E. Stapleton, G. L. Lewis, and F. Sherwood Taylor culled the sayings of Hermes from the work *The Silvery Water and the Starry Earth* by Ibn Umail (about 900–990 CE) ("The Sayings of Hermes Quoted in the Mā'al-waraqī of Ibn Umail," *Ambix* 3 [1949]: 69–90). For additional surveys of medieval Latin Hermetica, see Lynn Thorndike, *A History of Magic and Experimental Science During the First Thirteen Centuries of our Era* (New York: Columbia, 1923), 2.214–28; Paolo Lucentini, "Hermes Trismegistus II: Middle Ages," in *DGWE*, 479–83; Paolo Lucentini and Vittoria Perrone Compagni, "Hermetic Literature II: Latin Middle Ages," in *DGWE*, 499–529; Charles Burnett, "The Establishment of Medieval Hermeticism," in Peter Linehan and Janet L. Nelson, eds., *The Medieval World* (London: Routledge, 2001), 111–30; Paolo Lucentini, I. Parri, and V. Perrone Compagni, eds., *Hermetism from Late Antiquity to Humanism / La tradizione ermetica dal mondo tardo-antico all'Umanesimo. Atti del Convegno internazionale di studi, Napoli, 20–24 novembre 2001* (Turnhout: Brepols, 2003), with a helpful index of works attributed to Hermes on 769–75.

Artapanus

TH 1

Artapanus (Late Third to Second Centuries BCE) Quoted by Eusebius, Preparation for the Gospel *9.27.4–9*[1]

As a grown man, Moses bestowed many useful benefits upon humankind. He invented boats and devices for setting stones, Egyptian weapons, hydraulic and military implements, in addition to philosophy. Further, he divided the state (of Egypt) into thirty-six districts. He arranged for each of the districts the god to be worshiped, hieroglyphics for the priests, and that they (the gods) should be cats and dogs and ibises.[2] He also allotted a choice land for the priests.

He did all these things for the sake of preserving the monarchy secure for Chenephres.[3] Formerly, the masses were disordered and would at one time expel kings, at other times appoint them – often the same kings, but sometimes others. On account of these things, then, Moses was loved by the masses, and was deemed worthy by the priests of honor equal to a god. He was addressed as "Hermes" on account of his interpretation (*hermeneia*) of hieroglyphics.[4]

[1] The text used for the following translation is edited by Guy Schroeder and Édouard des Places, *La Préparation Évangélique livres VIII–IX–X*, SC 369 (Paris: Cerf, 1991), 270–72.

[2] On Hermes-Thoth as the inventor of hieroglyphic writing, compare Plato, *Phaedrus* 274c–75b; Diodorus, *Library of History* 1.16.1; Cicero, *Nature of the Gods* 3.22. See further Jasnow, "Book of Thoth," 331. The word used here (ἱερὰ γράμματα) could also refer to sacred writings. For the ibis selected as a sacred animal, see Herodotus, *Histories* 2.67 (ibises are embalmed at Hermopolis); Apion in Aelian, *Nature of Animals* 10.29 (the priests of Hermopolis say that the ibis is deathless). See further Carl R. Holladay, *Fragments from Hellenistic Jewish Authors volume 1: Historians* (Chico: Scholars Press, 1983), 232–34; John J. Collins in *OTP* 2.898–99, notes j–r.

[3] The reigning Pharaoh, or one of them (Artapanus indicates that Egypt had many kings at the time).

[4] Compare Acts 14:12 (Paul called "Hermes" because he is the chief speaker); Diodorus, *Library of History* 1.16.2: "He (Hermes) taught the Greeks the art of interpretation (τὰ περὶ τὴν ἑρμενείαν), for which reason he was called 'Hermes.'" Artapanus also called all the Jews "Hermiouth" – apparently a name related to Hermes (Holladay, *Fragments*, 205, 226).

Now when Chenephres observed the excellence of Moses, he was envious of him and sought to be rid of him on some specious pretext. So when the Ethiopians campaigned against Egypt, Chenephres supposed that he had found a convenient opportunity. He sent Moses against them as a general with an army. Nevertheless, he enlisted for Moses a host of farmers, supposing that he would easily be wiped out by the combatants on account of the weakness of the soldiers.[5]

When Moses came to the district called Hermopolis with about a hundred thousand farmers, he pitched his camp. He sent generals to occupy the region, and these fared brilliantly in battles … Moses's comrades founded a city in that place on account of the size of the army. They made the ibis sacred there because it destroys animals that kill people. They called it "Hermopolis" (the city of Hermes).[6]

[5] See further D. Runnalls, "Moses' Ethiopian Campaign," *Journal for the Study of Judaism* 14 (1993): 135–56.

[6] The types of benefits that Moses bestows (his founding of Hermopolis, the sacralization of the ibis) indicate that Artapanus identified Moses with the god or deified hero later called "Hermes Thrice Great." The consecration of the ibis may depend on a version of a story told by Josephus (*Antiquities* 2.246) in which Moses used ibises on his march to overcome serpents. The aid of the ibis against noxious animals was part of Greek cultural knowledge (Diodorus, *Library of History* 1.87.6; Plutarch, *Isis and Osiris* 74 [*Moralia* 381a]).

Cicero

TH 2

Cicero (Mid First Century BCE*),* On the Nature of the Gods *3.56*[1]

The first Mercury, whose father was Ouranos and his mother Day, is rather obscenely said to have his penis erect because he was aroused by the sight of Persephone. The second Hermes is the son of Valens and Phoronis; he is considered to be the same being as Trophonius under the earth. The third Hermes was born of the third Jove and Maia. From him and Penelope, they say, Pan was born. The fourth Hermes had the Nile for his father; the Egyptians hold it sacrilegious to pronounce his name. The fifth Hermes is the one whom the people of Pheneüs worship; he is said to have killed Argus and for this reason to have fled to Egypt and delivered laws and literature to the Egyptians.[2] The Egyptians call this Hermes {Theyn},[3] which is also their name for the first month of the year.[4]

[1] The text used for the following translation is edited by Arthur Stanley Pease, ed., *M. Tulli Ciceronis De natura deorum*, 2 vols. (Cambridge, MA: Harvard University Press, 1955–58), 2.1108–12.

[2] Similarly, Aelian says that the Egyptians received their laws from Hermes, or that Hermes specifically instructed Pharaoh Sesostris (*Varied History* 14.34; 12.4). Diogenes Laertius reports similar traditions (*Lives of Philosophers* 1.11). See further Bull, "Tradition of Hermes," 87–93.

[3] That is, Thoth.

[4] Cicero's testimony is taken over by Lactantius in FH 3a. See notes there.

Manilius

TH 3

Manilius (Early First Century CE*),* Astronomica *1.25–37*[1]

By the gift of the celestials to the lands of earth it was first granted to know this[2] more deeply.
For who if the gods concealed these things could filch by stealth the sky in which all things are governed?
Who with human intelligence would dare so great a deed –
To want to appear as a god when the gods are unwilling,
To make manifest the sublime paths and the deepest highway underground
And stars obedient to their own boundaries as they course through the void?
You are the prince and author, Cyllenian,[3] of so great a sacred art,
Through you, heaven in its depths is known along with its constellations,
The names and the courses of the signs, their dignities and powers,

[1] The text on which the following translation is based is edited by George P. Goold, *M. Manilii Astronimica* (Stuttgart and Leipzig: Teubner, 1998), 2. See further Josèphe-Henriette Abry, "Manilius," *DPA* 4.248–54.

[2] Manilius refers to the sky or the universe more broadly.

[3] That is, Hermes. The earliest Hermetic texts seem to have been astrological in nature. In the late first century BCE, Strabo observed that the priests of Egyptian Thebes (modern Luxor) attributed astronomical knowledge to Hermes (*Geography* 17.1.46). Around the same time, Diodorus reported that the philosopher Democritus learned astrology from the Egyptians (*Library of History* 1.98.3). Note also Pseudo-Eratosthenes, *Catasterismi* 43 (the planet Mercury "was given to Hermes because he was the first to define the cosmic order of heaven, to measure the stars, their ranks, their times, and to reveal the seasonal indications"); Hyginus, *Astronomy* 2.42 (Hermes was the first to institute the months and survey the courses of the stars).

So that the face of the sky might be more eminent, and so that not only the outer form,
But also the very power of reality be worshiped,
And so that the peoples might have a sense for God wherein he is greatest.

Thrasyllus

TH 4

Thrasyllus (Early First Century CE*)*, Pinax for Hieroclea *according to a Later Summary*[1]

He (Thrasyllus) also discusses how the so-called Hermes Thrice Great saw fit to customarily name each twelfth-part section of the chart.[2] For instance, he (Hermes) declared that the ascendant or constellation rising at the horizon was the "steering wheel" and indicator of fortune, a person's soul, the manner of one's life, as well as one's siblings.[3] The place after the ascendant signals a person's hopes. The third (place) indicates both action and siblings. The fourth he called the foundation of happiness, the indicator of ancestral possessions and the ownership of slaves. The fifth indicates good fortune. The sixth, by contrast, indicates <bad> fortune,

[1] The text used for the translation of this fragment is edited by Harold Tarrant, ed., *Thrasyllan Platonism* (Ithaca: Cornell University Press, 1993), 245–46. A "pinax" refers to an astrological table that astrologers used to determine the position of the planets at a certain day and hour without actual observation. It could refer more broadly to an astrological manual.

[2] The author refers to a birth chart (διάθεμα) filled out for clients who paid to learn their horoscope.

[3] Some of the technical terms used in this passage are discussed by Sextus Empiricus, *Against the Mathematicians* 5.12–14. To explain briefly: the astrologer draws a "birth theme" (διάθεμα τῆς γενέσεως) by determining four "centers," sometimes called "cardines." The first cardine is the "ascendant" (ὁροσκόπος) or indicator of the zodiacal degree rising at the eastern horizon at the moment of the subject's birth. The cardine after the ascendant is the midheaven (μεσουράνημα) in the center of the sky, then follows the descendant (δύσις) in the western horizon, and finally the anti-midheaven (ἀντιμεσουράνημα) in the 6 o'clock position below the earth. To each sign of the zodiac are assigned constant psychological and physical features. The planets and the signs that appear at the cardines especially reveal the client's fate. Superimposed on the signs of the zodiac is a second circle of "places" (τόποι), later called "houses" (οἶκοι, as already in Sextus Empiricus, *Against the Mathematicians* 5.34; compare Manilius, *Astronomica* 2.788–967; Firmicus Maternus, *Mathesis* 2.14–20). In most systems, there are twelve houses, each of which is assigned a particular topic such as parents, children, health, marriage, and so on. These topics were never standardized. The revolution of the zodiacal constellations within these stationary houses made possible more complex predictions. See further Beck, *Brief History*, 38–49.

punishment, and injuries. The seventh, in the place of setting, is indicative of death and a wife. The eighth (place) he called "life" and "livelihood." The ninth indicates trips abroad and life in a foreign land. The tenth or the <anti->midheaven, he said, indicates fortune, livelihood, life, children, sowing, deeds, honors, beginnings, and ruling offices. The eleventh zodiacal sign in the chart he called "good daimon." The twelfth, or the one that rises after the ascendant, he called "evil daimon," which indicates livelihood <and> the subjection of slaves.

Dorotheus of Sidon

TH 5a

Dorotheus of Sidon (Mid to Late First Century), Astrological Poem *(or* Pentateuch*) 2.20.1*[1]

A chapter. Knowledge of the places of the planets.

Look with this at the places of the planets and their portions, and know this as says the honored (and) praiseworthy by three natures, Hermes, the King of Egypt.[2]

TH 5b

Dorotheus Fragment II E 3 = Scholium to Hephaestion, Outcomes *(*Apotelesmatica*) 3.6.11*[3]

In every beginning, one must observe the four lots, namely chance, daimon, necessity, and love. It is unclear whether one must exclude necessity and love according to Hermes Thrice Great as Dorotheus reports in his fourth book narrating the views of the Egyptians.

[1] The translation used here is that of David Pingree, ed., *Dorothei Sidonii. Carmen Astrologicum: Interpretationem arabicam in linguam anglicam versam una cum Dorothei fragmentis et graecis et latinis*, BGRST (Stuttgart: Teubner, 1976), 224. Dorotheus's original Greek text does not survive complete. It was translated into Pahlavi (Middle Persian) around the third century CE, and into Arabic evidently around 800 CE.

[2] For Hermes as king, compare TH 7 (Athenagoras) below. Hermes as possessing three natures may reflect a later attempt to explain his name "Thrice Great."

[3] The Greek text used as a basis for the following translation is that of Pingree, *Carmen Astrologicum*, 433–34.

Philo of Byblos

TH 6a

Philo of Byblos (Early Second Century CE) Quoted in Eusebius, Preparation for the Gospel *1.9.24*[1]

Under these conditions, Sanchuniathon, a learned man and a meticulous researcher, yearning to know from all peoples events even from the beginning of time, the starting points of everything, replicated with wide-ranging thoughtfulness the teachings of Taautos.[2] Sanchuniathon knew that Taautos was the first man to live under the sun.[3] He is the one who devised the discovery of letters and began the writing of notes, upon which basis he devised the writing of his treatise.[4] The Egyptians call Taautos "Thouth," and the Alexandrians "Thoth," which the Greeks translated as "Hermes."

TH 6b

Philo of Byblos Quoted in Eusebius, Preparation for the Gospel *1.10.17–18*

Advancing into manhood, Kronos made use of the counsel and help of Hermes Thrice Great (for he was his scribe) to defend himself against his father Ouranos and to avenge his mother (Earth) . . . Then Hermes spoke magical words to the allies of Kronos and inspired them with a yearning to fight against Ouranos on behalf of Ge (Earth).[5]

[1] The text used as a basis for the following translation is edited by Jean Sirinelli and Édouard des Places, *La Préparation Évangélique livre I*, SC 206 (Paris: Cerf, 1974), 180, 194.

[2] Another name for Thoth (as is explained later). Sanchuniathon is reputedly an ancient Phoenician scholar whose dates, biography, and existence are disputed.

[3] Compare FH 21 (from Zosimus).

[4] Compare Plato, *Phaedrus* 274c–75b.

[5] Here a strange mix of Greek, Phoenician, and possibly Egyptian mythology generates a new story. See further Fowden, *Egyptian Hermes*, 162, 216–17.

Athenagoras

TH 7

Athenagoras of Athens (Mid to Late Second Century CE*),* **Embassy** ***28.3***[1]

When Alexander (the Great) and Hermes surnamed "Thrice Great" linked their own family with the gods – and ten thousand others I will not list individually – there is no reason left to doubt that they were considered gods by virtue of being kings.[2]

[1] The text used for the following translation is edited by Miroslav Marcovich, ed., *Athenagoras. Legatio pro Christianis* (Berlin: de Gruyter, 1990), 92.

[2] On Hermes as king, compare Dorotheus in TH 5. On the question of Hermes the elder's deification, see FH 41 (from Augustine, *City of God* 8.26, quoting *Ascl.* 37). In general, Augustine observes: "in all the literature of the pagans there are not found any, or scarcely any gods, who have not been men, to whom, when dead, divine honors have been paid" (*City of God* 8.26). On Athenagoras, see further Fowden, *Egyptian Hermes*, 162, 216–17. On the deification of ancient kings, see Nickolas P. Roubekas, *An Ancient Theory of Religion: Euhemerism from Antiquity to the Present* (London: Routledge, 2017), 93–114.

Virtues of Plants

TH 8

Virtues of Plants *(Second Century* CE*)*[1]

Epitome of the Medical Manual of Hermes Thrice Great according to His Astrological Knowledge and the Natural Emanations of the Stars Published for His Disciple Asclepius.

The plant of Aries is salvia.
The plant of Taurus is vervain.
The plant of Gemini is holy vervain.
The plant of Cancer is comfrey.
The plant of Leo is cyclamen.
The plant of Virgo is catmint.
The plant of Libra is scorpion's tail or heliotrope.
The plant of Scorpio is artemisia.
The plant of Sagittarius is red and blue-scarlet pimpernel.
The plant of Capricorn is herb of patience.
The plant of Aquarius is dragonwort.
The plant of Pisces is birthwort.

[1] The dating of this text follows Ian S. Moyer, "A Revised Astronomical Dating of Thessalus's *De virtutibus herbarum*," in Brooke Holmes, ed., *The Frontiers of Ancient Science: Essays in Honor of Heinrich von Staden* (Berlin: de Gruyter, 2015), 437–49. The text used for the following translation was published by Hans-Veit Friedrich, ed., *Thessalos von Tralles griechisch und lateinisch* (Meisenheim am Glan: Anton Hain, 1968), 43–44, 56–69. Friedrich explains that there are two recensions of *On the Virtues of Plants*, a longer one attributed to Thessalus (possibly Thessalus of Tralles, a famous medical doctor who died around 79 CE), and a shorter one ascribed to Hermes Thrice Great. I translate the prologue of the shorter recension along with §§25–28. The attribution to Hermes, if secondary, is still significant. When exactly the attribution occurred is unknown. See further Festugière, *Mystique*, 141–80; Festugière, *RHT*, 1.56–59, 143–60, 201–16; Jonathan Z. Smith, "Temple and Magician," 172–89; David Pingree, "Thessalus Astrologus," in Paul Oskar Kristeller, ed., *Catalogus Translationum et Commentariorum* 3 (Washington, DC: Catholic University of America Press, 1976): 83–86; Fowden, *Egyptian Hermes*, 162–66; Moyer, *Egypt*, 208–73.

One must gather these plants and extract their juices when the Sun is lord in Aries, and also when it is lord of each particular sign of each single plant and when the Moon is lord in trine with the sun or at the ascendant. Let it be the day and the hour of the house-ruler for the zodiacal sign. Thus you will be highly esteemed, as the teacher says, with regard to the cosmic and natural effects ...

Book of Hermes Thrice Great on Sacred Plants and Juicing

"O Hermes, you who have obtained blessed honor from the gods, in the progress of time, when your successes become known, people will worship you all the more! Ask now according to your desire. I will offer you all things gladly." This is what the god said to him.

Yet I (Hermes) barely heard, since I was so struck and overwhelmed in my mind as I gazed upon the form of the god.[2] Nevertheless, I inquired why I failed ... to achieve anything with the powers of Nechepso. The god answered: There was a king (called) Nechepso, a man of supreme wisdom and adorned with every virtue. He failed to learn all things from the divine voice, yet through his innate nobility he discovered the correspondences of stones and plants, and came to know the seasons and the places in which to pick the plants.[3]

You observe that all plants grow and diminish by astral emanation. The distinctive breath of the stars is most subtle and passes through all matter especially in those places where the earthly allotment of the stars exists aligned with the descent (of their energies) through the cosmos. I will show you evidence of this phenomenon that will confirm the remainder of what I say ...

[2] The shift to the first person indicates imperfect editing of the source. Originally, it was probably Thessalus who spoke in the first person. See the next note.

[3] Pharaoh Nechepso (along with the priest Petosiris) was the reputed author of astrological writings from the second century BCE. According to (probably the original) recension of *On the Virtues of Plants*, Thessalus found a book of Nechepso which discussed remedies based on correspondences between plants and zodiacal signs. (See the fragments edited by E. Riess, ed., *Nechepsonis et Petosiridis fragmenta magica* [Göttingen: Dieterich, 1892].) Yet Nechepso's remedies failed to work, forcing Thessalus to find a priest of Thebes (modern Luxor) to call up Asclepius the healing god. Thessalus's experiences were later assigned to Hermes even though Hermes was normally viewed as the teacher of Asclepius and the source of Nechepso's wisdom (Firmicus Maternus, *Mathesis* 3.1.1: 4, *proem* §5; the Salt Papyrus cited by Moyer, *Egypt*, 243). Clement of Alexandria in the late second century CE assigns certain medical books to Hermes (*Stromata* 6.4.37.3).

Refutation of All Heresies

TH 9

Refutation of All Heresies *(220–25 CE), 5.14.7*[1]

The right hand is a power of God whom Ignorance called "Rhea."[2] According to his image were born Attis, Mygdon, and Oinone . . . The right-hand power has authority over the harvests. Ignorance called him "Mena."[3] According to his image were born Boumegas, Ostanes, Hermes

[1] The text used for the following translation is edited by Miroslav Marcovich, *Hippolytus: Refutatio omnium haeresiorum* (Berlin: de Gruyter, 1986), 179–80; compare Bidez and Cumont, *Mages hellénisés*, 2.86. The author of this work is anonymous. For recent research on authorship, see Emanuele Castelli, "Saggio introduttivo: L'*Elenchos*, ovvero una 'biblioteca' contro le eresie," in Aldo Magris, ed., *'Ippolito.' Confutazione di tutte le eresie* (Brescia: Morcelliana, 2012), 34–46; Litwa, *Refutation*, xxvii–liii.

[2] In context, the author of *Ref.* quotes from a Peratic book entitled *Outlying Officials Dwelling as far as the Aether*. It appears to be some kind of manual identifying the true names of the heavenly bodies. The author of *Outlying Officials* starts with Saturn, envisioned as a primal ocean (compare the Egyptian Nun) surrounding the cosmos. From Saturn, the author works his way inward to identify the true names and companions of the five planets, the administrators of the air, the rulers of the hours of the night and day, a right- and left-hand power, three middle powers (the Fates), and an androgynous power identified with Eros. I begin the citation with the description of the right-hand power.

[3] J. Montserrat-Torrents identifies Mena (or perhaps Meis [Μείς], the Greek word for moon) with Men, a moon god of Asia Minor ("Les Pérates," *Compostellanum* 34 [1989]: 185–98 [193]; compare *Ref.* 5.8.4; 5.9.8 [Naassenes]). Hermes Thrice Great, as a form of Thoth, would qualify as a moon god. Here, however, it is probably Hermes's association with magic and astrology that links him to the moon. See the next note.

Thrice Great, Kourites, Petosiris, Zodarion, Berosus, Astrampsouchus, and Zoroastris.[4]

[4] All these "sons of the moon" are non-Greek sages, magicians, or diviners. Berosus (usually spelled Berossus) was a Babylonian priest, astrologer, and historian in the third century BCE. Ostanes was a Persian magus in the line of Zoroaster (see further Bidez and Cumont, *Mages hellénisés*, 1.165–212; 2.265–356; Van Bladel, *Arabic Hermes*, 48–54). Petosiris was a high priest of Thoth at Hermopolis in the late fourth century BCE, later associated with astrology. Hermes and Petosiris also appear together in Firmicus Maternus, *Mathesis* 4, *proem* §5. See further Pedro Pablo Fuentes González, "Néchepso-Pétosiris," *DPA* 4.601–15; Lichtheim, *Ancient Egyptian Literature*, 3.44–49; TH 10a from Pseudo-Manetho. Astrampsouchos was the name of one or several Persian magicians (Diogenes Laertius, *Lives of Philosophers* proem. 2). There is a love spell of "Astrapsoukos" in *PGM* 8.1. In *Zostrianos* (NHC VIII,1), "Strempsouchos" is mentioned as a guardian of souls (47.3). Marcovich equates Boumegas with the ancient Persian Gaumata (a magos of the Achaemenid era who had a brief reign as king). He also equates Ζωδάριον with Ὠάννης or the Mesopotamian god Ea (*Refutatio*, 180).

Pseudo-Manetho

TH 10a

Pseudo-Manetho (Third Century CE*),* Apotelesmatica *5.1–10*[1]

From the sacred books of the inner shrines, King Ptolemy,
And from hidden steles, which all-wise Hermes devised[2]
And inscribed by his own prescience of the celestial bodies,
After finding Asclepius his fellow counselor in prudent wisdom,[3]
I copied on my wax tablet and now offer it
As a flower basket for my Muse, the honey-sweet gift of bees.
Thus in the darkling night I discovered underneath a chorus of stars
An instruction that speaks with the threads of the Fates;
For no man devised the glory of so great a wisdom
Except Petosiris alone, a man most dear to me.[4]

[1] The text used for the following translation is edited by Robert Lopilato, "The *Apotelesmatika* of Manetho" (Ph.D. diss., Brown University, 1998), 108.

[2] For shrines and hidden steles compare SH 23.5; TH 12 from Iamblichus; *Disc. 8–9* (NHC VI,6) 61.18–62.20; *Three Steles of Seth* (NHC VII,5) 118.10–24. The Ptolemy addressed here is evidently Ptolemy II Philadelphus.

[3] Compare SH 23.6; Firmicus Maternus, *Mathesis* 3.1.1: "Petosiris and Nechepso in this (astrological doctrine) followed Asclepius and Hanubius. To them most powerful Hermes entrusted the secret"; *Mathesis* 4, *proem* §5: "We have written in these books all the things which Hermes and Hanubius handed down to Asclepius, which Petosiris and Nechepso explained."

[4] Petosiris was an Egyptian priest associated with astrological writings. For Petosiris associated with Hermes, see TH 9 from *Ref.* 5.14.7.

TH 10b

Pseudo-Manetho Quoted by George Syncellus (Early Ninth Century CE*),* Chronological Excerpts 72[5]

Our task henceforth is to treat small passages from the writings of Manetho of Sebennytos concerning the rule of the Egyptians. At the time of Ptolemy Philadelphus, he bore the title of high priest of the idols in Egypt.[6] He (Manetho) addressed himself to the same king Philadelphus, Ptolemy II, in his *Book of Sothis*, writing as follows:[7]

> Letter of Manetho of Sebennytos to Ptolemy Philadelphus.
>
> To the great and revered king Ptolemy Philadelphus, Manetho the high priest and scribe of the holy shrines in Egypt, by race a man of Sebennytos yet dwelling at Heliopolis, greetings to my master Ptolemy!
>
> We consider it necessary, greatest king, to investigate all those matters about which you willed. You have searched out the future happenings in the cosmos. As you ordered me, I will divulge to you the holy books written by my forefather Hermes Thrice Great which I learned (by heart) from the stelae located in the Seriadic land.[8] They were inscribed in a sacred language and hieroglyphic characters by Thoth, the first Hermes, and translated after the Flood from the sacred language into the Greek tongue [with hieroglyphic characters].[9] They were recorded in books by the son of Agathos Daimon, namely the second Hermes, father of Tat, in the inner shrines of Egypt's sanctuaries.[10]

5 The text for the following translation is edited by Alden A. Mosshammer, ed., *Ecloga Chronographica* (Leipzig: Teubner, 1984), 40–41.

6 Ptolemy Philadelphus reigned in Egypt from 285 to 247 BCE.

7 The Greek text of this paragraph is also edited by Felix Jacoby in *FGrH* 609 as testimony 11a from Manetho of Sebennytos.

8 Probably a reference to Egypt, assuming that "Seiriadic" refers to the star Sirius (Σείριος), harbinger of the Nile flood, and the astral form of Isis (Plutarch, *Isis and Osiris* 38 [*Moralia* 365f]). Josephus (*Antiquities* 1.68–71) says that the descendants of Seth set up two inscribed stelae that exist (in Josephus's day) in the land of Seiris (Σειρίδα; other MSS read Σιριάδα). Possibly Josephus meant some place closer to Israel or Babylon. See the proposals of G. J. Reinink, "Das Land 'Seiris' (Šir) and das Volk der Serer in jüdischen und christlichen Traditionen," *JSJ* 6 (1975): 72–85; Guy Stroumsa, *Another Seed: Studies in Gnostic Mythology* (Leiden: Brill, 1984), 138.

9 "With hieroglyphic characters" is probably a doublet of a similar phrase mentioned before. It is not impossible that after a universal Flood (in origin a Mesopotamian myth, not an Egyptian one) Greek was in use. But a Greek translation would not have been written with hieroglyphs.

10 Here I follow Scott (*Hermetica*, 3.491–92, n.6) in transposing the passage "from the stelae . . . of Egypt's sanctuaries" (ἐκ τῶν ἐν τῇ Σηριαδικῇ γῇ . . . τῶν ἱερῶν Αἰγύπτου) to this location in the quoted letter. In the text of Syncellus, it occurs before the letter, after the sentence: "At the time of Ptolemy Philadelphus, he bore the title of high priest of the idols in Egypt."

Farewell, my lord and king.[11]

This is what he says about the translation of the books by the second Hermes.[12]

[11] The Greek text of the letter is also edited by Felix Jacoby in *FGrH* 609 as fragment 25 from Manetho of Sebennytos. In the letter, the reference to Ptolemy as "Augustus" (Σέβαστος) – if meant as an official title – is anachronistic, as is the title "Hermes Thrice Great." These anachronisms may not, however, prove that the letter as a whole is a forgery. See the discussion of Laqueur, "Manetho" *RE* 14.1 (1928): 1100; Festugière, *RHT*, 1.74–75; William Adler, *Time Immemorial: Archaic History and its Sources in Christian Chronography from Julius Africanus to George Syncellus* (Washington, DC: Dumbarton Oaks, 1989), 58–60; Fowden, *Egyptian Hermes*, 30–31; Bull, "Tradition of Hermes," 48–59.

[12] This final comment by Syncellus indicates that the notice concerning Hermes's translation of the stelae originally belonged to Manetho's letter. Van Bladel argues that Syncellus's citation of the *Book of Sothis* was dependent upon a chronicle composed by the Alexandrian writer Pandorus around 400 CE (*Arabic Hermes*, 137–38).

Arnobius

TH 11

Arnobius, Against the Nations *2.13 (Early Fourth Century* CE*)*[1]

Meanwhile, you who show surprise, who marvel at the tenets of the learned and of philosophy, do you not consider it incredibly unfair to insult and mock us, as if we were mouthing follies and idiocies when you are found saying the same or similar things at which you laugh when said or stated by us? Here my debate is not with those who, scattered through the various bypaths of the schools, have created this and that party by divergence of views. It is *you* I address, you people who follow after Hermes, Plato, and Pythagoras, and you others who are of the same mind and march with unity of opinion through the same paths. You dare to laugh at us because we venerate and worship the father of and lord of nature, and because we give and entrust our hopes to him?[2]

[1] The text used for the following translation is edited by C. Marchesi, *Adversus nationes libri VII* (Turin: Paraviae, 1953), 80.

[2] A question raised by this passage is whether Arnobius envisioned philosophical followers of Hermes as an independent "sect" of his time. What Arnobius may have had in mind was Neoplatonist or gnostic groups that appealed to Hermes (among other sages) as an authority. In fact, Arnobius's own theology was significantly influenced by these groups or at least by their teachings. See further Jérôme Carcopino, *Aspectes mystiques de la Rome païenne* (Paris: L'artisan du Livre, 1942), 286–301; Festugière, *Mystique*, 261–312; E. L. Fortin, "The viri novi of Arnobius and the Conflict Between Faith and Reason in the early Christian Centuries," in D. Neiman and M. Schatkin, eds., *The Heritage of the Early Church: Essays in Honor of G. V. Florovsky* (Rome: Institute for Oriental Studies, 1973), 197–226; Fowden, *Egyptian Hermes*, 199–200; Moreschini, *Hermes Christianus*, 31–32; Van Oort, "Augustine and Hermes," 64–66.

Iamblichus

TH 12

Iamblichus, On the Mysteries *1.1–2, 8.4 (Early Fourth Century* CE*)*[1]

1.1 Hermes, the deity who presides over rational discourses, has long and rightly been considered common to all who practice the sacred arts. He who presides over true science concerning gods is one and the same throughout the universe. It is to him that our ancestors dedicated the discoveries of their wisdom, attributing all their own writings to Hermes . . .

1.2 If you put forward a philosophical question, we will judge this too for you by the canon of Hermes's stelae, which Plato and Pythagoras of old perused in order to establish their philosophy . . .[2]

8.4 With these elucidations, the solution of the matters in the treatises you claim to have read is clear. The writings that circulate under the name of Hermes contain Hermaic tenets, even if they often make use of philosophical language. For they were translated from the Egyptian language by men not unversed in philosophy.[3]

Yet Chaeremon – and however many others who treat cosmic first principles – explain the principles of the lowest level; and the tradents of the lore regarding the planets, the zodiac, the decans, hour-watchers, along with the so-called "dominant" and "leading" stars, only deal with the

[1] The text used for the following translation is edited by Édouard des Places, *Jamblique, les mystères d'Égypte*, 2nd edn. (Paris: Belles Lettres, 1989), 38–39, 197–98.

[2] Iamblichus, writing in the person of the Egyptian priest "Abammon," addresses the philosopher Porphyry who in his *Letter to Anebo* had been critical of Egyptian thought and practice. See further the introduction to Iamblichus prefaced to FH 16.

[3] Compare CH 16.1: "It (my discourse) will be entirely unclear when the Greeks eventually desire to translate our language to their own."

partitioned distribution of the principles.[4] Moreover, the contents of the *Salmeschiniaka* contain the smallest portion of the Hermaic system.[5] In addition, the appearance and disappearance of stars, along with the waxings and wanings of the moon, are entirely subsidiary in the Egyptian theory of causation.

The Egyptians do not claim that all things are physical. Rather, they distinguish the life of the soul and that of the intellect from the physical world, not only at the level of the universe, but also at our level (as individuals). They present consciousness and reason as independent principles responsible for crafting existing things.

They set up a Forefather as Craftsman of existing things, and they acknowledge a life-giving power both prior to heaven and in heaven.[6] They posit a pure consciousness existing above the cosmos, a single indivisible consciousness in the cosmos as a whole, and yet another consciousness partitioned among the heavenly spheres.

They do not simply theorize about these doctrines. Rather, they bid that we ascend through the practice of priestly theurgy to the regions that are higher, more universal, and superior to Fate, toward the Craftsman deity without the addition of matter or the taking alongside of anything else other than the observation of the critical time.

5. Hermes is the guide for this very journey. The prophet Bitys, moreover, translated it for King Ammon, having discovered it inscribed

[4] Chaeremon is usually identified both as an Egyptian priest and a Stoic philosopher living in the mid first century CE. Iamblichus responds to Porphyry who had said that, "Chaeremon and the others do not believe in anything prior to the visible worlds, stating that the basic principles are the gods of the Egyptians and that there are no other gods than the so-called planets, and those stars which fill up the zodiac, and all those that rise near them, and the sections relating to the decans, and the hour-watchers, and the so-called mighty rulers. Of these both their names and their treatments of diseases, their risings and settings, and their indications of future events can be found in the *Salmeschiniaka*" (frag. 5 Van der Horst, trans. Van der Horst, modified).

[5] The *Salmeschiniaka* was an astrological work existing by 150 BCE which survives only in fragments. Briant Bohleke calls it "a book of 72 pictures of celestial signs, their risings, settings, what they indicate for future events, and the five-day periods over which they are sovereign" ("In Terms of Fate: A Survey of the Indigenous Egyptian Contribution to Ancient Astrology," *Studien zur altägyptische Kultur* 23 [1996]: 11–46, at 17–19). Quotes from the work show that it also dealt with decans (Greenbaum, *Daimon*, 230), and probably clarified the position of the decans on the day a person was born. It was also a source for astrological writings attributed to pharaoh Nechepso and the priest Petosiris composed in the latter half of the second century BCE. The wisdom of these two figures was later attributed to Hermes. See further Fowden, *Egyptian Hermes*, 139–40; Grant Adamson, "The Old Gods of Egypt in Lost Hermetica and Early Sethianism," in *Histories of the Hidden God: Concealment and Revelation in Western Gnostic, Esoteric, and Mystical Traditions*, ed. April D. DeConick and Grant Adamson (London: Acumen, 2014), 58–86 at 60–62.

[6] Compare the "Forefather" in SH 2A.13 with the note there. The life-giving power in heaven would evidently be the Sun.

in hieroglyphic characters in the inner shrines around Saïs in Egypt.[7] He handed on the name of God that pervades the whole cosmos. There are many other treatises on the same subjects, so that you (Porphyry) are not correct, it seems to me, in referring all Egyptian doctrine to physical principles. In fact, they recognize many principles with regard to many substances, including supracosmic powers, which they worship by means of priestly ritual.

[7] For Bitys, compare FH 17 (from Iamblichus, *On the Mysteries* 10.7) and FH 21 (from Zosimus) with notes. According to Plato, the Athenian lawgiver Solon met Egyptian priests in Saïs (*Timaeus* 21e; compare *Critias* 113a–b).

Marius Victorinus

TH 13

Marius Victorinus, Commentary on Cicero's Rhetoric *1.39* *(Mid Fourth Century CE)*[1]

This is the origin of the twelve-hour period as it is remembered. At a certain time, Hermes Thrice Great, when he lived in Egypt, dedicated a certain sacred animal to Serapis. This animal urinated twelve times in the entire daylight period, always at an equal interval. From this practice, Hermes inferred that the day was divided into twelve hours. Ever since, this number of hours has been preserved.

[1] The text used for the following translation is edited by Thomas Riesenweber, ed., *C. Marius Victorinus, Commenta in Ciceronis Rhetorica accedit incerti auctoris tractatus de attributis personae et negotio*, BSGRT (Berlin: de Gruyter, 2013), 98.

The Emperor Julian

TH 14

The Emperor Julian Quoted in Cyril, Against Julian *5.33.6–9 (around 362 CE)*[1]

We must speak of the Egyptians as well.[2] They number among themselves the names of not a few sages – many of whom received their succession from Hermes. I refer to the Hermes who three times visited Egypt.[3]

[1] The text used for the following fragment is edited by Riedweg, *Gegen Julian*, 1.393.

[2] In context, Julian argues that God does not care solely for the Hebrews but visits every nation on earth.

[3] Possibly Julian assumes that Hermes was thrice incarnated. This point becomes clear in Hermias (TH 20b) and the *Passion of Artemius* (TH 24). Ammianus Marcellinus reports that Julian used to supplicate Hermes privately during the night (*Historical Events* 16.5.5). It is not clear, however, that he had Hermes Thrice Great specifically in mind.

Ammianus Marcellinus

TH 15

Ammianus Marcellinus (Mid to Late Fourth Century), Historical Events *21.14.5*[1]

We read these two verses in Menander the comic poet: "A daimon accompanies every man the moment he is born, and serves as his guide in the mysteries of life." Likewise from the eternal poems of Homer we come to understand that it was not celestial gods who conversed with brave men, or were present to help the fighters. Rather, they were visited by their familiar spirits.

Leaning upon the special support of these spirits, Pythagoras and Socrates increased in brilliance, along with Numa Pompilius, the earlier Scipio and, as some suppose, Marius, then Octavian – who first received the title "Augustus."[2] Add to these Hermes Thrice Great, Apollonius of Tyana, and Plotinus, who first dared to profess certain mystical teachings on this topic and to show in depth by what original principles these spirits were connected to mortal souls.[3] The spirits took these souls into their arms, as it were, and protected them as long as was permissible. To those they deemed pure and set apart from the dregs of sin by their immaculate fellowship with the body, they taught doctrines of a higher order.

[1] The text used as a basis for the following translation is edited by Wolfgang Seyfarth, *Ammiani Marcellini rerum gestarum libri qui supersunt*, 2 vols. (Leipzig: Teubner, 1999), 1.243.

[2] Pythagoras and Socrates are famous ancient Greek philosophers. See Plutarch's tractate *On the Daimonion of Socrates.* Numa was the second Roman king and philosopher. Scipio Africanus the Elder was a famous Roman general thought to have personally communed with Jupiter. Marius was a later general who saved Rome from northern invaders. Octavian/Augustus was the first official emperor of Rome.

[3] Hermes is connected to philosophers of a more mystical bent. For Plotinus's encounter with his guardian daimon, see Porphyry, *Life of Plotinus* 10.

Greek Magical Papyri

TH 16a

Greek Magical Papyri *(Second to Fourth Centuries* CE*)* *4.850–87*[1]

Solomon's trance spell effective for children and mature adults.[2]

I adjure you by the sacred and celestial gods not to pass on the procedure of Solomon to anyone and certainly not for frivolous reasons unless a matter of necessity compels you, lest perchance wrath be stored up for you.

The formula spoken: "(a listing of magical names) . . . Hear me, that is, my sacred voice, because I invoke your sacred names, and reveal to me concerning the matter I desire, through this man or child – since otherwise I will not defend your sacred and undefiled names. Come to me, you who became Hesies and were carried away by a river.[3] Inspire this man or child concerning that which I inquire . . .

Come to me through this person or child and explain to me with precision, since I speak your names which Thrice Great Hermes wrote in hieroglyphics at Heliopolis![4]

> (magical names follow, some of them compound names for deities) . . .
> Enter him and reveal to me the matter at hand!"

[1] The text used as a basis for the following translation is edited by Karl Preisendanz and Albert Henrichs, *Papyri Graecae Magicae. Die griechischen Zauberpapyri*, 2nd edn., 3 vols. (Munich: Saur, 2001), 1.102.

[2] The magician asks the gods to enter another person and through this person to speak the future or give advice on a particular topic.

[3] "Hesies" or "Esies" is an epithet of the deified dead often applied to Osiris whose body was thrown into the Nile, but who lives eternally in the Underworld.

[4] Compare TH 10b from Pseudo-Manetho.

TH 16b

Greek Magical Papyri *7.540–59*[5]

Lamp divination. Place an iron lamp in the eastern part of a pure house. Place on it a lamp not painted red (and) light it. Let the wick be made from new linen and light the censor. Then fumigate frankincense over vine wood. Let the boy be uncorrupted and pure.

Formula: (magical names) . . . Since I call upon you on this very day in this immediate moment! Make appear to this boy the light and the sun, MANE Osiris, MANE Isis, Anubis servant of all gods, and make the boy fall into a trance to see all the gods that attend this divination.

Appear to me in the divination, O noble-minded god, Thrice Great Hermes! Let him appear who <made> the four quarters of heaven and the four foundations of the earth. (magical names follow) . . . Come to me, you who are in heaven! Come to me, you who emerged from the egg! I adjure you by the one in the (magical names follow) . . . Speak, <while there appear the two gods in your company, THATH.[6] One god is called Sō, the other Aph.[7]

[5] The text used as a basis for the following translation is edited by Preisendanz and Henrichs, *Papyri Graecae Magicae*, 2.24–25.

[6] A form of Thoth.

[7] Compare *PGM* 5.247–49, 376–414. See further Mariangela Monaca, "Ermete e la divinazione nei papyri graecae magicae," in Lucentini and others, eds., *Hermetism from Late Antiquity*, 491–503.

Filastrius

TH 17

Filastrius, Diverse Heresies *10.2 (Late Fourth Century* CE*)*[1]

Hermes . . . Thrice Great taught that beyond God almighty humans ought to adore no other except the Sun himself. When he had made his way to the province of the Celts, we discern that he taught them and persuaded them to succumb to this same error.[2]

[1] The text used for the following translation is taken from F. Heylen, ed., *Filastrii episcopi Brixiensis. Diversarum hereseon liber*, CCSL 9 (Turnholt: Brepols, 1957), 221.

[2] Hermes's journey to the Celts is elsewhere unattested. Perhaps Filastrius confused Hermes with Zalmoxis, a disciple of Pythagoras (Herodotus, *Histories* 4.94–96; Plato, *Charmides* 156d–58b; *Ref.* 1.2.17; 1.25.1; see further Mircea Eliade, *Zalmoxis: The Vanishing God*, trans. Willard R. Trask [Chicago: University of Chicago Press, 1972], 21–75). Some form of Celtic sun worship is attested (Miranda Green, *The Gods of the Celts* [Totowa: Barnes and Noble, 1986], 46–71; Green, *Dictionary of Celtic Myth and Legend* [London: Thames & Hudson, 1992], 31–32, 202; Green, *Celtic Myths* [Austin: British Museum Press, 1993], 43–49). On Filastrius, see further Moreschini, *Hermes Christianus*, 49.

First Prologue to the Cyranides

TH 18

First Prologue to the Cyranides *(Late Fourth to Early Fifth Century* CE*)*[1]

This is the book of Cyranus <and> Hermes <called> {"three" from both} *The Book of Natural Virtues, Attractions, and Repulsions* composed from the first book of the *Cyranides* by Cyranus king of Persia and from the book of Harpocration the Alexandrian to his own daughter.

The first book of Cyranus as we have appended it is as follows.

Hermes Thrice Great received the greatest gift of God from angels. As a god himself, he handed on this book of mysteries to all receptive people. Do not hand it on to senseless men, but keep it to yourself as the greatest of possessions. If you are able, hand it on like a father to his children as a gift of equal value to priceless gold, a great possession for effective work, making them swear only to keep it safe, {my holy child}.[2]

This book was inscribed on an iron slab in Syriac letters in <a lake of Syria as I mentioned in> the previous archaic book which I translated.[3]

[1] The dating of the Greek Cyranides is based on the observations of Klaus Alpers, "Untersuchungen zum griechischen Physiologus und den Kyraniden," *Vestigia Bibliae* 6 (1984): 12–87 at 22. Galen already criticizes Pamphilus, an Alexandrian grammarian of the first century CE, for utilizing a treatise on astrological botany attributed to Hermes (Galen, *Mixing and Potency of Simple Medicines* 7, 11.798.1–15 [Kühn]). The Harpocration mentioned in the text as a source probably lived in the second or early third century CE. The text used as a basis for the following translation is edited by Dimitris Kaimakis, *Die Kyraniden* (Meisenheim am Glan: Anton Hain, 1976), 14–15. A Latin translation of a different Greek version can be found in Delatte, *Textes Latins*, 13–14. See further Heiduk, "Offene," 267–74.

[2] On the theme of secrecy, see Albert de Jong, "Secrecy I: Antiquity," *DGWE* 1050–54; von Stuckrad, "Secrecy as Social Capital," 239–52.

[3] Apparently the slab was found in the lake. For the motif of hiding imperishable tablets (later rediscovered), see SH 23.5. Compare Josephus, *Antiquities* 1.71; Philo of Byblos in Eusebius, *Preparation for the Gospel* 1.9.26; *Apocalypse of Paul* (NHC V,2) 2–3; *Disc. 8–9* (NHC VI,6) 62.1–27. See further Burns, *Apocalypse*, 55–57.

The present book called *Cyranis* concerns twenty-four stones, twenty-four birds, twenty-four herbs, and twenty-four fish along with each of their virtues blended and mixed with what remains for the purpose of healing – and indeed, the enjoyment and growth – of the mortal body. He[4] devised this book with the help of the almighty and all-powerful God. He devised it by his wisdom concerning the active powers and virtues of herbs, stones, fish, birds, the nature of animals and beasts along with their mixings, oppositions, and peculiar properties. Thus there has come to be from God to human beings a rich experimental knowledge.

After dividing the whole treatise of the *Cyranides* into three (parts), I clarified the material in alphabetical order as is recorded. The books are called *Cyranides* on account of being queens of the other inscribed books. They were discovered by Cyranus king of Persia.

[4] Evidently Hermes Thrice Great.

Augustine

TH 19a

Augustine, Against Faustus *13.1, 15 (around 400 CE)*[1]

13.1 (Faustus speaks): Thus as I said, the testimonies of the Hebrews contribute nothing to the Christian church which consists, it is agreed, more of Gentiles than of Jews. By all means, if, as is reported, there are other prophecies about Christ from the Sibyl or from Hermes who is called Thrice Great, or from Orpheus, or from other Gentile bards, these could help us to a certain extent come to faith – I mean us Gentiles who became Christians.[2]

13.15 (Augustine responds): If the Sibyl or the Sibyls or Orpheus or some Hermes or other and any bards, theologians, sages, or philosophers of the gentiles foretold or are said to have foretold something true concerning the son of God or God the father, it has indeed some value for beating back the foolish pride of the pagans, but does not amplify their authority. For we show that we worship that God about whom they were not able to remain silent, while they in part dared to teach their nations to worship idols and demons and in part did not dare to forbid it.

[1] For an introduction to Augustine, see FH 41 above. Faustus was perhaps the most famous Manichean intellectual in North Africa at the time. The following translation is based on the text edited by Joseph Zycha, *De utilitate credenda, de duabus animabus, contra Fortunatam, contra Adimantum, contra epistulam fundamenti, contra Faustum,* Corpus Scriptorum Ecclesiasticorum Latinorum 25.6.1 (Vienna: F. Tempsky, 1891), 377–78, 394.

[2] Similarly, Longinianus, a correspondent with Augustine, maintained the great antiquity and authority of the teachings of Hermes Thrice Great (*trismegisticis*) (Augustine, *Epistle* 234.1).

TH 19b

Augustine, City of God *18.8, 39*[3]

18.8 Thus when Saphrus reigned as the fourteenth king of Assyria, and Orthopolis reigned as the twelfth king in Sicyon, and Criasus the fifth king in Argus, Moses was born in Egypt. Through him, the people of God were freed from slavery in Egypt . . .
Some believe that during the reign of these kings lived Prometheus. Since he was esteemed their finest teacher of wisdom, it was said of him that he molded people out of clay. Nevertheless, it is not clear who the sages of his day were. His brother Atlas was reputed to have been a great astrologer . . .

But proceeding down to Cecrops king of Athens . . . during whose reign God, working through Moses, led his people out of Egypt, several dead people were brought into the ranks of the gods by blind and vain custom and by the superstition of the Greeks. Among these were Melantomice, wife of king Criasus, and Phorbas their son, who after his father was the sixth king of the Argives, Iasus son of Triopas their seventh king, along with their ninth king Sthenelas or Stheneleus or Sthenelus – variously spelled among different authors.

During these times, Hermes is also said to have lived. He was the grandson of Atlas from Atlas's daughter Maia, a fact that is paraded in popular literature as well. He was famous as an expert in many arts that he bestowed upon human beings. For this reason, after he died, they decided or even believed that he was a god.[4] . . .

18.39 In regard to philosophy, which professes to teach something about how people become happy, studies of this kind were famous in those lands around the time of Hermes, whom they called Thrice Great. This was long before the sages or philosophers of Greece, but after Abraham, Isaac, Jacob, Joseph, and doubtless after Moses himself. Indeed, during the time that Moses was born, Atlas the grand astrologer and brother of Prometheus is found to have lived. Atlas was the maternal grandfather of the elder Hermes. His grandson, in turn, was that Hermes called Thrice Great.

[3] The following translation is based on the text edited by Bernard Dombart and Alphonse Kalb, eds., *Sancti Aurelii Augustini. De Civitate Dei*, CCSL 48 (Turnholt: Brepols 1955), 598–99, 634–35.

[4] For Hermes deified, compare FH 41 (Augustine); TH 1 (Artapanus), TH 7 (Athenagoras), TH 20 (Hermias).

Hermias

TH 20

Hermias, Scholia on Plato's Phaedrus 2, *Scholia 2 and 45 (Early to Mid Fifth Century* CE*)*[1]

Scholion 2. Indeed, there have been many Sibyls, all of whom chose the prophetic life.[2] All of them, furthermore, chose for a particular reason to be called "Sibyls," just as Hermes Thrice Great is said to have sojourned many times to Egypt.[3] He remembered his identity and for three times was called "Hermes."[4]

Scholion 45. It is necessary for the soul restored to life to choose the philosophic life in order to be led upward.[5] If the soul lives its restored life philosophically and then takes leave of it, it is henceforth led upward. So if the soul lives these nine lives, and afterward a single restored life, as was said, there will be in all ten lives.[6] Since, then, the sojourn below earth for each soul is a thousand years, ten times one thousand makes ten thousand

[1] The text used for the following translation is edited by Carlo M. Lucarini and Claudio Moreschini, eds., *Hermias Alexandrinus in Platonis Phaedrum scholia* (Berlin: de Gruyter, 2012), 99.4–8; 176.5–15. See further Moreschini, *Hermes Christianus*, 131–32.

[2] Hermias comments on Plato, *Phaedrus* 244b: "We might also mention the Sibyl and others who use divinely inspired prophecy to foretell many things to many people and rectify them for the future."

[3] "Sojourned" represents ἐπιδημήσας. At this point, it is not clear that Hermes was thrice incarnated. This understanding becomes evident in the following scholion.

[4] Compare the emperor Julian (TH 14 = Cyril, *Against Julian* 768b); the *Passion of Artemius* (TH 24).

[5] Here Hermias comments on Plato, *Phaedrus* 248e–49a: "No soul returns to the place from which it came for ten thousand years, since its wings will not grow before then, except for the soul of the one who practices philosophy without deceit or who loves boys philosophically. If, after the third cycle of one thousand years, the last-mentioned souls have chosen such a life three times in a row, they grow their wings back, and depart in the three-thousandth year." Plato himself was probably inspired by Pindar, *Olympian Odes* 2.75–77: "But all who, remaining three times in both realms, have the resolution to keep their souls from wrongdoing, these complete the road of Zeus to the Tower of Kronos."

[6] The nine lives are those of a lover of wisdom, a lawful king, a statesman, a trainer or doctor, a prophet or priest, a poet, a manual laborer, a sophist, and a tyrant (Plato, *Phaedrus* 248d–e).

years. And since the person restored must become a philosopher three times, as he (Plato) says, then in turn three times one thousand becomes three thousand.

Perhaps he (Plato) took this figure from history, for Hermes surnamed Thrice Great lived as a philosopher here three times and the third time recognized himself.[7]

[7] In fact, the tradition of three philosophic lives from Plato may have influenced the theory of Hermes's triple incarnation. Self-recognition here would seem to refer to Hermes, like Pythagoras, recognizing his previous lives.

Cyril of Alexandria

TH 21

Cyril of Alexandria, Against Julian *1.41 (Mid Fifth Century* CE*)*

I suppose it is necessary to judge the Egyptian Hermes worthy of account and memory. He is the one they called "Thrice Great," whom they worshiped as a god at that time. Some people equated him with the one born of Zeus and Maia.[1] At any rate, he is the Egyptian Hermes, though he was an initiator who always loitered in the precincts of the idols. He is discovered to have thought carefully about the writings of Moses, though he did not use them in a way that was entirely correct and blameless; at any rate, it was partial.[2] So even Hermes received help.

Mention is made of him in particular writings which someone composed in fifteen books at Athens under the title *Hermaica*.[3] The author writes as follows about him in the first book. He introduces one of the priests saying: "So that we can come to matters which are in accord <. . .>. Have you really not heard our Hermes dividing all Egypt into portions and lots, measuring out the acres with a line, digging canals with irrigation channels, laying down laws, naming the regions after them, establishing the agreements of symbols, recently producing a list of rising stars, cutting plants, discovering and bestowing numbers, calculations, geometry, astronomy, astrology, music and literature?"[4]

[1] Compare TH 2 from Cicero.

[2] On the dating after Moses, see TH 19b from Augustine. On the use of Hebrew scripture, compare TH 29e from Michael Psellus.

[3] If these books contained Hermetic tractates, they indicate that a large portion of Hermetic literature has not survived.

[4] A fair summary of all the arts and sciences attributed to Hermes Thrice Great. Compare the inventions of Hermes-Moses in TH 1 from Artapanus and the occupations in SH 23.42.

John of Antioch

TH 22

John of Antioch, Historical Chronicle, *frag. 6.2 (Early Seventh Century* CE*)*[1]

After the death of Zeus, his son Faunus, also called Hermes, ruled as king over Italy for thirty-five years. He was a clever man and an astrologer. He was the first to discover the metal gold in the west and the smelting of metals. Realizing that his brothers envied him, he went into hiding. Hermes had about eighty brothers since Zeus coupled with many women to produce children.

Carrying much gold, he departed for Egypt to the tribe of Ham. After being received in honor, he lived there in pomp, wearing a golden robe and offering prophecies. He was a man of supreme learning. The Egyptians worshiped him, calling him a "god" because he foretold the future. He supplied them with money and so they called him "Bestower of Wealth." When Mestrem the king of Egypt from the tribe of Ham died, the Egyptians made Hermes king and he ruled for thirty-nine years.[2]

[1] The text used as a basis for the following translation is edited by Roberto, *Fragmenta ex Historia chronica*, 14.

[2] A later summary of this tradition can be found in the *Suda* under the headword Φαῦνος (Adler, *Suidae*, 4.707, §148). Compare also the *Excerpta Barbari* translated by Moreschini, *Hermes Christianus*, 127–28.

Isidore of Seville

TH 23

Isidore of Seville (560–636 CE), Etymologies *8.9.33, 49*[1]

33. Hermes, it is said, is the first to have invented the illusionary arts. They are called "illusionary" since they dazzle the eyes.[2]

49. Hermes is named from *hermeneia* in Greek, which in Latin means "interpreter." On account of his knowledge of many arts, he is called *Trismegistus*, that is "Thrice Great." Why they depict him with the head of a dog is explained by the fact that among all animals, the dog is considered to be the most clever and clear-sighted.[3]

[1] The text used for the following translation is edited by W. M. Lindsay, *Etymologiarum sive Originum libri xx*, 2 vols. (Oxford: Clarendon Press, 1911), 1.326–27, 356.

[2] The art of illusion (*praestigium*) is a way of referring to magic. Contrast FH 21a (from Zosimus), where Hermes repudiates magic. Isidore's testimony is repeated with slight expansion by Hincmar of Rheims (writing 860 CE): "And so we read that the devil first brought this (illusionary art) forth through Hermes, which is why the inventor of it is called Hermes: and no Christian can allow this devilish work to take place in front of him" (Rachel Stone and Charles West, trans., *The Divorce of King Lothar and Queen Theutberga: Hincmar of Rheims's "De Divortio"* [Manchester: Manchester University Press, 2016], 239, modified).

[3] Isidore is apparently referring to Hermanubis, a blending of Hermes-Thoth with the other Egyptian guide of souls, Anubis.

John of Damascus(?), Passion of Artemius

TH 24

John of Damascus(?), Passion of Artemius *26, 28, 30 (Eighth Century* CE*)*[1]

26. The Apostate,[2] supposing that Christ's martyr was some simpleton and unversed in Hellenic wisdom, scoffingly said to him: "So, then, you wretch, your Christ is twice born?[3] If you brag about this, why, the Hellenes too have men of the highest wisdom who have been born not just twice, but even three times! Hermes, surnamed Thrice Great, knew that he had come into the world three times, as his holy and wondrous books relate, and for this reason he is called Thrice Great."[4] . . .

28. (Artemius replies to Julian): "As for Hermes, whom you address as Thrice Great, he was an Egyptian man. He was raised according to Egyptian customs, married a wife, and produced children, the eldest of whom they call Tat. Hermes conversed with Tat and dedicated his discourses to him.[5] He also dedicated them to Asclepius of Epidaurus,

[1] The text for the following translation is edited by P. Bonifatius Kotter, *Die Schriften des Johannes von Damaskos V: Opera homiletica et hagiographica*, Patristische Texte und Studien 29 (Berlin: de Gruyter, 1988), 216–18. For John of Damascus (676–749 CE) as the author (a view proposed by F. Dölger), see *ibid.*, 185–87.

[2] Namely, the emperor Julian (reigned 361–63 CE). Julian addresses the soon-to-be-martyred Artemius, the Arian Christian governor of Egypt. According to legend, Artemius brought the relics of saints Andrew, Luke, and Timothy (early Christians mentioned in the New Testament) to Constantinople. When Artemius was himself canonized as a saint, he became famous as a healer of hernias and testicular diseases. See further Sam Lieu and Dominic Montserrat, *From Constantine to Julian: Pagan and Byzantine Views. A Source History* (London: Routledge, 1996), 210–23.

[3] Lactantius argued that Hermetic texts foretold the double birth of Christ, eternally from the Father and temporally from a human mother (*Divine Institutes* 4.8.1–12; 4.13.1–15).

[4] One can also translate: "Hermes, surnamed Thrice Great, came into the world three times (and) recognized himself."

[5] On the genealogy of Hermes, see Copenhaver 133, 164–65. Most of the discourses in CH are dedicated either to Tat or Asclepius.

the originator, so you say, of the art of medicine and the one to whom he explains his theology. It goes as follows:

> 'To conceive of God is difficult, but to speak of him is impossible.'[6] For he is three persons, uninterpretable in his essence and nature, and he has no likeness among mortals.[7] But those whom people call gods are swallowed up in a mass of deceitful fables.

Concerning the coming of Christ, moreover, Hermes relates some obscure prophecy that is not his own but that he derives from the theology of the Hebrews . . .

30. These are the advantages of your philosophers twice and thrice born as you so pompously declare! And these are the cheap tricks of my Christ meant for the salvation and restoration of the human race! To be sure, Pythagoras and Hermes lead the souls of human beings down to the dungeon of Hades, craftily introducing certain transmigrations and reincarnations, translocating them sometimes into non-rational animals and beasts and sometimes even dragging them down into fish and plants, dragging and pushing the soul through various cycles and revolutions.[8]

6 Compare SH 1, FH 25 (from Cyril), and FH 38 (from Gregory of Nazianzus).

7 That God is inexpressible because of the mystery of the Trinity is a Christian interpretation. For Hermes and Trinitarian speculation, see the *Addendum: The Reception of Hermetic Fragments from Cyril* following FH 35 above.

8 Compare FH 1c (from Tertullian).

Al-Kindī

TH 25a

Al-Kindī (Died 870) as Quoted by Ibn an-Nadīm, **Fihrist,** *9.1 (Composed in 987 CE)*[1]

Al-Kindī said that he examined a book that people (the Harrānians) regard as authoritative. It is *Chapters of Hermes on the Doctrine of God's Unity* which he wrote for his son most expertly on God's unity.[2] Philosophers who have exerted themselves will find no alternative to them and to professing their doctrine.[3]

TH 25b

Al-Kindī as Quoted by Ibn Nubāta (1287–1366 CE), **Commentary on the Epistle of Ibn Zaydūn**[4]

Al-Kindī said: "He (Hermes) is the author of *Poisonous Animals*. He was a physician and a philosopher, knowledgeable in the natures of medicines. He traveled around the earth, wandering in different countries, knowing the foundations of cities, their natures, and the natures of their peoples and their medicines."

[1] The translation used below is that of Van Bladel, *Arabic Hermes*, 89. See further Pinella Travaglia, "Al-Kindī," in *DGWE* 58–60.

[2] Van Bladel notes that, "It is possible that the title of the work is to be construed *Chapters of Hermes on (Monotheistic) Theology which He Wrote for His Son Most Expertly on Theology* " (*Arabic Hermes*, 89, n.109). The word translated "chapters" can also refer to "individual treatises or sections of a book" (*ibid.*, 89). Evidently the "son" is Tat.

[3] Van Bladel observes, "Because there is no reason to doubt the testimony of al-Kindī, one can assume that in the ninth century he had obtained a work attributed to Hermes in Arabic (the only language he could read) . . . The absences of other references to such works in Arabic literature probably means that these Hermetica did not find the audience that al-Kindī thought they deserved, and that they were lost in Arabic at an early stage" (*Arabic Hermes*, 90). Compare the later testimony of Ibn al-Qiftī (died 1248) cited by Van Bladel, *Arabic Hermes*, 91.

[4] The translation used here is that of Van Bladel, *Arabic Hermes*, 158.

Abū Maʿshar

TH 26a

Abū Maʿshar (Died 886 CE) as Quoted by Ibn Ǧulǧul of Cordova, The Generations of the Physicians and Philosophers, *5–10 (Composed in 987 CE)*[1]

Abū Maʿshar al-Balḫī the astrologer said in the *Book of the Thousands*: "The Hermeses are three.[2] The first of them is Hermes who was before the Flood. The significance of 'Hermes' is a title, like saying 'Caesar' and Ḫusraw' (which are titles). The Persians named him Wīwanghān, meaning 'the Just,' in their biographies of the kings. He is the one to whose philosophy the Harrānians adhere.[3] The Persians state that his grandfather

[1] The translation that appears below is taken with slight modification from Van Bladel, *Arabic Hermes*, 125–27. Its original source is Abū Maʿshar's *Book of Thousands*, a non-extant astrological work. Van Bladel notes that this work was "the main source of the Hermes legend in Arabic" (*Arabic Hermes*, 122). But Abū Maʿshar was not entirely original. Van Bladel traces his sources to the *Book of Sothis* ascribed to Manetho (see TH 10b) and to the Christian chronographical tradition (*ibid.*, 132–57). See also Van Bladel's "Sources of the Legend of Hermes in Arabic," in Lucentini and others, eds., *Hermetism from Late Antiquity*, 285–93; Massimo Pappacena, "La figura di Ermete nella tradizione Araba," in *ibid.*, 263–84; A. E. Affifi, "The Influence of Hermetic Literature on Moslem Thought," *Bulletin of the School of Oriental and African Studies* 13 (1949–51): 840–55; M. Plessner, "Hermes Trismegistus and Arab Science," *Studia Islamica* 2 (1954): 45–59.

[2] See on this point Charles Burnett, "The Legend of the Three Hermes and Abū Maʿshar's *Kitab al-Ulūf* in the Latin Middle Ages," *Journal of the Warburg and Courtauld Institutes* 39 (1976): 231–34; Mark D. Delp, ed., *De sex rerum principiis*, Corpus Christianorum Continuatio Mediaevalis 142 (Turnhout: Brepols, 2006), 5–8. Alexandra von Lieven attempts to trace the tradition of three Hermeses back to native Egyptian traditions in "Thot selbdritt: mögliche ägyptische Ursprünge der arabisch-lateinischen Tradition dreier Hermesgestalten," *Die Welt des Orients* 37 (2007): 69–77.

[3] Abū Maʿshar refers to a religious group located in the city of Harran in northwestern Mesopotamia who claimed Hermes as one of their prophets. See further Francis E. Peters, "Hermes and Harran: The Roots of Arabic-Islamic Occultism," in Michael M. Mazzaou and Vera B. Moreen, eds., *Intellectual Studies on Islam* (Salt Lake City: University of Utah, 1990), 186–215; Tamara M. Green, *The City of the Moon God: Religious Traditions of Harran* (Leiden: Brill, 1992),

was Ǧayūmart̲, that is Adam.[4] The Hebrews state that he is Enoch, which, in Arabic, is Idrīs."

Abū Ma'shar said, "He was the first to discuss the celestial phenomena of the movements of the stars, and his grandfather Ǧayūmart̲ taught him the hours of the nychthemeron.[5] He is the first who built temples and glorified God in them. He was the first to investigate medicine and to discuss it. He composed for his contemporaries odes in poetic meter and well-known verses on terrestrial and celestial things.

He was the first to give advance warning of the Flood, and he thought that a celestial catastrophe of fire and water would overwhelm the earth. His home was Upper Egypt; he chose that (place) and built the pyramids and cities of clay there. He feared that knowledge would pass away in the Flood, so he built the monumental temples; it is a mountain known as *birbā* in Aḫmīm, which he chiseled out, portraying in it all the arts and their uses in carvings, as well as pictures of all the instruments of the artisans, indicating the features of the sciences by illustrations, out of desire thereby to preserve the sciences forever for those after him, fearing that all trace of it would perish from the world."[6] . . .

"The Second Hermes, of the people of Babylon: He lived in the city of the Chaldeans, Babylon, after the Flood in the time of Naburīzbānī, who was the first to build the city of Babylon after Nimrod son of Kush.[7] He was skilled in the knowledge of medicine and philosophy, knew the natures of numbers, and his student was Pythagoras the Arithmetician. This Hermes renewed the knowledge of medicine, philosophy, mathematics that was lost during the Flood at Babylon." That is what Abū Ma'shar stated . . .

"The Third Hermes: He lived in the city of Egypt. He was after the Flood. He is the author of *Poisonous Animals*.[8] He was a philosopher and a physician, knowledgeable about the natures of lethal drugs and infectious animals. He traveled around in different countries, wandering in them,

124–90; David Pingree, "The Sābians of Harrān and the Classical Tradition," *International Journal of the Classical Tradition* 9 (2002): 8–35 at 23–26.

[4] In Zoroastrian tradition, Ǧayūmart̲ was the first human created by Ahura Mazda. He was sometimes represented as a culture hero as, for instance, in the epic poem *Shahnameh* (late tenth or early eleventh centuries CE). Zosimus says that Hermes-Thoth was Adam (FH 21a).

[5] That is, the hours in a complete day-night cycle.

[6] Aḫmīm, which the Greeks called "Chemmis" and "Panopolis," was a city in Upper Egypt and the reputed home of Zosimus the alchemist.

[7] Nimrod was the founder of Babylon according to Genesis 10:8–10. Naburīzbānī is apparently the famous Babylonian king Nebuchadnezzar II (ruled 604–562 BCE).

[8] Compare Manfred Ullmann, ed., *Das Schlangenbuch des Hermes Trismegistos* (Wiesbaden: Harrassowitz, 1994).

knowing the foundations of cities, their natures, and the natures of their peoples. He is the author of a valuable discourse on the art of alchemy; part of it is related to crafts like glass, stringing precious stones, implements of clay, and such things. He had a student who is known, whose name was Asclepius."[9]

TH 26b

Abū Maʿshar as Quoted by Ṣāʿid al-Andalusī, Exposition of the Generations of Nations *18.18–19.6; 39.7–16; 40.5–7 (Composed around 1068 CE)*[10]

(From a section on the Sciences among the Chaldean Nation)
According to us, the most famous and most respected of their (the Chaldeans') scholars is Hermes the Babylonian. He was in the time of the Greek philosopher Socrates. Abū Maʿshar Ǧaʿfar ibn Muḥammad ibn ʿUmar al-Balḫī stated in the *Book of the Thousands* that he was the one who restored many of the books of the ancients on the astral sciences and other kinds of philosophy that had perished, and that he composed many books on various sciences.[11]

Abū Maʿshar said, "The Hermeses are a group of different individuals. Among them is the Hermes who was before the Flood, whom the Hebrews claim is the prophet Enoch, who is Idrīs, peace be upon him. After the Flood were a number of them (that is, Hermeses) knowledgeable and discerning. The preeminent of these were two, the first of whom was the Babylonian we mentioned, and the second was the student of the philosopher Pythagoras and an inhabitant of Egypt."[12]

Ṣāʿid said, "Information has reached us about the doctrine of the Babylonian Hermes indicating his preeminence in science. This includes his doctrine on projection of the rays of the stars and his doctrine on the uniformity of the Houses of the celestial sphere. It also includes his book

[9] Van Bladel argues that this information regarding the third Hermes derives from al-Kindī (cited in TH 25b) (*Arabic Hermes*, 159–61). See further David Pingree, *The Thousands of Abū Maʿshar* (London: Warburg Institute, 1968), 14–19.

[10] The translation that appears below is taken with slight modification from Van Bladel, *Arabic Hermes*, 129–30.

[11] According to Abū Maʿshar's reckoning, this is the second (Babylonian) Hermes.

[12] According to TH 26a and Ibn Ǧulǧul (late tenth century CE), Pythagoras was in fact the student of Hermes.

on astrology such as the *Book of Latitude* and the *Book of Longitude* and *The Rod of Gold*."[13] . . .

(From a section on the Sciences among the Egyptian Nation)
A group of scholars reported that it was from the first Hermes, who lived in highest Upper Egypt, that all of the sciences that appeared before the Flood came. He is the one whom the Hebrews name Enoch, son of Jared, son of Mahala'il, son of Cainan, son of Enosh, son of Seth, son of Adam, upon him be peace.[14] He is the prophet Idrīs (Enoch), peace be upon him. They said that he was the first to discuss celestial substances and the movements of stars and he is the first who built temples and glorified God the Exalted in them. He was the first to investigate medicine. He composed for his contemporaries odes in poetic meter on terrestrial and celestial things.

And they say that he was the first to give advance warning of the Flood, and he thought that ruin would overtake the earth from water and fire. He feared that knowledge would pass away and that the arts would perish in the Flood, so he built the pyramids and the monumental temples in highest Upper Egypt. He portrayed in them all the arts and the instruments, indicating the features of the sciences by illustrations, out of desire thereby to preserve the sciences forever for those after him, fearing that all trace of it would perish from the world . . .

Among the ancient scholars in Egypt is the Second Hermes. He was a philosopher, traveling in the lands, wandering the cities, knowing the foundations of the (cities?) and the natures of the peoples. He wrote a great book on the art of alchemy and a book on poisonous animals.[15]

[13] The latter two works are also mentioned in the Prologue to *Six Principles of Nature* (TH 31b). For *The Rod of Gold*, see Van Bladel, *Arabic Hermes*, 28.

[14] Compare the genealogy in Genesis 5:1–24.

[15] According to Abū Maʿshar (TH 26a), this description fits the third Hermes, not the second.

Ibn an-Nadīm

TH 27

Ibn an-Nadīm, Fihrist *10 (Composed in 987* CE*)*[1]

Persons interested in the art of alchemy, which is the making of gold and silver from other metals, state that the first man who spoke about the science of this art was Hermes, the wise man and Babylonian, who moved to Egypt when the peoples were dispersed from Babylon. He was the king of Egypt, a wise man and philosopher, for whom the Art (alchemy) was validated, and about which he wrote a number of books. He observed the specific and spiritual properties of phenomena and his knowledge of the art of alchemy was substantiated by this investigation and observation. He also knew about the making of talismans and wrote many books about them . . .

There has been a difference of opinion about him. It is said that he was one of the seven attendants whom they established for the care of the seven (planetary) shrines, and that he was in charge of the Shrine of Mercury, by whose name he was called . . . It is related that for various reasons he migrated to the land of Egypt, which he ruled. He had many children, among whom were Tat, Sá, Ashmun, Athrīb and Quft.[2] He was, moreover, the wise man of his time.

When he died, he was buried in the building which is known in Cairo as Abū Hermes. The common people know it as the Two Pyramids. One of

[1] The *Fihrist* is an index of the books of all nations extant in Arabic in 987 CE on all the branches of knowledge known at that time. The translation used here with slight adaptation comes from Bayard Dodge, *The Fihrist of al-Nadīm: A Tenth-century Survey of Muslim Culture,* 2 vols. (New York: Columbia University Press, 1970), 2.843–48.

[2] Traditionally, Hermes's only son is Tat. The four other names seem to refer to places in Egypt. Ashmun is Ashmounein (or Hermopolis); Athrīb is Athribis, a religious center in the Delta; Quft is Coptos; and Sá may be Saïs.

them is his tomb while the other is the tomb of his wife, or it is said the tomb of his son, who succeeded him after his death . . .

Hermes wrote about the stars, incantations, and things incorporeal (*pneumas*).

The Books of Hermes about the Art:

Book of Hermes to his son about the Art; *Flowing Gold*; *To Tat about the Art*; the *Making of Knots*; *Secrets* . . .

Al-Mubaššir ibn Fātik

TH 28

Al-Mubaššir ibn Fātik, Selection of Wise Sayings (Muḫtār al-ḥikam) *7.8–10.19 (Compiled 1048–49 CE)*[1]

Hermes of the Hermeses was born in Egypt, in the city of Memphis there. In Greek he is "Irmīs," and then it was pronounced "Hirmīs." The meaning of "Irmīs" is "Mercury." He was also named, upon him be peace, "Trismīn"[2] among the Greeks; among the Arabs, "Idrīs"; among the Hebrews, "Enoch." He is the son of Jared, son of Mahala'il, son of Cainan, son of Enosh, son of Seth, son of Adam, upon them be peace.[3]

He was before the great deluge that inundated the world, that is, the first deluge. After it, there was another deluge that inundated the people of Egypt only. In the beginning of his career, he was a student of Agathos Daimon the Egyptian. Agathos Daimon was one of the prophets of the Greeks and the Egyptians; he is for them the second Ūrānī, and Idrīs is the third Ūrānī, upon him be peace[4] . . .

Hermes left Egypt and went around the whole earth. He returned to Egypt and God raised him to Himself there. God the Exalted said, "And We raised him to a high place."[5] That was after (he had lived) eighty-two years.

[1] The translation below is taken with slight adaptation from Van Bladel, *Arabic Hermes*, 185–88.

[2] Apparently Trismegistos, or Thrice Great.

[3] Compare the genealogy in Genesis 5:1–24.

[4] In context, Seth son of Adam had already been identified with the first Ūrānī. Scott (*Hermetica*, 4.249, n. 3) and Van Bladel (*Arabic Hermes*, 188) both connect the term to Harrān, making Ūrānī (or Urānī) an eponymous ancestor of the Harranians. In Hermetic literature, however Ouranos (or Uranus) is identified as an ancestor to Hermes (CH 10.5; FH 5a–b; compare TH 2 from Cicero). Perhaps those who succeeded Ouranos were thought to inherit his name; or the name Ouranos was taken to be a title that could be passed on (compare TH 26a from Abū Ma'shar).

[5] Qur'ān 19:57 in reference to Enoch or Idris.

In seventy-two languages he called the people of the entire earth's population to worship the Creator, the Mighty and High. God granted him wisdom so that he spoke to them in their different languages, taught them and educated them. He built for them a hundred and eight great cities, the smallest of which is Edessa.[6] He was the first who discovered astrology, and he established for each region a model of religious practice for them to follow which corresponded to their views. Kings were his servants, and the whole earth's population and the population of the islands in the seas obeyed him. Four kings served him; each one of them, by his order – upon him be peace – was in charge of the whole earth . . .

He preached God's judgment, belief in God's unity, humankind's worship (of God), and saving souls from punishment. He incited (people) to abstain piously from this world, to act justly, and to seek salvation in the next world. He commanded them to perform prayers that he stated for them in manners that he explained to them, and to fast on recognized days of each month, to undertake holy war against the enemies of the religion, and to give charity from (their) possessions and to assist the weak with it. He bound them with oaths of ritual purity from pollutants, menstruation, and touching the dead. He ordered them to forbid eating pig, donkey, camel, dog, and other foods. He forbade intoxication from every type of beverage, and stated this in the most severe terms.

He established many feasts for them at recognized times, and prayers and offerings in them. One (of these) is that of the entry of the sun into the beginnings (that is, the first degrees) of the signs of the zodiac. Another is that of the sightings of the new moon and that of the times of astrological conjunctions. And whenever the planets arrive at their houses and exaltations or are aspected with other planets, they make an offering. The offerings for what he prescribed include three things: incense, sacrificial animals, and wine. Of the first fruits of aromatic plants they offer roses. Of grains, they offer wheat and barley, of fruit, grapes, and of drink, wine.[7]

He promised them that a number of prophets would come after him, and he informed them that some of the characteristics of the prophet to be sent are that he will be free of all causes of blame and ailments, perfect

[6] On Hermes's worldwide travels and city-building, compare TH 25b (from al-Kindī); TH 37d (*Picatrix*). Van Bladel avers that al-Kindī and al-Mubaššir shared a common source for this tradition which either derived from the Harranians or older chronographic works (*Arabic Hermes*, 189–90).

[7] "They" here and below probably refers to the "Sabians" of Harran or Harranians. See further Pingree, "Sābians of Harrān," 8–35.

in all praiseworthy virtues, will not fail to answer correctly questions asked about anything in the heavens and the earth, and that he will indicate cures for every pain, and that his prayers will be answered in everything he asks for, including the sending down of rain, the lifting of ailments, and other sorts of requests. His doctrine and his preaching would be the doctrine by which the world becomes well and by which its prosperity increases.

He ordered people into three classes: priests, kings, and subjects. The rank of priest is above the rank of king, because the priest prays to God for himself, his king, and his subjects, while it is not for the king to pray to God the Exalted for anything other than for himself and his subjects, and it is not for the subjects to pray to God for anything that is not for themselves alone.

He was, upon him be peace, a man of dark[8] complexion, of full stature, bald, of handsome face, thick-bearded, of pleasant lineaments, and perfect arm-span, broad-shouldered, big-boned but of little flesh, with flashing, dark-lined eyes, unhurried in his speech, often silent, his limbs at rest; when he walked, he mostly kept his gaze toward the earth; he thought much; he was serious and stern. He moved his index finger when he talked. His period on the earth was eighty-two years.

There was on the bezel of his seal-ring that he wore every day: "Patience combined with faith in God bequeaths victory." And on the bezel of the seal-ring that he wore at religious feasts was "perfect joy at religious feasts is good works." And on the bezel of his seal-ring that he wore when he prayed for a dead person, "The time of death is the harvest of hope; death is a watchman never heedless." And on the belt that he always wore, "Consideration of the next life bequeaths security to body and soul from harmful accidents." On the belt that he wore to religious feasts, "Keeping religious duties and law is the fulfillment of religion, and the fulfillment of religion is the fulfillment of valor." On the belt that he wore at the time of prayer for the dead, "Whoever considers his soul is victorious, and his intercession with the Lord is his good works."

His religious law, the *hanīfī* community,[9] also known as the Right Religion, reached the eastern and western ends of the earth, and the north

[8] The word used here could also mean "white" or "ruddy" (Van Bladel, *Arabic Hermes*, 187, n.98).

[9] The *hanīfī* community is technically "pagan." The term, however, is used in a positive sense, since the *hanīfī* are assumed to be monotheistic and devout. See further Van Bladel, *Arabic Hermes*, 190–92.

and the south, and spread throughout the earth in its entirety until there remained no human on the face of the earth who did not practice this religion.[10] Their direction of prayer was towards the true south along the line of the meridian.[11]

[10] Much more than in Abū-Ma'shar (TH 26a–b), the emphasis here is on Hermes as the founder of the universal primordial religion, a religion with a certain resemblance to Islam.

[11] Van Bladel quotes a Latin summarizing adaptation of Al-Mubaššir's testimony under the title *Book of Ancient Moral Philosophers* (*Liber philosophorum moralium antiquorum*) (*Arabic Hermes*, 193–94). He hypothesizes that this late thirteenth-century Latin rendition "was known to the Italian scholars of the late fifteenth century, such as Ficino" (*ibid.*, 193). See further Franz Rosenthal, "Al-Mubashshir ibn Fâtik. Prolegomena to an Abortive Edition," *Oriens* 13–14 (1960–61): 132–58; Heiduk, "Offene," 229–33.

Michael Psellus

TH 29a

Michael Psellus, Allegory Regarding Tantalus = Opusculum *43, Lines 40–48 (around the Mid Eleventh Century* CE*)*[1]

The third opinion (among the Greeks about Zeus) is more historical and perhaps more true. For the myths agree that Zeus's father was Kronos and that he was born in the same place, namely Crete. They do not acknowledge where Kronos was buried in the world, but point out the mound over the tomb (of Zeus). Then the myths raise them above mortal nature, make them akin to the higher essence and transfer them to divine form.

Hermes Thrice Great assents to this teaching. Though he passed over the other myths, he welcomed this one in its unadulterated form. He even spurs on his own son Tat to imitate them (namely, Zeus and Kronos).[2]

TH 29b

Michael Psellus, Different Solutions to Natural Difficulties Addressed to His Own Disciples and to Other Inquirers = Opusculum 16, *Lines 34–37, 44–72*[3]

Why Some Infants are Defective and Others Sound

Reasonably you wonder why some infants brought to term have bodily defects such as uneven limbs and lameness from birth while others are sound and beautifully formed . . .

[1] For an introduction to Michael Psellus, see FH 43. The text used for the following translation is taken from J. M. Duffy and D. J. O'Meara, eds., *Michaelis Pselli Philosophica minora*, 2 vols. (Leipzig: Teubner, 1992), 1.154.

[2] Psellus evidently refers to CH 10.5.

[3] The text used for the following translation is taken from Duffy and O'Meara, eds., *Philosophica minora*, 48–50.

Now Hermes, writing about this subject to Ammon the wise ... says that, since the infant is formed not only part by part but with regard to its whole nature, and since the varied distribution of planetary powers flows down to it, by this means such and such a causal differentiation occurs.

If this explanation is unclear, I will clarify it for you. The outstanding representatives of Greek wisdom, in differentiating our nature, connect it to beings above this world as well as to bodies and principles in this world. Included among these are the planets. They assign our eyes to the sun and moon, our sense of smell to Aphrodite, our cranial membrane to Kronos, and so on with the other body parts. They assign them not only to the planets, but also to their decans as well as the fixed stars which shoot their rays toward the fetus.

Since the forms of the decans are various, and various are the planetary configurations, and the varying alignments of the fixed stars differ, the ray shot from each astral body toward the unborn child (has a different effect).[4] If the ray descends from a beneficent configuration, it makes the child's body part most sound ... but if it is not beneficent, then the body part is stunted.

For example, if Jupiter, who presides over an animal's head, brain, and all its membranes ... is arrayed in a good position and configured in trine with the moon,[5] when it shoots a ray toward the fetal brain, the principle powers shape the embryo correctly. But if a maleficent planet exerts influence on this part, it causes the opposite result. According to this Hermetic logic, then, bad-tempered and good-tempered babies are born, along with those who see straight and are cross-eyed.

All the mutually opposed outcomes result from the powers of the stars.

TH 29c

Michael Psellus, Defense of the Lawkeeper against Ophrydas = Oration *3 (around 1046–47 CE)*[6]

You put forth Zoroaster the Egyptian and Hermes Thrice Great whom legend says were self-taught.[7] Did some single Soul open its mouth to give

4 Compare TH 37c from the *Picatrix*.

5 That is, when Jupiter is three signs of the zodiac distant from the moon (which presides over growth). Compare *Ref.* 4.1.2.

6 The text used for the following translation is edited by George T. Dennis, *Michaelis Pselli. Orationes forenses et acta* (Leipzig: Teubner, 1994), 134. Compare Bidez and Cumont, *Mages hellénisés*, 2.35.

7 Zoroaster was usually considered to be Persian. Hermes is the Egyptian. Likely, something has dropped out of the text.

them lessons from some hidden vein? Not even the long-lived nymphs, if Plato is to be believed – through whom the "receptive of consciousness and intelligence" was added to the definition of humanity – are able to communicate knowledge to other sages as something that can be passed on.[8]

TH 29d

Michael Psellus, Accusation of the High Priest to the Synod = Oration *1*[9]

If you receive every vision indifferently, why do we not mention the vision of Thrice Great Hermes which Poimander – some daimon or other – revealed to him? For these visions are fearful and strange, manifesting and theologizing as they do about mist, deep gloom, a shining light, the father and the son.[10]

TH 29e

Michael Psellus, Scholium on CH 1.18[11]

It appears that this magician (Hermes) had no casual acquaintance with divine scripture.[12] Accordingly, he eagerly lays hands on the story of creation from scripture, not hesitating at times to copy out the plain text of Moses – as for instance the entire passage before us. For this saying: "And God said, 'Grow and increase!'" is clearly taken from Moses's creation story.[13]

[8] Plato, *Definitions* 415a–b: "human being: ... the only being capable of acquiring rational (*or*: discursive) knowledge" (ὃ μόνον τῶν ὄντων ἐπιστήμης τῆς κατὰ λόγους δεκτικόν ἐστιν).

[9] The text used for the following translation is taken from Dennis, *Orationes forenses*, 34.

[10] Compare CH 1.1–5, 9, 12.

[11] The text used for the following translation is taken from J. M. Duffy and D. J. O'Meara, eds., *Philosophica minora*, 2.154–55.

[12] The word translated "magician" here (γόης) could be rendered "juggler" or "charlatan." The term was frequently associated with activities condemned as "magical" (Fritz Graf, *Magic in the Ancient World*, trans. Franklin Philip [Cambridge, MA: Harvard University Press, 1997], 20–60). Psellus tried to delegitimize Hermes by casting him not as a philosopher or sage but as a kind of magician. Compare TH 23 from Isidore of Seville.

[13] Psellus glosses CH 1.18 ("Increase in increasing and multiply in multitude, all you creatures and craftworks!") to the effect that Hermes was dependent upon "Moses's creation story," evidently Gen 1:28 ("Be fruitful and multiply, and fill the earth and subdue it"). In context, the passages differ considerably. The text in Genesis exhorts the first human(s) to take dominion over the earth, whereas CH 1.18 encourages humanity to recognize its own inner divinity. Psellus seeks to score a polemical point: that Hermes depended upon Moses, a point already affirmed by Cyril (TH 21). See further C. H. Dodd, *The Bible and the Greeks* (London: Hodder & Stoughton, 1935), 99–200.

Yet Hermes hardly preserved the simplicity, clarity, directness, purity, and in general the divine cast of divine scripture. Rather, he gushes – as he usually does – with the affective rhetoric characteristic of Greek sophists. He is diverted from the straight path into allegories, errors, and fairy tales, or is constrained (to do so) by Poimandres.

Who this Poimandres was is not a hidden matter. Among us (Christians) he would perhaps be called the ruler of the cosmos, or one of his lackeys.[14] For the devil is a thief, twisting our own stories – not so that his people might learn reverence, but so that by using the terminology and concepts of truth they can shape and make their own irreverence into something more persuasive and acceptable . . .

If perchance some other barbarian race worshiped the creator and king of the universe according to their own ancestral notions and laws, I am unable to say. Yet it has been demonstrated by many that the Hebrews' worship of God was famous throughout the inhabited world and that their laws were older than even this Hermes along with any other Greek sage.[15]

TH 29f

Michael Psellus, Opusculum *10.40–51*[16]

I will speak to you a hidden discourse as well. This discourse a wise Greek sage declared in secret sayings as his theology. I refer to Hermes called "Thrice Great" among the Hellenes. In one of his discourses which he entitled *Pure Consciousness*, he ranked the eternities (*or:* aeons) after God, then consciousness, then soul, heaven after it, followed by nature, time, and generation.

He also arranged what depended upon each of these: the Good dependent upon God, the same upon eternity, intellectual motion upon consciousness, life on soul, the revolution and counter-revolution upon heaven, motion and change upon time, what is mutable and fluid upon nature, and finally life and death dependent upon generation.[17]

[14] Paul called the devil "the god of this world/cosmos" (2 Corinthians 4:4); the implication is that Poimandres is the devil or one of his underlings. Ephesians 6:12 indicates that there are multiple world rulers.

[15] Yet Hermes is in fact an Egyptian sage (compare TH 29g from Psellus). For the strategy of asserting Moses's chronological priority with respect to Hermes, compare TH 19b from Augustine.

[16] The text used for the following translation is edited by Paul Gautier, *Michaelis Pselli. Theologica I* (Leipzig: Teubner, 2002), 39.

[17] Compare CH 11.2: "God makes eternity; eternity makes the cosmos; the cosmos makes time; time makes becoming. The essence . . . of God is [the Good]; . . . the essence of eternity is identity; of the

In certain respects, Hermes philosophizes in common with Orphics and Chaldeans, in other respects he inserts his own ideas.

TH 29g

Michael Psellus, Opusculum *18.26–33*[18]

God as Good

About this issue (that God alone is good) all the extraordinary sages concur – Egyptians, Greeks, and before all of them the one called "Hermes Thrice Great." He, setting out to declare the Good, left aside the soul's habits, virtues, and qualities that descend from above to below. Rather he defined it as "the One before all," from which other things are and are called good not essentially but by participation, as passively experiencing the Good.[19]

TH 29h

Michael Psellus, Opusculum *106.136–43*[20]

The Mixing Bowl

The theologian Hermes in his discourses to Asclepius speaks somewhat as follows (I do not recall the exact words): consciousness does not reside in all people, but some, by brushing themselves clean, prepare their souls to be receptive of it. These people gather before a mixing bowl and God casts the one having consciousness into it. "Receive," he says, "the most lovely treasure, you purified soul!"[21]

cosmos, order; of time, change; of becoming, life and death. But the energy of God is mind and soul; the energy of eternity is permanence and immortality; of the cosmos, recurrence and counterrecurrence; of time, increase and decrease; of becoming, quality <and quantity.>"

18 The text used for the following translation is edited by Westerink and Duffy, *Michael Psellus. Theologica II*, 98.

19 Compare CH 2.16: "The Good is what is inalienable and inseparable from God, since it is God himself. All other immortal gods are given the name 'good' as an honor, but God is the Good by nature, not because of honor. God has one nature – the Good. In God and the Good together there is but one kind, from which come all other kinds. The Good is what gives everything and receives nothing; God gives everything and receives nothing; therefore God is <the> Good, and the Good is God."

20 The text used for the following translation is edited by Gautier, *Theologica I*, 422.

21 Compare CH 4.4: "He (the Craftsman) filled a great mixing bowl with it (consciousness) and sent it below, appointing a herald whom he commanded to make the following proclamation to human hearts: 'Immerse yourself in the mixing bowl if your heart has the strength, if it believes you will rise up again to the one who sent the mixing bowl below, if it recognizes the purpose of your coming to be.'" See further Copenhaver, 131.

You see how the finest inheritance of the Greeks has come down to us, although they differ in terminology. For we call it "Holy Spirit," while they name it "total Consciousness" and "imported Consciousness."

TH 29i

Michael Psellus, Extract from a Codex in the Bodleian Library (Arch. Seld. B 18, of the Sixteenth Century, Folio 192 Verso)[22]

But it is necessary to smooth and polish the objects by water treatment, mist treatment, distillation, sublimation, and whatever (term) <Pibechius>[23] the sage borrowed from Ostanes and locked up, so to speak, in language before passing it on in his art. I mean that he obscures the confused mixture of materials, their weighing, their gold coloration as well as the instruments like the furnace and the oven.

Hermes did the same thing before him. Accordingly, they called his book about these matters *The Key*.[24] Anubis alone attempted to explain Hermes's *Treatise in Seven Books*, but not even he did so in a clear fashion.

[22] The text used as a basis for the following translation is edited by Bidez and Cumont, *Mages hellénisés*, 2.309.

[23] The Greek here reads Πηχυαῖος (Pechyaius).

[24] *The Key* is also the title given to CH 10 (manifestly a different tractate).

Emerald Tablet

TH 30a

Emerald Tablet (Tabula Smaragdina, *Translated into Latin, Mid Twelfth Century*)[1]

True it is, without falsehood, certain and most certain: that which is above is like that which is below, and that which is below is like to that which is above, to accomplish the wonders of a single reality.

[1] Julius Ruska dated the composition of the *Emerald Tablet* sometime between 600 and 750 CE (*Tabula Smaragdina: Ein Beitrag zur Geschichte der hermetischen Literatur* [Heidelberg: Carl Winter, 1926], 166). It was originally written in Arabic. It belonged to the end of a book called *Kitāb sirr al-ḫalīqā* (*Book of the Secrets of Creation*) attributed to Apollonius of Tyana (the Arabic "Balīnūs"). In this work, "Balīnūs" relates the contents of an emerald tablet that he discovered in Hermes's subterranean crypt (TH 30b). It is disputed whether the *Book of the Secrets of Creation* was a translation from a Greek work or a new composition in Arabic. For the Arabic text, see Ursula Weisser, *Das "Buch über das Geheimnis der Schöpfung" von Pseudo-Apollonios von Tyana* (Berlin: de Gruyter, 1980). The Latin text, translated here, appears in several versions. Hugo of Santalla made a translation of the entire *Book of the Secrets of Creation* probably between 1145 and 1151. His Latin text of the *Emerald Tablet* is edited by Françoise Hudry, "Le *De secretis naturae* du pseudo-Apollonius de Tyane: Traduction latine par Hugues de Santalla du *Kitāb sirr al-ḫalīqa* de Balīnūs," in "Cinq traités alchimique médiévaux," *Chrysopoeia* 6 (1997–99): 1–153 at 152. It serves as the basis of TH 30b. An independent translation of the *Emerald Tablet* was made slightly earlier by another scholar, possibly Plato of Tivoli (between 1134 and 1145). This version was used by Albert the Great (1200–80) and Arnald of Villanova (1235–1311) and was edited by Dorthea Waley Singer and Robert Steele, "The Emerald Table," *Proceedings of the Royal Society of Medicine, Section of the History of Medicine* 21 (1927): 485–501 at 492. Their text is used as a basis for TH 30a. A similar Latin text is edited by Ruska, *Tabula*, 2. Ruska explores the differences between the Arabic and Latin versions in *ibid.*, 116–23. See further Quispel, "Gnosis and Alchemy: the Tabula Smaragdina," in van den Broek, ed., *From Poimandres*, 303–34; Heiduk, "Offene," 258–63. For the later European reception of the *Emerald Tablet*, see Thomas Hofmeier, "Exotic Variations of the Tabula smaragdina," in *Magia, alchimia*, 1.540–62; Didier Kahn, ed., *Hermès Trismégiste, La Table d'Émeraude et sa tradition alchimique* (Paris: Belles Lettres, 1994); Jean-Marc Mandosio, "La Tabula smaragdina nel Medioevo latino, I. La Tabula smaragdina e i suoi commentari medievali," in Lucentini and others, eds., *Hermetism from Late Antiquity*, 681–96; Irene Caiazzo, "La Tabula smaragdina nel Medioevo latino, II. Note sulla fortuna della Tabula smaragdina nel Medioevo latino," in *ibid.*, 697–714.

As all things were from one, by mediation of a single one, so all things were born from this one reality by a single process of adaptation.[2]

Its father is the Sun; its mother the Moon.[3]

The Wind carried it in its womb, the Earth is its nurse.

Here is the father of every talisman throughout the whole world.[4] Its power is complete.

If it be turned toward earth, it will separate earth from fire, the subtle from the gross.

Smoothly, with great ability, it rises from earth to heaven; again it descends to earth and receives the power of things on high and of things below.

Thus you will possess the glory of the splendor of the world; therefore all darkness will flee from you.

This is the strong strength of all strength, for it conquers every subtle reality and passes through every solid object. In this way, this world was created.

From this source will come wondrous correspondences whose mode of operation is here established.

Thus I was called Hermes, since I have the three parts of the whole world's wisdom.[5]

Now what we have said about the operation of the sun is complete.

[2] Here taking *meditatione* as an error for *mediatione*, which better corresponds to the Arabic original (Ruska, *Tabula*, 117).

[3] Sun and Moon are sometimes taken to refer to gold and silver, respectively. Here, however, they better relate to fire and water, since wind (air) and earth come next (summing up the four elements). Bernard D. Haage observes: "The Philosopher's Stone has the Sun (Fire, philosophical Sulphur, which bestows a gold colour) for its father, the Moon (Water, philosophical Mercury, which gives a silver colour and is the matrix of the Stone) for its mother. The wind (Air, the 'Volatile' that is the rising vapor in a heated distillation still . . .) carries the Stone aloft like a seed, and the earth (. . . in which the minerals grow, likewise the mercurial humus of the Stone) nourishes the Stone and brings it to maturity" ("Alchemy II: Antiquity–12th Century," in *DGWE* 24–25).

[4] The reference is apparently to the Philosophers' Stone, for which see Mark Haeffner, *The Dictionary of Alchemy: From Maria Prophetissa to Isaac Newton* (London: Aquarius, 1991), 240–43; Claus Priesner and Karin Figala, eds., *Alchemie: Lexikon einer hermetischen Wissenschaft* (Munich: Beck, 1998), 215–20.

[5] The reference may be to magic, alchemy, and astrology (compare TH 30b, end). In TH 34 (*Fifteen Stars, Stones, Plants, and Talismans*), the four sciences associated with Hermes are astrology, physics, magic, and alchemy.

TH 30b

Emerald Tablet *(Translated into Latin by Hugo of Santalla, 1145–51 CE)*

"For these are the secrets of Hermes which, to guard them from less learned men, he buried with himself inscribed (and resting) in his own hands as mentioned above. Over it (his tomb), he erected a statue, thereby denying open access to the less discerning. The one who takes care to study them diligently will obtain the leadership in philosophy over all one's contemporaries."

These are the words that Apollonius wrote at the end of his book, without any explanation. He said: "Entering an underground crypt, I saw a tablet of emerald[6] between the hands of Hermes, a truth inscribed in an intricate web of words:

> 'Higher things from lower things, lower things from higher things,
>
> The operation of wonders from one, just as all things draw their origin from one and the same thing, by one and the same administration of the plan.
>
> Its father is the Sun, its mother is the Moon; the wind raises them in her body, the earth becomes sweeter.
>
> You, then, children of talismans, workers of wonders, perfect in your discernment, if earth arises, prudently, extensive<ly>, and with the industry of wisdom lead it out of the subtle fire which excels all grossness and bluntness.
>
> Led out from earth, it will ascend to heaven; it will slip down from heaven to earth, containing the power and potential of higher and lower things.
>
> Hence all darkness is illumined by it, whose power clearly transcends whatever is subtle, and penetrates every gross thing.
>
> This operation is able to subsist in accord with the make-up of the superior world.
>
> This is what Hermes the philosopher calls the triple wisdom and the triple science.'"

[6] Emerald, or more generally green stone, is the stone that corresponds to Hermes. Compare the "turquoise steles" in *Disc. 8–9* (NHC VI,6) 61.27, 29.

Prefaces to the Composition of Alchemy *and the* Six Principles of Nature

TH 31a

*Chester's Preface (*Praefatio Castrensis*) to the* Book on the Composition of Alchemy *(*Liber de Compositione Alchemiae, *1144 CE)*[1]

We read in the *Histories of Ancient Divine Matters* that there were three philosophers each called Hermes. The first of these was Enoch, known by the two names "Hermes" and "Mercury." Second, there was Noah also called "Hermes" and "Mercury." The third was Hermes who reigned in Egypt after the Flood and maintained his reign for a long time.[2] This was the one called "Threefold" by our ancestors on account of his accruing three virtues bestowed on him, clearly, by the lord God. He was king, philosopher, and prophet.[3] It was this Hermes who after the Flood was the first inventor and promoter of all arts and disciplines, both liberal and mechanical.

All who came after him walked in his path and closely imitated his footsteps. What more can I say? It would be a long and difficult task at

[1] The text used as a basis for the following translation is Julius Ruska, "Zwei Bücher de Compositione Alchemiae und ihre Vorreden,"*Archiv für Geschichte der Mathematik, der Naturwissenschaft und der Technik* 11 (1928): 28–37. The preface is ascribed to Robertus Castrensis (Robert of Chester, not the same man as Robert of Ketton) and dated to 1144 CE. Ruska, however, argued that the *Praefatio Castrensis* was a thirteenth- or early fourteenth-century forgery dependent upon the linguistically similar prologue to the *Septem tractatus Hermetis* (*ibid.*, 28–37; Delp, *De sex rerum*, 6). Lee Stavenhagen hypothesized that additions were made to an original text that went back to the twelfth century ("The Original Text of the Latin *Morienus*," *Ambix: The Journal of the Society for the Study of Alchemy and Early Chemistry* 17 [1970]: 1–12). For a defense of the traditional dating, see Robert Halleux, "The Reception of Arabic Alchemy in the West," in Roshdi Rashed, ed., *Encyclopedia of the History of Arabic Science*, 3 vols. (London: Routledge, 1996), 3.886–902 at 889–90. See further Michela Pereira, "I Septem Tractatus Hermetis: note per una ricerca," in Lucentini and others, eds., *Hermetism from Late Antiquity*, 651–80 at 655–58, 674; Heiduk, "Offene," 248–53.

[2] Compare TH 26 from Abū Ma'shar.

[3] Compare TH 37b from the *Picatrix* 3.7 (Hermes as "king, prophet, and sage").

present to call to mind the honors and deeds of so great a man of virtue. Though we have not explained his peculiar teaching in the translation of this divine book – for my ability as a scholar and a writer is meager – I introduced his name in the prologue of this book since he was the first to devise and publish it.

This, then, is the divine book, and one full of divinity. In it is contained the true and complete approval of the two Testaments, Old and New. If, then, anyone studies this book at length and fully understands it, the truth and power of the Testaments and also both kinds of life cannot utterly escape him. This is the book called *Concerning the Composition of Alchemy*.

Since your Latin world does not yet know the meaning and system of alchemy, I will clarify it in the present discourse. I presented this word, though unknown and astonishing, in order to clarify it by definition. Hermes the philosopher and others who lived after him defined the word in the following way. In the book *On the Changing of Substances*, for instance, "alchemy" is a material substance taken from one and composed by one, which alternately brings together the precious substances by their affinity and effect, and naturally transforms these same substances by a natural mixture into things of a superior nature.[4]

We will explain the definition in what follows; the process and its procedure will be treated at length. We, though our abilities are still untried and our skill at Latin slight, have endeavored to translate from Arabic into Latin this extensive and magnificent work.

TH 31b

Anonymous Preface to The Six Principles of Nature *(between 1147 and 1180)*[5]

We read in the ancient histories of divine matters that there were three philosophers. The first of these was Enoch who was also called "Hermes" or "Mercury." The second was Noah, who likewise was named "Hermes" and "Mercury." The third was dubbed "Hermes Mercury Threefold" because he was eminent as a king, philosopher, and prophet. He it was who, after the Flood, ruled the kingdom of Egypt with consummate

[4] The insistence on a unitive cause is reminiscent of the *Emerald Tablet* (TH 30a–b).

[5] The text that serves as the basis for this translation is edited by Lucentini and Delp, *De sex rerum principiis*, 147. See further Lucentini, "Hermetic Literature II: Latin Middle Ages," in *DGWE*, 499–529 at 504, 512–13.

justice. He excelled in the liberal and mechanical arts and was the first to explain astronomy clearly.[6]

He brilliantly composed *The Golden Bough*, *The Book of Longitude and Latitude*, *The Book of Election*, and *Ezich* which constitutes guidelines for aligning the planets and for the device that measures the altitude of stars – along with many other works.[7]

This Threefold or Thrice Great was the first to spread abroad alchemy as one of his pursuits. Morienus the consummate philosopher gave great attention to this in his writings; with long labors he began to investigate the secret nature of alchemy.[8] He wrote on this subject with subtlety and finally composed the discipline.[9]

[6] Compare TH 26a–b from Abū Maʿshar.

[7] For information about the Arabic book *Golden Bough* or *Rod of Gold*, see Van Bladel, *Arabic Hermes*, 28. Hermann of Carinthia (about 1100–60 CE) says that in the *Rod of Gold* (*Aurea Virga*), Hermes revealed the words spoken to him by his familiar spirit (*On Essences*, 72vD, Burnett). Compare TH 15 from Ammianus Marcellinus.

[8] Morienus was a Byzantine Christian hermit reported to have dwelt near Jerusalem. According to Arabic sources, he initiated the Islamic prince Khālid ibn Yazīd into the art of alchemy. See further Lee Stavenhagen, *A Testament of Alchemy* (Hanover: University Press of New England, 1974), 51–69; Ahmad Y. al-Hassan, "The Arabic Original of *Liber de compositione alchemiae*," *Arabic Sciences and Philosophy* 14 (2004): 213–31.

[9] See further Ch. Peuch, "Hermès troi fois incarné. Sur quelques témoignages négligés relatifs à Hermétisme," *Revue des Études Grecques* 59–60 (1946–47), xi–xiii; Heiduk, "Offene," 177–96.

Book of the Twenty-Four Philosophers

TH 32

Book of the Twenty-Four Philosophers *(Late Twelfth Century* CE*)*[1]

When twenty-four philosophers came together, only one question remained for them: what is God?[2] They by joint counsel deferred the date and agreed to convene again at a set time to propose their own definitions about God individually so that from their distinctive definitions they might establish by communal agreement some assured assertion about God.

[1] The text used as a basis for the following translation is edited by Françoise Hudry, *Liber viginti quattuor philosophorum* (Turnholt: Brepols, 2007), 3–5. The *Book of the Twenty-four Philosophers* is a Latin work attested in manuscripts as early as the twelfth century CE. It consists of twenty-four definitions of God, each reputedly given by different philosophers. The initial definition of the work is attributed to Hermes Thrice Great first by Alexander Nequam (1157–1217 CE), followed by several other medieval writers. The whole book begins to be ascribed to Hermes in the 1300s (Hudry, *Liber*, xxv–xxx), although other manuscripts leave the work anonymous. Hudry judges that the work's doctrinal content goes back to the early third century and stems from the intellectual melting pot of Alexandria (*Liber*, xxviii, xxii). She argues more specifically that the work can be traced back to a composition of the Latin philosopher Marius Victorinus in the mid fourth century CE (*Le livre des XXIV philosophes. Résurgence d'un texte du IVe siècle* [Paris: J. Vrin, 2009], 113–46). See further Peter Dronke, *Hermes and the Sibyls: Continuations and Creations* (Cambridge: Cambridge University Press, 1990), 23–26; Antonella Sannino, "Berthold of Moosburg's Hermetic Sources," *Journal of the Warburg and Courtauld Institutes* 63 (2000): 243–58 at 251–52; Bernard McGinn, *The Harvest of Mysticism in Medieval Germany 1300–1500* (New York: Herder & Herder, 2005), 42–45; Lucentini, "Hermetic Literature II: Latin Middle Ages," in *DGWE*, 499–529 at 503–4, 510–11; Ebeling, *Secret History*, 52–54; Heiduk, "Offene," 196–226; David Porreca, "How Hidden was God? Revelation and Pedagogy in ancient and medieval Hermetic Writings," in DeConick and Adamson, eds., *Histories of the Hidden God*, 137–48 at 142–43.

[2] Compare SH 28 where Hermes defines God as, "The Craftsman of the universe, a Consciousness most wise and eternal." This definition has a certain resemblance to later definitions in the *Book of Twenty-four Philosophers*. For instance, definition 20 presents God as living from his own intellect or consciousness (*solus sui intellectu vivit*); definition 12 speaks of God's wisdom (*sapientiae*) and definition 13 refers to God's eternity (*sempiternitas*).

1. God is a monad giving birth to a monad mirroring back upon himself a singular brilliance.[3]
2. God is an infinite sphere whose center is everywhere and whose circumference is nowhere.[4]

[3] The word translated "brilliance" (*ardor*) also signifies "heat" or "flame." For God as monad, compare CH 4.10–11. For further parallels from ancient philosophy, see Hudry, *Livre des XXIV*, 24–29, 150; Zénon Kaluza, "Comme une branche d'amandier en fleurs. Dieu dans le Liber viginti quattuor philosophorum," in Lucentini and others, eds., *Hermetism from Late Antiquity*, 99–126.

[4] This much-repeated definition is attributed to Hermes more rarely, but is included here for the sake of completeness. For ancient philosophical parallels, see Hudry, *Livre des XXIV*, 35–42, 152. For later citations, see Nicholas of Cusa, *On Learned Ignorance*, 2.12 §162; *On the Bowling Game (De Ludo Globi)* 2.84. See further Michael Keefer, "The World Turned Inside Out: Revolutions of the Infinite Sphere from Hermes to Pascal," *Renaissance and Reformation* 24 (1988): 303–13; Francesco Paparella, "La metafora del cerchio: Proclo e il Liber viginti quattuor philosophorum," in Lucentini and others, eds., *Hermetism from Late Antiquity*, 127–38.

Book of Alcidus

TH 33

Book of Alcidus on the Immortality of the Soul *2.15* *(Late Twelfth Century* CE*)*[1]

Popular opinion has consecrated to Hermes Thrice Great the undeserved honors of deity out of consummate admiration for his excellence.[2] When he was nearing the final end of his life, a company of disciples rose and stood around him.

"Thus far, my children," he said, "I, expelled from my fatherland, have lived as a sojourner and an exile. Now, safe and secure, I seek my fatherland again. When after a little while, I am fully released from my bodily chains and depart, see to it that you do not bewail me as if I were dead. I return to that best and blessed city in which all the citizens do not know death and corruption, a city governed by the single, sole, and supreme God. As long as all people desire to obey his supremely just rule, they are united by the fullness of his inestimable and inviolable goodness, and filled with his wondrous sweetness.

I confess to you, my children, that life is the true one. In it, all effects of changeability are excluded, its citizens cling inseparably to the eternal Good and enjoy true beatitude. For that life which many people consider to be the only one is rather to be called death. Nor is there one single

[1] The text used as a basis for the following translation was edited by Paolo Lucentini, *Liber Alcidi de immortalitate animae: Studio e edizione critica* (Naples: Oriental Institute, 1984), 47–49. For an introduction, see *ibid.*, lx–xcv, with comments on provenance (possibly Sicily) and dating on *ibid.*, xcviii–cix. The work is a dialogue, a consolation, and an allegorical vision. It is set in imaginary Greece at the end of the first century CE. The main character, Alcidus, mourns the death of his brother. There appears to him first a pompous young rhetor symbolizing the outer self. His speech leaves Alcidus deeply grieved. Then a radiant ancient sage, the inner self, attacks the rhetor's speech and drives him away. He brings Alcidus true comfort by affirming the immortality of the soul and the body's resurrection.

[2] For Hermes deified, compare FH 41 (Augustine), TH 1 (Artapanus), TH 7 (Athenagoras), TH 19b (Augustine), TH 20 (Hermias).

(mortal life), but many – as many, I would say, as there are hindrances to the virtues of the highest deity, as many as there are clouds of ignorance, as many as there are failures to fulfill sacred vows, and all the other (sins) in which our mortal condition is entangled.

Therefore dry your tears, my children! For this dissolution in which occurs the unloading of the corruptible burden brings with it no calamitous end, but offers to me a glorious return![3] There is no reason to mourn when you devote your father to the glory of true life. Thus far I have gasped as one about to receive the prize of deathlessness which the divine steadfastness of my soul, providence, sobriety, justice, and the unimpaired worship of deity has earned for me.[4]

You yourselves will follow your father and find him in the fatherland – and surely you will not fail to know me in my transformed state. This is because each person, by that single immense light of goodness which God is, when the darkness of unknowing is dispersed, will recognize – more truly than I am able to tell – all his fellow citizens. You will follow me, I say, if you most wholly venerate the virtues of which justice is chief. By this (virtue), I earnestly exhort you: despise the multitude of gods and worship with supplication that one who constructed the entire mechanism of the world's body and shut up souls in these earthly prisons."[5]

When they stood around him pouring out tears instead of joy, he said: "Silence. For I know not what wondrously sweet music echoes in my ears, whose immensely pleasing melody I confess that I have never more fully attended to. For it is much different than these reverberations in musical instruments by which we enjoy the symphony that procures and preserves good habits. I cannot for lack of experience describe (the sound) which the swiftness of the wondrous firmament produces by the mixing of high and low notes, with the seven celestial spheres veering in a contrary direction."[6]

Up to this point the words trailed from Hermes's moving lips and a glow of superlative brightness beamed from his face. Then Hermes spoke no more, and his soul flew away from his corpse.

3 On death as dissolution, see CH 8.4, 11.15, 12.15–16.

4 Devotion was central to Hermetic spirituality. See SH 2B.2 with notes.

5 The Christian author attempts to revise the memory of Hermes such that polytheism is despised. Compare FH 2 (from *Idols do not Exist*) and VH 2 ("one God"). Contrast Cyril, who accused Hermes of "loiter[ing] in the precincts of idols" (TH 21). For souls shut up in bodies, see SH 23.38–42, 49.

6 For the cosmology, compare Plato, *Timaeus* 37c–38d. See further Dominique Proust, "The Harmony of the Spheres from Pythagoras to Voyager," *Proceedings of the International Astronomical Union* 260 (2009): 358–67; Andrew Barker, "Pythagorean Harmonics," in Carl A. Huffmann, ed., *A History of Pythagoreanism* (Cambridge: Cambridge University Press, 2014), 185–203.

Fifteen Stars, Stones, Plants, and Talismans

TH 34

Fifteen Stars, Stones, Plants, and Talismans *(Twelfth to Mid Thirteenth Century CE)*[1]

Among the many other goods which the ancient and wisest fathers of philosophy told, Hermes, father of the philosophers – the most ancient sage, and as it were the single one from many philosophers who were blessed by God – published this book for <Agathos Daimon>.[2] He divided it into four parts since it principally deals with the powers of four phenomena, namely stars, plants, stones, and talismans (*figuras*). Contained in it and <. . .> is a model for later sages in order that their wisdom might not be buried in obscurity.

He (Hermes) said: "The one who makes wisdom alive will not die." Again: "That man is counted as holy whose exemplary deeds are lauded in this age. Every person who is wise and famous for good habits is a philosopher. Wise is the person who knows reality as it is and as it can be tested. After this," he said, "I see that every true reality has a manifestation, form, weight, color and, as a person comes to completion in something, it is produced through <. . .> this very thing." . . .

He also said: "There are four things in the world which cannot be banished from the whole or fully joined with it, and these are called the four elements. Similarly, four things are understood to be established on high which are judged to be unmoving, incorruptible, and unattainable . . .

[1] The presumed Greek original of this work has been lost. An Arab astronomer published a version of this text with comments in the eighth century CE. This version was then translated into Latin probably in the later twelfth or thirteenth century (Lucentini and Compagni, *I testi*, 47–48). Here I translate the Latin text published by Louis Delatte, *Textes Latins*, 241–44. See further Festugière, *RHT*, 1.160–86; Thorndike, "Traditional Medieval Tracts," 224–27; Paolo Lucentini, "Hermetic Literature II: Latin Middle Ages," in *DGWE*, 499–529 at 515; Heiduk, "Offene," 311–13.

[2] The Latin text reads *Abhydimon*.

These are the sun, moon, stars, and sky. Moreover, I observe that the four directions on earth cannot be a single direction for a person who only stands on one point of the world. In the same way, it is impossible for four years to be a single temporal experience. I say this to illustrate the four noble sciences, namely astrology, physics, magic, and alchemy."

Hermes also said: "Blessed is the one who knows what he sees, understands what he hears, while thinking realizes what he thinks about, and while seeking realizes what he seeks, how he seeks it, and when. Blessed is the one who tests because testing is the root of all knowledge. Therefore, whoever is naturally disposed to test, a true test arises from visible things, testable things, tasteable things, moving things, and apart from these, no true test is found.

It must be learned what each sage thirsts to learn, a sage both parsimonious and greedy for riches. It must be noted also that higher nature has four forms: namely, a generating, nourishing, weakening, and corrupting form."

Hermes also said: "There are four humors, namely blood, phlegm, bile, and black bile. Similarly, there are four elements, namely fire, air, water and earth. Moreover, there are four things in which all incidentals consist, namely wealth, poverty, life, and death. Let it be known that there are two things by which we understand that the things we know are either good or evil, that is, a curse and its opposite."

Hermes said, "Briefly I wish to explain things that I found amidst the discourses of certain sages. For I found that there are fifteen things that are indispensable among sages, namely among those who want to bring some work into realization through astronomy or magic. For let it be known that there are fifteen stars amidst the others called "fixed" which are of great power and significance. Some of these are beneficent and grant a long and happy life, while others bestow a short and impoverished life."

Book of the Beibenian Stars

TH 35

Book of the Beibenian Stars *(Early Thirteenth Century* CE*)*[1]

This is the book of Hermes, head of all sages, extracted from other books like a blossom from the power of the stars and from the depth of their knowledge, a knowledge which no one else knew except he alone.

Hermes said: "I will tell you about the matters of Fortune. They will be the source of your joy and benefit. This is what God set and set up in the stars called 'beibenian.'[2] He gave them rule over us. These may be in the same degree as the ascendant or in the tenth or seventh or in the same degree as the sun or moon. For setting planets will be unfavorable for those who are born. When there will be a star from these aforementioned places, it signifies the high standing of the one born, if God wills. It also signifies the outcome for that rank, an outcome uncredited and unimagined in the human heart. Moreover, if you find them (in aspect) with other stars in places already

[1] The doctrines of the *Liber de stellis beibeniis* may date back to the third century BCE, though the earliest known version dates to 379 CE. This originally Greek work was successively translated into Pahlavi (Middle Persian), Arabic (by the early ninth century CE), and Latin. The attribution of the work to Hermes appears first in the Arabic versions and continues in the Latin tradition. The text translated here is the Latin version made by Salio of Padua in Toledo around 1218 CE. The text is edited by Paul Kunitzsch in *Hermetis Trismegisti Astrologia et Divinatoria*, ed. Gerrit Bos, among others, Hermes Latinus 4.4 (Turnhout: Brepols, 2001), 57–59. An English translation of a Hebrew version of the introduction is translated by Fabrizio Lelli in *ibid.*, 125. See further Paolo Lucentini, "Hermetic Literature II: Latin Middle Ages," in *DGWE*, 499–529 at 515; Paul Kunitzsch, "Origin and History of *Liber de stellis beibeniis*," in Lucentini and others, eds., *Hermetism from Late Antiquity*, 449–60.

[2] That is, the "fixed" stars (as opposed to wandering planets, meteors, and so on).

mentioned – especially if they be southern or northern stars like the beibenian stars, and especially if they be in luminous degrees – they will be of superior force."

Now I will explain to you the pronunciation of the beibenian stars, their judgment, force, places, signs, degrees, and temperaments (in aspect) with other stars, if God so wills.

Albert the Great

TH 36a

Albert the Great, Book of Minerals *1.1.4 (around 1254 CE)*[1]

Hermes, in the book that he wrote on the power of stones, seems to say that the generative cause of stones is a certain power, which, he says, is one in all things. Nonetheless, on account of the variety of things it produces, it is called by diverse names. He gives as an example the light of the Sun, which alone produces all things; but when it is dispensed, no longer acting through a single power in the things acted upon, it produces various effects. He chose to assign this power first of all to Mars as its source. Nevertheless, it varies greatly in proportion to the effects of the light from other stars and of the material that receives it, as we said; and hence different kinds of stones and metals are produced in different places.

TH 36b

Albert the Great, Book of Minerals *2.1.2*[2]

Yet Hermes and certain followers, mostly Indians, who differ on many points concerning the universal power, said that the powers of all things below originate in the stars and constellations of the heavens. All these powers are poured down into all lower things by means of the circle called *Alaur*, which is, they said, the first circle of the constellations.

[1] For an introduction to Albert the Great, see FH 44 above. The text used for the following translation is edited by Augustus Borgnet, *B. Alberti Magni. Opera omnia vol. 5. Mineralium libri quinque* (Paris: Vivès, 1890), 5. See further Loris Sturlese, "Saints et magiciens: Albert le Grand en face d'Hermès Trismégiste," *Archives de Philosophie* 43 (1980): 615–34.

[2] The text used for the following translation is edited by Borgnet, *Opera, vol. 5*, 26.

These powers descend into natural things either nobly or ignobly: nobly when the materials receiving these powers are more like things above in their brightness and transparency; ignobly, when the materials are confused and foul, so that the heavenly power is, as it were, suppressed. Therefore they say that this is the reason why precious stones, more than anything else, have wondrous powers, since they are in substance more like things above in their brightness and transparency. On this account, some of them say that precious stones are starry elements.

TH 36c

Albert the Great, Book of Minerals *2.2.10*[3]

Hermes says that there are wondrous powers in stones and likewise in plants, by means of which whatever occurs for skilled magicians can happen naturally, if their powers are well understood.

TH 36d

Albert the Great, Book of Minerals *3.2.3*[4]

For this reason Hermes, leader and father of alchemy, says that if thin sheets of silver are smeared with salt of Ammon and vinegar and suspended over an alembic, a sort of vessel, then the silver plates change into an azure color. Then, if the sheets are reduced to ash with sulphur so as to become powder, then stirred with vinegar and *zeruph*, a kind of herb, the azure will be fermented and perfected.[5]

TH 36e

Albert the Great, On Sleep and Waking *3.1.5 (1254–57 CE)*[6]

One must by long study, noble habits, and ordered emotions call back the soul from exterior to interior things. One must close off the routes so that the tumults of the senses that operate in waking consciousness do not draw

[3] The text used for the following translation is edited by Borgnet, *Opera, vol. 5*, 40.

[4] The text used for the following translation is edited by Borgnet, *Opera, vol. 5*, 78.

[5] Albert describes further recipes of Hermes in *Book of Minerals* 4.3, 6. See further Sylvain Matton, "Hermès Trismégiste dans la littérature alchimique médievale," in Lucentini and others, eds., *Hermetism from Late Antiquity*, 621–50 at 632–37.

[6] The text used for the following translation was edited by Borgnet, *B. Alberti Magni. Opera Omnia, vol. 9. De somno et vigilia* (Paris: Vivès, 1890), 184.

out the soul toward external things. Then, if this is performed over a long period, a more certain divination comes about. It is more certain because the phantasms received through the senses and the passions that drag the soul toward other things vanish away. This is the reason why Hermes and the other students of divination hid themselves away in desert caves.

TH 36f

Albert the Great, On Ethics *10.2.3 (around 1260 CE)*[7]

The life according to the works of contemplation is superior to human life. A human life accords with works that are human. Humankind is twofold. With respect to consciousness, first of all, a person is constituted as the connecting link to God.[8] In this respect, says Hermes Thrice Great, one has nothing bestial in oneself.[9] . . .

(True) life is the working of contemplative consciousness divorced from passions and the composite (self).[10] This life does not fit humanity unless consciousness turns away from the body as much as possible. This kind of activity and happiness is not human, but divine.

TH 36g

Albert the Great, On Animals *22.1.5 (1258–63 CE)*[11]

Regarding the properties of humankind, the most important is that which Hermes writes about to Asclepius. It is this: humanity alone is the connecting link between God and the world in that humanity has divine consciousness within. Through consciousness, humanity is at times elevated above the world so that even the stuff of this world obeys human conceptions. We see this phenomenon in those brilliantly endowed from

[7] The text used for the following translation was edited by Borgnet, *B. Alberti Magni. Opera Omnia, vol. 7. Ethicorum libri x* (Paris: Vivès, 1891), 627, 629.

[8] Compare *Ascl.* 6: humankind "has been put in the happier place of middle status so as to cherish those beneath and be cherished by those above . . . Of all living things, consciousness equips only the human, exalts it, raises it up to understand the divine plan."

[9] Compare Albert, *On Ethics* 10.2.3: "In its perfect state, humankind possesses nothing bestial, as Hermes Thrice Great says."

[10] The composite self is evidently the soul-body unit that Plotinus referred to as the συναμφότερον (*Enneads* 1.1.5; 1.1.6–7; 1.4.14; 2.3.9).

[11] The text used for the following translation is edited by Hermann Stadler, ed., *De animalibus libri xxvi nach der Cölner Urschrift*, 2 vols. (Münster: Aschendorff, 1916–21), 2.1354.

birth. These people, by means of their souls, propel the transformation of worldly bodies with the result that they are reputed to be miracle-workers.

Thus even in that part by which humanity is entangled in the world, it is not subject to it, but stands above it as governor. Hence arises the bewitching powers of one mind that cause hindrance or enhancement in the mind of another through vision or some other faculty of perception.

Hermes further testifies: if one ever willingly subjects oneself to the world, one is deprived of human dignity and receives animal characteristics. This person is called a pig due to lust, a dog due to irascibility, a lion due to rapaciousness, and so on.[12] ... Still, if a person advances to the upper reaches of human thought, one draws to oneself both the body and the world since the soul is born to excel both body and world.

TH 36h

Albert the Great, On Animals *25.2*[13]

When Hermes says that the basilisk is born in glass, he does not understand an actual basilisk. Rather, he has in mind a certain alchemical elixir by which metals are transmuted.[14]

TH 36i

Albert the Great, On Causes and the Procession of the Whole *1.4.3 (1267–68 CE)*[15]

The most ancient originators of philosophy – the Thrice Great, Apollo, Hermes the Egyptian, Asclepius the disciple of the Thrice Great – placed the mode of this influx in the first principle which penetrates all things.[16] The first principle is from itself the essence of all things ...

[12] Compare CH 12.4: "But those human souls that do not have mind as a guide are affected in the same way as souls of animals without reason ... they never cease their irrational anger and irrational longing"; FH 40 (from Gaius Iulius Romanus).

[13] The text used for the following translation is edited by Stadler, *De animalibus*, 2.1562.

[14] In *On Animals* 22.2.1 §91, Hermes indicates that the reindeer can change color like a basilisk. Then in 23.24, §51, Hermes is cited as supporting the view that an egg laid by an old rooster in dung hatches into a basilisk. Albert himself does not credit this latter report.

[15] The text used for the following translation was edited by Borgnet, *B. Alberti Magni. Opera Omnia, vol. 10. Liber de causis et processu universitatis* (Paris: Vivès, 1891), 414.

[16] The distinction between the Thrice Great and Hermes the Egyptian suggests that Albert conceived of multiple persons called Hermes as was common in the Arabic tradition (for instance, TH 26 from Abū Maʿshar).

Thus Hermes speaks these words: "God is all that is."[17] He is so in two respects: in himself and in the second god whom he produces. In himself, he is solely what he is in himself. In the second god whom he produces from himself, he is in all things the totality of what they are in that he formed and made all things according to the image of his divinity.[18] For this reason, many kinds of gods, as he says, were produced.[19]

[17] Compare *Ascl.* 20: "he (God) is one and all."

[18] For the second god, compare *Ascl.* 8; FH 36 (from Marcellus of Ancyra).

[19] Compare *Ascl.* 19: "There are many kinds of gods, of whom one part is intelligible, the other sensible."

Picatrix

TH 37a

Picatrix *3.6 (Translated into Latin in the Late Thirteenth Century* CE*)*[1]

Perfect Nature

Moreover, Hermes said, "When I desired to understand and to extract the secrets of the working of the world and its quality, I set myself over a pit profoundly deep and dark. From it, a violent wind blew. On account of its darkness, I was unable to look into it. When I sent a lit candle down into it, it was immediately extinguished by the wind.

Some time later, a handsome man of stately authority appeared to me in a dream. He spoke to me in the following way: "Take a lit candle and place it in a glass lantern so that it is not extinguished by the violence of the wind. Then put it into the pit, excavate its center, and quickly draw out a talisman. When you have drawn it out, the talisman will extinguish the wind of the pit and you will be able to hold the light there. Then dig out the four corners of the pit. From them, draw out the secrets of the world, the perfect nature, its qualities, as well as the generative principles of all things."

I asked him who he was. He responded: "I am perfect nature."[2] . . .

[1] The text used for the following translation is edited by David Pingree, *Picatrix: The Latin Version of the Ghāyat Al-Hakīm* (London: Warburg Institute, 1986), 113. The Arabic original of this work (called *The Aim of the Sage*) goes back to the middle of the eleventh century CE, and possibly somewhat earlier. The author of the work is unknown, although it came to be attributed to the mathematician and astronomer Maslama ibn Ahmad al-Majrītī (died between 1005 and 1008 CE). A Spanish translation (or rather adaptation) of the work was made between 1256 and 1258 CE. This translation informed the Latin translation that was made shortly thereafter. The Latin translation was widely distributed throughout Europe. See further Pingree, "Some of the Sources of the *Ghāyat al-Hakīm*," *Journal of the Warburg and Courtauld Institutes* 43 (1980): 1–15; Béatrice Bakhouche, Frédéric Fauquier, and Brigitte Pérez-Jean, *Picatrix: Un traité de magie médiéval* (Turnhout: Brepols, 2003), 21–38; Heiduk, "Offene," 298–308.

[2] Compare CH 1.2: "'Who are you?' I (Hermes) asked. 'I am Poimandres,' he said."

Some people questioned Hermes the sage: "By what means are knowledge and philosophy joined?" He answered: "By perfect nature." Again they asked: "What is the root of knowledge and philosophy?" He said: "Perfect nature." Then they questioned him more precisely: "What is the key by which knowledge and philosophy are opened?" He responded: "Perfect nature." Then they inquired of him: "What is perfect nature?"

He answered: "Perfect nature is the spirit of a philosopher or sage linked with the planet governing him. He is the one who opens the locked rooms of knowledge, the one from whom are understood the things which otherwise could hardly be understood. His activities proceed in a natural way and just as directly in sleep as in waking.

So it is clear from the foregoing what perfect nature is. It comports itself toward the sage or philosopher just as a teacher to a student. It initially teaches him in basic and easy matters, then, step by step, proceeds to greater and more difficult lessons until the student is made perfect in knowledge. In this way, perfect nature works by its own power and influence by disposing the mind of the philosopher according to its natural inclination.

Understand that the foregoing must be committed to memory. From the foregoing, one must conclude that it would be impossible for someone to approach this knowledge unless he were naturally inclined to it as much by his own virtue as by the disposition of the planet ruling in his horoscope.

TH 37b

Picatrix *3.7*[3]

The Threefold Office

The sages who made prayers and sacrifices to the planets in mosques performed the foregoing.[4] While the planet revolved across eight degrees of the sky, they made a sacrifice of a single animal. Likewise, when it declined by another eight degrees, they made another sacrifice. They say that Hermes commanded them to do this in their mosques or churches. The sages who knew the aforementioned Hermes affirmed that he was the master of three flourishing offices, namely king, prophet, and sage.[5]

[3] The text used for the following translation is edited by Pingree, *Picatrix*, 113.

[4] That is, prayer to the planets.

[5] Compare TH 31a (Chester's Preface); 31b (Preface to the *Six Principles of Nature*).

TH 37c

Picatrix *3.11*[6]

Recipe for Magic Oil

Hermes wrote about a wondrous potion that works many wonders. He made it in this fashion. He took an entire human head of one recently dead and placed it in a large jar. With it, he put eight ounces of fresh opium, eight ounces of human blood, and eight ounces of sesame oil, enough to submerge the aforementioned (head). He then sealed the mouth of the jar with clay and put it over a steady-burning charcoal fire for a complete twenty-four hours. Afterward, he removed it from the fire and allowed it to cool. He then strained the mixture, keeping the face submerged. He discovered that everything had liquefied into an oil-like substance, which he stored away.

He used to say that in this oil existed many wonders. First among them was the ability to see whatever one wishes. If you light a lamp from this oil, or anoint yourself with it, or put a little bit of it in someone's food, you will see whatever you wish.[7]

TH 37d

Picatrix *4.3*[8]

Hermes's Great City

They (the Chaldeans) assert that Hermes originally constructed a certain temple of images by means of which he knew the volume of the Nile facing the mountain of the moon.[9] This man also built a temple to the Sun. He knew how to hide himself from people so that no one standing with him was able to see him.

It was he, too, who in the east of Egypt constructed a city twelve miles long within which he constructed a castle. The castle had four gates at each of its four quarters. On the eastern gate, he placed the form of an eagle; on the western gate, the form of a bull; on the southern gate, the form of a

[6] The text used for the following translation was edited by Pingree, *Picatrix*, 160.

[7] The source for this potion is apparently a Hermetic book called *Hedeytoz*, from which a number of other recipes derive (Pingree, *Picatrix*, 159–60).

[8] The text used for the following translation was edited by Pingree, *Picatrix*, 188–89.

[9] The mountain of the moon probably designates the Rwenzori mountain range of eastern equatorial Africa. They support glaciers and are one source for the Nile waters.

lion, and on the northern gate, he constructed the form of a dog.[10] Into these images, he introduced spiritual essences that spoke by projecting their voices.[11] No one could enter the gates of the city except by their permission. There he planted trees in the midst of which was a great tree that offered the produce of all fruits.

On the top of the castle, he had built a tower thirty cubits high. On the top of the tower, he ordered to be placed a round dome. Its color changed every day until the seventh day after which it returned to its initial color. Moreover, each day the city corresponded with the color of the dome, and thus the city shone with each aforementioned color for that day.

In the environs of the tower, there was abundant water in which many kinds of fish lived. In the vicinity of the city, Hermes arrayed diverse images of whatever sort he desired. Their health-giving power made the city's inhabitants healthy, free from all deformity and languishing diseases.

The name of the aforementioned city was Adocentyn.[12]

TH 37e

Picatrix *12.39*[13]

Instructions for Talismans

Hermes Thrice Great explained in his book *On Talismans* his system of reckoning for when he attached talismans for each and every part of the human body and under which faces of the zodiacal signs to construct them.[14]

(For instance,) take pure gold and make a seal image in which you draw the figure of a lion when the sun rises in Leo in the first or second face in

[10] The animals correspond – except for the dog – to the four animals that came to represent the four Evangelists: lion, bull, eagle, and human. Compare Revelation 4:7.

[11] The animation of statues recalls the discussion in *Ascl.* 24, 37. See further FH 41 (from Augustine).

[12] "Adocentyn" is apparently a garbled version of Ashmounein, the Egyptian name for Hermopolis Magna in Middle Egypt.

[13] The text used for the following translation is edited by Pingree, *Picatrix*, 82. It appears in Scarpi 2.35 as his fragment 34.

[14] The "face" (Latin *facies*) refers to the third part of a zodiacal sign. Compare the testimony of Michael Psellus (TH 29b). In *Picatrix* 2.10, Hermes (also called *Mercurius*) gives information on how to represent figures (for instance, Saturn, Venus, a fox) on gems (Pingree, *Picatrix*, 65, 67, 69). Compare also the *Book of the Planets* ascribed to Hermes (*Mercurius*) in *Picatrix* 3.3 (Pingree, *Picatrix*, 97–98).

the ascendant or midheaven position with the Moon not in her house,[15] and with the lord of the ascendant not in aspect with Saturn or Mars or moving in the opposite direction.[16] Then tie this seal image around the waist or near the kidneys. I know by experience that the one who carries this seal image suffers no harm in time to come.[17]

[15] The planets have dominion over particular signs of the zodiac that are called their "houses" (see TH 4 from Thrasyllus). The house of the Sun is Leo; the house of the Moon is Cancer.

[16] The "lord of the ascendant" refers to a planet whose house is rising in the east. To be "in aspect" means that a planet "looks upon" another planet that is either two, three, four, or six signs away on the zodiacal chart.

[17] Hermes was associated with magic and magical talismans in a number of works copied in the Middle Ages. The author of the *Speculum Astronomiae* 11 (Zambelli, 243–45) preserves the titles of some of these works including the *Liber praestigiorum* (*Book of Illusions*), the *Liber imaginum Mercurii* (*The Book of the Images of Mercury*), the *Liber Saturni* (*Book of Saturn*). These works are further discussed by Lynn Thorndike, "Traditional Medieval Tracts concerning engraved Astrological Images," in *Mélanges Auguste Pelzer: Études d'histoire littéraires et doctrinale de la Scolastique médiévale* (Leuven: Higher Institute of Philosophy, 1947), 217–74 at 227–48.

Nicholas of Cusa

TH 38a

Nicholas of Cusa (1401–64 CE), On the Gift of the Father of Lights *2, Number 102 (1446 CE)*[1]

Although God is thus everything in everything, humanity is nevertheless not God. One can, however, admit the saying of Hermes Thrice Great in soundness of understanding. He said that God is named with the name of all things and all things with the name of God. As a result, a person can be called a god made human.[2]

TH 38b

On Beryl *7 (1458 CE)*[3]

Fourthly, observe that Hermes Thrice Great calls the human being a second god.[4] For just as God is the creator of real entities and natural forms, so the human is creator of conceptual entities and artificial forms.

[1] For an introduction to Nicholas of Cusa, see FH 45. The text used for the following translation is edited by Paulus Wilpert, *Nicolai de Cusa Opera Omnia 4. Opuscula 1: De Deo abscondito, De quaerendo deum, De filiatione dei, De dato patris luminum, Coniectura de ultimis diebus, De genesi* (Hamburg: Meiner, 1959), 176–77.

[2] Compare *Ascl.* 6: "A human being is a great wonder, a living thing to be worshiped and honored: for he changes his nature into a god's, as if he were a god (*in naturam dei transit, quasi ipse sit deus*)."

[3] The text used for the following translation is Nicolaus of Cusa, *De beryllo*, ed. H. G. Senger and C. Bormann, *Opera Omnia* XI.1 (Hamburg: Meiner, 1988), 9.1–10.2.

[4] This is a distinctive interpretation of Nicholas bearing on *Ascl.* 6 (humanity transmutes into divine nature to become a quasi-god); *Ascl.* 7 (there is something divine in humanity); *Ascl.* 36 (humans can create a divine nature; compare also CH 12.1). Strictly speaking, however, it is the cosmos that is presented as a second god (*Ascl.* 8). Nicholas glossed *Ascl.* 8 with the words: *nota quomodo deus de deo*, or "note how god emerges from God," with apparent reference to humanity (Pasquale Arfé, ed., *Cusanus-Texte III. Marginalien. 5. Apuleius. Hermes Trismegistus aus Codex Bruxellensis 10054–56* [Heidelberg: Winter GMBH, 2004], 112). In *On Surmises* (*De coniecturis*) 2.14 (§§143–44), he says

These rational entities do not exist unless they are likenesses of the human intellect just as the creatures of God are likenesses of the divine intellect. Therefore, humanity has intellect, which, in its creative power, is the likeness of divine intellect. Hence humanity creates a likeness of the likenesses of the divine intellect just as extrinsic and artificial figures are likenesses of intrinsic natural forms.[5]

that, "the human is a god, though not independently, because one is human. One is a human and thus god. The human is a world, yet not all things in a strict sense, because one is human. The human, then, is either a small world or a human world. The very sphere of humanity encompasses god and the whole world by a human potential. Thus a human being is a human god and, as a god, able in a human way to be a human angel, a human beast, a human lion or bear, or anything whatsoever. For within humanity there is a potential for all things to exist in their own way. Thus in humanity are enfolded all things in a human way as all things are enfolded in the universe in a universal way, because there exists a human world. All things, finally, are wrapped up in humanity in a human way, for the human is a god. Humanity is a unity, which is an infinity contracted in a human way."

[5] See further Karl Bormann, *Nikolaus von Kues: "Der Mensch als zweiter Gott"* (Trier: Cusanus Institute, 1999); Bernd Irlenborn, "Der Mensch als zweiter Gott? Anmerkungen zur *Imago dei*-Lehre des Nikolaus von Kues,"*Freiburger Zeitschrift für Philosophie und Theologie* 47 (2000): 381–401; Martin Thurner, "Explikation der Welt und mystische Verinnerlichung. Die hermetische Definition des Menschen als 'secundus deus' bei Cusanus," in Lucentini and others, eds., *Hermetism from Late Antiquity*, 245–60.

Bibliography

Modern Editions and Translations of Hermetic Writings

Copenhaver, Brian P., trans. *Hermetica: The Greek Corpus Hermeticum and the Latin Asclepius in a New English Translation with Notes and Introduction.* Cambridge: Cambridge University Press, 1992.

Holzhausen, Jens, trans. *Das Corpus Hermeticum Deutsch.* 2 vols. Stuttgart-Bad Cannstatt: Friedrich Frommann Verlag, 1997.

Mahé, Jean-Pierre. "Fragments hermétiques dans les papyri Vindobonenses graecae 29456r° et 29828r°." Pages 51–64 in *Mémorial André-Jean Festugière: Antiquité païenne et chrétienne.* Ed. E. Lucchesi and H. D. Saffrey. Cahiers d'orientalisme. Geneva: Cramer, 1984.

Hermès en Haute-Égypte. 2 vols. Bibliothèque Copte de Nag Hammadi 3, 7. Québec: University of Laval, 1978–82.

"La création dans les Hermetica." *Recherches Augustiniennes* 21 (1986): 3–53.

Nock, A. D. and A.-J. Festugière, eds. *Corpus Hermeticum.* 4 vols. Paris: Belles Lettres, 1945–54.

Paramelle, Joseph and Jean-Pierre Mahé. "Extraits hermétiques inédits dans un manuscrit d'Oxford." *Revue des Études Grecques* 104 (1991): 109–39.

"Nouveaux parallèles grecs aux Définitions Hermétiques arméniennes." *Revue des Études Arméniennes* 22 (1990–91): 115–34.

Poltronieri, Chiara, ed. *La pupilla del mondo.* Venice: Marsilio, 1994.

Ramelli, Ilaria, ed. *Corpus Hermeticum: Testo Greco, Latino e Copto. Edizione e commento di A.D. Nock e A.-J. Festugière, ed. dei testi ermetici copti e commento di Ilaria L. E. Ramelli.* Milan: Bompiani, 2005.

Salaman, Clement, Dorine van Oyen, William D. Wharton, and Jean-Pierre Mahé. *The Way of Hermes: New Translations of "The Corpus Hermeticum" and "The Definitions of Hermes Trismegistus to Asclepius."* Rochester, VT: Inner Traditions, 2000.

Scarpi, Paolo. *La rivelazione segreta di Ermete Trismegisto.* 2 vols. Rome: Arnoldo Mondadori, 2009–11.

Scott, Walter with A. S. Ferguson. *Hermetica: The Ancient Greek and Latin Writings which Contain Religious or Philosophic Teachings Ascribed to Hermes Trismegistus.* 4 vols. Oxford: Clarendon Press, 1924–36.

Siegert, Folker, ed., and Karl-Gottfried Eckart, trans. *Das Corpus Hermeticum einschliesslich der Fragmente des Stobaeus. Münsteraner Judaistische Studien 3*. Münster: Lit, 1999.

Wiontzek-Hermetica-Stiftung, ed., with introductions and commentaries by Maria Magdalena Miller. *Die Hermetischen Schriften: Corpus Hermeticum*. Hildesheim: Georg Olms, 2009.

Reference Works

Adler, Ada, ed. *Suidae Lexicon. Lexicographi Graeci*. 5 vols. Stuttgart: Teubner, 1967–71.

Diels, Hermann and Walther Kranz, eds. *Fragmente der Vorsokratiker, griechisch und deutsch*. 6th edn. Berlin: Weidmann, 1954.

Glare, P. G. W., ed. *Oxford Latin Dictionary*. Oxford: Clarendon Press, 1968–82.

Hanegraaff, Wouter J., ed. *Dictionary of Gnosis and Western Esotericism*. Leiden: Brill, 2006.

Lampe, G. W. H. *A Patristic Greek Lexicon*. Oxford: Clarendon Press, 1961.

Latte, Kurt. *Hesychii Alexandrini Lexicon*. Vols. 1–2. Hauniae: Ejnar Munksgaard, 1953–66.

Liddell, Henry George, Robert Scott, and P. G. W. Glare, eds. *A Greek-English Lexicon with Revised Supplement*. Oxford: Clarendon Press, 1996.

Pauly, A., G. Wissowa, Wilhelm Kroll, and Karl Mittelhaus, eds. *Paulys Realencyclopädie der classischen Altertumswissenschaft*. 83 vols. Munich: Alfred Druckenmüller, 1893–1982.

Primary Sources

Aelian. *De natura animalium*. Ed. Manuela García Valdés, Luis Alfonso Llera Fueyo, and Lucía Rodríguez-Noriega Guillén. BSGRT. Berlin: de Gruyter, 2009.

Aeschylus. *Oresteia: Agamemnon, Libation-Bearers, Eumenides*. Ed. Alan H. Sommerstein. Loeb Classical Library. Cambridge, MA: Harvard University Press, 2008.

Albert the Great. *De animalibus libri xxvi nach der Cölner Urschrift*. Ed. Hermann Stadler. 2 vols. Beiträge zur Geschichte der Philosophie des Mittlealters 15–16. Münster: Aschendorff, 1916–21.

Albertus Magnus on Animals: A Medieval "Summa Zoologica." Trans. Kenneth F. Kitchell Jr. and Irven Michael Resnick. Baltimore: Johns Hopkins University Press, 1999.

Opera omnia. Ed. Augusti Borgnet. 38 vols. Paris: Ludovicum Vivès, 1890–1899.

Commentarii in Iob. Ed. Melchior Weiss. Freiburg: Herder, 1904.

Alcinous. *Enseignement des doctrines de Platon*. Ed. John Whittaker. Paris: Belles Lettres, 1990.

Ammianus Marcellinus. *Rerum gestarum libri qui supersunt*. Ed. Wolfgang Seyfarth. 2 vols. BSGRT. Leipzig: Teubner, 1978.

Anaxagoras of Clazomenae. *Fragments and Testimonia: A Text and Translation with Notes and Essays*. Ed. Patricia Curd. Toronto: University of Toronto Press, 2007.

Apuleius. *Opera quae Supersunt*. Ed. C. Moreschini. 3 vols. BSGRT. Stuttgart: Teubner, 1991.

Rhetorical Works. Ed. Stephen Harrison. Oxford: Oxford University Press, 2002.

Arfé, Pasquale, ed. *Cusanus-Texte III. Marginalien. 5. Apuleius. Hermes Trismegistus aus Codex Bruxellensis 10054–56*. Heidelberg: Winter, 2004.

Aristides, Aelius. *The Complete Works*. Trans. Charles A. Behr. 2 vols. Leiden: Brill, 1981.

Aristides of Athens. *The Apology of Aristides on behalf of the Christians*. Ed. J. Rendel Harris and J. Armitage Robinson. Texts and Studies 1:1. Cambridge: Cambridge University Press, 1891.

Aristotle. *Opera*. Ed. Olof Gigon. 2nd edn. 5 vols. Berlin: de Gruyter, 1960–87.

Arnobius. *Adversus nationes libri VII*. Ed. C. Marchesi. Corpus Scriptorum Latinorum Paravianum. Torino: Giovanni Battista & Co., 1953.

Athanassakis, Apostolos N., and Benjamin M. Wolkow. *The Orphic Hymns: Translation, Introduction, and Notes*. Baltimore: Johns Hopkins University Press, 2013.

Athenaeus. *Deipnosophistae. The Learned Banqueters*. Ed. S. Douglas Olson. 8 vols. LCL. Cambridge, MA: Harvard University Press, 2006–12.

Athenagoras. *Legatio pro christianis*. Ed. Miroslav Marcovich. Patristische Texte und Studien 31. Berlin: de Gruyter, 1990.

Augustine. *Confessioni*. Ed. Manlio Simonetti. 5 vols. Scrittori greci e latini. Milan: Lorenzo Valla, 1992–97.

Contra Faustum Manicheum. Ed. Joseph Zycha. CSEL 25.1. Vienna: Tempsky, 1891.

Scripta contra Donatistas. Ed. Michael Petschenig. Vienna: Tempsky, 1908.

De Civitate Dei. Ed. Bernard Dombart and Alphonse Kalb. 2 vols. Corpus Christianorum Series Latina 7–48. Turnholt: Brepols, 1955.

Letters 211–270, 1–29* (Epistulae)*. Trans. Roland Teske. The Works of Saint Augustine II.4. Hyde Park, NY: New City Press, 2005.

Babrius and Phaedrus. Ed. and trans. Ben Edwin Perry. Loeb Classical Library. Cambridge, MA: Harvard University Press, 1965.

Bardaisan. *The Book of Laws and Countries: Dialogue on Fate of Bardaisan of Edessa*. Trans. H. J. W. Drijvers. Asen: Van Gorcum & Co., 1965.

Beatrice, Pier Franco. *Anonymi monophysitae Theosophia: An Attempt at Reconstruction*. Supplements to *VC 56*. Leiden: Brill, 2001.

Bernabé, Alberto. *Poetae Epici Graeci Testimonia et Fragmenta Pars II: Orphicorum et Orphicis similium testimonia et fragmenta*. 3 vols. BSGRT. Leipzig: K. G. Saur, 2004–7.

Berthelot, M. and M. Ch.-Em.. Ruelle, eds. *Collections des anciens alchimistes grecs II. Texte grec.* London: Holland Press, 1963.

Boethius. *The Consolation of Philosophy.* 4.6. Trans. David R. Slavitt. Cambridge, MA: Harvard University Press, 2008.

Brock, Sebastian. "A Syriac Collection of Prophecies of the Pagan Philosophers." *Orientalia Lovaniensia Periodica* 14 (1983): 203–46.

"Some Syriac Excerpts from Greek Collections of Pagan Prophecies." *VC* 38 (1984): 77–90.

Cedrenus, Georg. *Historiarum compendium.* Ed. Luigi Tartaglia. *Bollettino dei Classici 30.* Rome: Bardi, 2016.

Censorinus. *De die natali/Über den Geburtstag: Lateinisch und deutsch.* Ed. Kai Brodersen. Darmstadt: Wissenschaftliche Buchgesellschaft, 2012.

Chaeremon. *Egyptian Priest and Stoic Philosopher: The Fragments Collected and Translated with Explanatory Notes.* Ed. Pieter Willem van der Horst. Études Préliminaires aux Religions Orientales 101. Leiden: Brill, 1984.

Charisius, Flavius Sosipatrus. *Artis grammaticae libri v.* Ed. Charles Barwick and F. Kühnert. BSGRT. Stuttgart and Leipzig: Teubner, 1997.

Charlesworth, James, ed. *Old Testament Pseudepigrapha.* Anchor Bible Reference Library. 2 vols. New York: Doubleday, 1983–85.

Cicero. *De finibus bonorum et malorum.* Ed. Claudio Moreschini. BSGRT. Leipzig: K. G. Saur, 2005.

De natura deorum. Ed. Arthur Stanley Pease. 2 vols. New York: Arno, 1979.

De re publica, de legibus. Ed. Clinton Walker Keyes. LCL. Cambridge, MA: Harvard University Press, 1928.

Clement of Alexandria. *Stromata, Quis dives salvetur.* Ed. Otto Stählin, Ludwig Früchtel, and Ursula Treu. GCS 15, 17. 4th edn. Berlin. Akademie, 1970–85.

Cumont, Franz and Franz Boll, eds. *Catalogus Codicum Astrologorum Graecorum.* 12 vols. Brussels: Lamertin, 1898–1959.

Cyprian. *The Complete Works of Saint Cyprian of Carthage.* Ed. Phillip Campbell. Merchantville, NJ: Evolution, 2013.

Cyril of Alexandria. *Gegen Julian Teil 1: Buch 1–5.* Ed. Christoph Riedweg. Die Griechischen Christlichen Schriftsteller der ersten Jahrhunderte (GCS) Neue Folge 20. Berlin: de Gruyter, 2016.

Gegen Julian Teil 2: Buch 6–10 und Fragmente. Ed. Wolfram Kinzig and Thomas Brüggemann. Die Griechischen Christlichen Schriftsteller der ersten Jahrhunderte (GCS) Neue Folge 21. Berlin: de Gruyter, 2017.

Damascius. *Problems and Solutions Concerning First Principles.* Trans. Sara Ahbel-Rappe. Oxford: Oxford University Press, 2010.

Delatte, Louis. *Textes Latins et vieux française relatifs aux Cyranides.* Paris: Librairie E. Droz, 1942.

Didymus of Alexandria. *Kommentar zum Ecclesiastes (Tura Papyrus), Teil III, Kommentar zu Ecclesiastes Kap. 5 und 6* in Zusammenarbeit mit dem

Ägyptischen Museum zu Kairo, unter Mitwirking v. L. Koenen. Ed. J. Kramer. Bonn: Rudolf Habelt, 1970.

Psalmenkommentar (Tura Papyrus), Teil II, Kommentar zu Psalm 22–26,10. Ed. M. Gronewald. Bonn: Rudolf Habelt, 1968.

Diels, H. *Doxographi Graeci*. 4th edn. Berlin: de Gruyter, 1965.

Dindorf, Ludwig. *Chronicon Paschale ad exemplar Vaticanum*. Volume 1. Bonn: Weber, 1832.

Diocles of Carystus. *A Collection of the Fragments with Translation and Commentary*. Ed. Philip J. van der Eijk. 2 vols. Studies in Ancient Medicine 22. Leiden: Brill, 2000–1.

Diodorus of Sicily. *Bibliothèque historique*. Ed. Françoise Bizière. Budé. Paris: Les Belles Lettres, 1972–.

Diogenes Laertius. *Vitae philosophorum*. Ed. Miroslav Marcovich. Stuttgart: Teubner, 1999.

Dorotheus of Sidon. *Carmen Astrologicum: Interpretationem arabicam in linguam anglicam versam una cum Dorothei fragmentis et graecis et latinis*. Ed. David Pingree. BSGRT. Stuttgart: Teubner, 1976.

Edelstein, E. J. and L. *Asclepius: A Collection and Interpretation of the Testimonies*. 2 vols. Baltimore: Johns Hopkins University Press, 1945.

Ephrem the Syrian. *Hymns*. Trans. Kathleen E. McVey. Classics of Western Spirituality. New York: Paulist Press, 1989.

Epictetus. *The Discourses as Reported by Arrian*. Trans. W. A. Oldfather. Loeb Classical Library. Cambridge, MA: Harvard University Press, 1925.

Erbse, Hartmut. *Fragmente griechischer Theosophien*. Hamburg: Hanischer Gilden, 1941.

Euripides. Ed. Arthur S. Way. 3 vols. LCL. Cambridge, MA: Harvard University Press, 1988.

Eusebius of Caesarea. *La Préparation Évangélique*. Ed. Jean Sirinelli, Édouard des Places, Odile Zink, and Guy Schroeder. 9 vols. SC 206, 266, 228, 262, 215, 369, 292, 307, 338. Paris: Cerf, 1974–87.

Eusebius. *Gegen Marcell, Über die kirchliche theologie, die Fragmente Marcells*. Ed. Erich Klostermann and Günther Christian Hansen. 3rd edn. Die Griechischen Christlichen Schriftsteller, Eusebius Werke 4. Berlin: Akademie, 1991.

Faulkner, Raymond O., trans. *The Ancient Egyptian Book of the Dead*. Ed. Carol Andrews. London: British Museum, 1985.

Filastrius Brixiensis. *Diversarum Hereseon Liber*. Ed. F. Heylen. Corpus Christianorum Series Latina 9. Turnholt: Brepols, 1957.

Firmicus Maternus. *Matheseos Libri VIII*. Trans. Jean Rhys Bram. Park Ridge, NJ: Noyes Press, 1975.

Galen. *Opera Omnia*. Ed. C. G. Kühn. Tomus XI. Leipzig: Knobloch, 1826.

On the Doctrines of Hippocrates and Plato. Ed. Philip de Lacy. 2nd edn. 3 vols. Corpus Medicorum Graecorum 5.4.1.2. Berlin: Akademie, 1978–84.

De Usu Partium Libri XVII. Ed. George Helmreich. 2 vols. Leipzig: Teubner, 1907.

On Semen. Ed. Phillip de Lacy. Corpus Medicorum Graecorum V 3,1. Berlin: Akademie, 1992.

On the Usefulness of the Parts of the Body. Περὶ χρείας μορίων. De usu partium. Trans. Margaret Tallmadge May. 2 vols. Ithaca: Cornell University Press, 1968.

Gregory of Nazianzus. *Discours 27–31 (Discours théologiques)*. Ed. Paul Gallay. SC 250. Paris: Cerf, 1978.

Hermann of Carinthia. *De Essentiis: A Critical Edition with Translation and Commentary*. Ed. Charles Burnett. Studien und Texte zur Geistesgeschichte des Mittlealters 15. Leiden: Brill, 1982.

[Hermes Trismegistus], *De triginta sex decanis*. Ed. Simonetta Feraboli. Corpus Christianorum Continuatio Mediaevalis 144. Turnholt: Brepols, 1994.

"Le livre sacré sur les decans." Ed. C.-E. Ruelle. *Revue de Philologie* 32 (1908): 247–77

Astrologia et Divinatoria. Ed. Gerrit Bos, Charles Burnett, Thérèse Charmasson, Paul Kunitzsch, Fabrizio Lelli, and Paolo Lucentini. Hermes Latinus 4.4. Turnhout: Brepols, 2001.

Hermias Alexandrinus. *In Platonis Phaedrum scholia*. Ed. Carlo M. Lucarini and Claudio Moreschini. BSGRT 2010. Berlin: de Gruyter, 2012.

Herodotus. *Historiae*. Ed. Carl Hude. 3rd edn. 2 vols. Oxford: Clarendon Press, 1933.

Hesiod. *Theogony, Works and Days, Testimonia*. Ed. and trans. Glenn W. Most. Loeb Classical Library. Cambridge, MA: Harvard University Press, 2006.

Hippocrates. *De la Génération, De la nature de l'enfant, Des maladies IV, Du foetus de huit mois*. Ed. Robert Joly. Budé. Paris: Belles Lettres, 1970.

The Hippocratic Treatises "On Generation," "On the Nature of the Child," "Diseases IV." Ed. Iain M. Lonie. Berlin: de Gruyter, 1981.

Die hippokratische Schrift von der Siebenzahl in ihrer vierfachen Überlieferung. Ed. W. H. Roscher. Paderborn: Schöningh, 1913.

Hippocrates IV. Trans. W. H. S. Jones. Loeb Classical Library. Cambridge, MA: Harvard University Press, 1931.

Hippocrates X. Trans. Paul Potter. Loeb Classical Library. Cambridge, MA: Harvard University Press, 2012.

Holladay, Carl R. *Fragments from Hellenistic Jewish Authors, Volume 1: Historians. Texts and Translations Pseudepigrapha Series 10*. Chico, CA: Scholars Press, 1983.

Homer. *The Iliad*. Trans. A. T. Murray and rev. William F. Wyatt. 2 vols. LCL. Cambridge, MA: Harvard University Press, 1999.

The Odyssey. Trans. A. T. Murray and rev. George E. Dimock. 2 vols. LCL. Cambridge, MA: Harvard University Press, 1995.

Horace. *Odes and Epodes*. Trans. Niall Rudd. Loeb Classical Library. Cambridge, MA: Harvard University Press, 2004.

Horapollo. *Hieroglyphics*. Trans. George Boas. Bollingen Series 23. New York: Pantheon, 1950.

Hudry, Françoise. "Le *De secretis naturae* du pseudo-Apollonius de Tyane: Traduction latine par Hugues de Santalla du *Kitāb sirr al-ḫalīqa* de

Balīnūs," in "Cinq traités alchimique médiévaux," *Chrysopoeia* 6 (1997–99): 1–153.

Hudry, Françoise, ed. *Liber viginti quattuor philosophorum*. Turnholt: Brepols, 2007.

Hyginus. *De Astronomia*. Ed. Ghislaine Viré. Leipzig: Teubner, 1992.

Iamblichus. *De Anima. Text, Translation, and Commentary*. Philosophia Antiqua 92. Leiden: Brill, 2002.

In platonis dialogos Commentariorum fragmenta. Ed. John M. Dillon. Philosophia Antiqua 23. Leiden: Brill, 1973.

Jamblique, les mystères d'Égypte. Ed. Édouard des Places. 2nd edn. Paris: Belles Lettres, 1989.

De mysteriis. Ed. and trans. Emma C. Clarke, John M. Dillon, and Jackson P. Hershbell. WGRW 4. Atlanta: SBL, 2003.

Inwood, Brad, ed. *The Poem of Empedocles. A Text and Translation with an Introduction*. 2nd edn. Toronto: University of Toronto Press, 2001.

Irenaeus of Lyon. *Contre les hérésies livres I–V*. Ed. Adelin Rousseau and Louis Doutreleau. SC 100, 153, 211, 263–64, 294. Paris: Cerf, 1965–82.

Isidore of Seville. *On the Nature of Things*. Trans. Calvin B. Kendall and Faith Wallis. Translated Texts for Historians 66. Liverpool: Liverpool University Press, 2016.

Etymologiarum sive Originum libri xx. Ed. W. M. Lindsay. 2 vols. Oxford: Clarendon Press, 1911.

Jackson, Howard M., ed. *Zosimos of Panopolis on the Letter Omega*. SBL Texts and Translations 14. Missoula, MT: Scholars Press, 1978.

Jacob of Edessa. *Hexaemeron seu In opus creationis libri septem*. Ed. A. Vaschalde. Corpus Scriptorum Christianorum Orientalium 97. Scriptores Syri 48. Leuven: L. Durbecq, 1953.

Hexaemeron seu In opus creationis libri septem. Ed. I.-B. Chabot. Corpus Scriptorum Christianorum Orientalium. Scriptores Syri 56. Paris: Republic, 1928.

Jacoby, Felix, ed. "Manetho (?) von Sebennytos (609)." *Die Fragmente der griechischen Historiker Part I–III*. Published by Brill Online Reference Works. Consulted online February 3, 2017. doi: 10.1163/1873–5363 boj a609.

Jasnow, Richard and Karl-Theodor Zauzich, eds. *The Ancient Egyptian Book of Thoth: A Demotic Discourse on Knowledge and Pendant to the Classical Hermetica*. 2 vols. Wiesbaden: Harrassowitz, 2005.

John of Antioch. *Fragmenta ex Historia chronica*. Ed. Umberto Roberto. Texte und Untersuchungen zur Geschichte der altchristlichen Literatur 154. Berlin: de Gruyter, 2005.

Julian. *The Works of the Emperor Julian*. Ed. Wilmer Cave Wright. Loeb Classical Library. Cambridge, MA: Harvard University Press, 1980–93.

Justin Martyr. *Apologies*. Ed. Denis Minns and Paul Parvis. Oxford Early Christian Texts. Oxford: Oxford University Press, 2009.

Kahn, Didier, ed. *Hermès Trismégiste, La Table d'Émeraude et sa tradition alchimique*. Paris: Belles Lettres, 1994.

Kaimakis, Dimitris. *Die Kyraniden*. Meisenheim am Glan: Anton Hain, 1976.
Lactantius. De Opificio dei. *La création de dieu*. Ed. Béatrice Bakhouche and Sabine Luciani. Monothéismes et Philosophie. Turnhout: Brepols, 2009.
De ira dei – Vom Zorne Gottes. Ed. H. Kraft and A. Wlosok. Darmstadt, 1957.
Épitomé des Institutions Divine. Ed. Michel Perrin. SC 335. Paris: Cerf, 1987.
Institutions divines livre IV. Ed. Pierre Monat. SC 377. Paris: Cerf, 1992.
Epitome Divinarum Institutionum. Ed. Eberhard Heck and Antonie Wlosok. BSGRT. Stuttgart and Leipzig: Teubner, 1994.
Divinarum Institutionum libri septem. Ed. Eberhard Heck and Antonie Wlosok. BSGRT. Berlin: de Gruyter, 2005–7.
Lichtheim, Miriam. *Ancient Egyptian Literature: A Book of Readings*. 3 vols. Berkeley: University of California Press, 1973–80.
Litwa, M. David, ed. *Refutation of All Heresies: Translated with an Introduction and Notes*. WGRW 40 Atlanta: SBL Press, 2016.
Löhr, Gebhard. *Verherrlichung Gottes durch Philosophie: Der hermetische Traktat II im Rahmen der antiken Philosophie- und Religionsgeschicthe*. WUNT 97. Tübingen: Mohr Siebeck, 1997.
Long, A. A. and D. N. Sedley. *The Hellenistic Philosophers: Translations of the Principal Sources with Philosophical Commentary*. 2 vols. Cambridge: Cambridge University Press, 1987.
Lucentini, Paolo. *Liber Alcidi de immortalitate animae: Studio e edizione critica*. Naples: Oriental Institute, 1984.
Lucian. *Oeuvres*. Ed. Jacques Bompaire. 4 vols. Budé. Paris: Belles Lettres, 1993–2008.
Lucretius. *De rerum natura libri sex*. Ed. William Ellery Leonard and Stanley Barney Smith. Madison: University of Wisconsin Press, 1942.
Lydus, John. *Liber de mensibus*. Ed. Richard Wuensch. BSGRT. Stuttgart: Teubner, 1967.
On the Months (De Mensibus). Ed. and trans. Anastasius C. Bandy. Lewiston, NY: Edwin Mellen, 2013.
Macrobius. *Saturnalia*. Ed. Robert A. Kaster. 3 vols. Loeb Classical Library. Cambridge, MA: Harvard University Press, 2011.
Commentaire au songe de Scipion. Ed. and trans. Mireille Armisen-Marchetti. 2 vols. Budé. Paris: Belles Lettres, 2003.
Majercik, Ruth. *The Chaldean Oracles: Text, Translation, and Commentary*. Studies in Greek and Roman Religion 5. Leiden: Brill, 1989.
Manetho. Trans. W. G. Waddell. Loeb Classical Library. Cambridge, MA: Harvard University Press, 1980.
Manilius. *Astronomica*. Ed. George P. Goold. BSGRT. Leipzig. Teubner, 1985.
Marcovich, Miroslav, ed. *Hippolytus. Refutatio omnium haeresium*. PTS 25. Berlin: de Gruyter, 1986.

Marcus Aurelius Antoninus. *Ad se ipsum libri xii*. Ed. Joachim Dalfen. BSGRT. Leipzig: Teubner, 1979.

Marius Victorinus. *Commenta in Ciceronis Rhetorica accedit incerti auctoris tractatus de attributis personae et negotio*. Ed. Thomas Riesenweber. BSGRT. Berlin: de Gruyter, 2013.

Martianus Capella. *The Marriage of Philology and Mercury*. Trans. William Harris Stahl, Richard Johnson, and E. L. Burge, 2 vols. New York: Columbia University Press, 1977.

Mertens, Michèle. *Zosime de Panopolis: Mémoires authentiques. Les alchimistes grecs IV/1*. Paris: Belles Lettres, 1995.

Meyer, Marvin, ed. *Nag Hammadi Scriptures: The International Edition*. New York: HarperOne, 2008.

Migne, J.-P., ed. *Patrologia Graeca*. 162 vols. Paris: Garnier, 1857–86.

Nicholas of Cusa. *De Docta Ignorantia*. Ed. Ernest Hoffmann and Raymund Klibansky. Leipzig: Meiner, 1932.

Opera Omnia 3. De coniecturis. Ed. Joseph Koch and Karl Bormann. Hamburg: Meiner, 1972.

Opera Omnia 4. Opuscula 1: De Deo abscondito, De quaerendo deum, De filiatione dei, De dato patris luminum, Coniectura de ultimis diebus, De genesi. Ed. Paulus Wilpert. Hamburg: Meiner, 1959.

Nickelsburg, George W. E. and James C. VanderKam. *1 Enoch: A New Translation based on the Hermeneia Commentary*. Minneapolis: Fortress, 2004.

Numenius. *Fragments*. Ed. Édouard des Places. Budé. Paris: Belles Lettres, 1973.

Ocellus Lucanus. *Text und Kommentar*. Ed. Richard Harder. Neue Philologische Untersuchungen 1. Berlin: Weidmann, 1926.

Origen of Alexandria. *Contra Celse*. Ed. Marcel Borett. 5 vols. SC 132, 136, 147, 150, 227. Paris: Cerf, 1967–76.

Traité des principes. Ed. Henri Crouzel and Manlio Simonetti. 5 vols. SC 252–53, 268–69, 312. Paris: Cerf, 1978.

Ovid. *The Art of Love, and Other Poems*. Ed. J. H. Mozley and G. P. Goold. 2nd edn. LL. Cambridge, MA: Harvard University Press, 1979.

Page, D. L. *Greek Literary Papyri*. 2 vols. Loeb Classical Library. Cambridge, MA: Harvard University Press, 1942.

Parmenides of Elea. *Fragments*. Ed. David Gallop. Phoenix 1. Toronto: University of Toronto Press, 1984.

Pausanias. *Description de la Grèce*. Ed. Michel Casevitz, Jean Pouilloux, and François Chamoux. 4 vols. Budé. Paris: Belles Lettres, 1992–2005.

Pelikan, Jaroslav and Valerie Hotchkiss. *Creeds & Confessions of Faith in the Christian Tradition*, 3 vols. New Haven: Yale University Press, 2003.

Philo of Alexandria. *Opera*. Ed. Leopold Cohn and Paul Wendland. 7 vols. Berlin: de Gruyter, 1962–63.

De Animalibus: The Armenian Text with an Introduction, Translation, and Commentary. Ed. Abraham Terian. Studies in Hellenistic Judaism 1. Atlanta, GA: Scholars Press, 1981.

Piccione, R.-M. "Sulle fonti e le metodologie compilative di Stobeo." *Eikasmos* 5 (1994): 281–317.

Piccardi, Daria Gigli. *La "Cosmogonia di Strasburgo."* Florence: Giorgio Pasquali, 1990.

Pindar. *The Olympian and Pythian Odes.* Ed. Basil L. Gildersleeve. New York: American Book Company, 1885.

Pingree, David, ed. *Picatrix: The Latin Version of the Ghāyat Al-Hakīm.* London: Warburg Institute, 1986.

Plato. *Opera.* Ed. E. A. Duke, W. F. Hicken, W. S. M. Nicoll, D. B. Robinson, and J. C. G. Strachan. 5 vols. OCT. Oxford: Clarendon Press, 1995.

Pliny. *Natural History.* Trans. H. Rackham. 2nd edn. 10 vols. LCL. Cambridge, MA: Harvard University Press, 1983.

Plotinus. *Opera.* Ed. Paul Henry and Hans-Rudolf Schwyzer. 3 vols. Oxford: Oxford University Press, 1964–82.

Plutarch. *Moralia in Fifteen Volumes.* Ed. Harold Cherniss and William C. Helmbold. vol. 12. Cambridge, MA: Harvard University Press, 1968.

Porphyry. *De l'abstinence.* Ed. and trans. Jean Bouffartigue. 3 vols. Paris: Belles Lettres, 1977.

Introduction. Trans. Jonathan Barnes. Oxford: Clarendon Press, 2003.

Opuscula selecta. Ed. Augustus Nauck. BSGRT. Leipzig: Teubner, 1886.

Sentences: Études d'introduction texte grec et traduction française, Commentaire. Ed. Luc Brisson. 2 vols. Histoire des Doctrines de l'Antiquité Classique 33. Paris: J. Vrin, 2005.

Lettre à Anébon l'Égyptien. Ed. Henri Dominique Saffrey and Alain-Philippe Segonds. Paris: Belles Lettres, 2012.

To Gaurus on How Embryos are Ensouled and on What is in Our Power. Trans. James Wilberding. London: Bristol Classical Press, 2011.

To Marcella. Text and Translation with Introduction and Notes by Kathleen O'Brien Wicker. Texts and Translations Graeco-Roman Religion Series 10. Atlanta, GA: Scholars Press, 1987.

Fragmenta. Ed. Andrew Smith. BSGRT. Stuttgart: Teubner, 1993.

Posidonius. *Posidonius I–II.* Ed. I. G. Kidd. 2 vols. Cambridge: Cambridge University Press, 1988.

Preisendanz, Karl and Albert Henrichs, eds. *Papyri Graecae Magicae. Die griechischen Zauberpapyri.* 2nd edn. 3 vols. Munich: Saur, 2001.

Pritchard, James B. *Ancient Near Eastern Texts Relating to the Old Testament.* 3rd edn. Princeton: Princeton University Press, 1969.

Proclus. *In Platonis rem publicam commentarii.* Ed. Wilhelm Kroll. 2 vols. Leipzig: Teubner, 1901.

In Platonis Timaeum Commentaria. Ed. Ernst Diehl. 3 vols. Leipzig: Teubner, 1903–6.

Psellus, Michael. *Philosophica minora.* Ed. J. M. Duffy and D. J. O'Meara. 2 vols. BSGRT. Leipzig: Teubner, 1992.

Orationes forenses et acta. Ed. George T. Dennis. BSGRT. Leipzig: Teubner, 1994.

Theologica I-II. Ed. Paul Gautier, L. G. Westerink, and J. M. Duffy. BSGRT. Munich: K. G. Saur, 2002.

Pseudo-Apollodorus. *Bibliotheca*. Ed. Richard Wagner. Stuttgart: Teubner, 1965.

Pseudo-Eratosthenes, *Catasterismi*. Ed. Alexander Olivieri. Leipzig: Teubner, 1897.

Pseudoklementinen I: Homilien. Ed. Bernard Rehm and Georg Strecker. 3rd edn. Berlin: Akademie, 1992.

Pseudo-Hippocrates, *The Heart*. Pages 347–51 in *Hippocratic Writings*. Ed. G. E. R. Lloyd. Trans. I. M. Lonie. New York: Penguin, 1978.

Pseudo-Justin. *Ouvrages apologétiques: Exhortation aux grecs (Marcel d'Ancyre?), Discours aux grecs, sur la monarchie*. Ed. Bernard Pouderon. SC 528. Paris: Cerf, 2009.

Pseudo-Plato. *Axiochus*. Ed. Jackson P. Hershbell. Texts and Translations 21. Chico, CA: Scholars Press, 1981.

Pseudo-Plutarch. *Opinions des Philosophes*. Ed. G. Lachenaud. Budé. Paris: Belles Lettres, 1993.

Ptolemy. *Tetrabiblos*. Ed. and trans. F. E. Robbins. Cambridge, MA: Harvard University Press, 1940.

Quodvultdeus. *Opera Quodvultdeo Carthaginiensi episcopo tributa*. Ed. R. Braun. Corpus Christianorum Series Latina 60. Turnholt: Brepols, 1976.

The Creedal Homilies. Conversion in Fifth-century North Africa. Trans. Thomas Macy Finn. Ancient Christian Writers 60. New York/Mahwah: Newman Press, 2004.

Rahlfs, Alfred and Robert Hanhart. *Septuaginta, id est Vetus Testamentum graece iuxta LXX interpretes*. 2nd edn. Stuttgart: Deutsche Bibelgesellschaft, 2006.

Sallustius. *Concerning the Gods and the Universe*. Ed. A. D. Nock. Cambridge: Cambridge University Press, 1926.

Schenke, Hans-Martin, Hans-Gebhard Bethge, and Ursula Ulrike Kaiser, eds. *Nag Hammadi Deutsch: Studienausgabe*. Berlin: de Gruyter, 2007.

Schmidt, Carl, ed. *Pistis Sophia*. Trans. Violet MacDermot. NHS 9. Leiden: Brill, 1978.

The Books of Jeu and the Untitled Text in the Bruce Codex. Trans. Violet MacDermot. NHS 13. Leiden: Brill, 1978.

Schneemelcher, Wilhelm and Edgar Hennecke. *New Testament Apocrypha*. Trans. R. McL. Wilson. 2nd edn. 2 vols. Louisville, KY: Westminster John Knox, 1992.

Seneca. *Epistles 93–124*. Trans. Richard M. Gummere. Cambridge, MA: Harvard University Press, 1925.

Moral Essays. Ed. John Basore. 3 vols. Cambridge, MA: Harvard University Press, 1920–25.

Servius. *Servii Grammatici qui fervntvr in Vergilii carmina commentarii*. Ed. Georg Thilo and Hermann Hagen. Leipzig: Teubner, 1881–1902.

Sextus Empiricus. *Opera*. Ed. Hermann Mutschmann and J. Mau. 4 vols. BSGRT. Leipzig: Teubner, 1912–61.

Simpson, William Kelly, ed. *The Literature of Ancient Egypt: An Anthology of Stories, Instructions, Stelae, Autobiographies, and Poetry*. 3rd edn. New Haven: Yale University Press, 2003.

Stobaeus, Ioannes. *Anthologium*. Ed. Curt Wachsmuth and Otto Hense. 2nd edn. 5 vols. Berlin: Weidmann, 1958.

Stone, Rachel and Charles West, trans. *The Divorce of King Lothar and Queen Theutberga: Hincmar of Rheims's "De Divortio."* Manchester: Manchester University Press, 2016.

Strabo. *Géographie*. Ed. Germaine Aujac, Raoul Baladié, François Lasserre, Benoît Laudenbach, and Jehan Desanges. 15 vols. Budé. Paris: Belles Lettres, 1966–2003.

Stavenhagen, Lee. *A Testament of Alchemy, Being the Revelations of Morienus, Ancient Adept and Hermit of Jerusalem to Khalid ibn Yazid ibn Mu'awiyya, King of the Arabs of the Divine Secrets of the Magisterium and Accomplishment of the Alchemical Art*. Hanover: University Press of New England, 1974.

Syncellus, George. *Ecloga Chronographica*. Ed. Alden A. Mosshammer. BSGRT. Leipzig: Teubner, 1984.

Taylor, C. C. W. *The Atomists Leucippus and Democritus: Fragments*. Toronto: University of Toronto Press, 1999.

Tertullian. *Opera*. Ed. E. Dekkers, A. Gerlo, and A. Kroymann. 2 vols. CCSL 1.1, 1.2. University of Toronto Press, 1999. Turnholt: Brepols, 1954.

Contre les Valentiniens Tome 1. Ed. Jean-Claude Fredouille. SC 280. Paris: Cerf, 1980.

De Anima. Ed. J. H. Waszink. VCSup 100. Leiden: Brill, 2010.

Thales. Wöhrle, Georg and Richard McKirahan. *The Milesians: Thales*. Traditio Praesocratica 1. Berlin: de Gruyter, 2014.

Theophrastus of Eresos. *Sources for his Life, Writings, Thought, and Influence*. Ed. William Fortenbaugh, Pamela Huby, R. W. Sharples, and Dimitri Gutas. Philosophia Antiqua. 2 vols. Leiden: Brill, 1992.

Thom, Johan C., ed. *Cosmic Order and Divine Power. Pseudo-Aristotle, On the Cosmos: Introduction, Text, Translation and Interpretive Essays. SAPERE 23*. Tübingen: Mohr Siebeck, 2014.

[Timaeus Locrus], *On the Nature of the World and the Soul: Text, Translation, and Notes*. Ed. Thomas H. Tobin. Texts and Translations 26. Chico, CA: Scholars Press, 1985.

Totti, Maria. *Ausgewählte Texte der Isis- und Sarapis-Religion. Subsidia Epigraphica 12*. Hildesheim: Georg Olms, 1985.

Vanderlip, Vera F. *The Four Greek Hymns of Isidorus and the Cult of Isis*. Toronto: Hakkert, 1972.

Vergil. *Eclogues, Georgics, Aeneid I–VI*. Trans. H. Rushton Fairclough, revised by G. P. Goold. Loeb Classical Library. Cambridge, MA: Harvard University Press, 1999.

Vettius Valens. *Anthologiarum libri novem*. Ed. David Pingree. Leipzig: Teubner, 1986.

Vinzent, Markus, ed. *Markell von Ankyra: Die Fragmente. Der Brief an Julius von Rom. Supplements to VC 39*. Leiden: Brill, 1997.

Von Arnim, Johannes, ed. *Stoicorum veterum fragmenta*. Leipzig: Teubner, 1903–24.

Ullmann, Manfred, ed. *Das Schlangenbuch des Hermes Trismegistos*. Wiesbaden: Harrassowitz, 1994.

Wilson, Walter, ed. *The Sentences of Sextus. Wisdom Literature from the Ancient World 1*. Atlanta: Society of Biblical Literature, 2012.

Žabkar, Louis V. *Hymns to Isis in Her Temple at Philae*. Hanover: University Press of New England, 1988.

Zambelli, Paola. *The Speculum Astronomiae and its Enigma: Astrology, Theology and Science in Albertus Magnus and his Contemporaries*. Boston Studies in the Philosophy of Science 135. Dordrecht: Kluwer Academic, 1992.

Zonaras, John. *Lexicon ex tribus codicibus manuscriptis*. Ed. Iohannes Augustus Henricus Tittmann. 2 vols. Amsterdam: Hakkert, 1967.

Secondary Sources

Adamson, Grant. "The Old Gods of Egypt in Lost Hermetica and Early Sethianism." Pages 58–86 in *Histories of the Hidden God: Concealment and Revelation in Western Gnostic, Esoteric, and Mystical Traditions*. Ed. April D. DeConick and Grant Adamson. London: Acumen, 2014.

Adler, William. *Time Immemorial: Archaic History and its Sources in Christian Chronography from Julius Africanus to George Syncellus*. Washington, DC: Dumbarton Oaks, 1989.

Affifi, A. E. "The Influence of Hermetic Literature on Moslem Thought." *Bulletin of the School of Oriental and African Studies* 13 (1949–51): 840–55.

al-Hassan, Ahmad Y. "The Arabic Original of *Liber de compositione alchemiae*." *Arabic Sciences and Philosophy* 14 (2004): 213–31.

Allen, James P. *Genesis in Egypt: The Philosophy of Ancient Egyptian Creation Accounts*. New Haven: Yale Egyptological Seminar, 1988.

"Ba." Volume 1, pages 161–62 in *The Oxford Encyclopedia of Ancient Egypt*. Ed. Donald B. Redford. 3 vols. Oxford: Oxford University Press, 2001.

Alpers, Klaus. "Untersuchungen zum griechischen Physiologus und den Kyraniden." *Vestigia Bibliae* 6 (1984): 12–87.

Assmann, Jan. *Religion and Cultural Memory: Ten Studies*. Stanford: Stanford University Press, 2006.

Death and Salvation in Ancient Egypt. Trans. David Lorton. Ithaca: Cornell University Press, 2001.

Bagnall, Roger S. *Egypt in Late Antiquity*. Princeton: Princeton University Press, 1993.

Bain, David. "Μελανῖτις Γῆ: An Unnoticed Greek Name for Egypt: New Evidence for the Origins and Etymology of Alchemy?" Pages 205–26 in *The World of Ancient Magic: Papers from the First International Samson Eitrem Seminar at the Norwegian Institute at Athens, 4–8 May 1997*. Ed. David R. Jordan, Hugo Montgomery, and Einar Thomassen. Bergen: John Grieg AS, 1999.

Bakhouche, Béatrice, Frédéric Fauquier, and Brigitte Pérez-Jean, trans. *Picatrix: Un traité de magie médiéval*. Turnhout: Brepols, 2003.

Barker, Andrew. "Pythagorean Harmonics." Pages 185–203 in *A History of Pythagoreanism*. Ed. Carl A. Huffmann. Cambridge: Cambridge University Press, 2014.

Barton, Tamsyn. *Ancient Astrology*. London: Routledge, 1994.

Bayliss, Grant. D. *The Vision of Didymus the Blind: A Fourth-century Virtue-Origenism*. Oxford: Oxford University Press, 2015.

Beatrice, Pier Franco. "Hermetic Tradition." Pages 429–31 in *Augustine Through the Ages: An Encyclopedia*. Ed. Allan D. Fitzgerald. Grand Rapids, MI: Eerdmans, 1999.

"Pagan Wisdom and Christian Theology according to the *Tübingen Theosophy*." *Journal of Early Christian Studies* 3 (1995): 403–18.

Beck, Roger. *A Brief History of Ancient Astrology*. Malden: Blackwell, 2007.

Beck, Edmund. *Ephräms Polemik gegen Mani und die Manichäer im Rahmen der zeitgenössischen griechischen Polemik und der des Augustinus*. Corpus Scriptorum Christianorum Orientalium 391. Louven: Secretariat of the Corpus SCO, 1978.

Bellitto, Christopher M., Thomas M. Izbicki, and Gerald Christianson, eds. *Introducing Nicholas of Cusa: A Guide to a Renaissance Man*. New York and Mahwah, NJ: Paulist Press, 2004.

Bidez, Joseph and Franz Cumont. *Mages hellénisés: Zoroastre, Ostanès et Hystaspe d'après la tradition grecque*. 2 vols. Paris: Belles Lettres, 1938.

Bleeker, C. J. *Hathor and Thoth: Two Key Figures of the Ancient Egyptian Religion*. Leiden: Brill, 1973.

Bodson, Liliane. "Attitudes toward Animals in Greco-Roman Antiquity." *International Journal for the Study of Animal Problems* 4 (1983): 312–20.

Bohleke, Briant. "In Terms of Fate: A Survey of the Indigenous Egyptian Contribution to Ancient Astrology in Light of Papyrus CtYBR inv. 1132 (B)." *Studien zur altägyptische Kultur* 23 (1996): 11–46.

Bolshakov, Andrey O. "Ka." Volume 2, pages 215–17 in *The Oxford Encyclopedia of Ancient Egypt*. Ed. Donald B. Redford. 3 vols. Oxford: Oxford University Press, 2001.

Bormann, Karl. *Nikolaus von Kues: "Der Mensch als zweiter Gott."* Trier Cusanus Lecture Heft 5. Trier: Cusanus Institute, 1999.

Bouché-Leclercq. *L'astrologie grecque*. Paris: E. Leroux, 1899.

Bousset, Wilhelm. "Zur Dämonologie der späteren Antike." *Archiv für Religionswissenschaft* 18 (1915): 134–72.

Kyrios Christos: A History of the Belief in Christ from the Beginnings of Christianity to Irenaeus. Trans. John E. Steely. Nashville, TN: Abingdon Press, 1970.

Boylan, Patrick. *Thoth, the Hermes of Egypt: A Study of Some Aspects of Theological Thought in Ancient Egypt*. London: Oxford University Press, 1922.

Brock, Sebastian. *The Luminous Eye: The Spiritual World Vision of Saint Ephrem*. Kalamazoo, MI: Cistercian Publications, 1992.

Bull, Christian H. "The Tradition of Hermes: The Egyptian Priestly Figure as a Teacher of Hellenized Wisdom." Ph.D. diss., University of Bergen, 2014.

"The Notion of Mysteries in the Formation of the Hermetic Tradition." Pages 399–425 in *Mystery and Secrecy in the Nag Hammadi Collection: Ideas and Practices. Studies for Einar Thomassen at Sixty*. Ed. Einar Thomassen, Christian H. Bull, Liv Ingeborg Lied, and John D. Turner. NHMS 76. Leiden: Brill, 2012.

Burns, Dylan M. *Apocalypse of the Alien God: Platonism and the Exile of Sethian Gnosticism*. Philadelphia: University of Pennsylvania Press, 2014.

Burnett, Charles. "The Establishment of Medieval Hermeticism." Pages 111–30 in *The Medieval World*. Ed. Peter Linehan and Janet L. Nelson. London: Routledge, 2001.

"The Legend of the Three Hermes and Abū Ma'shar's Kitab al-Ulūf in the Latin Middle Ages." *Journal of the Warburg and Courtauld Institutes* 39 (1976): 231–34.

Burton, Anne. *Diodorus Siculus Book 1 Commentary. Études Préliminaires aux Religions Orientales 29*. Leiden: Brill, 1972.

Busine, Aude. "Hermès Trismégiste, Moïse et Apollonius de tyane dans un Oracle d'Apollon." *Apocrypha* 13 (2002): 227–44.

Calabi, Francesca, ed. *Arrhetos Theos: L'ineffabilità del primo principio nel medio platonismo*. Pisa: ETS, 2002.

Carcopino, J. "Sur les traces de l'hermétisme africain." Pages 207–314 in *Aspectes mystiques de la Rome païenne*. Paris: L'artisan du Livre, 1941.

Castelli, Emanuele. "Saggio introduttivo: L'*Elenchos*, ovvero una 'biblioteca' contro le eresie." Pages 34–46 in *"Ippolito." Confutazione di tutte le eresie*. Ed. Aldo Magris. Brescia: Morcelliana, 2012.

Copenhaver, Brian P. "Hermes Theologus: The Sienese Mercury and Ficino's Hermetic Demons." Pages 149–84 in *Humanity and Divinity in Renaissance and Reformation: Essays in Honor of Charles Trinkaus*. Ed. John W. O'Malley, Thomas M. Izbicki, and Gerald Christianson. Leiden: Brill, 1993.

Magic in Western Culture: From Antiquity to the Enlightenment. Cambridge: Cambridge University Press, 2015.

Courcelle, Pierre. "Le corps-tombeau." *Revue des études anciennes* 78 (1966): 101–22.

Daley, Brian E. *Gregory of Nazianzus*. London: Routledge, 2006.

Delcourt, Marie. *Hermaphrodite: Mythes et rites de la bisexualité dans l'antiquité classique*. Paris: University Presses of France, 1958.

Denzey Lewis, Nicola. *Cosmology and Fate in Gnosticism and Graeco-Roman Antiquity: Under Pitiless Skies*. Nag Hammadi and Manichaean Studies 81. Leiden: Brill, 2013.

Derchain, Ph. "L'authenticité de la inspiration égyptienne dans la Corpus Hermeticum," *Revue de l'Histoire des Religions* 161 (1962): 175–98.

Derchain, Maria-Theresia and Philippe. "Noch einmal Hermes Trismegistos." *Göttinger Miszellen* 15 (1975): 7–10.

Derchain-Urtel, Maria-Theresia. *Thot à travers ses épithètes dans les scènes d'offrandes des temples d'époque gréco-romaine*. Brussels: Egyptology Foundation Queen Elizabeth, 1981.

Dickerman, S. O. "Some Stock Examples of Animal Intelligence in Greek Psychology." *Transactions of the American Philological Association* 42 (1911): 123–30.

Digeser, Elizabeth DePalma. *The Making of a Christian Empire: Lactantius and Rome*. Ithaca: Cornell University Press, 2000.

Dieleman, Jacco. *Priests, Tongues, and Rites: The London-Leiden Magical Manuscripts and Translation in Egyptian Ritual (100–300 CE)*. Religions in the Greco-Roman World 153. Leiden: Brill, 2005.

Dodd, C. H. *The Bible and the Greeks*. London: Hodder & Stoughton, 1935.

Dodds, E. R. *Proclus. Elements of Theology*. 2nd edn. Oxford: Clarendon Press, 1963.

Dodge, Bayard. *The Fihrist of al-Nadīm: A Tenth-century Survey of Muslim Culture*. 2 vols. New York: Columbia University Press, 1970.

Dörrie, Heinrich. *Der hellenistische Rahmen des kaiserzeitlichen Platonismus Bausteine 36–72: Text Übersetzung, Kommentar. Volume 2 of Der Platonismus in der Antike*. Stuttgart-Bad Cannstatt: Friedrich Fromman, 1990.

Dowling, Maurice James. "Marcellus of Ancyra: Problems of Christology and the Doctrine of the Trinity." Ph.D. diss., Queen's University, Belfast, 1987.

Dragona-Monachou, Myrto. "Divine Providence in the Philosophy of the Empire." Pages 4461–490 in *ANRW* II.36.7. Ed. Wolfgang Haase. Berlin: de Gruyter, 1994.

Dronke, Peter. *Hermes and the Sibyls: Continuations and Creations*. Cambridge: Cambridge University Press, 1990.

Dunand, Françoise and Christiane Zivie-Coche. *Gods and Men in Egypt 3000 BCE to 395 CE*. Ithaca: Cornell University Press, 2004.

Dunn, Geoffrey D. *Tertullian*. London: Routledge, 2004.

Ebeling, Florian. *The Secret History of Hermes Trismegistus: Hermeticism from Ancient to Modern Times*. Trans. David Lorton. Ithaca: Cornell University Press, 2007.

Ehrman, Bart D. *Forgery and Counterforgery: The Use of Literary Deceit in Early Christian Polemics*. Oxford: Oxford University Press, 2013.

Eliade, Mircea. *Zalmoxis: The Vanishing God: Comparative Studies in the Religions and Folklore of Dacia and Eastern Europe*. Trans. Willard R. Trask. Chicago: University of Chicago Press, 1972.

Evans, Erin. *The Books of Jeu and the Pistis Sophia as Handbooks to Eternity: Exploring the Gnostic Mysteries of the Ineffable*. Nag Hammadi and Manichean Studies 89. Leiden: Brill, 2016.

Festugière, A.-J. *Hermétisme et mystique païenne*. Paris: Aubier-Montaigne, 1967.

"Le Style de la '*Korē Kosmou*.'" *Vivre et Penser* 2 (1942): 15–57.

La Révélation d'Hermès Trismégiste. 4 vols. Paris: Gabalda, 1949–54.

Finamore, John F. *Iamblichus and the Theory of the Vehicle of the Soul*. Chico, CA: Scholars Press, 1985.

Flamand, Jean-Marie. "Cosmogonie de Strasbourg." *DPA*. Ed. Richard Goulet. 5 vols. Paris: CNRS Editions, 1994: 2.478–80.

Fortin, E. L. "The viri novi of Arnobius and the Conflict Between Faith and Reason in the early Christian Centuries." Pages 197–226 in *The Heritage of the Early Church: Essays in Honor of G. V. Florovsky*. Ed. D. Neiman and M. Schatkin. Rome: Institute for Oriental Studies, 1973.

Foucault, Michel. "What is an Author?" Pages 262–75 in *Contemporary Literary Criticism*. Ed. R. C. Davis and R. Scheifer. 3rd edn. New York: Longman, 1994.

Fowden, Garth. *The Egyptian Hermes: A Historical Approach to the Late Pagan Mind*. Cambridge: Cambridge University Press, 1996.

Frankfurter, David. *Religion in Roman Egypt: Assimilation and Resistance*. Princeton: Princeton University Press, 1998.

Franses, P. Desiderius. *Die Werke des hl. Quodvultdeus Bischofs von Karthago gestorben um 453*. Münich: J. J. Lentnerschen, 1920.

Fraser, Kyle A. "Zosimos of Panopolis and the Book of Enoch: Alchemy as Forbidden Knowledge." *Aries* 4 (2004): 125–47.

Gager, John G. *Moses in Greco-Roman Paganism*. Nashville, TN: Abingdon, 1972.

Gantz, Timothy. *Early Greek Myth: A Guide to Literary and Artistic Sources*. Baltimore: Johns Hopkins University Press, 1993.

Gersh, Stephen. *Middle Platonism and Neoplatonism: the Latin Tradition*. 2 vols. Notre Dame: University of Notre Dame Press, 1986.

Gilhus, Ingvild Saelid. *Animals, Gods and Humans: Changing Attitudes to Animals in Greek, Roman and early Christian Ideas*. London: Routledge, 2006.

Giversen, S. "Hermetic Communities?" Pages 49–54 in *Rethinking Religion: Studies in the Hellenistic Process*. Ed. J. P. Sorensen. Copenhagen: Museum Tusculanum, 1989.

González, Pedro Pablo Fuentes. "Néchepso-Pétosiris." Pages 601–15 in *DPA* volume 4. Paris: CNRS, 2005.

Graf, Fritz. *Magic in the Ancient World*. Trans. Franklin Philip. Cambridge, MA: Harvard University Press, 1997.

Grafton, Anthony. *Forgers and Critics: Creativity and Duplicity in Western Scholarship*. Princeton: Princeton University Press, 1990.

Green, Miranda. *The Gods of the Celts*. Totowa: Barnes and Noble, 1986.

Dictionary of Celtic Myth and Legend. London: Thames & Hudson, 1992.

Celtic Myths. Austin: British Museum Press, 1993.

Green, Tamara M. *The City of the Moon God: Religious Traditions of Harran*. Leiden: Brill, 1992.

Greenbaum, Dorian Gieseler. *The Daimon in Hellenistic Astrology: Origins and Influence*. Leiden: Brill, 2016.

Griffiths, John Gwyn, ed. *Plutarch's de Iside et Osiride*. Cardiff: University of Wales Press, 1970.

The Divine Verdict: A Study of Divine Judgment in the Ancient Religions. Studies in the History of Religions 52. Leiden: Brill, 1991.

Gundel, Wilhelm. *Dekane und Dekansternbilder: Ein Beitrag zur Geschichte der Sternbilder der Kulturvölker*. Studien der Bibliothek Warburg 19. Hamburg: J. J. Augustin, 1936.

Neue astrologische Texte des Hermes Trismegistos: Funde und Forschungen auf dem Gebiet der antiken Astronomie und Astrologie. Abhandlungen der Bayerischen Akademie der Wissenschaften N.F. 12. Munich: Bavarian Academy of Sciences, 1936.

Haeffner, Mark. *The Dictionary of Alchemy: From Maria Prophetissa to Isaac Newton*. London: Aquarius, 1991.

Halleux, Robert. "The Reception of Arabic Alchemy in the West." Volume 3, pages 886–902 in *Encyclopedia of the History of Arabic Science*. Ed. Roshdi Rashed. 3 vols. London: Routledge, 1996.

Hanegraaff, Wouter J. "Altered States of Knowledge: The Attainment of Gnōsis in the Hermetica." *International Journal of the Platonic Tradition* 2 (2008): 128–63.

"Hermetism." Volume 2, pages 1135–39 in *The Oxford Guide to the Historical Reception of Augustine*. Ed. Karla Pollmann and Willemien Otten. 3 vols. Oxford: Oxford University Press, 2013.

Hani, Jean. *La religion Égyptienne dans la pensée de Plutarque*. Paris: Belles Lettres, 1967.

Hanson, R. P. C. "The Date and Authorship of Pseudo-Anthimus '*De Sancta Ecclesia*.'" *Proceedings of the Royal Irish Academy* 83c (1983): 251–54.

Hatzimichali, Myrto. *Potamo of Alexandria and the Emergence of Eclecticism in Late Hellenistic Philosophy*. Cambridge: Cambridge University Press, 2011.

Hegedus, Tim. *Early Christianity and Ancient Astrology*. Patristic Studies 6. New York: Lang, 2007.

Heiduk, Matthias. "Offene Geheimnisse – Hermetische Texte und verborgenes Wissen in der mittelalterlichen Rezeption von Augustinus bis Albertus Magnus." Ph.D. diss., Albert-Ludwigs-Universität, 2007.

Hornung, Erik. *Conceptions of God in Ancient Egypt: The One and the Many*. Trans. John Baines. Ithaca: Cornell University Press, 1982.

The Secret Lore of Egypt: Its Impact on the West. Trans. David Lorton. Ithaca: Cornell University Press, 2001.

Hudry, Françoise. *Le livre des XXIV philosophes. Résurgence d'un texte du IVe siècle*. Paris: J. Vrin, 2009.

Irlenborn, Bernd. "Der Mensch als zweiter Gott? Anmerkungen zur *Imago dei*-Lehre des Nikolaus von Kues." *Freiburger Zeitschrift für Philosophie und Theologie* 47 (2000): 381–401.

Iversen, Erik. *Egyptian and Hermetic Doctrine*. Copenhagen: Museum Tusculanum, 1984.

Jackson, Howard. "Κόρη Κόσμου: Isis, Pupil of the eye of the world." *Chronique d'Égypte* 61 (1986): 116–35.

Johnston, Sarah Iles. "Animating Statues: A Case Study in Ritual." *Arethusa* 41 (2008): 445–77.

Jung, C. G. *Psychology and Alchemy*. Trans. R. F. C. Hull. London: Routledge & Kegan Paul, 1953.

Kaldellis, Anthony. *Hellenism in Byzantium: The Transformations of Greek Identity and the Reception of the Classical Tradition*. Cambridge: Cambridge University Press, 2007.

Mothers and Sons, Fathers and Daughters: The Byzantine Family of Michael Psellos. Notre Dame: University of Notre Dame Press, 2006.

Keefer, Michael. "The World Turned Inside Out: Revolutions of the Infinite Sphere from Hermes to Pascal." *Renaissance and Reformation* 24 (1988): 303–13.

Kingsley, Peter. "An Introduction to the Hermetica: Approaching Ancient Esoteric Tradition." Pages 17–40 in *From Poimandres to Jacob Böhme: Gnosis: Hermetism and the Christian Tradition*. Ed. Roelof van den Broek and Cis van Heertum. Amsterdam: In de Pelikaan, 2000.

Ancient Philosophy, Mystery, and Magic. Empedocles and Pythagorean Tradition. Oxford: Clarendon Press, 1995.

"From Pythagoras to the *Turba philosophorum*: Egypt and Pythagorean Tradition." *Journal of the Warburg and Courtland Institutes* 57 (1994): 1–13.

Klingshirn, William E. and Mark Vessey, eds. *The Limits of Ancient Christianity: Essays on Late Antique Thought and Culture in Honor of R. A. Markus*. Ann Arbor: University of Michigan Press, 1999.

Klotz, David. *Caesar in the City of Amun: Egyptian Temple Construction and Theology in Roman Thebes*. Monographies Reine Élisabeth 15. Turnhout: Brepols, 2012.

Koenen, L. "Die Prophezeiungen des 'Töpfers.'" *Zeitschrift für Papyrologie und Epigraphik* 2:3 (1968): 178–209.

Lane Fox, Robin. *Pagans and Christians*. New York: Alfred A. Knopf, 1987.

Laszlo, Gallusz. *The Throne Motif in the Book of Revelation*. Library of New Testament Studies 427. London: Bloomsbury, 2014.

Letrouit, Jean. "Hermétisme et alchimie: contribution à l'étude du Marcianus graecus 299 (= M)." Volume 1 pages 85–112 in *Magia, alchimia, scienza dal '400 al '700: L'influsso di Ermete Trismegisto*. Ed. Carlos Gilly and Cis van Heertum. 2 vols. Venice: Centro di, 2002.

Lewy, Hans. *Chaldean Oracles and Theurgy: Mysticism, Magic and Platonism in the Later Roman Empire*. Cairo: French Institute of Oriental Archaeology, 1956.

Lienhard, Joseph T. *Contra Marcellum: Marcellus of Ancyra and Fourth-century Theology*. Washington, DC: Catholic University of America Press, 1999.

Lieu, Sam and Dominic Montserrat. *From Constantine to Julian: Pagan and Byzantine Views. A Source History*. London: Routledge, 1996.

Lincoln, Bruce. *Theorizing Myth: Narrative, Ideology and Scholarship*. Chicago: University of Chicago Press, 1999.

Lindsay, Jack. *The Origins of Alchemy in Graeco-Roman Egypt*. New York: Barnes & Noble, 1970.

Lopilato, Robert. "The *Apotelesmatika* of Manetho." Ph.D. diss., Brown University, 1998.

Lucentini, Paolo. "L'Ermetismo magico nel secolo XIII." Pages 409–50 in *Sic itur ad astra: Studien zur Geschichte der Mathematik und Naturwissenschaften: Festschrift für den Arabisten Paul Kunitzsch zum 70. Geburtstag*. Ed. Menso Folkerts and Richard Lorch. Wiesbaden: Harrassowitz, 2000.

Lucentini, Paolo, I. Parri, and V. Perrone Compagni, eds. *Hermetism from Late Antiquity to Humanism / La tradizione ermetica dal mondo tardo-antico all'Umanesimo. Atti del Convegno internazionale di studi, Napoli, 20–24 novembre 2001.* Instrumenta Patristica et Mediaevalia 40. Turnhout: Brepols, 2003.

Lucentini, Paolo and V. Perrone Compagni. *I testi e i codici di Ermete nel Medioevo*. Florence: Polistampa, 2001.

Logan, Alistair H. B. "Marcellus of Ancyra (Pseudo-Anthimus), 'On the Holy Church': Text, Translation, and Commentary." *Journal of Theological Studies* 51 (2000): 81–112.

Löw, Andreas. *Hermes Trismegistos als Zeuge der Wahrheit: Die christliche Hermetikrezeption von Athenagoras bis Laktanz.* Theophaneia 36. Berlin: Philo, 2002.

"L'Asclepio ermetico nel secolo XII." Pages 397–420 in *From Athens to Chartres. Neoplatonism and Medieval Thought. Studies in honour of Edouard Jeaneau.* Ed. Haijo Jan Westra. Leiden: Brill, 1992.

Mahé, Jean-Pierre. "Stobaei Hermetica XIX,1 et les *Définitions* hermétiques Arméniennes." *Revue des Études Grecques* 94 (1981): 523–25.

"Mental Faculties and Cosmic Levels in the Eighth and the Ninth." Pages 73–83 in *The Nag Hammadi Texts in the History of Religions: Proceedings of the International Conference at the Royal Academy of Sciences and Letters in Copenhagen, September 19–24, 1995*. Ed. Søren Giversen, Tage Petersen, and Jørgen Podemann Sørensen. Copenhagen: C. A. Reitzel, 2002.

Mansfeld, Jaap. *Heresiography in Context: Hippolytus' Elenchos as a Source for Greek Philosophy*. Leiden: Brill, 1992.

Mansfeld, Jaap and D. T. Runia. *Aëtiana: The Method and Intellectual Context of a Doxographer. Volume 1: The Sources*. Philosophia Antiqua 73. Leiden: Brill, 1997.

McGinn, Bernard. *The Harvest of Mysticism in Medieval Germany 1300–1500.* Vol. 4 of *The Presence of God: A History of Western Christian Mysticism*. New York: Herder & Herder, 2005.

McGuckin, John A. *St. Gregory of Nazianzus: An Intellectual Biography*. Crestwood, NY: St. Vladimir's Seminary Press, 2001.

Megino, Carlos. "Presence in Stoicism of an Orphic Doctrine of the Soul quoted by Aristotle (*De Anima* 410b 27 = *OF* 421)." Pages 139–46 in *Tracing Orpheus: Studies of Orphic Fragments in Honour of Alberto Bernabé*. Ed. Miguel Herrero de Jáuregui. Sozomena 10. Berlin: de Gruyter, 2011.

Mertens, Michèle. "Sur la trace des anges rebelles dans les traditions ésotériques du début de notre ère justqu'au xviie siècle." Pages 383–98 in *Anges et démons. Actes du colloque de Liège et de Louvain-la-Neuve 25–26 novembre 1987*. Ed. J. Ries and H. Limet. Louvain-la-Neuve: Centre d'histoire des Religions, 1989.

"Zosimos of Panopolis." Volume 7, pages 405–8 in *New Dictionary of Scientific Biography*. Ed. Noretta Koertge. 7 vols. Farmington Hills, MI: Gale, 2008.

"Alchemy, Hermetism and Gnosticism at Panopolis c. 300 AD: The Evidence of Zosimus." Pages 165–76 in *Perspectives on Panopolis: An Egyptian Town from Alexander the Great to the Arab Conquest: Acts from an International Symposium held in Leiden on 16, 17 and 18 December 1998*. Ed. Arno Egberts. Leiden: Brill, 2002.

Meuthen, Erich. *Nicholas of Cusa: A Sketch for a Biography*. Trans. David Crowner and Gerald Christianson. Washington, DC: Catholic University Press, 2010.

Monaca, Mariangela. "Ermete e la divinazione nei papyri graecae magicae." Pages 491–503 in *Hermetism from Late Antiquity*. Ed. Lucentini and others. Turnhout: Brepols, 2003.

Montserrat-Torrents, J. "Les Pérates." *Compostellanum* 34 (1989): 185–98.

Morenz, Siegfried. *Egyptian Religion*. Trans. Ann E. Keep. Ithaca, NY: Cornell University Press, 1973.

Moreschini, Claudio. *Dall'Asclepius al Crater Hermetis: Studi sull'Ermetismo latino tardo-antico e rinascimentale*. Pisa: Giardini, 1985.

Hermes Christianus: The Intermingling of Hermetic Piety and Christian Thought. Trans. Patrick Baker. Turnhout: Brepols, 2011.

"La sapienza pagana al servizio della dottrina trinitaria secondo lo pseudo Didimo di Alessandria." *Augustinianum* 54 (2014): 199–216.

"Dal *pneuma* ermetico allo Spirito cristiano." *Studi Classici e Orientali* 61 (2015): 451–60.

Moreschini, Claudio and Enrico Norelli. *Early Christian Greek and Latin Literature: A Literary History*. Trans. Matthew J. O'Connell. 2 vols. Peabody: Hendrickson, 2005.

Moyer, Ian S. *Egypt and the Limits of Hellenism*. Cambridge: Cambridge University Press, 2011.

"A Revised Astronomical Dating of Thessalus's *De virtutibus herbarum*." Pages 437–49 in *The Frontiers of Ancient Science: Essays in Honor of Heinrich von Staden*. Ed. Brooke Holmes and Klaus Dietrich-Fischer. Berlin: de Gruyter, 2015.

Mussies, Gerard. "The Interpretatio Judaica of Thot-Hermes." Pages 89–120 in *Studies in Egyptian Religion Dedicated to Professor Jan Zandee*. Ed. M. Heerma van Voss, D. J. Hoens, G. Mussies, D. van der Plas, and H. te Velde. Leiden: Brill, 1982.

Neugebauer, O. and H. B. Van Hoesen, *Greek Horoscopes*. Philadelphia: American Philosophical Society, 1959.

Neugebauer, O. and Richard A. Parker. *Egyptian Astronomical Texts 1. The Early Decans*. Providence, RI: Brown University Press, 1960.

Egyptian Astronomical Texts III. Decans, Planets, Constellations and Zodiacs. Providence, RI: Brown University Press, 1969.

Nock, A. D. "Exegesis of Timaeus 28c." *VC* 16 (1962): 79–86.

Essays on Religion and the Ancient World. Ed. Zeph Stewart. 2 vols. Cambridge, MA: Harvard University Press, 1972.

"Two Notes." *VC* 3 (1949): 48–56.

Norden, Eduard. *Agnostos Theos: Untersuchungen zur formengeschichte religiöser Rede*. Leipzig: Teubner, 1913.

Norris, Frederick W. *Faith Gives Fullness to Reasoning: The Five Theological Orations of Gregory Nazianzen: Introduction and Commentary. Supplements to VC 13*. Leiden: Brill, 1991.

Oellacher, H. "Papyrus- und Pergamentfragmente aus Wiener und Münchner Beständen." Volume 2, pages 182–88 in *Miscellanea Giovanni Galbiati*. 3 vols. Fontes Ambrosiani 26. Milan: Hoepli, 1951.

Osborne, Catherine. *Dumb Beasts and Dead Philosophers: Humanity and the Humane in Ancient Philosophy and Literature*. Oxford: Clarendon Press, 2007.

Parlebas, Jacques. "L'origine égyptienne de l'appellation 'Hermès Trismégiste.'" *Göttinger Miszellen* 13 (1974): 25–28.

Parvis, Sara. *Marcellus of Ancyra and the Lost Years of the Arian Controversy 325–345*. Oxford: Oxford University Press, 2006.

Pépin, Jean. "Grégoire de Nazianze, lecteur de la littérature hermétiques." *VC* 36 (1982): 251–60.

"Cosmic Piety." Pages 408–36 in *Classical Mediterranean Spirituality: Egyptian, Greek, Roman*. Ed. A. H. Armstrong. London: SCM Press, 1989.

Perrin, Michel. *L'homme antique et chrétien: l'anthropologie de Lactance 250–325*. Paris: Beauchesne, 1981.

Peters, Francis E. "Hermes and Harran: The Roots of Arabic-Islamic Occultism." Pages 186–215 in *Intellectual Studies on Islam*. Ed. Michael M. Mazzaou and Vera B. Moreen. Salt Lake City: University of Utah, 1990.

Petty, Robert. *Fragments of Numenius of Apamea: Translation and Commentary, Platonic Texts and Translations 7*. Westbury, Wiltshire: Prometheus Trust, 2012.

Peuch, Ch. "Hermès troi fois incarné. Sur quelques témoignages négligés relatifs à Hermétisme." *Revue des Études Grecques* 59–60 (1946–47): xi–xiii.

Pingree, David. "Some of the Sources of the *Ghāyat al-Hakīm*." *Journal of the Warburg and Courtauld Institutes* 43 (1980): 1–15.

The Thousands of Abū Ma'shar. London: Warburg Institute, 1968.

"Thessalus Astrologus." Pages 83–86 in *Catalogus Translationum et Commentariorum* 3. Ed. Paul Oskar Kristeller. Washington, DC: Catholic University of America Press, 1976.

"The Sābians of Harrān and the Classical Tradition." *International Journal of the Classical Tradition* 9 (2002): 8–35.

Plessner, M. "Hermes Trismegistus and Arab Science." *Studia Islamica* 2 (1954): 45–59.

Porreca, David. "The Influence of Hermetic Texts on Western European Philosophers and Theologians (1160–1300)." Ph.D. diss., University of London, 2001.

"How Hidden was God? Revelation and Pedagogy in ancient and medieval Hermetic Writings." Pages 137–48 in *Histories of the Hidden God: Concealment and Revelation in Western Gnostic, Esoteric, and Mystical Traditions*. Ed. April D. DeConick and Grant Adamson. London: Acumen, 2014.

Possekel, Ute. "Bardaisan and Origen on Fate and the Power of the Stars." *Journal of Early Christian Studies* 20 (2012): 515–41.

Priesner, Claus and Karin Figala, eds. *Alchemie: Lexikon einer hermetischen Wissenschaft*. Munich: Beck, 1998.

Proust, Dominique. "The Harmony of the Spheres from Pythagoras to Voyager." *Proceedings of the International Astronomical Union* 260 (2009): 358–67.

Quispel, Gilles. "Hermes Trismegistus and Tertullian." *VC* 49 (1989): 188–90.

Ray, J. D. *Archive of Hor*. London: Egypt Exploration Society, 1976.

Reitzenstein, Richard. *Die Göttin Psyche in der hellenistischen und frühcrhistlichen Literatur*. Heidelberg: Carl Winters, 1917.

Reydams-Schils, G. *Thinking through Excerpts: Studies on Stobaeus*. Monothéismes et Philosophie. Turnhout: Brepols, 2011.

Rosenthal, Franz. "Al-Mubashshir ibn Fâtik. Prolegomena to an Abortive Edition." *Oriens* 13–14 (1960–61): 132–58.

Roubekas, Nickolas P. *An Ancient Theory of Religion: Euhemerism from Antiquity to the Present*. London: Routledge, 2017.

Runnalls, D. "Moses' Ethiopian Campaign." *Journal for the Study of Judaism* 14 (1993): 135–56.

Ruska, Julius. *Tabula Smaragdina: Ein Beitrag zur Geschichte der hermetischen Literatur*. Heidelberg: Carl Winter, 1926.

"Zwei Bücher de Compositione Alchemiae und ihre Vorreden." *Archiv für Geschichte der Mathematik, der Naturwissenschaft und der Technik* 11 (1928): 28–37.

Russell, Norman. *Cyril of Alexandria*. London: Routledge, 2000.

Saffrey, H. D. "Réflexions sur la pseudonymie Abammôn-Jamblique." Pages 307–18 in *Traditions of Platonism: Essays in Honour of John Dillon*. Ed. John Clearly. Aldershot: Ashgate, 1999.

Sallmann, Klaus. *Die Literatur des Umbruchs von der römischen zur christlichen Literatur 117 bis 284 n. Chr*. Handbuch der Lateinischen Literatur der Antike vol. 4. Munich: Beck'sche, 1997.

Sannino, Antonella. "Berthold of Moosburg's Hermetic Sources." *Journal of the Warburg and Courtauld Institutes* 63 (2000): 243–58.

Sauneron, Serge. *The Priests of Ancient Egypt New Edition*. Trans. David Lorton. Ithaca: Cornell University Press, 2000.

Schwartz, Jacques. "La *Korē Kosmou* et Lucien de Samosate (a propos de Momus et de la creation de l'homme)." Pages 223–33 in *Le Monde Grec: pensée, littérature, histoire, documents. Hommages a Claire Préaux*. Ed. J. Bingen. Brussels: University of Brussels, 1975.

Scott, Thomas McAllister. "Egyptian Elements in Hermetic Literature." Ph.D. diss., Harvard Divinity School, 1987.

Searby, Denis Michael. "The Intertitles in Stobaeus: Condensing a Culture." Pages 23–70 in *Thinking through Excerpts: Studies on Stobaeus*. Ed. Gretchen J. Reydams-Schils. Turnhout: Brepols, 2011.

Sfameni Gasparro, Giulia. "The Hellenistic face of Isis: Cosmic and Saviour Goddess." Pages 40–72 in *Nile into Tiber. Egypt in the Roman World:*

Proceedings of the IIIrd International Conference of Isis Studies, Faculty of Archaeology, Leiden University, May 11–14 2005. Ed. Laurent Bricault, Miguel John Versluys, and Paul G. P. Meyboom. Religions in the Graeco-Roman World 159. Leiden: Brill, 2007.

"L'ermetismo nelle testimonianze dei Padri." Pages 261–308 in *Gnostica et Hermetica. Saggi sullo gnosticismo e sull'ermetismo*. Rome: Ateneo, 1982.

"La gnosi ermetica come iniziazione e mistero." Pages 309–30 in *Gnostica et Hermetica. Saggi sullo gnosticismo e sull'ermetismo*. Rome: Ateneo, 1982.

Sharples, Robert W. "Aristotelian Theology after Aristotle." Pages 1–40 in *Traditions of Theology: Studies in Hellenistic Theology, its Background and Aftermath*. Ed. Dorothea Frede and André Laks. Leiden: Brill, 2002.

Silverman, David P. "Divinity and Deities in Ancient Egypt." Pages 9–87 in *Religion in Ancient Egypt: Gods, Myths, and Personal Practice*. Ed. Byron E. Shafer. Ithaca: Cornell University Press, 1991.

Singer, Dorthea Waley and Robert Steele. "The Emerald Table." *Proceedings of the Royal Society of Medicine, Section of the History of Medicine* 21 (1927): 485–501.

Siniscalco, Paolo. "Ermete Trismegisto profeta pagano della rivelazione cristiana: La fortuna di un passo ermetico (*Asclepius* 8) nell'interpretazione di scrittori cristiani." *Atti dell'Accademia delle Scienze di Torino* 101 (1966–67): 83–117.

Smith, Jonathan Z. *Map is Not Territory: Studies in the History of Religions*. Chicago: Chicago University Press, 1978.

Smith, Mark. *The Liturgy of the Opening of the Mouth for Breathing*. Oxford: Griffith Institute, Ashmolean Museum, 1993.

Sorabji, Richard. *Matter, Space and Motion: Theories in Antiquity and their Sequel*. Ithaca: Cornell University Press, 1988.

Animal Minds and Human Morals: The Origins of the Western Debate. Ithaca: Cornell University Press, 1993.

Stapleton, H. E., G. L. Lewis, and F. Sherwood Taylor. "The Sayings of Hermes Quoted in the Mā'al-waraqī of Ibn Umail." *Ambix* 3 (1949): 69–90.

Stavenhagen, Lee. "The Original Text of the Latin *Morienus*." *Ambix* 17 (1970): 1–12.

Sterling, Gregory E. "'The Queen of the Virtues': Piety in Philo of Alexandria." *Studia Philonica Annual* 18 (2006): 103–23.

Stroumsa, Guy G. *Another Seed: Studies in Gnostic Mythology*. Leiden: Brill, 1984.

Sturlese, Loris. "Saints et magiciens: Albert le Grand en face d'Hermès Trismégiste," *Archives de Philosophie* 43 (1980): 615–34.

Tardieu, Michel "Bitys." Volume 2. Pages 113–15 in *DPA*. Ed. Richard Goulet. Paris: CNRS, 1994.

Tarrant, Harold. *Thrasyllan Platonism*. Ithaca: Cornell University Press, 1993.

Taylor, F. Sherwood. "A Survey of Greek Alchemy." *Journal of Hellenic Studies* 50 (1930): 109–39.

Teeter, Emily. *Religion and Ritual in Ancient Egypt*. Cambridge: Cambridge University Press, 2011.

te Velde, H. *Seth, God of Confusion*. Leiden: Brill, 1967.

Thissen, Heinz J. "KMHΦ – Ein Verkannter Gott." *Zeitschrift für Papyrologie und Epigraphik* 112 (1996): 153–60.

Thorndike, Lynn. *A History of Magic and Experimental Science during the First Thirteen Centuries of our Era.* Vol. 2. New York: Columbia University Press, 1923.

"Traditional Medieval Tracts concerning engraved Astrological Images." Pages 217–74 in *Mélanges Auguste Pelzer: Études d'histoire littéraires et doctrinale de la Scolastique médiévale.* Leuven: Higher Institute of Philosophy, 1947.

Tröger, Karl-Wolfgang. "Die hermetische Gnosis." Pages 97–120 in *Gnosis und Neues Testament. Studien aus Religionswissenschaft und Theologie.* Berlin: Gütersloh, 1973.

Tugwell, Simon and Leonard E. Boyle. *Albert & Thomas: Selected Writings.* New York: Paulist Press, 1988.

Valantasis, Richard. *Spiritual Guides of the Third Century: A Semiotic Study of the Guide-Disciple Relationship in Christianity, Neoplatonism, Hermetism, and Gnosticism.* Minneapolis: Fortress, 1991.

Van Bladel, Kevin. *The Arabic Hermes: From Pagan Sage to Prophet of Science.* New York: Oxford University Press, 2009.

van den Broek, R. "Religious Practices in the Hermetic 'Lodge': New Light from Nag Hammadi." Pages 77–96 in *From Poimandres to Jacob Böhme: Gnosis: Hermetism and the Christian Tradition.* Ed. R. van den Broek and Cis van Heertum. Amsterdam: In de Pelikaan, 2000.

Van den Kerchove, Anna. *Le voie d'Hermès: Pratiques rituelles et traités hermétiques.* Leiden & Boston: Brill, 2012.

van der Horst, P. W. "The Way of Life of the Egyptian Priests according to Chaeremon." Pages 61–71 in *Studies in Egyptian Religion Dedicated to Professor Jan Zandee.* Ed. M. Heerma van Voss, D. J. Hoens, G. Mussies, D. van der Plas, and H. te Velde. Leiden: Brill, 1982.

van Oort, Johannes. "Augustine and Hermes Trismegistus: An Inquiry into the Spirituality of Augustine's 'Hidden Years.'" *Journal of Early Christian History* 6 (2016): 55–76.

Versnel, H. S. *Ter Unus: Isis, Dionysus, and Hermes: Three Studies in Henotheism.* Leiden: Brill, 1990.

Volokhine, Youri. "Le dieu Thot et la parole." *Revue de l'histoire des religions* 221 (2004): 131–56.

von Stuckrad, Kocku. "Jewish and Christian Astrology in Late Antiquity – A New Approach." *Numen* 47 (2000): 1–40.

"Secrecy as Social Capital." Pages 239–52 in *Constructing Tradition: Means and Myths of Transmission in Western Esotericism.* Ed. Andreas B. Kilcher. Aries 11. Leiden: Brill, 2010.

von Lieven, Alexandra. "Thot selbdritt: mögliche ägyptische Ursprünge der arabisch-lateinischen Tradition dreier Hermesgestalten." *Die Welt des Orients* 37 (2007): 69–77.

Walter, Jochen. *Pagane Texte und Wertvorstellungen bei Lactanz. Hypomnemata 165.* Göttingen: Vandenhoeck & Ruprecht, 2006.

Weisheipl, James A. *Albertus Magnus and the Sciences: Commemorative Essays 1980*. Toronto: Pontifical Institute of Mediaeval Studies, 1980.

Weisser, Urusula. *Das "Buch über das Geheimnis der Schöpfung" von Pseudo-Apollonios von Tyana*. Ars Medica 2. Berlin: de Gruyter, 1980.

West, Stephanie. "The Greek Version of the Legend of Tefnut." *Journal of Egyptian Archaeology* 55 (1969): 161–83.

Wildberg, Christian. "*Corpus Hermeticum*, Tractate III: The Genesis of a Genesis." Pages 139–64 in *Jewish and Christian Cosmogony in Late Antiquity*. Ed. Lance Jenott and Sarit Kattan Gribetz. Texte und Studien zum Antiken Judentum 155. Tübingen: Mohr Siebeck, 2013.

Wildung, Dietrich. *Imhotep und Amenhotep. Gottwerdung im alten Ägypten*. Munich: Deutscher Kunstverlag, 1977.

Williams, Steven J. *The Secret of Secrets: The Scholarly Career of a Pseudo-Aristotelian Text in the Latin Middle Ages*. Ann Arbor: University of Michigan Press, 2003.

Wlosok, Antonie. *Laktanz und die philosophischen Gnosis: Untersuchungen zu Geschichte und Terminologie der gnostischen Erlösungsvorstellung*. Heidelberg: Carl Winter, 1960.

Yates, F. A. *Giordano Bruno and the Hermetic Tradition*. Chicago: University of Chicago Press, 1964.

Zandee, Jan. "Der androgyne Gott in Ägypten: Ein Erscheinungsbild des Weltschöpfers." Pages 240–78 in *Religion im Erbe Ägyptens: Beiträge zur spätantiken Religionsgeschichte*. Ed. Manfred Görg. Wiesbaden: Harrasowitz, 1988.

Zuntz, Günther. *Persephone: Three Essays on Religion and Thought in Magna Graecia*. Oxford: Clarendon Press, 1971.

Index

Printed in Great Britain
by Amazon